Equity PEDAGOGY

TEACHING DIVERSE STUDENT POPULATIONS

Kalisha A. Waldon, Ph.D. | Traci P. Baxley, Ed.D.

Kendall Hunt

publishing company

Cover image: Shutterstock.com

Kendall Hunt
publishing company

www.kendallhunt.com

Send all inquiries to:
4050 Westmark Drive
Dubuque, IA 52004-1840

Contents

Preface

It is our goal for *Equity Pedagogy: Teaching Diverse Student Populations* to contribute to existing pedagogy, which empowers pre-service educators and practitioners to harness the collective knowledge, histories, and experiences students and local communities through curricula and pedagogies that counter the dominant narrative and silences marginalized voices. We invite the readers to instead infuse the counterstories and highlight the perspectives and voices of the marginalized so that they are integral parts of the teaching and learning. The chapters that follow contain culturally diverse perspectives of curriculum and instruction that asks the readers to engage in self-reflective practices regarding their potential biases, misconceptions, and personal cultural competencies. Readers are also invited to consider how the *Voices in the Field* give credence to why multicultural education is needed, and why and how we should embrace pedagogical practices that are culturally responsive and engaging. Finally, each chapter concludes with *Practical Encounters* in which the editors offer case studies, real-world applications, and hands-on activities designed to engage the reader in applicable interactions that connect to the theory introduced in the chapter.

The Introduction is designed to make the case for why multicultural education is imperative for educators. The author introduces a typology of multicultural education that seeks to integrate diverse scholarship on what *should* be the conceptualization of multicultural education in institutional practice.

Chapter 1 begins with an introduction to the history and the goals of multicultural education. Key theorists and frameworks within in the field of multicultural education are discussed from a surface-level approach to a more critical one.

Chapter 2 then provides an overview of why students' culture and identities should matter and introduces activities that get the readers to reflect on their own cultural values and how they may align with or marginalize groups of students in their classrooms. The chapter also defines culture and discusses identity stage models associated with various cultural groups.

Chapter 3 delves deeper into why culture matters. The chapter situates culture within the discussion of culturally responsive teaching and why it is needed in our schools. Traditional classrooms and instruction are critiqued through the offering of the *Curriculum Connections Instructional Model*. The authors posit that there are multiple domains of the learner and that they all are central to understanding the complexity of students' personal and academic lives.

Chapter 4 focuses on the importance of the inclusion all students, including students with disabilities and students whose first language is not English (ELL). In this chapter, the authors thoroughly inform the readers about current laws and mandates that protect the rights of students with disabilities. The chapter includes practical strategies for working with students with 501 Plans and Individualized Educational Plans. In addition, the *Voice in the Field* dispels myths regarding ELL learners, while offering strategies to scaffold their learning.

Chapter 5 addresses the issue of poverty and how often low-socioeconomic families and students are viewed from a deficit perspective. The chapter calls for educators to embrace the strengths of these students through the inclusion of strategies and classroom practices that honor and support students who live in poverty, thus leading to equitable learning opportunities.

Religious bias is captured in Chapter 6. An often controversial topic, the author uses great care in discussing the role of religion in education and what teachers need to know to avoid forms of religious suppression or oppression in the classroom. "Well-meaning, yet unprepared teachers can be detrimental to young religious minority students by inadvertently ostracizing them." The author includes practical and meaningful ways to introduce religion in a public school classroom setting.

Assumptions today about children not being aware of gender or sexuality are outdated. We are living in an age when LGBTQ issues and people are part of mainstream media. Chapter 7 investigates the need for the inclusion of sexual orientation topics/issues within multicultural education classrooms and current school climate for students or families who may identify as LGBTQ (Lesbian, Gay, Bisexual, Transgender, and Queer/Questioning). The author concludes with suggestions on how to successfully integrate curricula that highlight LGBTQ themes into the classroom.

Chapter 8 provides an overview of the essential components of multicultural lesson planning. The authors demonstrate a method for successfully aligning lesson objectives, instruction, and assessment(s) through a multicultural lens. Strategies to ensure the inclusion of the needs of diverse students and diverse voices and perspectives are discussed.

One essential component to lesson planning is evaluation. "Evaluations, when used properly, can be tools to understanding your students better and to designing lessons that are data-driven and purposeful." The authors of Chapter 9 discuss the pros and cons of both traditional standardized testing and authentic assessments. They also explore what assessment should look like in a multicultural classroom. Issues with testing and evaluation are explored alongside strategies to determine whether assessments are culturally biased. *The Voice in the Field* discusses ways in which the playing field can be leveled.

Chapter 10 advocates for providing students with opportunities of choice, voice, and spaces for critical discourse, in an effort to bring about personal liberation and societal transformation. The chapter also explores types of literacies and how language arts can be taught through a multiculturally inclusive lens that encourages students to read texts from the perspectives of marginalized groups, as well as empower students to re-create narratives from various standpoints. The authors introduce methods to use multiple genres of literature for social action and for emphasizing alternative perspectives.

The traditional historical narrative has been one that has sought to paint America has the hero, or the story of "a superior people, destined to become the most powerful force in the world" while discounting "the human suffering that resulted from this very trajectory of power." Chapter 11 advocates for the reframing of the traditional American narrative to one that is multicultural and aligns with the aims and goals of the NCSS (National Council of Social Studies) and NAME (National Association of Multicultural Education). The author provides practical examples and strategies.

Chapter 12 explores how the STEM subject/field has traditionally been viewed, perceived, or taught from a monolithic perspective. The authors discuss the importance of including diverse voices in the STEM curriculum and providing students opportunities to see themselves in the curriculum. This is key to marginalized groups of students pursuing degrees and occupations in STEM fields. A practical application for designing and implementing STEM curricula with a multicultural focus will end the chapter.

In Chapter 13, the authors advocate for the necessity to create safe spaces for art integration into the public school curriculum. The chapter highlights the academic, social, and personal benefits of fine arts, while sharing the realities of groups of students who will be denied the opportunities to engage in fine arts if not for the inclusion of it into the school curriculum. The chapter introduces the reader to practical approaches, strategies, and belief systems that art specialists, educators, and teaching artists have identified as successful when they work with children in schools.

The critical pedagogy theoretical framework which is the foundation for *Equity Pedagogy: Teaching Diverse Student Populations* creates a space in which the authors of this textbook present their content. From a multicultural stance, they highlight the principles and ideas intended to challenge the way in which traditionally marginalized groups are depicted or excluded from curriculum and instruction. This text confronts issues related to racism, sexism, classism, ableism, and heterosexism through relevant theory, practical examples, and engaging, current case studies.

Acknowledgments

We would like to take the opportunity to thank the authors of each chapter who contributed their content expertise and knowledge to this textbook. Your contributions and those of the *Voices in the Field* and *Practical Encounters* made our desire to provide a counter to traditional pre-service texts come to life. In addition, we would like to extend a special appreciation to Ramonia Rochester for her diligence and patience in being an extra set of eyes on each and every chapter of this book. Her feedback was significant to the quality of the final manuscript. We also would like to say a heartfelt thank you to Dr. Carlos Diaz for writing the foreword for *Equity Pedagogy: Teaching Diverse Student Populations.* We are honored to have an endorsement from a significant scholar in the field of Multicultural Education. Finally, thank you to Kendall Hunt and the amazing team members that have assisted us every step of the way. Your support and expertise were integral in our publishing journey. We are thankful and grateful for our village.

Dedication

We dedicate this book to our children who provide the context and meaning for the work we do every day. May what we pour into each preservice teacher we educate, each workshop we deliver on diversity and equity pedagogy, and every article we write to contribute to the field provide more opportunities for all of you to grow and live in a world that will accept you for who you are. Let our work inspire you to fight for social justice and continue to ask thoughtful, engaging questions along the way. May your educational experiences be liberating and transformative!

Foreword

One of the most vexing challenges in the preparation of new teachers is how to encourage them to be "multi-culturally literate." The nation's teaching force, as well the majority of prospective teachers, is predominantly White, middle-class, and female. Students in the public school system are increasingly much more diverse than the professionals who teach them. When life experiences between teachers and students diverge, it is critical that the professional education of teachers bridges this gap.

Waldon and Baxley's *Equity Pedagogy: Teaching Diverse Student Populations* represents a valuable tool to assist teacher educators in addressing the needs of culturally and ethnically diverse students. Although intended primarily as a text for undergraduate teacher preparation, it is also a valuable resource which could be employed in the continuing education of veteran teachers.

This edited book does a thorough job of presenting research, theory, and providing ample classroom and practical examples. It defines multicultural education and makes clear that demography in the United States argues strongly for greater educational equity in its schools. Schoorman provides a valuable typology to measure the levels of integration of multicultural education. Many schools in this nation which feel they are applying multicultural principles would belong in Schoorman's Level One: The Compliance Model. Educators need to conceptualize and attempt to reach Schoorman's higher levels of multicultural integration.

Teaching Diverse Student Populations makes it clear that effective education for culturally/ethnically diverse students goes far beyond establishing clear curricular standards and aligning these with classroom instruction. Positive classroom and school climates are absolutely critical for the achievement of all students, but particularly for those students who have been historically underserved in the public schools of the United States. Whether we are describing students with disabilities, LGBTQ students, gender elements in schools, race, ethnicity, or socioeconomic class, this text makes it abundantly clear that the often-cited claim "We treat all of our students equally" is a myth, not supported by research.

A notable observation in this text is that "Students may become immersed in educational environments that undermine their value" (p.67). While it is deplorable if this happens to any student, all students are not equally at risk for this possibility. Educators are more likely to have lower expectations and engage in "deficit thinking" when encountering students of color or those from low-income households. In a nation where the groups from which these students emanate are on the increase, further under-education of these groups is not only inappropriate, but if continued, will affect future prosperity for the entire nation.

This book also contains a unique chapter on the role of religion in public schools and reminds the reader that educators can teach varying religious perspectives (when they are germane to the subject) without advocating any particular one. When educators are unsure about this standard, they often avoid any mention of religion in the classroom in order to play it safe.

The text is rife with practical examples of "culturally responsive pedagogy" as well as a chapter on cultural bias in evaluation and one concerning special education. These point out that testing is an area where cultural bias is often found. Cultural bias is sometimes present in screening methods for various special education programs. One of the more blatant examples of this is the underrepresentation of students of color in gifted programs.

Baxley and Waldon remind the reader that students should not be viewed through the lens of what they do not bring to school (deficit ideology) but rather by what they do possess (funds of knowledge). When educators focus primarily on student deficits, teacher expectations are almost sure to be lowered. These expectations have a significant impact on students' academic achievement. While it is very important for students to emerge from high schools with sufficient skills to be viable in the workplace or pursue higher education, a purely skills-based approach to public education is myopic. This will diminish other significant goals of education such as cultural, political, historical, media, and geographical literacy. Fixation on state or national standardized test scores will often sacrifice these other areas, since they are rarely the subjects of standardized tests.

Gatens reminds the reader that a sound social studies program must be embedded with multicultural content and result in graduates who are able to see their own nation and the world, not just through their own eyes, but also through the eyes of others. Burnaford and colleagues provide a unique chapter in a multicultural text: the role of arts education. The arts have often been regarded as ancillary subjects to core academics. This chapter makes a persuasive case that the arts are universal and are an excellent way to reach students' creative and expressive abilities. Every community contains local artists which may be tapped into in order to enhance education in many art forms.

As a veteran multicultural educator, I have faced the challenge of stretching current and future teachers' perspectives to encompass those different from themselves. This is not an easy task since the most common reference for individuals for what is "normal" in schools and society is their own lived experiences. *Equity Pedagogy: Teaching Diverse Populations* presents many of the key concepts in multicultural education as well as provides a number of "voices from the field" which give these ideas authenticity. Another challenge faced by multicultural educators is the question, "Well, I see what you mean in theory, but what does this idea look like when you try to use it in the classroom?". This text provides current and future teachers with a plethora of classroom examples as well as numerous resources for further study. It strikes a proper balance between theory and practice.

Multicultural education recognizes that, in order to reduce inequity in schools, educators must be willing to acquire additional multicultural content knowledge, as well as evaluate their pedagogy for culturally responsive methods. Both of these commitments require additional work. Reducing inequity will always take more work than rationalizing why it will always be with us. For the readers of this book who are willing to make those commitments, the rewards for you and your students will last a lifetime.

Carlos F. Diaz
Professor Emeritus
Florida Atlantic University

Voices in the Field Contributors

Jillian Berson, M.Ed.

Jillian Berson is a high school English teacher in South Florida. She is currently pursuing her doctoral degree in Curriculum and Instruction at Florida Atlantic University in Boca Raton, Florida. With degrees in English Literature and Multicultural Education, her current research involves incorporating post-structuralist feminist ideals into the existing high school English curriculum.

Martha Brown, Ph.D.

Dr. Brown is a professor, educational consultant, researcher, and program evaluator. She has studied and practiced restorative justice since 2010, and her area of expertise is in restorative justice in education (RJE). She teaches online courses in restorative justice at Simon Fraser University, British Columbia, Canada, and works with schools and school districts that wish to adopt RJE.

Carlos Diaz, Ed.D.

Dr. Diaz is Professor Emeritus at Florida Atlantic University. He has a plethora of experience as a distinguished educator, researcher, presenter and writer. He has written widely in the area of multicultural education and has served as an advocate of multicultural education on both the local, state, national, and international levels. His areas of scholarship include multicultural curriculum theory; equity in US education; Latino education; global education and multicultural infusion in the social studies curriculum. In 2016, he was a Fulbright Specialist Scholar to KPH College in Vienna, Austria.

Julie Hector, M.Ed.

Julie Hector is a doctoral student at Florida Atlantic University (FAU) in the Curriculum, Culture, and Educational Inquiry program in the College of Education. She is currently working on her dissertation, which focuses on the historical, political, and social implications of the 2012 banning of Tucson Unified School District's Mexican American Studies program. She has a Masters in Teaching Spanish, and is currently teaching Spanish at the Karen Slattery Educational Research Center for Child Development at FAU. She has worked as a graduate assistant for The Center for Holocaust and Human Rights Education (CHHRE), and has also taught undergraduate Spanish courses through FAU's Department of Languages, Linguistics, and Comparative literature.

Mirynne O'Conner Igualada, Ph.D.

Dr. Igualada received her Ph.D. in Culture, Curriculum and Educational Inquiry at Florida Atlantic University. She served as a social studies teacher for eight years before becoming the Supervisor of Gifted and Talented Programs for Broward County Public Schools. She has written, reviewed and implemented lesson plans for Pearson and McGraw Hill. She is now an Associate Director with the Florida Partnership. Her scholarly interests include the impact of policy implementation on equity and access initiatives related to accelerated mechanisms.

Sabrina F. Sembiante, Ph.D.

Dr. Sembiante is an Assistant Professor of TESOL/Bilingual Education from Florida Atlantic University. She earned her doctoral degree from the University of Miami in Language and Literacy Learning in Multilingual

Settings, with a focus on early childhood bilingualism. Her research focuses primarily on the development of emergent bilingualism and biliteracy in young Spanish-speaking children, and the instructional practices supporting children's academic discourse development in dual language contexts. She frames her research from sociocultural and systemic functional linguistic perspectives. Her research has been published in Language and Education, Bilingual Research Journal, Journal of Research in Childhood Education, and Curriculum Inquiry.

Rachayita Shah, Ph.D.

Dr. Shah works as a Program Manager at Florida Atlantic University's (FAU) Center for Holocaust and Human Rights Education (CHHRE), where her responsibilities include facilitating teacher professional development, providing curriculum consultations to K-12 teachers, and managing Holocaust and human rights oriented events. She has taught undergraduate and graduate courses at FAU, which focused on multicultural and global education. Her areas of research include teacher professional development, curriculum and instruction, multicultural education, and Holocaust and human rights education.

Leila Shatara, M.Ed.

Leila Shatara earned both her undergraduate and graduate degrees at FAU and is currently enrolled in their Doctoral Educational Leadership and Research Methodology program. She has been an educator for over two decades and has served in many capacities ranging from being a teacher to being a principal. She has taught elementary, middle, high school, and college level courses throughout her career. Ms. Shatara currently serves as the Vice President of the Council of Islamic Schools of North America (CISNA) and is an Islamic school educational consultant.

Samantha N. Uribe, Ph. D.

Dr. Uribe is an Instructor of TESOL/Bilingual Education at Florida Atlantic University. She earned her doctoral degree from Florida Atlantic University in Curriculum and Instruction with a specialization in TESOL. She worked for Broward County Public Schools as an elementary school teacher, school-based ESOL Program Coordinator, and district-based administrator in the Bilingual/ESOL Department. Her research interests include infusion of ESOL instructional strategies within teacher education and professional learning experiences as well as the benefits of modeling and scaffolding best practices for preservice teachers.

Michelle Vaughan, Ph.D.

Dr. Vaughan is currently an Assistant Professor at Florida Atlantic University in the Department of Curriculum, Culture, and Educational Inquiry. She teaches courses in curriculum design, action research, school reform, and trends in curriculum and instruction. She works with local school districts to train teachers in curriculum design and modification for students with disabilities and continuously supports the inclusion efforts of all school districts through her publications and scholarship. Additionally, Dr. Vaughan studies teacher growth and change through action research, online learning, and the integration of technology into practice.

Chapter Contributors

Ilene Allgood, Ed.D.

Dr. Ilene Allgood's primary areas of specialization and research include Religion and public schooling, genocide and peace studies, and curriculum and strategies to counteract bias and alleviate prejudice. She has published several peer-reviewed articles and book chapters and has presented her work at the National Association for Multicultural Education (NAME), National Council for the Social Studies (NCSS), and the American Educational Research Association (AERA) conferences. She is the recipient of two prestigious awards that recognize outstanding teaching at Florida Atlantic University -- The University Award for *"Excellence and Innovation in Teaching Undergraduates"* and the North Campus Achievement Award for *"Exceptional Faculty."* A Senior Instructor in the College of Education, Department of Curriculum, Culture and Educational Inquiry at Florida Atlantic University, Dr. Allgood is dedicated to advancing equity in education, and has been preparing pre and in-service teachers in critical multicultural education for two decades.

Roxanna Anderson, Ph.D.

Dr. Anderson received her Ph.D. in psychological development from New York University. She was awarded the Dissertation of the Year from the Women's Studies Commission, and selected to present at the American Psychological Association at their annual conference held in Washington, DC. Recently, she co-authored an article entitled, The Psychological, Economic, and Sociological Roots of Violence: A Multidisciplinary Approach. In 2015, she was selected from hundreds of applicants to be one of 30 Faculty Scholars for the Phi Theta Kappa International Honor Society (PTK), for a two-year term.

Traci P. Baxley, Ed.D.

Dr. Baxley is an Associate Professor in the Department of Curriculum, Culture and Educational Inquiry at Florida Atlantic University. She has worked in PreK-20 educational systems for over 20 years. She earned a doctorate degree in Curriculum and Instruction with a specialization in Literacy at Florida Atlantic University. Her areas of scholarship include: critical literacy; multicultural literature; racial identity development; and social justice education addressing the academic and social success of students of color. She has published in international and national peer reviewed journals including *Taboo: The Journal of Culture and Education*, *International Journal of Critical Pedagogy*, and *Urban Education*. Most recently she co-authored a book entitled *Invisible Presence: Feminist Counter-Narratives of Young Adult Novels Written by Women of Color* (Baxley & Boston, 2014).

Gail Burnaford, Ph.D.

Dr. Gail Burnaford is the Director of Research and Evaluation at the John F. Kennedy Center for the Performing Arts in Washington, DC. She is a former high school English teacher and preschool teacher. Dr. Burnaford has been an evaluator on numerous projects with organizations including the Chicago Arts Partnerships in Education (CAPE), the Ravinia Music Festival, and the Smart Museum at the University of Chicago. She has served as a Principal Investigator for Department of Education Model Dissemination Grants and Professional Development Grants and for the Music In Education National Consortium project funded by the Fund for the Improvement of Post-Secondary Education (FIPSE). She has presented at the International Congress for

School Effectiveness and Improvement (ICSEI) in Barcelona, Spain, the World Conference on Arts Education (UNESCO) in Lisbon, Portugal, and the European and International Symposium for Evaluating the Impact of Arts and Cultural Education on Children and Young People in Paris, France. Gail is the author of numerous articles and books, including *Teaching and Learning in 21st Century Learning Environments* (Burnaford, Brown, 2014), *Arts Integration Frameworks, Research and Practice: A Literature Review* (Burnaford, 2007), and *Renaissance in the Classroom: Arts Integration and Meaningful Learning* (Burnaford, Aprill, Weiss, 2001).

Aquil Charlton

Aquil Charlton is a visionary musician and educator who applies his entrepreneurial background & artistic practice toward his vision for a more just society. He is passionate about providing imaginative spaces combined with educational tools that empower and validate people from systemically marginalized communities. Aquil is the founding director of ALT-City, the first contemporary ensemble of Chicago Public Schools All City Arts program since 1970. He is also a 2015-16 Artist-In-Residence at the University of Chicago's Arts Incubator. Aquil is currently developing a traveling music education practice called Mobile Music Box, which was launched in June 2016.

Tunjarnika Coleman-Ferrell, Ed.D

Dr. Coleman-Ferrell is a Dean of Academic Affairs at Palm Beach State College. Her experiences reflect 14 years as a Professor at Palm Beach State College and over 15 years as an Adjunct Professor at Florida Atlantic University where she teaches courses in Foundations of Education, Teaching Diverse Populations and Educational Measurement and Evaluation. She is dedicated to raising the awareness of the critical nature of the role of educators in our society while challenging the conversations regarding accountability and championing the importance of equity in the Pre-K-16 classroom on the local, state and national level.

Allyson L. Copeland, MA.

Allyson Hall has worked in the Florida University System for over 6 years. As the coordinator of Online Programs at a local For-Profit college, she helped to find solutions for students who were technologically disadvantaged. As an Instructional Designer at Florida Atlantic University, she helps faculty develop curriculum and implement effective teaching strategies through digital mediums. Allyson holds a Bachelor of Science degree in Telecommunications from the University of Florida and a Master of Arts degree in Sociology from Florida Atlantic University. She is currently pursuing a doctorate degree in Curriculum and Instruction at Florida Atlantic University. She continues to teach Multicultural Education courses at local colleges and universities with a focus on the intersectionality of Race, Class, and Gender in education.

Rosanna M. Gatens, Ph.D.

Dr. Gatens received the Ph.D. in Modern European History from the University of Pittsburgh. Her research and writing in the area of Holocaust education focuses on the relationship between Holocaust education and education for democracy. She chairs the Grades 9-12 Curriculum development committee of the Florida Commissioner's Task Force on Holocaust Education. From 2002 until 2015, she served as Director of Florida Atlantic University's Center for Holocaust and Human Rights Education where she played a leading role in southern Florida in connecting schools, religious and civic organizations to regional and national networks seeking to advance human rights for all. She received the 2008 Human Relations Award, American Jewish Committee of South Florida, the 2009 International Relations Award from the Florida Council for the Social Studies and the Florida Atlantic University TIAACREFF Community Service Award in 2011. She is an adjunct instructor in the Department of Curriculum, Culture and Critical Inquiry

Dominic Grasso, M.Ed

Dominic Grasso currently serves as the LGTQ Program Coordinator of Broward County Schools. He is completed up his Doctoral Degree in Curriculum & Instruction in 2016, with an area of specialization in Multicultural & LGBTQ Issues in Education, at Florida Atlantic University. His dissertation examined elementary school teacher perceptions regarding the inclusion of LGBTQ themed literature and curriculum.

Susan Gay Hyatt, Ph.D.

Dr. Hyatt is the Co-Founder and Co-Executive Director of Blue Planet Writers' Room, a non-profit creative writing center dedicated to creating international collaborations through the arts. She received her PhD in Curriculum and Instruction from Florida Atlantic University in 2014 after working for twenty years as a teaching artist and theater arts educator. Dr. Hyatt believes firmly in the efficacy of the arts as a means to bridge cultures and foster diversity.

Dana Hamadeh, MA.

Dana Hamadeh earned a Bachelor of Science in Computer Engineering and a Master of Education in Curriculum and Instruction with a minor in Mathematics. Some of her professional experiences include over 10 years of teaching college mathematics, supervising student learning center for physics and mathematics, managing million dollar STEM grant programs, and serving as Associate Dean of STEM Academic Affairs at Palm Beach State College. She continues to develop and present dynamic and interactive staff, faculty, and student workshops and seminars on various academic and professional-related topics. She feels privileged and blessed to wake up every morning doing what she loves to do.

Brianna Joseph

Brianna Joseph is a doctoral student in the Department of Exceptional Student Education at Florida Atlantic University. She is a member of the Council for Exceptional Children and multiple special education divisions. Her research interests include health and fitness promotion for young adults with developmental disabilities and adolescents with learning disabilities. Brianna earned her master's degree in Exceptional Student Education from Florida Atlantic University.

Chasity O'Malley, Ph.D.

Chasity O'Malley is a Professor of Anatomy and Physiology at Palm Beach State College. She taught at the college level in Biology for 16 years in very diverse settings, from large 4 year universities to a small private liberal arts college to community colleges. She received her Bachelor of Science from Heidelberg University and her Ph.D training from Tulane University. Her research focuses on the effects of physical forces on yeast growth and genetics. Her PhD project flew aboard Space Shuttle Atlantis during STS-115. Through her many experiences in research (including assisting with 6 payloads aboard NASA shuttles), she has strove to be a strong woman in science to provide a relatable role model for young women looking into science.

Jeanette McCune

Jeanette McCune has been Director of DC School and Community Initiatives at the John F. Kennedy Center for the Performing Arts since 2001, leads programming with Washington, D.C. public and charter schools including collective impact initiatives and in-depth model partnerships in 22 schools, manages Kennedy Center performance access programs for under-resourced communities in the greater Washington, DC metropolitan area, and serves as leader for youth initiatives. Jeanette's expertise and interests are in building partnerships in high-risk schools and community settings, and serving populations of impoverished, minority, and disabled citizens.

Iris Minor, MSW.

Iris Minor is a research assistant and full-time doctoral student in the Curriculum and Instruction program at Florida Atlantic University. She received her Master's degree in Social Work from Barry University and a Bachelor's degree in Social Work from the University of Alabama. She was awarded the Presidential Fellowship in 2016–2017 and most recently the Graduate Diversity Fellowship 2017. Her current scholarship focuses on examining the implications of multicultural education toward building STEM resiliency amongst historically marginalized groups and culturally responsive pedagogy as a means for closing the achievement gap in the science and mathematics fields.

Nanette Missaghi, M.A.
Nanette Missaghi is the director of the Collaborative Urban Educator Program at the University of St. Thomas. Her responsibilities include recruitment and retention of pre-service teachers of color, budget oversight, graduate student advising, and faculty trainer/coach of equity and culturally responsive pedagogy for instruction and curriculum in teacher and special education. Co-facilitator of the AACTE Network Improvement Community (NIC) initiative on the Retention of black and Latino men in teacher education, Nanette provides consulting services in racial equity, culturally responsive pedagogy, curriculum reconstruction and race relations. She is co-author of *Eden Prairie Schools- A Case Study* with Dr. Melissa Krull, Chapter 11 of *More Courageous Conversations About Race* by Glenn E. Singleton, Corwin Press, Thousand Oaks California, 2013. She also writes a blog called CultureIntel at www.cultureintel.com and is a licensed Intercultural Development Inventory (IDI) coach.

Eliana Carvalho Mukherjee
Eliana Mukherjee has over 20 years of work experience in all aspects of education, including teaching, administration, research, planning, curriculum development and teacher training. She was the Director of the American International School of Costa Rica for two years, and she taught elementary school in the United States for five years. She has worked on research projects for the World Bank on school improvement and for Harvard University on early language and literacy development. She worked as Assistant Professor in the Peace Education M.A. program at the United Nations mandated University of Peace for six years. Additionally, she worked as a consultant for the UNESCO International Bureau of Education in developing guidelines for curriculum developers and teacher training institution in Angola. Mrs. Mukherjee earned her B.S. in Mass Communications from Emerson College and her Ed.M. in Administration, Planning and Social Policy from Harvard University. She is pursuing her Ph.D. at Florida Atlantic University in Curriculum, Culture, and Educational Inquiry. Mrs. Mukherjee currently works as a Professor in the teacher education program at Palm Beach State College, Florida.

Kathleen Randolph, M.Ed.
Kathleen M. Randolph is a doctoral candidate and university supervisor in the Department of Exceptional Student Education at Florida Atlantic University. Her research interests include using technology to provide immediate feedback to teachers, and using applied behavior analysis in the classroom to support teachers and students with high-incidence disabilities. Kathleen earned her master's degree in Special Education, and two post-master's certifications in Graduate Study in Educational Leadership and Special Education Supervision from Duquesne University.

Kimberly Rhoden, M.Ed.
Kimberly Rhoden is a Florida certified teacher and educational leader. She has worked as a classroom teacher, language arts trainer, curriculum coach, Title I-Part D liaison, and professional development facilitator. Ms. Rhoden has helped implement core reading and writing programs for elementary and middle schools and has received several awards throughout her career including: Chappie James "Most Promising Teacher", Daytona Beach Jaycees *Outstanding "Young" Educator, and Unsung Heroes –ING.*

Ramonia R. Rochester, MA.
Ramonia R. Rochester is a doctoral candidate, AACTE Holmes Scholar and Presidential Fellow 2014–2016 of Curriculum and Instruction at Florida Atlantic University, specializing in media literacy education policy for K-12 and teacher preparation. Her scholarship includes work in international and comparative education, critical pedagogy, and social communication theories of education. Ramonia is passionate about developing media literacy education's capacity to sustain participatory democracy and mitigate the negative effects of media's pervasive influence on 21st century society. Her current research examines modes for rectifying the disconnect between media education policy and practice, and attending to inequities associated with information access and education for critical media consumption. To this end, she most recently published "Amazing Ourselves to Death: A critical review" of one author's view of Neil Postman's theories concerning the negative effects of

media communication technology on public literacy. Her presentations include a study of the transectionalities between media, religious habitus, and the organization of social justice spaces in educational practice, made at Trinity College's Graduate Symposium in Ireland and the European Conference on Education in England, UK.

Dilys Schoorman, Ph.D.

Dr. Schoorman is Chairperson and Professor in the Department of Curriculum, Culture and Educational Inquiry in the College of Education at Florida Atlantic University where she teaches courses in Multicultural/ Global Education, Curriculum, and Critical Theory. She is well aware, at a personal and professional level, of the national and international struggles around issues of diversity and the violent consequences that come with our inability to see difference as an asset, not a hindrance, to our democracy.

Kalisha Waldon, Ph.D.

Dr. Waldon currently holds the position of *Professor II* at Palm Beach State College. She has worked in the PreK-20 system for almost 15 years as an administrator, teacher/professor, professional development facilitator, and mentor. She has a doctorate degree in Curriculum and Instruction with an emphasis in multicultural education/critical multiculturalism. Her areas of scholarship include K-12 reading education, religious education, critical media literacy, and multicultural education. Kalisha has conducted professional development trainings for educators, served on school accreditation teams, and is passionate about empowering others to strive for excellence. She co-authored a chapter on teaching the African American student in E.N. Ariza & S.I. Lapp (Eds). *Literacy, Language, and Culture.*

Kyla L. Williams, Ph.D.

Kyla L. Williams is an Associate Professor of Mathematics and Honors College Coordinator at Broward College in Coconut Creek, FL. She holds a B.S. in Mathematics Education and Pure Mathematics, a M.S. in Mathematics Education, and a Ph.D. in Curriculum and Instruction. Williams also holds a Florida Teaching Certificate in 6–12 Mathematics and has 13 years of experience teaching high school and college-level mathematics. Her educational specializations include, but are not limited to: Multicultural Education in Mathematics, Culturally Responsive Pedagogy, and the Implementation of Critical Thinking in Mathematics. She is a member of the Florida Chapter of the National Association of Multicultural Education (NAME) and Delta Sigma Theta Sorority, Inc.

Cynthia L. Wilson, Ph.D.

Dr. Cynthia L. Wilson is a Professor in the Department of Exceptional Student Education at Florida Atlantic University. She is the 2015-2017 President of the Higher Education Consortium for Special Educators, a national organization that represents major university programs that prepare personnel for special education leadership roles. Dr. Wilson's research and instructional focus emphasizes the preparation of educators to implement research-based, effective practices to improve educational opportunities for special education students, learners at-risk for academic failure, and to increase the effectiveness of university-school partnerships. She obtained her doctoral degree in Special Education with a cognate in Higher Education from Florida State University.

INTRODUCTION

Why Do We Need Multicultural Education?
Reclaiming Our Roles as Professionals in a Democracy

Dilys Schoorman, Ph.D.

The trouble is not that schools don't work; they do. They're excellent machines for achieving historically accepted purposes. . . . What is now encompassed by the one word "school" are two very different kinds of institutions that, in function, finance and intention, serve entirely different roles. Both are needed for our nation's governance. But children in one set of schools are educated to be governors; children in the other set of schools are trained for being governed. . . . In suburban schools are children of the rich, who grow up to privilege and anesthetic oblivion to pain – and who then use the servants produced by ghetto schools. The former are given the imaginative range to mobilize ideas for economic growth; the latter are provided with the discipline to do the narrow tasks the first group will prescribe.

Jonathan Kozol[1]

Pre-reading Activity

Reflect on your K-12 education. To what extent did your education perpetuate or interrupt the stratification described by Kozol in the quotation presented above?

Notes on reading this chapter

To the extent that is possible, please read this chapter as if you were participating in a dialogue with me, the writer. Talk back; pause to reflect; ask questions; agree or disagree; consider your emotions as you read. My hope is that you are cognitively active, not passive, as you read. You should read all your texts in this way.

Author biases

I believe that . . .

- Education is our single best hope against bigotry. Yet it has also been a particularly effective tool for the perpetuation of bigotry and discrimination.
- Educators operate on the front lines of our quest for a better world. Thus it matters, how educators think, what they know, and how they are supported. It is a matter of national importance and global survival.
- What are your beliefs about education and the role of educators? How might we educate the next generation of students (and their educators) for a democratic and justice-oriented world?

The Rationale and Context for Multicultural Education

Scholars have framed education as an essential facet of the public good. That is, they view the purpose of education as serving not only the individual learner but also the public who benefits from a well-educated citizen, professional and leader (Baldwin, 1963; Dewey, 1916; Giroux, 2013). For these scholars, education is central to the maintenance and preservation of democracy, because an informed voting public is key to successful governance of, for and by the people. Yet, an examination of the historical and contemporary experiences of a diverse range of people reveals that education has fallen short of these ideals (Bigelow, 2008; Spring, 2013; Zinn, 2003). Although for many school is/was a place of pleasant memories, intellectual safety and profound growth, for others, it has been a site of intellectual and psychological violence, negligence and/or boredom (Acuna, 2014; Adams, 1995; Anderson, 1988; Gonzalez, 1996; Lomawaima & McCarty, 2006; Takaki, 1989; Watkins, 2001; Woodson, 1933). These discrepancies are indicators of injustices that ought to be remedied by education, not caused by it. This chapter draws on these discrepancies in historical and contemporary educational experiences to provide a backdrop for understanding why and how multicultural education should be implemented. Critical multiculturalism is presented as a central organizing framework for our identity as a professional and a typology that illustrates the potential framing of multiculturalism in schools is offered. As you review these ideas, consider how your own educational experiences, including your educator preparation program, resonate with the observations made and/or provide an alternate view for how education for a democratic and socially just world might be pursued. Consider also how you can ensure that your future classroom instruction embodies the principles of critical multiculturalism rather than blindly perpetuating problematic and fundamentally inequitable practices.

Contemporary concerns about stratification in education emerge in the context of the standardized testing and accountability regimes that have exacerbated the historic disparities between/ among students of diverse groups (Alquist, Gorski & Montano, 2011). Although for many years, scholars have sounded the alarm against standardized tests (Karp, 2016; 2014; Kohn, 2015; 2000; 1999; Kozol, 2006; 2005; Meier, 2003), it is only recently that many educators, parents, students and now, even politicians have finally agreed that our children are tested too much and that the recent accountability movement that has swept public education in the USA in the form of high stakes standardized tests has led to a narrowed curriculum, joyless classrooms and punitive systems of assessments (Ravitch, 2014; Rose 2011; School Board of Palm Beach County, Florida, 2014; Watkins, 2012; Zernike, 2015). Few, beyond private testing companies, have experienced long-term benefits. The fact now remains that we have sacrificed the education of many students, particularly those of historically marginalized backgrounds, by turning them off the love of learning through test-prep oriented curriculum that required diverse students to demonstrate standardized, yet narrow learning outcomes in high stakes, culturally and linguistically inhospitable conditions. Students in private schools, where most policy makers send their children, have not had to perform or learn under these circumstances. Thus we are witness to a two tiered system built on inequity and hypocrisy: what is good enough for your child, is not good enough for mine.

Contemporary social and political realities in the USA also reveal the urgent need for curriculum reform in the direction of multicultural education. The anticipated demographic shift where those of White racial identities will no longer be majority in the USA among children by 2020 and adults by 2045 (Ware, 2015), highlights the urgent need for a significant reconceptualization in the role of educators in preparing us, individually and collectively, to successfully live and work in this multicultural, multilingual, multi-religious globally interconnected world. In contrast, each of the following speaks to the adverse affects social and political realities have on particular communities while privileging corporate and economic elites. Individually and collectively, they reveal a searing and sobering revelation about our nation's underlying attitudes towards diversity and democracy.

- Social and political discourse about difference (see Southern Poverty Law Center, 2016)
- Recent social advocacy movements such as the Occupy Movement (see Giroux, 2012) and Black Lives Matter (see Gray & Finley, 2015; Hoffman, Granger, Vallejos & Moats, 2016)
- DREAMers in support of Immigration Reform (see Preston, 2012), together with legislative and judicial (in)action on a range of issues including restricted access to voting and the dismantling of key race-based protections in the Voting Rights Act (Rutenberg, 2015),

- Restricted access to reproductive health services for women even as we are bombarded with advertisements for products supporting men's reproductive health (Joffe & Parker, 2015),
- Opposition to access to affordable health care (see Ungar, 2010),
- Corporatization of incarceration (Alexander, 2012),
- Environmental (in)justice (Taylor, 2014),
- Political intransigence on gun violence and gun sales, despite the multiple mass shootings (see New York Times Editorial Board, 2016; Gabor, 2016; Kristof, 2016)
- Deliberate political negligence in cities that have caused gentrification in Chicago (Stovall, 2014), lead poisoning in the water in Flint (Ganim & Tran, 2016; Kennedy, 2016), and
- Urban blight and entrenched corruption in US cities; for example, Ferguson and Detroit (Friedersdorf, 2015; Zavatarro, 2014)

These examples highlight the need for leaders to be well-educated on and capable of working with diverse constituents and advocating for the needs of all groups. We can no longer afford leaders who are inept and/or bigoted in their decision making in the context of diversity. The question, then, is who is responsible for this education? And how will it be implemented?

Historical Legacies and Contemporary Realities

Critical multicultural education also responds to the long history of discrimination and its ongoing legacy still experienced by groups such as Native Americans, African Americans, Latinos and Asians. Ladson Billings (2006) discusses this legacy in terms of the historical, economic, sociopolitical and moral debt owed to these groups for the inequitable policies that have prevented them from equal participation in US democracy; this includes the lack of access to an equitable education. The pursuit of equity in the context of historic patterns of educational discrimination lies at the center of the social justice imperatives of education. Achieving this goal involves a process that Freire (2000) has dubbed conscientization: becoming critically aware of these patterns of power and marginalization, the methods by which they are enacted and the potential for individual and collective agency to struggle against them. Freire revealed how traditional education perpetuated patterns of oppression among politically marginalized groups and called for education to be emancipatory, where one acquired the knowledge and skills for transformation of inequitable systems. While such an injunction applies to all aspects of education, this imperative is particularly salient in the education of future teachers and administrators.

While multiple examples of institutional discrimination in education abound in US educational history, two cases are presented as a contextual backdrop for understanding the ideas presented in this chapter. The first is historical, focused on the Native American Boarding Schools set up in the USA in the late 1800s. The second is the more contemporary case of the Mexican American Studies program in Tucson Unified School District that was banned in 2012. As readers you are encouraged to learn more about these cases through additional research, as what is presented is only a 'snapshot' of a more complex set of decisions and experiences. Each case offers us an opportunity to consider how perspectives of white supremacy play a role in educational policy and practice and to contemplate the role that educators play in these circumstances.

Learning from Our Past: Native American Boarding Schools

In 1819 the Civilization Fund Act paved the way for the use of education as a means for cultural transformation designed to strip Native American children of their native culture and identity. This model for Native American education called for the establishment of off-reservation boarding schools, an arrangement deliberately designed to separate Native Americans children from their parents. This occurred despite the existence of bilingual schools among the Choctaws and the Cherokees where the literacy level was higher than the white populations of some states. By the end of the century, congress had made school attendance mandatory for Native American children and families were penalized for non-compliance.

Multiple, interconnected rationales governed this educational policy. Education offered a more efficient and economical alternative to war as the government's way to "deal with" the Native American populations. Political rhetoric framed Native Americans as "uncivilized" and as "savages" allowing for education to be viewed as a process of "civilizing" as well as "Christianizing" the students. There was the possibility that education could, in a generation, cause Native Americans to accept White American Protestant capitalistic values governing trade and property to facilitate smoother and efficient transfer of lands away from Native American ownership. Thus, education became a tool of oppression where cultural genocide was perpetuated.

The educational alternative to war appeared to be a more humane alternative to the military edict, "The only good Indian is a dead Indian." Instead, General Richard Henry Pratt advocated that through education one could, "Kill the Indian and save the man [sic]." The Carlisle Boarding School, founded in 1879 by Pratt, was the first of many Native American Boarding Schools set up around the nation. Boarding schools were harsh, traumatic, militarized experiences. At these schools, students pursued agriculture and basic skills in reading, writing and arithmetic. They were penalized for speaking their native languages. At many schools the children were undernourished and were engaged in labor more than they focused on education and academic achievement. In 1928, the Meriam Report was commissioned to review practices in the boarding schools, resoundingly criticized their practices. This education had failed to prepare students academically, socially, psychologically or vocationally for life either in reservation or non-reservation contexts (Lomawaima & McCarthy, 2006).

Students who were subjected to these experiences speak of the trauma they experienced and loss of identity that drove further social wedges between the generations. They also describe their own youthful ways of resistance to this indoctrination, including a refusal to speak at all when deprived of their mother tongue. Teachers who worked at these schools clearly assumed they were doing their duty as they administered what hindsight would reveal as brutal, racist and unjust.

What lessons might we learn from this history? How do contemporary attitudes towards cultural assimilation to a mainstream identity, or bilingualism mirror this history? What are the different ways in which to view student resistance to an unjust or irrelevant curriculum?

Learning from Recent History: The Mexican American Studies Program

The Mexican American Studies (MAS) program of the Tucson Unified School District (TUSD) was initiated in 1998 in the context of broader historical concerns about commitments towards desegregation and racial integration amid persistent academic achievement gaps between White and Latino/a students. Launched in 2002 in one high school classroom and later expanded to multiple high school classes, middle schools and elementary schools, the curriculum focused on Mexican American history and culture. At the high school level, courses were offered as electives, but counted towards core class requirements in social studies and language arts.

The program was grounded in the principles of critical pedagogy and was explicitly dedicated to developing Latino/a identity, history and culture where the indigenous funds of knowledge of students, their families and communities were viewed as integral to academically rigorous curriculum, pedagogy that supported social engagement through respectful relationships among teachers, students and parents.

Although more likely to have lower 9th and 10th grade GPAs, speak English as their second language and from lower socioeconomic backgrounds, the MAS participants who had initially failed the state standardized tests prior to enrolling in the program outperformed their non-MAS peers on the re-take of the tests and in graduation rates. Despite this success, a state bill [HB 2281] explicitly designed to eliminate the program was passed in 2010 and, threatened with a 10% cut in funding, the Tucson Unified School District was forced to disband the program. The bill stipulated against classes that: 1. Advocate ethnic solidarity, rather than treating pupils as individuals; 2. Promote resentment toward a race or class of people; 3. Are designed primarily for pupils of a particular ethnic group; or 4. Promote the overthrow of the US government (Acuna, 2014).

Although a state audit supported continuation of the program, and despite protests by the community, the threat of funding cuts ultimately resulted in the banning of the program in 2012. Documentary and media reports reveal primary source evidence of high levels of student intellectual and social engagement, curricular rigor and vitality, educator talent and commitment as well as alarming expressions of racism, bigotry and ignorance by key decision makers. Efforts are under way to re-introduce culturally relevant studies into the district's offerings, while versions of the MAS program are being adopted in other parts of the country.

In this case, we see how students, including those of non-Latino backgrounds, responded positively to the curriculum and pedagogy; yet state officials operating in a political climate hostile to Latinos saw it fit to target what has been viewed as one of the nation's best exemplars of ethnic studies. What lessons might we, as multicultural educators, learn from this case? Why would a policy such as HB 2281 be developed? Why would a program that supports academic achievement be targeted?

A comparison of the nature of curriculum and experiences of student learning in the two cases reveals that education is never a politically, culturally, or philosophically neutral process and that education has a powerful potential to oppress or empower. Oppression was evident in the case of the Native American Boarding Schools while empowerment emerged in the Mexican American Studies program. Education as a process of conscientization facilitates a clearer understanding of whether – regardless of its accompanying rhetoric - an educational policy or practice further perpetuates a stratified educational experience for students in increasingly re-segregated schools or interrupts such inequity. It is crucial that all future educators develop a critical awareness of this history so that egalitarian and open-minded educators do not unintentionally and blindly replicate these patterns of institutional discrimination on the one hand and, on the other, are equipped to handle the successful implementation of and struggle for critical multicultural education.

Gunnar Pippel / Shutterstock.com

Critical Multicultural Education

Not everything labeled "multicultural" is desired practice. Multicultural scholars have developed typologies that differentiate between approaches that represent restrictively targeted efforts or superficial adaptations and the desired approaches that are integrative and aimed at broad-based structural transformation (see Banks 2001a; Grant & Sleeter, 2007; Nieto, 1994; Sleeter & Grant, 2009). The desired approaches in each typology are based on principles of social justice and democracy and are referred to as critical multicultural education. Less desired approaches are based on perspectives of *cultural* differences (sometimes through deficit orientations) attributed to marginalized *individuals* or groups with limited reference to positions of privilege, policies and/ or practices that create difference. In contrast, critical multiculturalism "gives priority to structural analysis of unequal power relationships, analyzing the role of institutional inequities, including *but not necessarily limited to* racism" (May & Sleeter, 2010, p. 10; italics in original). Each of these typologies promotes a broad conceptualization of diversity, critical awareness of structural inequalities, and the need for education to interrupt these inequities through an explicit connection between education and its role in a democracy and culturally relevant pedagogy that draws on students' interests and funds of knowledge as a catalyst for knowledge generation and academic achievement.

Banks' (2001b) identification of multiple dimensions of multicultural education underscores the fact that multicultural education encompasses the content of the curriculum, pedagogical approaches, the goals of prejudice reduction, the understanding of the politics of how knowledge is constructed and whose knowledge is privileged and extends beyond individual teachers and classes to the culture of the school itself. The central idea here is that meaningful multicultural education entails more than a single lesson, unit, month, grade, teacher or target group. It must be central to the core philosophy of educational policy and practice within a given system; whether that system is a school, a district or an educator preparation program.

Too often these discussions of the implementation of multicultural education are presented as if they are a matter of individual educator choice, rather than as a program or institutional commitment. It is crucial that pre-service and in-service educators see a commitment to issues of social justice at a *programmatic* level, rather than at the level of individual and isolated classrooms. How might we integrate the principles of critical multicultural education as central to our institutions (e.g. schools or programs)? Drawing on the curricular typologies as a heuristic, a typology of the framing of multiculturalism within institutions, schools, and educator preparation programs and their impact on educators' perceptions and practices in contexts of diversity is offered. We, both pre- and in-service educators, are encouraged to consider how the explicit and implicit messages about multicultural education shape our perspectives and practices as equitable educators in contexts of diversity.

Conceptualizing Multicultural Education: A Typology

Building on the curricular typologies in multicultural education, the following typology seeks to integrate diverse scholarship on what *should* be the conceptualization of multicultural education in institutional practice. The four levels of the typology highlight the assumptions about the purpose of education, values emergent in schools, institutions, and educator preparation programs, and the role of the educator in contemporary education. It highlights key ideational constructs to facilitate analysis and reflection on the philosophical underpinnings and social justice commitments of critical multicultural educators. Actual educational contexts may offer much wider variation than suggested the four levels of the typology. [See Table 2.1]

Not included in this discussion are approaches that adopt an explicitly deficit perspective of difference or those that espouse "color blind" perspectives where culture and difference are viewed as irrelevant. Educators might also espouse rhetoric supporting the success of "all" students without necessarily paying attention to the differences among them. This undifferentiated categorization glosses over difference or re-frames difference as a generic "other." Educators who claim to "not see color, but only humans" fail to grapple with difference that lies at the basis of structural inequalities and interpersonal prejudice.

Level 1: The Compliance Model

Educator preparation programs typically respond to diversity matters as a function of existing policies. While policies have been crucial for establishing equity, programs that seek compliance with externally-driven standards of diversity as their goal, frequently fall short of broader commitments to social justice, which are more difficult to mandate or require. Consequently, following Freire's (2000) analysis of the pedagogy of the oppressed, compliance-oriented programs yield compliance-oriented educators who use externally-imposed requirements as their primary compass for professional practice. As a result, concerns about "closing the achievement gap" cause educators to focus on the achievement of students of diverse under-served groups, but largely because educational policies or accreditation standards require them to do so. As such, the focus becomes the test scores of diverse groups of students rather than, as Ladson Billings (2006) so cogently argued, the inequities in policies

Table 1:   A typology for understanding multicultural education

LEVELS OF MULTICULTURAL EDUCATION

Level 1: The Compliance Model
Target: Students who are "different" from mainstream
Purpose: Assimilation
Values: "Equality" often guised as standardization; tolerance/ accommodation of difference
Focus in educator preparation: Pedagogy (differentiated instruction based on perceived "learning styles"); "strategies" focus. [i.e. change in teacher's instruction]
Role of teachers: Compliant; curricular technicians
Expected role of learners: Expectations of passive (i.e. unquestioning) acceptance of status quo; dutiful followers of instructions. Students who do not fit this mold are labeled "rebellious" or "problems."
Comments from scholars: Such an approach has led to de-skilling of teachers; perpetuation of existing inequities.

Level 2: The Culturally Liberal Model
Target: Students of all backgrounds.
Purpose: Bi-/multi-cultural identity development; acquiring 'mainstream' and culture-specific knowledge; multi-perspectival knowledge
Values: Difference as positive; self-reflection
Focus in educator preparation: White/ "mainstream" teachers encouraged to engage in self-reflection; focus on pedagogy and curriculum adaptation. [i.e. change in teacher attitudes]
Role of teachers: Facilitator of learning; teacher as curricular decision maker
Expected role of learners: Active learners in student-centered curriculum; cultural border crossers.
Comments from scholars: The focus on cross-cultural differences alone will not address the fundamental bases for inequality.

Level 3: The Advocacy Model
Target: Institutional practice (curriculum, policies, practices); the "system"
Purpose: Critical consciousness building among educators
Values: Equity
Focus in educator preparation: Understanding empowering v. disempowering potentiality of school policies and practices; Social construction of difference; historical and sociopolitical perspectives. [i.e. change school policies, practices]
Role of teachers: Equity leader; views education/ curriculum as a catalyst for equity and social justice.
Expected role of learners: Caring and conscious about social/ structural inequities; engaged learners in democratically organized spaces
Comments from scholars: The achievement gap will not be closed until the opportunity gap/ educational debt has been acknowledged and addressed.

Level 4: The Democratic Community Model
Target: School and community
Purpose: Education as democratic practice; development of democratic schools
Values: Community engagement; school-community partnerships; social justice
Focus in educator preparation: Experiential learning; Participatory Action Research; Academic Service Learning; comfort with/ ability to engage with multiple community voices
Role of teachers: Engaged public intellectual; moral activist
Expected role of learners: Active engagement in/with the community; view their role as educated members of the community 'giving back' or 'giving to' the ongoing development of local communities.
Comments from scholars: Democratic schools that are linked with their communities (rather than merely individual teachers or classrooms) are the fundamental organizational unit for multicultural practice

and practices that underlie those numerical discrepancies. Committed to the value of equality, frequently translated into 'one-size-fits-all' assumptions, even well-intended educators make assimilation the goal of education, with little regard for the relevance or the fairness of those standardized outcomes.

Contemporary manifestations of the compliance model in classrooms may not be overtly hostile to students of diverse underserved backgrounds, as were the educators of the Native American Boarding Schools. Many teachers pursue pedagogical adaptation based on students' cultural backgrounds, learning styles or perceived needs. However, school systems that adopt the compliance model are typically preoccupied with instructional "strategies" for addressing achievement gaps; yet they rarely question the relevance of the curriculum or its goals (Schoorman & Bogotch, 2010). Both teachers and students increasingly are evaluated on observations of teacher behaviors based on pre-determined checklists and rubrics rather than assessing the conceptual complexity or instructional decision making of the teacher. What today's uncritical educator might not realize is that engaging in strategies linked to students' perceived learning styles, leading successfully to learning outcomes that are intolerant of or hostile to cultural identities or personal goals might actually be doing significant harm. Similarly, educators might draw on the use of culturally representative texts, but without questioning the authenticity of those representations for students in the class (see Zittleman & Sadker, 2002 for more information on curriculum biases). Concerns for parity in achievement may well yield "pull out" or "drill and kill" practices that have proven to be ineffective in long-term learning (Kohn, 2011). Such a quest may deny these students opportunities to participate in art, music or PE, subjects deemed "extra" or "special" and therefore extraneous to the goal of compliance regarding the test scores of under-served students. Consequently, they run the risk of engaging in cultural assimilation more like the joyless, tedious and personally irrelevant practices of the Native American Boarding Schools, rather than moving towards successful academic achievement through a holistic approach grounded in critical multicultural education (more like the Mexican American Studies Program) that moves well beyond compliance with external mandates.

As the two cases reveal, state policies on diversity are often misguided as well. If policies regarding the education of diverse students are based on assimilationist or deculturalization models, compliance could well entail the perpetuation of inequity and institutional racism. In Florida, the state that ranks third in the nation as a host of immigrants, the revision of accomplished educator practices led to the deletion of *diversity* and *critical thinking* from the state standards that govern teacher preparation. What message does this send schools and educator preparation programs about what teachers need? It is therefore incumbent on school leaders, deans and educator preparation faculty to help professionals to question policies in ways that are appropriate to the contexts in which they work. However, compliance-oriented programs are less likely to support such questioning among their students.

As a teacher educator, I have witnessed the compliance orientation among my students, frequently engendered through years of conditioning through grading policies and external reward systems. These pre-service or in-service educators are typically pre-occupied with following directions dutifully, are disconcerted by flexible rules that encourage creative, independent and critical thought, and express their frustrations with the unlearning of old learning habits with pleas such as, "Just tell me what to do!" Compliant educators are often de-skilled practitioners who are largely "transmitters" of received curriculum, whose interaction with curriculum is technical (how to) rather than conceptual (what should/could). Instead of developing educators as decision makers who use their professional judgment to identify the best course of action in a given unique situation, compliance orientations - a consequence of what Freire referred to as a "banking approach" in education - result in practitioners who are dutiful rule-followers regardless of the rule's intent or impact. How does this characterize your teacher preparation and how do you think this would impact your future teaching?

To be clear, this critique does not advocate unbridled adversarial stances, nor does it condemn compliance with rules and regulations required for appropriate governance. It also does not rule out the value of mainstream knowledge that could serve as cultural capital for marginalized groups. It does, however, advocate for schools and programs that systematically prepare educators who are intellectually "wide awake" to the restrictiveness of rules, standards and policies, especially in the context of historically underserved populations. As evident in the model of the Mexican American Studies program, this entails preparing and supporting educators who will find ways to help students to acquire the cultural capital needed to survive in culturally inhospitable contexts without losing their sense of self.

Level 2: The Culturally Liberal Model

This model exemplifies classrooms that are responsive to students, rather than to external mandates or edicts, and is an approach to multiculturalism that is inclusive of the needs of students of a wide range of backgrounds. Consequently, those who belong to the White mainstream are also encouraged to examine their (often unexplored) cultural identities and the manner in which this heritage shapes their worldviews especially in the context of cultural diversity. Hence, it is not just the culture and identity of those traditionally underserved that is the focal point. In accepting cultural identity as "normal" (i.e. shared and experienced by all human beings), difference, itself, also becomes less threatening and more comfortable. Educators who are able to model comfort with difference and who demonstrate how the presence of diversity is an asset rather than a challenge to institutional decision making, will advance crucial learning towards equity and social justice.

Unlike the compliance model, where we engage with diversity because we "have to", here educators engage with diversity because we *want to* and are focused on the well-being of students. In this model, teachers are framed as facilitators of collectively generated knowledge, rather than as transmitters of fixed knowledge, while students recognize their legitimate and active role in the knowledge construction process, underscoring their own views as one of many. Students' knowledge and backgrounds are deemed a catalyst, rather than a barrier, for effective learning and curricula representative of diverse perspectives and student-centered learning are the norm. Cultural relevance in content and in instruction was evident in the MAS program, whereas it was clearly absent in the case of the Native American boarding schools. For students of historically marginalized groups, the injunction is that they become bicultural, learning their own histories as well mainstream knowledge (Freire & Macedo, 1987).

Two leading proponents of cultural responsiveness, Ladson-Billings (1995) and Gay (2013), highlight the importance of a humanizing pedagogy that results in academic success, cultural competence and critical consciousness that facilitates the questioning of an inequitable status quo. The student-centered and culturally-sensitive orientation of the culturally liberal model makes it appealing as an ultimate goal for multicultural integration in schools and educator preparation programs. However, many schools and educator preparation models focus on aspects of culture but do not adequately address the critical consciousness about structural barriers that maintain patterns of inequality. This task is taken on by the next model.

Level 3: The Advocacy Model

This model frames multicultural educators as leaders and advocates for equity in education. Consequently, professional preparation of educators facilitates their critical conscientization to acknowledge that education is not neutral, that curricular and policy decisions frequently result in differential benefits across individuals and groups, and that the goal of education is to facilitate equity. The focus of this model is on institutional structures, including but not limited to educational policies and practices that contribute to inequitable outcomes for students. This underscores the assumption that it is the structures - not the students, their families or their teachers – that should change. Multicultural education efforts undertaken within this model espouse an explicitly counter-hegemonic (e.g. anti-racist; anti-sexist; anti-classist; anti-homophobic etc.) standpoint and frame education as an inherently social justice endeavor.

Although scholars in the field of multicultural education have long advocated for this perspective, schools and teacher preparation programs have frequently fallen short in their ability to embrace multiculturalism at this level. Critical analysis of structures that privilege or marginalize groups have been central to the calls for social justice in education of leaders of underserved groups (see Ayers, Quinn & Stovall, 2009; Bogotch & Shields, 2014). However, the interrogation of and the rescinding of privilege accrued through the current system is much more difficult for those who have benefited from the status quo. Unlearning and re-structuring are daunting, despite our awareness of the egregious harm of mainstream education practices on students of underserved backgrounds. At a practical level, the status quo is, too often, the only familiar system of educational governance. Educators of the advocacy model recognize difference as socially constructed for the purposes of deliberate social stratification. For them, there is no option but to change. Such change is desired across the entire school/ program culture and not isolated to particular classes, teachers or dimensions of educational activity.

The transformation advocated in this model is not necessarily unknown. The education afforded to the privileged already exemplifies choices and opportunities that should be made available to all students: freedom from the oppressive regime of standardized testing, curriculum that is culturally relevant and personally meaningful, opportunities for challenging curriculum such as AP and honors classes, the presence of highly qualified teachers, school environments that are physically and socially safe and classrooms where learning is joyful, intellectually engaging and humanizing. In addition to the student-centeredness of the previous model, education for advocacy will require more effort in curriculum development, as curriculum is adapted to reflect principles of problem posing and critical pedagogy. Consciousness raising about whose knowledge is privileged, clear understandings of the philosophical underpinnings of curriculum, rigorous, engaging curriculum and an explicit commitment to principles of equity and social justice will be central goals of such educator preparation programs. Several exemplars of this work exist through organizations such as, Rethinking Schools (www.RethinkingSchools.org), Chicago Grassroots Network (http://grassrootscurriculum.org), Teaching for Tolerance (www.tolerance.org), and publications related to curriculum by critical multicultural educators (Sleeter, 2005; Grant and Sleeter, 2008; May & Sleeter, 2010).

Central to these exemplars is the role of the teacher as an autonomous and knowledgeable professional capable of developing and/or adapting curriculum, analyzing existing practice and advocating for students who are underserved by existing structures and policies. Consequently, the expected role of students is one of engaged equity advocates who see direct connections between their classroom-based learning and their social context. It is expected that the educational experiences of these students will serve them well as equity leaders in the future.

Level 4: The Democratic Community Model

This final model is somewhat different from the rest. Framed around the descriptions of democratic schools by Apple and Beane (1995), inspired by the work of community educators such as Jane Addams (1910/1961) and Paulo Freire (2000), and drawing on the underlying philosophies of historical exemplars such as the Rough Rock Demonstration School (Lomawaima & McCarty, 2002), the Freedom Schools of the 1964 (Emery, Braselmann, & Gold, 2004), and, contemporaneously, educator preparation programs of Center X, at the University of California, Los Angeles (Quartz, Priselac & Franke, 2009), this approach to multicultural education re-centers the school within the context of its surrounding community. Here schools reclaim their role as community centers that cannot operate separately from local communities. Schools and their communities serve as mutually beneficial resources. Curriculum emerges from and is responsive to the needs of the community and draws on the knowledge of community members as curriculum content. Students engage in learning activities that benefit the community and recognize their obligations, as educated citizens, to serve and contribute positively to building their communities. This stands in stark contrast to the Native American Boarding Schools, where schools made students irrelevant in their own communities.

Center X honors graduates such as Ramon Antonio Martinez, for his use of Spanish in the classroom despite Proposition 227, which banned the speaking of Spanish in California's classrooms (https://centerx.gseis.ucla.edu/our-work/ed-spotlights). This is the antithesis of the compliance model. This conceptualization of the role of the school vis-à-vis its community is, sadly, alien to the conceptualizations exemplified in most educator preparation programs. Thus it is crucial for us to contemplate how educators might be prepared for such a context, especially when most educators have not experienced this education themselves. It is unclear if most educator preparation programs even want to espouse such a model. And if they do, what might they look like? Ayers (2010) raised a parallel question when he asked, "What does it mean concretely – and distinctly – then, to be an excellent teacher in and for a democratic society? What makes a democratic classroom unmistakable?" (p. 3).

Reclaiming Your Own Education

In his 1963 address to teachers, Baldwin, an African American well-aware of the ravages of institutionalized discrimination, noted,

> The paradox of education is precisely this – that as one begins to become conscious one begins to examine the society in which he [or she] is being educated. The purpose of education, finally, is to create in a person the ability to look at the world for himself [or herself], to make his [or her] own decisions . . . to ask questions of the universe, and then learn to live with those questions, is the way he [or she] achieves his [or her] own identity. But no society is really anxious to have that kind of person around. What societies really, ideally, want is a citizenry which will simply obey the rules of society. If society succeeds in this, that society is about to perish. The obligation of anyone who thinks of himself [or herself] as responsible is to examine society and try to change it and to fight it – at no matter what risk. This is the only hope society has. This is the only way societies change (p. 42).

This chapter has attempted to follow Baldwin's challenge to teachers by raising critical consciousness about the historical role of education in emancipating on the one hand or maintaining stratification on the other. It is hoped that you have begun to ask questions about your own education, both current and past, and then make decisions about the questions you wish to ask and the changes for which you wish to fight. Thus, if as current or future educators we are to achieve the hopeful transformation that Baldwin envisions, we must first be able to ask questions of our own education and reclaim all lost opportunities for critical consciousness-raising.

The principles of critical pedagogy that underlie critical multiculturalism remind us that instead of relying on teachers as the source of received knowledge, learners must be active co-creators of the knowledge that emerges in programs of study and in schools. For many years, we have focused on constructing the role of the *teacher* in this dynamic. However, it is important that we first claim the role of *learners* as active partners in the democratic process of teaching and learning. Learners committed to the values of social justice will actively counter efforts that will de-skill, de-professionalize or disempower students and future educators. In so doing, these learners will also help their teachers move towards social justice practices as well.

A crucial early (and ongoing) step in resisting professional socialization that restricts our intellectual curiosity and/or moral capacity as we challenge the inequities of the system in which we work, is developing a critical self-awareness of our own biases and blinders and our role in limiting the potential for equity and social justice. It includes recognizing our own privilege (or positioning) in a stratified system, and consciously unlearning any previous or current socialization towards simple, unquestioning obedience (as Baldwin cautions) or training for subservience (as Kozol cautions). To what extent has our own education – as teachers or students - been part of the problem(s) we are trying to address vs. the solution(s) we seek? In what ways might we reclaim the emancipatory and critical potential of the education processes in which we participate?

As teacher/leader educators and as pre-service and in-service educators, we must view course content, instruction and assignments as opportunities for critical engagement and social justice advocacy in the democratization of education. This would mean not settling for minimal competency standards dictated by standardized syllabi, rubrics and assignments, but aspiring to additional levels of accomplishment commensurate with principles of critical multicultural education. Current trends and issues, whether they be standardized testing, accountability systems, teacher evaluations, performance-based funding, textbooks, accreditation and educator preparation standards should be scrutinized for their potential for democratization or stratification. Additionally, we should seize all opportunities for engagement in community-oriented democratic practice that links our work as professionals with our civic responsibilities to forge safe and hospitable communities dedicated to egalitarianism and inclusiveness.

It might appear that the burden of history and legacies of discrimination could make teaching itself rather daunting. Furthermore, critical multiculturalism and the goals of equity, democracy and social justice represent lofty and idealistic goals. Under these circumstances, it is important for educators who understand the broader scope of multiculturalism not to give up doing the few things that they *can* do for fear of not being able to achieve everything that *should* be done. Through critical awareness of the historical legacy of educational discrimination, educators will be able to connect their actions on the micro level of classroom practice or with individual students with macro level patterns of equity and justice. Conscientization alerts us to the need to uncover the philosophical and political rationales, both hidden and explicit, of the curriculum in which we participate, so that we might resist contemporary manifestations of historical patterns of marginalization and stratification. The urgency for the education system to support the development of professionals, leaders, and citizens who are comfortable with difference and committed to democratic practice is evident in the divisive politics, humanitarian crises and stratified access to basic human rights both in the USA and around the world. It will require, in part, conscious and explicit critical multicultural teacher and leader education programs to be adopted system-wide.

All multicultural educators participate in a journey towards the ideal levels of systemic change, even as we acknowledge current realities in our daily struggles and collective challenges. If one views one's professional responsibilities in terms of small but significant steps in a much longer journey, it would be possible to appreciate the small victories of everyday practice. Such a journey can begin at any time, in any context, at any level of action as an educator or as a student. What matters is our commitment as educators to engage in pedagogy that interrupts and works against the historic legacies of discrimination and stratification. As current and future educators it will be up to us to serve as society's leaders in this collective journey.

Endnote

1. See: Jennes, G. (1976, August 9). Jonathan Kozol, Boston's fenced-out teacher, still slashes away at U.S. schools. *People, 6* (6). Retrieved from: http://www.people.com/people/archive/article/0,,20066758,00.html

References

Acuna, R. (2014). *Occupied America: A history of Chicanos* (8th ed.). Upper Saddle River, NJ: Pearson.

Adams, D. W. (1995). *Education for extinction: American Indians and the boarding school experience 1875-1928*. Lawrence, KS: University Press of Kansas.

Addams, J. (1910/1961). *Twenty years at Hull House*. New York, NY: Signet.

Ahlquist, R., Gorski, P. & Montano, T. (2011). *Assault on kids: How hyper-accountability, corporatization, deficit ideologies, and Ruby Payne are destroying our schools*. New York, NY: Peter Lang.

Alexander, M. (2012). *The new Jim Crow: Mass incarceration in the age of color blindness*. New York, NY: New Press.

American Educational Research Association. (2015). Position statement on use of Value Added Models (VAM) for the evaluation of educators and educator preparation programs. Retrieved from: http://edr.sagepub.com/content/early/2015/11/10/0013189X15618385.full.pdf+html

Anderson, J. D. (1988). *The education of Blacks in the South, 1860-1935*. Chapel Hill, NC: University of North Carolina Press.

Apple, M. & Beane, J. (Eds.). (1995). *Democratic schools*. Alexandria, VA: ASCD.

Ayers, W., Quinn, T. & Stoval, D. (Eds.). (2009). Handbook of social justice. New York, NY: Routledge.

Ayers, W. (2010). Teaching in and for democracy. *Curriculum and Teaching Dialogue, 12*(1-2), 3-10.

Baldwin, J. (1963, December 21). A talk to teachers. *The Saturday Review*, 42-44; 60.

Banks, J. A. (2001a). Approaches to multicultural curriculum reform. In J. A. Banks & C. M. Banks (Eds.), *Multicultural education: Issues and perspectives* (4th ed., pp. 225-246). New York, NY: Wiley.

Banks, J. A. (2001b). Multicultural education: Characteristics and goals. In J. A. Banks & C. M. Banks (Eds.), *Multicultural Education: Issues and Perspectives* (4th ed., pp. 3-30.) New York: Wiley.

Banks, J. A. (2004). Multicultural education: Historical development, dimensions, and practice. In J. A. Banks & C. M. Banks (Eds.). *Handbook of research in multicultural education* (2nd ed., pp. 3-29). San Francisco, CA: Jossey Bass.

Bigelow. B. (2008). *A people's history, a people's pedagogy*. Available at: http://zinnedproject.org/about/a-peoples-history-a-peoples-pedagogy/

Bogotch, I. (2008). Social justice as an educational construct. In I. Bogotch, F. Beachum, J. Blount, J. Brooks & F. English, *Radicalizing educational leadership: Dimensions of social justice* (pp. 79-112). Rotterdam, The Netherlands: Sense Publishers.

Bogotch, I., & Shields, C. (Eds.). (2014). *International handbook of social [in]justice and educational leadership*. New York, NY: Springer.

Dewey, J. (1916). *Democracy and education*. New York, NY: Macmillan.

Emery, K., Braselmann, S. & Gold, L. R. (2004). *Mississippi freedom school curriculum*. Retrieved from: http://www.educationanddemocracy.org/FSCfiles/A_02_Introduction.htm

Freire, P. (2000). *Pedagogy of the oppressed* (30th anniversary ed.). New York, NY: Continuum.

Friedersdorf, C. (2015, March 5). *Ferguson's conspiracy against Black citizens: How the city's leadership harassed and brutalized their way to multiple civil rights violations*. Retrieved from: http://www.theatlantic.com/national/archive/2015/03/ferguson-as-a-criminal-conspiracy-against-its-black-residents-michael-brown-department-of-justice-report/386887/

Gabor, T. (2016). Confronting gun violence in America. London, UK: Palgrave.

Ganim, S., & Tran, L. (2016, January 13). How tap water became toxic in Flint, Michigan. CNN. Retrieved from: http://www.cnn.com/2016/01/11/health/toxic-tap-water-flint-michigan/

Gay, G. (2010). *Culturally responsive teaching: Theory, research, and practice*. New York, NY: Teachers College Press.

Gay, G. (2012). Our children need . . . "education for resistance". *Journal of Educational Controversy 6*, (1). Available at: http://cedar.wwu.edu/jec/vol6/iss1/8

Gay, G. (2013). Teaching to and through Cultural Diversity. *Curriculum Inquiry 43*(1): 48–70.

Giroux, H. (2013). Neoliberalism's war against teachers in dark times. *Cultural Studies Critical Methodologies 13*(6), 458-468.

Gonzalez, G. (1996). Chicano educational history: A legacy of inequality. *Humboldt Journal of Social Relations, 22*(1), 43-56.

Gorski, P. C. (2009). What we're teaching teachers: An analysis of multicultural teacher education coursework syllabi. *Teaching and Teacher Education, 25*, 309-318.

Grant, C. & Sleeter, C. (2009). *Turning on learning: Five approaches for teaching plans for race, class, gender and disability.* (5th ed.). New York, NY: Wiley.

Grant, C. & Sleeter, C. (2011). *Doing multicultural education for achievement and equity.* (2nd. ed.) New York, NY: Routledge.

Gray, B. M. & Finley, S. C. (2015). God is a while racist: Immanent atheism as a religious response to Black Lives Matter and state-sanctioned anti-Black violence. *Journal of Africana Religions, 3*(4), 443-453.

Hoffman, L., Granger, N., Vallejos, L. & Moats, M. (2016). An existential-humanistic perspective on Black Lives Matter and contemporary protest movements. *Journal of Humanistic Psychology*, 1-17.

Joffe, C. & Parker, W. (2015). Race, reproductive politics and reproductive health care in contemporary United States. *Contraception Journal, 86*, 1-3. http://www.arhp.org/publications-and-resources/contraception-journal/july-2012

Karp, S. (2014). The problems with the Common Core. *Rethinking Schools, 28*(2), 10-17.

Karp, S. (2016). ESSA: NCLB repackaged. *Rethinking Schools 30*(3). Available at: http://www.rethinkingschools.org/archive/30_03/30-3_karp.shtml

Kennedy, M. (2016, April 20). Lead-laced water in Flint: A step-by-step look at the makings of a crisis. *National Public Radio*. Retrieved from: http://www.npr.org/sections/thetwo-way/2016/04/20/465545378/lead-laced-water-in-flint-a-step-by-step-look-at-the-makings-of-a-crisis

Kristof, N. (2016, June 16). Some extremists fire guns and other extremists promote guns. *New York Times*. Retrieved from: http://www.nytimes.com/2016/06/16/opinion/some-extremists-fire-guns-and-other-extremists-promote-guns.html?&moduleDetail=section-news-3&action=click&contentCollection=Opinion&region=Footer&module=MoreInSection&version=WhatsNext&contentID=WhatsNext&pgtype=article

Kohn, A. (1999). *The schools our children deserve: Moving beyond traditional classrooms and "tougher standards"*. Boston, MA: Houghton Mifflin.

Kohn, A. (2000). *The case against standardized testing: Raising the scores, ruining the schools*. Portsmouth, NH: Heinemann.

Kohn, A. (2011, April 27). Poor teaching for poor children in the name of reform. *Education Week*, Available at: http://www.alfiekohn.org/article/poor/

Kohn, A. (2015). *Schooling beyond measure and other unorthodox essays about education.* Portsmouth, NH: Heinemann.

Kozol, J. (2005). *The shame of the nation: The restoration of Apartheid schooling in America*. New York, NY: Random House.

Kozol, J. (2006, March/April). Standardized testing: The do or die agenda. *Principal*, 19-22.

Kozol, J. (2013). *Fire in the ashes: Twenty-five years among the poorest children in America*. New York, NY: Random House.

Ladson-Billings, G. (1995). But that's just good teaching! The case for culturally relevant pedagogy. *Theory into Practice, 34*(3), 159-165.

Ladson-Billings, G. (2006). From the achievement gap to the educational debt: Understanding achievement in US schools. *Educational Researcher, 35*(7), 3-12.

Loewen, J. W. (2008). *Lies my teacher told me: Everything your American history textbook got wrong*. New York, NY: New Press.

Lomawaima, T. & McCarty, T. (2002). When tribal sovereignty challenges democracy: American Indian education and the democratic ideal. *American Educational Research Journal, 39*, (2), 279-305.

Lomawaima, T. & McCarty, T. (2006). *To remain an Indian: Lessons in democracy from a century of Native American education*. New York, NY: Teachers College Press.

May, P. & Sleeter, C. (2010). Introduction. In P. May & C. Sleeter (Eds.). *Critical multiculturalism: Theory and praxis.* (pp. 1-16). New York, NY: Routledge.

Meier, D. (2003). *In schools we trust: Creating communities of learning in an era of testing and standardization.* Boston, MA: Beacon Press.

New York Times Editorial Board. (2016, June 16). The N.R.A.'s complicity in terrorism. *New York Times.* Retrieved from: http://www.nytimes.com/2016/06/16/opinion/the-nras-complicity-in-terrorism.html?action=click&contentCollection=us&module=NextInCollection&region=Footer&pgtype=article&version=newsevent&rref=collection%2Fnews-event%2F2016-orlando-shooting

Nieto, S. (1994, Spring). Affirmation, solidarity and critique: Moving beyond tolerance in multicultural education. *Multicultural Education*, 9-12, 35-37.

Preston, J. (November 30, 2012). Young immigrants say it's Obama's time to act. *New York Times.* Retrieved from: http://www.nytimes.com/2012/12/01/us/dream-act-gives-young-immigrants-a-political-voice.html?_r=0

Quartz, K. H., Priselac, J. & Franke, M. L. (2009). Transforming public schools: A synthesis of research findings from UCLA's Center X. *Equity and Excellence in Education, 42*(3), 313-326.

Ravitch, D. (2014). *Reign of error: The hoax of the privatization movement and the danger to America's public schools.* New York, NY: Vintage Books.

Rose, M. (2011, Spring). The mismeasure of teaching and learning: How contemporary school reform fails the test. *Dissent*, 32-38.

Rutenberg, J. (2015, July 29). A dream undone: Disenfranchised. *New York Times Magazine.* Retrieved from: http://www.nytimes.com/2015/07/29/magazine/voting-rights-act-dream-undone.html

School Board of Palm Beach County, Florida. (2014). Resolution on accountability. Accessed on March 14. 2016 at: http://www.flstopcccoalition.org/files/0C1D9C09-6BE4-4C73-A5D0-4F94E25AC059--AEFCBA12-88C0-48A5-853E-1D1FA7336A23/pbcsresolution-on-accountability-2.pdf

Schoorman, D. & Bogotch, I. (2010). Conceptualisations of multicultural education among teachers: Implications for practice in universities and schools. *Teaching and Teacher Education, 26*, 1041-1048.

Sleeter, C. (2005). *Un-standardizing curriculum: Multicultural teaching in the standards-based classroom.* New York, NY: Teacher College Press.

Sleeter, C. & Grant, C. E. (2009). *Making choices for multicultural education: Five approaches to race, class, and gender.* Hoboken, NJ: John Wiley & Sons, Inc.

Spring, J. (2013). *Deculturalization and the struggle for equality: A brief history of the education of dominated cultures in the United States.* New York, NY: McGraw-Hill.

Stovall, D. (2014, October 30). Cities in revolt: Chicago. Praxis Center, Kalamazoo College. Retrieved from: http://www.kzoo.edu/praxis/cities-in-revolt-chicago/

Takaki, R. (1989). *Strangers from a different shore: A history of Asian Americans.* Boston, MA: Little, Brown and Company.

Taylor, D. (2014). *Toxic communities: Environmental racism, industrial pollution and residential mobility.* New York, NY: New York University Press.

Ungar, R. (2010, December 28). The truth about the opposition to healthcare. *Forbes.* Retrieved from: *http://www.forbes.com/sites/rickungar/2010/12/28/the-truth-about-the-opposition-to-health-care-reform/#3e13b7dd2e24.*

Watkins, W. (2001). *The White architects of Black education: Ideology and power in America, 1865-1954.* New York, NY: Teachers College Press.

Watkins, W. (2012). *The assault on public education: Confronting the politics of corporate school reform.* New York, NY: Teachers College Press.

Woodson, C. G. (1933). *The mis-education of the Negro.* Trenton, NJ: Africa World Press.

Zavattaro, S. M. (2014). Organizational implosion: A case study of Detroit, Michigan. *Administration & Society, 46*(9), 1071-1091.

Zernike, K. (October 24, 2015). Obama administration calls for limits on testing in schools. *New York Times.* Retrieved from http://www.nytimes.com/2015/10/25/us/obama-administration-calls-for-limits-on-testing-in-schools.html

Zinn, H. (2003). *A people's history of the United States.* New York, NY: Harper Collins.

Zittleman, K. & Sadker, D. (2002). Gender bias in teacher education texts: New (and old) lessons. *Journal of Teacher Education, 53*(2), 168-180.

Voice in the Field: Make Your Voices Heard

Leila Shatara, M. Ed.

Why does my 17-year-old daughter have to be subjected to "Are you happy with what your people did in Paris" a day after the Paris attacks? As a Muslim and an American, it pains me to know that we are constantly being told we cannot be both Muslim and American or that we must choose one or the other. This personal narrative will explore why we as multicultural educators must help society move past this.

My daughter had just stepped onto her college campus when a stranger approached her and angrily shouted at her. She was taken aback but was strong enough to respond, "Those are not my people." She went on to explain what the belief system in Islam and how "those people" were killing more Muslims than non-Muslims. Why does she have to sit through classes where students and even sometimes instructors repeatedly make derogatory comments about Muslims and claim they are just repeating facts? If news channels and newspapers reported on every death caused by guns, we would think the country was at war with itself with 53,272 incidents in 2015 alone. Imagine if you saw 13, 429 reports on deaths by firearms on the news in a year, that would be an average of 36 reports a day! (Gun Violence Archive, 2015). Imagine what you would think and how you would feel. Then everyone would be demanding a war on guns not a war on terror.

Media, politics, and a war machine that makes many people rich and powerful by merely instilling fear is hard at work. The mainstream media and the ideologies of the dominant population often decide what you see and how often and with what intensity. Most people do not stop to question messages in the media that perpetuate fear of Muslims and other marginalized groups thus inciting an emotional response that does not challenge but instead perpetuate overgeneralizations, stereotypes, and untruths across groups of people. Attacks on Muslims have increased significantly since 9/11 and the recent terrorist attacks across the world. Innocent Muslims have thus been affected by the radical behavior of a group of Muslims. One example of this was when my 15-year-old son and I sat in a hospital waiting room for his post op exam. A stranger, a man in his late 50's, began to direct some vulgar remarks towards us and became loud and more vulgar because we did not respond or react. He eventually began to shout obscenities about Islam, Allah, and Muhammad and said he was voting for Trump so he could kick all of our _____out of America. I shifted to stand up as I was going to call the security guard, and he shouted, "Watch out she's got a bomb!" Eventually security escorted him away and we had to have someone check in on us the rest of day to make sure we were safe. Why did my son who was recovering from his fourth surgery in 3 ½ months have to endure the hatred, vulgarity, and demeaning comments from this absolute stranger filled with venomous hate?

In a room of about 100 people, a woman did stand up and put him in his place and it is people like her who will make things right. I did not know her nor did she know us, but she recognized an injustice and stood and raised her voice above that man's voice to shut him down. It will take many more people to stand up and raise their voices, voices demanding fair treatment of others and justice for all.

Educators can make a difference by instructing differently, exposing students to a curriculum that critically examine text and opens minds to challenge the status quo. Teachers should teach about Islam and Muslims, go to a nearby mosque and meet Muslims, read and watch things from a Muslim perspective and understand more of the realities for Muslims. Teachers have the power to change history while it is being made. Hate comes from fear and fear is instilled based on ignorance that has often been passed down from generation to generation, through the media and societal injustices, and also through the traditional curriculum. Education is the key to unlocking the hearts and minds of people who just do not know. Educators should teach students to be analytical thinkers, to ask questions, to demand answers, and to understand what it means to live in a just society. Students should be taught to think from different perspectives, to see another person's ideas as valid even if they do not agree, to be able to solve problems while working with others, and to be able to stand up with courage and speak on behalf of those who cannot speak for themselves is the truest form of education.

We should have learned some lessons from our history by now. How many groups must we vilify and demonize to propel our own agendas? Do not swallow every lie, every half-truth; every tale the media spins to instill fear. Remember it was not too long ago that White Americans felt that Blacks did not deserve to be treated as equal human beings and justified it by using the Bible. It was not long ago that Jews in America were afraid to identify themselves as such and changed their names in fear of persecution. Just as we see it as absurd now only a few decades later, so is the idea that all Muslims are terrorists and enemies of democracy and the West. How many genocides, how many holocausts will it take for humanity to learn the lesson that human rights and justice is for all? We cannot wait another 50 or 60 years of increased Islamophobia until we realize how wrong this is and how detrimental it is to our fabric as a civil and just society.

CHAPTER 1

What Is Multicultural Education?

Eliana Carvalho Mukherjee

As the semester neared completion, students in Mr. Paul's class were rewarded with the viewing of the award winning movie *Glory*. This was relevant to the course since the class was concluding the Civil War portion of an 11th Grade United States History class. The school is comprised of predominantly White students, with minorities being about 20% of the student population. The movie tells the story of the first African American regiments created during the Civil War. Mr. Paul believed he had obtained a copy of the movie that removed some of the gore and, especially the occasional foul language, particularly the use of the derogatory "n-word" in a scene. Unfortunately, Mr. Paul did not obtain the edited copy and was surprised to hear a character in the movie shout "n-----, soldiers" very loudly in the scene. With the period coming to an end, Mr. Paul deeply apologized for the mistake. In the class that followed, one of the White student asked, "Why can't White people use the n-word?" This prompted students to look at the two African American students in the class to see their reactions and perhaps provide an answer.

Mr. Paul responded by saying, "Do not used that word, no matter what color (and) let's get back to discussing the experiences of African American soldiers in the Civil War." Mr. Paul was really buying time to get advice on how to address this issue.

Submitted by Geoffrey Periard

Questions to ponder:

1. What did Mr. Paul do that went beyond traditional teaching?
2. In what way was Mr. Paul afraid to address this issue in the classroom?
3. Did the teacher's race impact his comfort level in addressing this topic in the classroom?
4. How could Mr. Paul have addressed this from a historical perspective?
5. How would this scenario look different for a teacher who practiced or embraced the goals of multicultural education?

Introduction

Multicultural education is a process of education reform that promotes equitable learning opportunities for *all* students. In this chapter, a brief historical overview of the development of multicultural education will be provided. The definition of multicultural education will be offered, along with some of its goals. The chapter will then explain some of the leading theories of multicultural education and the scholars who promote them. The theoretical frameworks will provide information on different approaches to multicultural education, and these will be compared and presented from a surface level approach to a more critical approach to multicultural education. Throughout the chapter, active learning questions and activities will stimulate your thinking and encourage you to apply what you are reading to your own experience.

The Civil Rights Movement and Desegregation

Multicultural education is rooted in the Civil Rights Movement of the 1950s and 1960s. Of supreme importance is the 1954 *Brown v. Board of Education* decision that found segregation unconstitutional and forced schools to desegregate; however, desegregation did not occur automatically due to massive resistance (Gay, 2004a). The Civil Rights Act of 1964 added muscle to that ruling and required the end of racial segregation in schools. Consequently, schools in the South were forced to integrate. However, the expectation was that black students were to integrate into White schools instead of White students attending predominantly Black schools. The concern was centered on access to schools; curriculum and instruction (and its lack of relevance to Black students) were largely ignored. Inspired by the Civil Rights Movement, different groups' demands for educational equality grew louder (Gay, 2004a). Groups challenged society on the basis of discrimination and particularly targeted education. Several groundbreaking laws and court decisions recognized the educational rights of minorities and set in motion reforms that addressed the needs of minority students. The following chart from the Teaching Tolerance website (http://www.tolerance.org) includes an outline of the struggle for integration in the United States.

1849	The Massachusetts Supreme Court rules that segregated schools are permissible under the state's constitution. (Roberts v. City of Boston)
1857	With the Dred Scott decision, the Supreme Court upholds the denial of citizenship to African Americans and rules that descendants of slaves are "so far inferior that they had no rights which the white man was bound to respect."
1868	The Fourteenth Amendment is ratified, guaranteeing "equal protection under the law"; citizenship is extended to African Americans.
1875	Congress passes the Civil Rights Act of 1875, which bans racial discrimination in public accommodations.
1883	The Supreme Court strikes down the Civil Rights Act of 1875 finding that discrimination by individuals or private businesses is constitutional.
1896	The Supreme Court authorizes segregation in Plessy v. Ferguson, finding Louisiana's "separate but equal" law constitutional. The ruling, built on notions of white supremacy and black inferiority, provides legal justification for Jim Crow laws in southern states.
1927	The Supreme Court finds that states possess the right to define a Chinese student as non-white for the purpose of segregating public schools. (Gong Lum v. Rice)
1947	In a precursor to the Brown case, a federal appeals court strikes down segregated schooling for Mexican American and White students. (Westminster School Dist. v. Mendez)
1952	The Supreme Court hears oral arguments in Brown v. Board of Education.
1954	In a unanimous opinion, the Supreme Court in Brown v. Board of Education overturns Plessy and declares that separate schools are "inherently unequal." The Court delays deciding on how to implement the decision.
1955	In Brown II, the Supreme Court orders the lower federal courts to require desegregation "with all deliberate speed." Between 1955 and 1960, federal judges held more than 200 school desegregation hearings.
1957	The Arkansas National Guard was sent to protect nine black students integrating Central High School in Little Rock, Arkansas.
1959	25,000 young people march in Washington, D.C., in support of integration. Officials in Prince Edward County, Virginia voted to close their public schools rather than integrate them. The Supreme Court ordered the county to reopen its schools on a desegregated basis in 1964.
1960	In New Orleans, federal marshals shielded Ruby Bridges, Gail St. Etienne, Leona Tate and Tessie Prevost from angry crowds as they enrolled in school.
1964	The Civil Rights Act of 1964 was adopted. Title IV of the Act authorized the federal government to file school desegregation cases. Title VI of the Act prohibited discrimination in programs and activities, including schools, receiving federal financial assistance.
1971	The Court approved busing, magnet schools, compensatory education and other tools as appropriate remedies to overcome the role of residential segregation in perpetuating racially segregated schools. (Swann v. Charlotte-Mecklenberg Board of Education)

1972	Title IX of the Educational Amendments of 1972 was passed prohibiting sex discrimination in any educational program that received federal financial assistance.
1974	The Supreme Court ruled that the failure to provide instruction to those with limited English proficiency violates Title VI's prohibition of national origin, race or color discrimination in school districts receiving federal funds. (Lau v. Nichols)
1975	Public Law 94-142 was passed, guaranteeing free and appropriate education for students with exceptionalities.
1988	School integration reaches its all-time high; almost 45% of Black students in the United States are attending majority-White schools.
1992	The Supreme Court further speeds the end of desegregation cases, ruling that school systems can fulfill their obligations in an incremental fashion. (Freeman v. Pitts)
2003	A federal district court case affirms the value of racial diversity and race-conscious student assignment plans in K-12 education. (Lynn v. Comfort)
	A study by Harvard's Civil Rights Project finds that schools were more segregated in 2000 than in 1970 when busing for desegregation began.

Markus Mainka / Shutterstock.com

From Desegregation to Ethnic Studies

As the battle for desegregation in public schools was underway, many Black educators recognized that Black students were entering classrooms in schools where their White teachers and White peers did not know anything about them or had adopted negative societal images. Minority groups advocated for more accurate and positive portrayals of themselves in school curricula during the Civil Rights Movement. Subsequently, the 1960s saw the emergence of Ethnic Studies or ethnic studies courses, which were separate courses or programs that taught in depth the history, perspective, experience, and knowledge of a particular minority group. Art, literature, history, and political science are common topics covered in Ethnic Studies courses. Examples of courses in Ethnic Studies include Chicano Studies, Women's Literature, African American History, Native American Studies, Asian Diaspora, etc., sprouted up on college campuses out of concern for minority students on these campuses. According to the National Association for Ethnic Studies (NAES), students of color began to call for more courses that reflected their histories, curriculum that spoke to the needs of marginalized groups of people, as well as the hiring of professors of color (http://ethnicstudies.org/about/naes-history/).

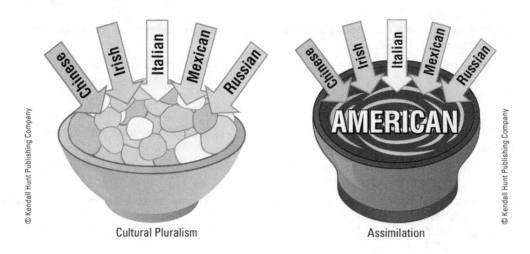

Cultural Pluralism

Assimilation

One recent example of an Ethnic Studies program on the grade school level may be found in Tucson, Arizona. The students taking courses in the Ethnic Studies/Mexican American Studies Program made gains academically, socially, culturally, and personally. While the students enrolled in the courses felt empowered, actually enjoyed learning about their family's history that traditionally was omitted from the curriculum, and their graduation rates increased, the program was dismantled. Outsiders felt that the students were being taught to resent others and that the program was anti-American. Tom Horne, Arizona's then attorney general, declared the program was in violation of all provisions of House Bill 2281, which mandates classes in Arizona may not: (1) be designed primarily for pupils of a particular ethnic group; (2) teach political views that encourage the overthrow of the U.S. government; (3) promote resentment toward a race or class of people; and (4) advocate ethnic solidarity (Arizona House Bill 2281, 2010). This example, although current, represents common challenges faced when implementing multicultural education and diversity in the public school system during the 1960s Banks (2014).

During the Civil Rights period, a shift began to occur. There was a slow swing from assimilationist thinking towards that of cultural pluralism. The assimilationist perspective is akin to that of the melting pot theory. This theory posits that cultural groups "melt together" to form a national identity; however in the process of becoming American, they are asked to strip themselves of who they are or what makes them unique as individuals becomes indistinguishable. The graphic above illustrates this point.

Cultural pluralism is the harmonious coexistence of differences where members of groups seek to understand each other. The pluralistic perspective views diversity as desirable and as an asset. It is the active engagement with diversity (Eck, 2006). This perspective is akin to that of the salad bowl theory. This theory maintains that while individuals come to the U.S. and contribute to American society, aspects of their culture do not have to be forsaken. They can still maintain their cultural identity while being an American. The graphic above illustrates this point.

In pluralistic classrooms, students' backgrounds are valued and maintained, and cultural knowledge and experiences are encouraged to be part of the learning experiences for all members of the classroom. In addition, there is a sense of mutual respect, genuine care and a sense of community

From Ethnic Studies to Multicultural Education

The 1970s brought efforts to change the content of curriculum to be more multicultural in nature. Brewing issues of discrimination and prejudice compelled schools to change curriculum to be more inclusive- to include minority groups and to foster positive relationships (La Belle & Ward, 1994). A shift took place during this time from Ethnic Studies to Multicultural Education. Even though curriculum was changing in this period, traditional teaching strategies persisted that were mainly teacher-centered.

In the 1980s, scholars emerged who advocated a form of multicultural education that was integrated into the curriculum along with pedagogy that was inclusive. Some of the scholars included James Banks, Gloria Ladson-Billings, Geneva Gay, Carl Grant, Sonia Nieto, and Christine Sleeter, among others. These multicultural education scholars called for structural changes in schools, where multicultural education was an integral part of the curriculum, environment, and teaching strategies. However, multicultural educators faced political resistance. The 1983 influential report, *A Nation at Risk*, indicated that the U.S. education system was, at best, mediocre, and that the U.S. was lagging behind other nations. Multicultural education efforts were perceived as a weakness to students' academic achievement (Sleeter & Grant, 2009). The idea was that multicultural education would be taking up valuable instructional time needed for students to master core subject areas. This was a catalyst for the development and refinement of core content standards, accountability, and standardized testing. In the 1990s, schools across the U.S. began implementing various forms of conflict resolution programs, spurred by issues of racial, ethnic, and religious tensions (Sleeter & Grant, 2009).

Multicultural education continues to evolve and improve. Meeting the needs of our diverse student population is central in education reform and multicultural efforts. Many contemporary multicultural education scholars promote a critical approach, which includes multicultural content, an examination of power and asymmetrical power relations, and a pedagogy that is action-oriented, dialogical, and student-centered. At the heart of a critical approach is action; a critical approach requires that learners become deliberate in their actions and seek out justice.

Defining Multicultural Education

Multicultural education has been defined in different ways (see, for example, Banks, 2014; Bennett, 2002; Nieto, 2012). The National Association for Multicultural Education (NAME) provides a contemporary definition of multicultural education. They posit that multicultural education is a process that should pervade all aspects of schooling - school practices, policies, etc., so that all students can reach their highest academic potential. Moreover, multicultural education should equip students with the skills, knowledge, and dispositions they need to actively work to challenge societal injustices and practices that marginalize groups of people. Multicultural education should assist students in their development of positive self-identities through the inclusion of their funds of knowledge into the curriculum. Schools must be open to address issues of race, sex, class, sexual orientation, religion, etc., on varying levels. To review NAME's definition of multicultural education, please visit this website: http://www.nameorg.org/definitions_of_multicultural_e.php.

Sleeter and Grant (2009) wrote, "Multicultural education has emerged as an umbrella concept that deals with race, culture, language, social class, gender, and disability. Although some educators still apply it only to race, it is the term most frequently extended to include additional forms of diversity" (p. 33). Indeed, multicultural education is relevant and appropriate for all teachers and students.

It is important to remember that multicultural education is not a monolithic approach to education. There are no national standards for multicultural education nor a packaged program that can nicely fit into any school or curriculum. The way in which multicultural education is approached very much depends on the school and community context. The manner and depth at which it is approached and implemented will vary depending on the teacher and school; this will be addressed later in this chapter when the theories of multicultural education is discussed. In the meantime, to better understand multicultural education, it is helpful to consider its goals.

Goals of Multicultural Education

The following are some of the goals integral to multicultural education.

- Ensure that all students learn basic skills and achieve academic success.
- Develop a sense of solidarity and care among all members of the school community.
- Provide equitable equal educational opportunities for all students.
- Assist students in developing their own interests and career goals.
- Assist students in developing a healthy sense of self.

- Teach students to develop an understanding and respect for others, and the ability to see through multiple perspectives.
- Develop students' critical thinking and decision-making skills
- Encourage students' to take responsibility for their actions.
- Foster understanding of issues of justice and encourage participation in the promotion of equity and the elimination of oppressive ideologies and systems.
- Develop positive interpersonal and intercultural communication skills.
- Develop an understanding of issues surrounding their communities and in the world.
- Practice the principles of democracy in the schools and classrooms.
- Foster a caring learning community and employ teaching strategies that are reflective of and relevant to the students.

The Need For Multicultural Education Today

Multicultural Education is increasingly important in responding to changing demographics in the United States. Yet, traditional U.S. schools still tend to represent dominant groups and reflect dominant values and belief systems (i.e. male, heterosexual, middle class, European-American), thus marginalizing other groups. This in effect reproduces inequalities (Banks, 2010; Ladson-Billings, 1995; Gay, 2004, 2010; Sleeter, 2004, 2005; Sleeter & Grant, 2009). Banks (2010) wrote, "A curriculum that focuses on the experiences of mainstream Americans and largely ignores the experiences, cultures, and histories of other ethnic, racial, cultural, language, and religious groups has negative consequences for both mainstream students and students of color" (p. 242). Despite efforts to improve the educational outcomes of all students, there is a persistent achievement gap in U.S. schools, with African American, Hispanic/ Latino, and Native American students faring academically far below their White counterparts (Hanushek, 2014). Sleeter (2004) points to the deficit perspective that too many educators hold of minority students (i.e. that they are less educated, are culturally deprived, have undesirable characteristics, etc.). Although we have come very far from the segregated era of Jim Crow, much work still needs to be done, and multicultural education today is as relevant as ever.

Consider this: the academic year that began in 2014 was the first year in which the total White student population was less than 50 percent (National Center for Education Statistics, 2014). We now have a minority majority – the total number of minority students in the public school system is greater than the number of White students. In the following pie chart (Figure 1.1), you can see the breakdown of the student enrollment

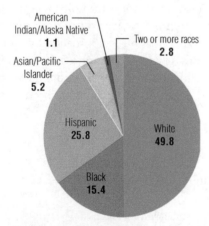

Figure 1.1. 2014 U.S. Elementary and Secondary School Enrollment
Source: Eliana Carvalho Mukherjee. Adapted from National Center for Education Statistics, 2014, http://nces.ed.gov/programs/digest/d15/tables/dt15_203.50.asp.

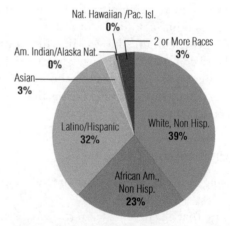

Figure 1.2. 2015 Florida Student Demographics
Source: Eliana Carvalho Mukherjee. Adapted from Florida Department of Education, https://edstats.fldoe.org.

in U.S. schools for the year 2014. Although Whites still represent the single largest student group in the U.S., there is a growing population of racial and ethnic minorities.

Florida is one of the most populated and diverse states. The pie chart above (Figure 1.2) shows the breakdown of the student demographics in Florida schools in 2015. The breakdown reveals a spread of racial diversity. Demographics for other states can be found by visiting the State's department of education website.

Interestingly, an examination of the teacher demographics in Florida for 2015 shows that the breakdown is very different (see Figure 1.3). In Figure 1.2 we see that the percentage of White students in Florida is 39 percent, but that percentage is starkly different for teachers. Seventy percent of Florida teaching force is White. While it is certainly true that White teachers can be exceptional educators of minority students, it does point to the need for a more diverse teaching force. It also suggests that teacher education programs must include courses and experiences for teachers to develop the skills, knowledge and dispositions for working with diverse student populations.

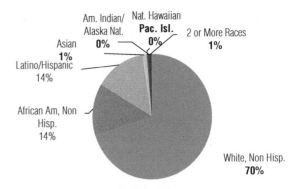

Figure 1.3:   2015 Florida Instructional Staff Demographics
Source: Eliana Carvalho Mukherjee. Adapted from Florida Department of Education, http://www.fldoe.org/accountability/data-sys/edu-info-accountability-services/pk-12-public-school-data-pubs-reports/staff.stml.

> **Active Learning**
> Find out what the demographics of your local school district is like.
> - How does it compare with the national demographics in Figure 1.1?
> - How does it compare with the demographics in Florida (Figure 1.2)?

Cultural, racial, and ethnic diversity are certainly not the only differences in student population. There is also great diversity in religious beliefs, gender identity and sexual orientation; language, social class, and ability, among others. Furthermore, the high level of poverty in the U.S., especially for groups of color, requires attention and response by the education system. Multicultural education attempts to address these issues and ensure that all students, regardless of their background and identity, have the opportunity to receive a quality education.

Multicultural Education Theories

This section will introduce six leading multicultural scholars who advanced our understanding of multicultural education. As you read this section, you will probably see some similarities among the theories or multicultural frameworks. The section will conclude with a synthesis of the theories and how they relate to one another.

James Banks

James Banks is one of the first scholars of multicultural education in the United States, often referred to as the father of multicultural education. His research and writing on multicultural education began in the 1970s and has influenced generations of educators and scholars. Here, two of his conceptualizations of multicultural education will be discussed.

Five dimensions of multicultural education. Banks's research led him to distinguish Five Interrelated Dimensions of Multicultural Education (2014):

Content integration: This is when teachers integrate content, perspectives, ideas, and examples from various sources and cultures into the curriculum. Banks (2014) noted that many people understand multicultural education simply as content integration, which is problematic because this limited perspective does not address the other fundamental components of multicultural education. An example of content integration would be a sixth grade language arts teacher including multicultural literature, such as *Roll of Thunder, Hear My Cry* by Mildred D. Taylor and *A Single Shard* by Linda Sue Park as literature circle (book group) choices.

Knowledge construction process: Banks explained this dimension when he wrote, "Teachers help students to understand how knowledge is created and how it is influenced by the racial, ethnic, gender, and social-class positions of individuals and groups" (2014, pp. 37-38). It includes the examination of what counts as "truth" and question whose "truth" is being promoted. For example, a high school U.S. history teacher who notices that the textbook does not include any information about the Japanese internment camps during World War II might investigate this with her students and have them consider why this topic was excluded from the U.S. History textbook.

Prejudice reduction: Teachers and schools intentionally implement strategies to help students have positive attitudes towards others. As students learn more about and have more experiences with groups different than themselves, they will grow more comfortable with differences, and prejudice can be reduced. A teacher working on this may, for example, incorporate cooperative learning groups and team projects so that students have experiences working on shared goals with their diverse peers.

Equity pedagogy: Banks explained: "An equity pedagogy exists when teachers use techniques and teaching methods that facilitate the academic achievement of students from diverse racial, ethnic, and social-class groups" (2014, p. 39). Teachers who practice equity pedagogy know the social and cultural backgrounds of the students and use this knowledge in their teaching in order to make connections between the students' lives and the content that is being taught. An example of this would be a teacher in a school with Native American students using storytelling techniques for teaching. She would have the students read "An Indian Father's Plea" by Robert Lake and have the students discuss the reading in groups then write letters back to the author reflecting on what they learned and connections they made with the text.

Empowering school culture: Banks recognized that the most effective approach to multicultural education is one in which the entire school is changed so that there is a culture of equality and where all students feel included and empowered. The entire school adopts the ethos that all students can succeed. Banks (2014) suggests that the use of fair (authentic) assessments and the elimination of tracking are indicative of this dimension.

Four levels of transformed curriculum. Banks' research also revealed different levels of multicultural curricula integration. He explained four levels at which curriculum is transformed, with the lowest level being the most superficial (and most commonly utilized) to the highest level being empowering and action-oriented (Banks, 2014).

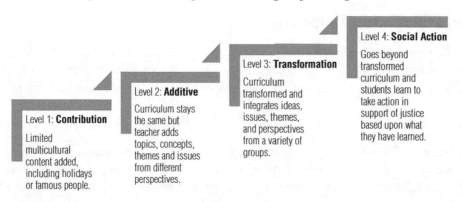

Level 4: **Social Action**
Goes beyond transformed curriculum and students learn to take action in support of justice based upon what they have learned.

Level 3: **Transformation**
Curriculum transformed and integrates ideas, issues, themes, and perspectives from a variety of groups.

Level 2: **Additive**
Curriculum stays the same but teacher adds topics, concepts, themes and issues from different perspectives.

Level 1: **Contribution**
Limited multicultural content added, including holidays or famous people.

Banks' Levels of Multicultural Curricula Integration

Level 1: Contributions approach. This is when a teacher adds some content about different cultural groups, but it is very limited. It typically includes the recognition of major holidays or famous people. Example of the contribution approach would include a kindergarten teacher doing an activity for Chinese New Year (like coloring a dragon red), writing their "dream" on Martin Luther King, Jr.'s birthday, or a school having a multicultural fair (bringing food and dressing up). These activities are enjoyable, but students' learning about cultural and ethnic groups remain superficial.

Level 2: Additive approach. At this level, the curriculum does not fundamentally change, but the teacher adds topics, concepts, themes, and issues from different perspectives into the existing curriculum. For example, a science teacher might add a unit on famous female scientists like Marie Curie, or a literature teacher might add a novel by a Native American author, like Leslie Marmon Silko. What's often reality in schools, is that you will mostly see the contributions or additive approaches in traditional classrooms

Level 3: Transformation approach. This level is where curriculum is fundamentally changed and transformed to incorporate ideas, issues, themes, and perspectives from a variety of groups. Banks wrote, "Major goals of this approach include helping students to understand concepts, events, and people from diverse ethnic and cultural perspectives and to understand knowledge as a social construction" (2014, p. 55). Social construction refers to the idea that people create knowledge; what may be true and real to one group may be understood differently by another. An example of the transformed approach is when a school's history curriculum is rewritten to integrate perspectives of multiple people and groups. For instance, in the study of European colonization, the perspective of those who were colonized would be given as much attention as the experience of the Europeans. Another examples is the Chicago Grassroots Curriculum Taskforce whose mission "seeks to build a movement towards liberatory education in all schools and communities whereby [all stakeholders] co-shape empowering, inspirational, meaningful, accurate, and challenging curriculum so students can better analyze, prepare for, and resolve greater challenges in Chicago's community and around the world" (grassrootscurriculum.org).

Level 4: Social action approach: At this level, the curriculum has been transformed, but it goes beyond the integration of multiple perspectives. Students learn to take action toward injustices based on what they have learned. Banks (2014) states that students at the social action level "pursue projects and activities that allow them to make decisions and to take personal, social, and civic actions related to the concepts, problems, and issues they have studied" (p. 55). For example, after learning about the history of oppression of Native Americans, students might develop and implement a plan to change the mascot of their school that is offensive to Native Americans. Another example would be for students to create counternarratives to media texts that often portray their cultural group in derogatory ways as in the case of Waldon's (2015) study in critical media literacy with Black adolescent youth.

Active Learning

Analyze your own schooling using Banks's four levels as a framework.

- Which level would characterize the approach toward multicultural education in your own school experience?
- Which level would you have preferred? Why?

Christine Sleeter and Carl Grant

In the 1980s, multicultural education scholars Christine Sleeter and Carl Grant developed a typology, or classification, of five approaches to multicultural education that emerged from their research (2007, 2009). These five approaches will be explained.

Teaching the exceptional and culturally different. The main goal in this type of multicultural education is to help students fit into the structures that already exist. Sleeter and Grant (2009) wrote, "The goal of this approach is to equip students with the cognitive skills, concepts, information, language, and values required to American society in order to hold a job and function within the society's existing institutions and culture" (p. 44). It is assimilationist in its ideology, and it preserves the status quo. Sink and swim approaches to bilingual education and other ESL programs reflect the assimilationist approach.

Human relations. In this form of multicultural education, the emphasis is on developing students' positive attitudes towards differences, including "feelings of unity, tolerance, and acceptance within existing social structures" (Sleeter & Grant, 2009, p. 86). There is a deliberate effort to reduce prejudice and stereotyping amongst the different groups while helping students feel positive about themselves. Teaching techniques for this approach include cooperative learning groups, where students must collaborate in order to achieve a common goal. This approach, however, does not address institutional inequities; there is limited, if any, examination as to why discrimination and equality exist.

Single-group studies. Teachers and schools who adopt this approach focus on a single minority group for in-depth study. It has its roots in the 1960s ethnic studies. This approach helps to foster acceptance, understanding, and empathy for the group. Sleeter and Grant (2014) said that the main goal in this form of multicultural education is to "empower oppressed groups and develop allies" (p. 123). Single-group studies usually involve learning about the history and experience of a given group, how they have been victimized, and current issues they face. The intention is to empower learners to take social action on behalf of the group. A critique of this approach, though, is that it does not change the main curriculum; it is typically an "add on" to the existing curriculum. Examples of single-group studies include Lesbian, Gay, Bisexual, and Transgender (LGBT) Studies, Arab American Literature, and African American History.

Multicultural education. The emphasis of in this approach is the promotion of respect, equality and cultural pluralism. It fosters the idea that there is strength and value in diversity. Acceptance of alternative lifestyles and perspectives is encouraged, and equal opportunity addressed. Critical thinking is taught, and bilingual instruction is offered. Students learn about social justice issues, and develop an understanding of human rights. The curriculum is changed to commonly present diverse perspectives, experiences, contributions, and represent diverse cultural and ethnic groups as well as sexes. This approach requires community involvement, and teachers use students' experiences and backgrounds to support their learning. It is most effective when the entire school adopts this approach to curriculum and instruction.

Education that is multicultural and social reconstructionist (2007)/Multicultural social justice education (2009). When Sleeter and Grant first wrote about the five types of multicultural education in the 1980s, they referred to this last approach as "Education that is multicultural and social reconstructionist" (2007). This last type of multicultural education is, as the name implies, reflective of the social reconstructionist philosophy of education that views the purpose of schooling as a means to change the world for better. The belief in this form of multicultural education is that there is a need to reconstruct society in order to better serve the interests of all groups. Students need to learn to question society or the hidden ideologies that are ingrained in the fabric of society and see through what is commonly accepted as "truths" which can lead to the acceptance of injustice and cruelty. In later editions of their work, Sleeter and Grant renamed this as "Multicultural social justice education" (2009). Although the name has changed, the concepts have not. This form of multicultural education has equity and justice as central concerns. Teachers guide students to understand issues, learn to become empowered to make decisions and take actions for social justice and a more humane and equitable society. Students become prepared for the "real world" and develop the necessary skills to bring about positive change. To bring about justice, solidarity is needed across differences (Sleeter & Grant, 2009), and this multicultural social justice education emphasizes the practice of democracy, where everyone is valued and participates.

Active Learning

As someone who is studying to be a teacher, you will likely be required to observe teachers in the field.

- Which of the five types of multicultural education do the teachers you have observed practice?
- What criteria did you use to make that determination?

Sonia Nieto

Like others in this chapter, Sonia Nieto's work in multicultural education emerged in the 1980s. Her definition of multicultural education is one that is commonly referred to today. She wrote:

> Multicultural education is a process of comprehensive school reform and basic education for all students. It challenges and rejects racism and other forms of discrimination in schools and society and accepts and affirms the pluralism (ethnic, racial, linguistic, religious, economic, gender, and sexual orientation, among others) that students, their communities, and teachers reflect. Multicultural education permeates the school's curriculum and instructional strategies as well as the interactions among teachers, students, and families and the very way that schools conceptualize the nature of teaching and learning. Because it uses critical pedagogy as its underlying philosophy and focuses on knowledge, reflection, and action (praxis) as the basis for social change, multicultural education promotes democratic principles of social justice. (Nieto, 2012, p. 42)

Note that Nieto's conceptualization of multicultural education calls for whole school reform. Let us explore what she means by considering the four ways that she said schools implement multicultural education. Similar to the other categories of multicultural education, Nieto's (1994) typology also moves from a superficial, add-on approach to one that is critical and justice-oriented.

Tolerance. A school characterized by tolerance simply emphasizes getting along with people who are different and denies or ignores the significance of differences. Nieto (1994) wrote, "To tolerate differences means that they are endured, not necessarily embraced" (p. 3). Differences are accepted, but the goal is for those students to assimilate. Traditional curriculum and instruction persist, although topics, issues, and themes from multicultural perspectives are sometimes added.

Acceptance. A school that practices acceptance acknowledges that differences are important to people. The school adopts the cultural pluralism perspective, and differences are respected. The integration of multiple perspectives and diverse content is more systematic.

Respect. In a school whose approach reflects respect, differences are viewed as positive, and learning about diversity is intentionally promoted. Curriculum at this level is multicultural and anti-racist, presenting multiple perspectives and experiences. Teachers collaborate and parents are welcomed.

Active Learning

- In which type of schools (i.e. Tolerance, Acceptance, Respect, or Affirmation, solidarity and critique) would you want to teach? Why?
- Which of the four types reflects your own education?

Affirmation, solidarity, and critique. In this type of school, a commitment to social justice issues goes beyond the classroom. All members of the school community engage with the issues of culture and identity and understand that culture is dynamic and not fixed. Conflicts are not avoided but addressed through dialogue and learning about each other. Curriculum is interdisciplinary and multicultural, and student-centered, active learning is the norm. Student empowerment is promoted, and students "learn, reflect, question, and work to make the world a better place" (Nieto, 1994, p. 6). There are strong links between school, families, and the community, and there is a sense of belonging.

Geneva Gay and Gloria Ladson-Billings

The instruction in multicultural education is as important as the curriculum. Ladson-Billings (1995) and Gay (2004, 2010) advocate for culturally relevant teaching, which Gay defines as "using the cultural knowledge, prior experiences, frames of reference, and performance styles of ethnically diverse students to make learning encounters more relevant to and effective for them" (2010, p. 31). It requires teachers to know and use students' cultural lenses as a basis for teaching. Teachers must make an effort to relate what is being taught to the experiences and interests of students. This approach is clearly student-centered. Culturally responsive teaching views culture and various perspectives as assets and as a starting point for planning lessons. Ladson-Billings (1995) stresses that a strong, dynamic and "synergistic" relationship between home, school and community exists in culturally relevant pedagogy, where teachers become part of students' communities (p. 467). It requires a dialogical, collaborative relationship between teachers and students in order for knowledge to emerge, and teachers help students recognize, acknowledge, and critique social inequities (Ladson-Billings, 1995). The emphasis is on the local context of the students, and teachers' expectations of students must remain high. An example of a teacher practicing culturally relevant teaching would be a middle school teacher in an urban, high poverty school implementing an interdisciplinary lesson on food deserts, that is relevant to students' lives. A food desert is an area where affordable healthy food is difficult to find. In this lesson, students would work together, look up statistics on food deserts and food insecurity, map out their own community and locate where healthy, affordable food can be found, if at all. Students would then present their research to the town council or local new media in order to advocate for access to healthy, affordable food. Note that Chapter 9 of this textbook will delve deeper into culturally responsive teaching.

Continuum of Multicultural Education

Categories and classifications can be useful to aid in our understanding of concepts, but we must remember that reality is usually not so neat, orderly, and exact. Nonetheless, they help us make sense of situations, and, in this case, of how teachers and schools implement multicultural education.

The approaches taken in multicultural education can be categorized on a continuum from surface on one side to social action/social justice on the other. To generalize, the surface side of the continuum includes

Table 1.   A continuum of multicultural education.

	Surface ←			→ Critical	
James Banks	Contributions Additive		Transformative	Social Action	
Christine Sleeter and Carl Grant	Teaching the Exceptional and Culturally Different Human Relations	Single Group Studies	Multicultural Education	Education that is Multicultural and Social Reconstructionist (2007) Multicultural Social Justice Education (2009)	
Sonia Nieto	Tolerance	Acceptance	Respect	Affirmation, solidarity, and critique	

the token, superficial inclusion of multicultural content and an emphasis on everyone getting along. Surface multicultural education efforts "fail to confront directly the deep-seated inequalities that exist in schools" (Nieto, 2002, p. 7). In the middle of the continuum we can find curriculum and instruction that either focuses on a given cultural group or curriculum that has been rewritten to include various multicultural perspective. Then at the critical side continuum, the entire school curriculum and culture is transformed. At this end, multiculturalism is seen as an asset, and curriculum and instruction is presented through various perspectives and experiences. Stereotypes, prejudice, discrimination, racism, and other types of intolerance, injustice, and oppression are deeply addressed at this level. Students at this end also learn to use their knowledge in order to act for equality and justice. Sleeter suggests that multicultural educators also examine with their students the relationship between power and schools and question what passes as truth – an awareness that knowledge is socially constructed (2004, 2005). Contemporary multicultural educators advocate for this critical approach.

Table 1 shows the continuum of multicultural education theories, placing them in categories from "surface," or superficial approaches to multicultural education on the left, to the more critical approaches on the right. The approaches on the left side of the continuum ("surface" multicultural education) positions different cultural and ethnic groups as "other," while the critical approach acknowledges the uniqueness of everyone and promotes a shared sense of responsibility to our common humanity.

Conclusion

This chapter provided an overview of multicultural education in the United States. What began with ethnic studies in the 1960s evolved into a school reform movement where cultural pluralism is promoted, diverse perspectives and knowledge is integrated into the curriculum, and where students work toward social justice. The theories of multicultural education were explained and compared, showing the range of approaches from a surface, superficial style, to a critical model that is advocated by contemporary scholars and practitioners of multicultural education.

References

Banks, J. A. (2010). Approaches to multicultural curriculum reform. In J. A. Banks & C. A. McGee-Banks (Eds.), *Multicultural education: Issues and perspectives*, (7th ed., pp. 233–254). Hoboken, NJ: Wiley.

Banks, J. A. (2014). *An introduction to multicultural education* (5th ed.). Boston, MA: Pearson.

Bennett, C. I. (2002). *Comprehensive multicultural education: Theory and practice* (5th ed.). Boston: Allyn and Bacon.

Eck, D. L. (2006). *What is Pluralism?* Harvard University's The Pluralism Project. Retrieved from http://pluralism.org/what-is-pluralism/.

Gay, G. (2004a). Beyond Brown: Promoting equality through multicultural education. *Journal of Curriculum and Supervision*, *19*(3), 193–216.

Gay, G. (2004b). The paradoxical aftermath of Brown. *Multicultural Perspectives*, *6*(4), 12-17.

Gay, G. (2010). *Culturally responsive teaching: Theory, research, and practice* (2nd ed.). New York, NY: Teachers College Press.

Hanushek, E. (2014). Achievement gap. In D. C. Phillips (Ed.), *Encyclopedia of Educational Theory and Philosophy*. (pp. 5–7) doi: http://dx.doi.org.ezproxy.fau.edu/10.4135/9781483346229.n9

La Belle, T. J. & Ward, C. R. (1994). *Multiculturalism and education: Diversity and its impact on schools and society*. Albany, NY: State University of New York Press.

Ladson-Billings, G. (1995). Toward a theory of culturally relevant pedagogy. *American Educational Research Journal*, *32*(3), 465-491.

National Association for Multicultural Education. (n.d). Definitions of Multicultural Education. Retrieved from http://www.nameorg.org/definitions_of_multicultural_e.php.

National Center for Education Statistics. (2014). Digest of Education Statistics: 2014. Retrieved from http://nces.ed.gov/programs/digest/d14/.

Nieto, S. (1994). Affirmation, solidarity and critique: Moving beyond tolerance in multicultural education. *Multicultural Education*, *1*(4), 9–12, 35–38.

Nieto, S. (2002). Profoundly multicultural questions. *Educational Leadership, 60*(4), 6–10.

Nieto, S. *(2012)*. Defining multicultural education for school reform. In S. Nieto & P. Body (Eds.), *Affirming diversity: The sociopolitical context of multicultural education.* (6th ed., pp. 40-59). Boston, MA: Pearson.

Sleeter, C. E. (2004). Critical multicultural curriculum and the standards movement. *English teaching: Practice and critique, 3*(2), 122-138.

Sleeter, C. E. (2005). *Un-standardizing curriculum: Multicultural teaching in the standards-based classroom.* New York, NY: Teachers College Press.

Sleeter, C. E. & Grant, C.A. (2007). *Making choices for multicultural education: Five approaches to race, class and gender* (5th ed.) Hoboken, NJ: John Wiley & Sons, Inc.

Sleeter, C. E. & Grant, C. A. (2009). *Making choices for multicultural education: Five approaches to race, class, and gender.* (6th ed.) Hoboken, NJ: Wiley.

Waldon, K. A. (2015). *Black adolescents' critical encounters with media and the counteracting possibilities of critical media literacy.* If Unpublished: (Unplublished doctoral dissertation). Florida Atlantic University, Boca Raton, FL, USA. Else, if published: (ProQuest Dissertations Publishing, 3730732). Retrieved from xxxdatabase (Access or Order Number). Florida Atlantic University, Boca Raton, FL, USA.

Voice in the Field: Collateral Damage I

Traci P. Baxley

Kalisha A. Waldon

As multicultural educators it is important for us to create spaces in our classrooms that engage all students and that intersect with their lived realities (including current events in the media) and what is transpiring within the walls of the classroom. Sometimes doing this interrupts what we have planned for the day; however these teachable moments provide us with opportunities to make learning relevant for our students, to connect with them personally, and to practice a classroom culture of care. It is through these intentional student-centered spaces that our students thrive academically and trust us as their teachers.

Vignette

Mrs. Harris, a language arts teacher of a sixth grade gifted class, assigned a creative writing assignment to her students. The theme for the writing was "Youth Violence." Mrs. Harris told her students to be as creative as they liked and that they could choose between three writing styles: informative essay, prose or poetry. Thomas, a sensitive, bright African American male (the only Black male in the class), wrote the following poem for the assignment. After reading the poem (which was later nominated to win an award and was published in a local newspaper), Mrs. Harris never discussed the poem with Thomas, nor did she discuss the social issue that was transpiring in the media, she never gave him any feedback on his paper.

I CAN'T BREATHE. . .

Written by Thomas Baxley III, 12 years old

I'm a young black male in a society that seems to not value people who look like me;
I am aghast when I see violence against young brown-skinned boys by police brutality.
I'm confused, sad, bewildered, puzzled . . . aren't the officers in blue suppose to Serve and Protect;
Who's protecting me from the violence . . .seems more like neglect.

I can't breathe!

On the computer there are stories about Trayvon Martin who held nothing but skittles and iced tea;
How did Zimmerman get away with making Trayvon the perpetrator on TV?
Michael Brown had both of his hands in the air surrendering, some witnesses say;
But that would be the last moment of his life as his body lay in the street for more than 4 hours that day.
Obeying universal rules and buying snack,
Doesn't make sense to shoot someone in the back,
This is making me sad, angry and confused,
Of this really twisted unexplained news.

I can't breathe!

Tamir Rice was only 12 years old like me, how could he be gone so early and so violently;
He never got a chance to say I'm a just a kid playing in the park, please don't hurt me.
Eric Garner's last words ring in my ears as I try to make sense of the violence against black youth like me;
Can't you see that I can't breathe. Give me space, Hear my words, Get to know who I am and you will see.
Choking someone to death is extreme,
And even more so . . . killing a tween!
This makes me devastated, enraged and perplexed
And it makes me think . . .it could happen to me next.

I can't breathe!

They think, boys like me with dark colored skin
In a hoodie with some friends is a sin;
Some White police officers are not understanding;
That negative stereotype is not upstanding.
BANG! BANG! BANG! the shots would ring out
One by one. . .
Not even realizing what they had done.
They think, "whoops another dumb boy was killed"
"He's probably been smoking weed with a gun, another job fulfilled."
I can't breathe! Do you even know who I am?
I am a gifted 'A' student, I am a talented actor, I am a brilliant pianist;
I am a great athlete with goals and dreams of one day being a neuroscientist.
The actions of a few create unrest, mistrust, division and affect us all; Give young black boys and opportunity
    to succeed and fail, but pick us up when we fall.
Don't make judgments, don't assume, don't stereotype because it often ends badly for young black boys;
Nonviolent protest, education, and know our words are not just loud noise.

I can't breathe. . .

This vignette was not just created to get you thinking about multiculturalism in the classroom. It was also provided to give you an indication of the types of things occur in classrooms today. The vignette is actually a real-world situation that transpired in a sixth grade classroom. Consider the following questions as you reflect upon what transpired and how you would have handled the situation if you were the teacher.

1. Did Mrs. Harris fail this student? Why/Why not?

2. What is Mrs. Harris' role as an educator in addressing the social issue in Thomas' paper?

3. Is Mrs. Harris obligated to address current racial issues?

4. In ignoring (or not addressing) the issue does Mrs. Harris further marginalizes? Silences?

5. Are you comfortable with having dialogue like this in your classrooms?

Here is another example of how students internalize and reflect upon injustices and systems of oppression in their world. Opportunities for critical discourse and writing about these experiences or about their wonderings create safe spaces for them to grapple with these important issues.

Racism 2016

By: Tiffany Rhoden, 10th grader
A bitter part of history still lingers in our present.
As images of scars and wounds stay fresh with pain and sin.
Destined to plague our future and seemingly here to stay,
Its soul is everlasting and will not go away.\

Its home is a segregated city-where neighbors look more like kin
Its schools are shells for integration-though divisiveness lurks within
Its streets are plagued with men in blue whose job is to protect and serve
Yet on the ground in a pool of blood is a man who "got what he deserved."

And so it thrives in our courtrooms - cloaked in a judge's chamber,
Where lengthy sentences are tossed about to those "who pose a danger".
Fueled by the work of lawmakers, whose aim is to please the voters,
Ridding our society of criminals whom we identify mostly by color.

Making its way in our economy - defined by rich and poor,
Where climbing the corporate ladder leaves many behind a closed door.
Wealth handed down through generations - by institutions like Big Banks,
Leave many with a thing called "privilege" and others below the ranks.

Can it still survive in a nation that is presumed above the rest?
Where hard work, talent and effort should land one among the best?
Can its echo be heard across a land, where a White House is home to a Black man?

Take one look in a mirror and let me know if it can.

Questions to Ponder:

1. What real world issues does Tiffany address in her poem?

2. Would you feel comfortable discussing the issues presented in your classroom? Why or why not?

3. How could you as a teacher engage her and others in the classroom?

Multicultural Education Theoretical Frameworks Chart

Name: _____

Instructions: For this assignment you will complete the chart located below after you have finished the readings and watched this unit's videos. The checkable options listed below include levels in each of the theorists' MCE frameworks. Choose all of the levels within each theorist's framework that align with the appropriate Dimension of Multicultural Education.

Hint: *Every box may not be filled in when you are complete this worksheet. There could be some levels that fit into the same box, there may be some "gray area" between boxes.* In other words everyone's chart will not look exactly alike when you are complete. However, there should be a general pattern and you should be able to defend why you select your theorists' levels in the chosen boxes.

Five Dimensions of Multicultural Education	Banks' Approaches to Multicultural Curriculum Integration	Sleeter & Grant's Five Approaches to Multicultural Education	Nieto's Levels of Multicultural Integration
1. Content Integration	☐ Contributions Approach ☐ Additive Approach ☐ Transformative Approach ☐ Social Action Approach ☐ N/A Not Applicable	☐ Teaching the Culturally Different ☐ Human Relations ☐ Single Group Studies ☐ Multicultural Education ☐ Multicultural and Social Reconstruction	☐ Monoculture ☐ Tolerance ☐ Acceptance ☐ Respect ☐ Affirmation, Solidarity, Critique
2. Knowledge Construction	☐ Contributions Approach ☐ Additive Approach ☐ Transformative Approach ☐ Social Action Approach ☐ N/A Not Applicable	☐ Teaching the Culturally Different ☐ Human Relations ☐ Single Group Studies ☐ Multicultural Education ☐ Multicultural and Social Reconstruction	☐ Monoculture ☐ Tolerance ☐ Acceptance ☐ Respect ☐ Affirmation, Solidarity, Critique
3. Equity Pedagogy	☐ Contributions Approach ☐ Additive Approach ☐ Transformative Approach ☐ Social Action Approach ☐ N/A Not Applicable	☐ Teaching the Culturally Different ☐ Human Relations ☐ Single Group Studies ☐ Multicultural Education ☐ Multicultural and Social Reconstruction	☐ Monoculture ☐ Tolerance ☐ Acceptance ☐ Respect ☐ Affirmation, Solidarity, Critique
4. Prejudice Reduction	☐ Contributions Approach ☐ Additive Approach ☐ Transformative Approach ☐ Social Action Approach ☐ N/A Not Applicable	☐ Teaching the Culturally Different ☐ Human Relations ☐ Single Group Studies ☐ Multicultural Education ☐ Multicultural and Social Reconstruction	☐ Monoculture ☐ Tolerance ☐ Acceptance ☐ Respect ☐ Affirmation, Solidarity, Critique
5. Empowering School Culture & Social Structure	☐ Contributions Approach ☐ Additive Approach ☐ Transformative Approach ☐ Social Action Approach ☐ N/A Not Applicable	☐ Teaching the Culturally Different ☐ Human Relations ☐ Single Group Studies ☐ Multicultural Education ☐ Multicultural and Social Reconstruction	☐ Monoculture ☐ Tolerance ☐ Acceptance ☐ Respect ☐ Affirmation, Solidarity, Critique

CHAPTER 2

The Relevance of Culture and Identity: Why It Matters

Nanette Missaghi

Ms. Forest has just recently graduated with her Bachelor's degree in elementary education from a university in Georgia. She is extremely motivated and excited to finally have a classroom of her own. Ms. Forest loves Georgia and wishes to stay there to teach; however, she cannot find a teaching job. She applies to various states and gets offered a teaching position at a new public school in Miami, Florida. Ms. Forest decides to move to Miami because she wants to live near the beautiful beaches that she has seen in all the movies.

On the first day of school her students walk into the classroom and her mouth unintentionally drops opened. She realizes that her classroom consists of students all different cultural groups, which was much different from her pre-service internship experience. Throughout her schooling her professors mentioned multiculturalism, in definition, but she had not had to put any of the principles of multiculturalism into practice. She takes a deep breath, welcomes the students to her class, and teaches her first day. When she got home later that evening, she broke down and cried. She realized that she had nothing in common with any of them. She asked herself, "How can I teach them?"

-Vignette Contributed by Mai Lyn Colangelo, Elementary School Teacher

Chapter Purpose

"How can I teach them?" How many educators do you think have asked this question throughout the years? How many educators do you think come prepared to teach students from cultural groups that are different from their own? What is culture? Is it something to study? Does everybody have it? Why is culture so important to the teaching and learning process? Why do educators need to understand culture? Isn't it enough that they are expected to master content knowledge and methods courses? This chapter will address these questions, and provide opportunities for you to begin a journey of self-reflection of your own culture, and how it can impact your students and your teaching practices.

It is common in education to approach the topic of culture from the student perspective. Several multicultural education scholars highlight the need for teachers to learn about the cultures of their students and families, and figure out how to incorporate those cultures and funds of knowledge into their classroom instruction and their lesson plans (Ladson-Billings 1995, 2008; Gay 2000; Sleeter, 2011). What is missing from this discourse is the educator knowing culture and their personal cultural identity. As a precursor to cultural competence pedagogy or culturally responsive teaching, educators should embrace the following:

1. An understanding of the definition and nature of culture.
2. An understanding of the basic tenets of cultural identity within the context of teaching diverse student populations.
3. An understanding of their own culture and its impact on teaching.
4. A commitment to a journey of cultural self-reflection and the affirmation of others.

This cultural self-knowledge will ground educators in a full understanding of culture itself and how it manifests itself in you, your students, colleagues, and in other relationships. As stated previously, this chapter will encourage you, as educators, to learn about the nature of culture, your personal cultural identity, and how your culture informs your teaching.

Culture Defined

Culture. The most basic definition of culture is described as a *way of life of a group of people*. We have come to know that it is more complex than simply *a way of life*. The word culture has become very popular in American society and used in many different contexts like business culture, pop culture, tech culture, and cultural appropriation. Culture means different things to people in these varied fields and situations. The classic definition of culture by James Banks (2010)–used in this chapter–is as follows:

> The essence of a culture is not its artifacts, tools, or other tangible cultural elements but how the members of the group interpret, use, and perceive them. It is the values, symbols, interpretations, and perspectives that distinguish one people from another in modernized societies; it is not material objects and other tangible aspects of human societies. People within a culture usually interpret the meaning of symbols, artifacts, and behaviors in the same or in similar ways. (p.8)

Traditionally in the educational setting, culture describes the backgrounds of students and how they learn. It should also takes into consideration students' implicit and explicit funds of knowledge, ways of speaking, traditions, and backgrounds.

Every country has a dominant culture that houses its language, governance, education, beliefs, and family structures. In the United States, the dominant culture is English-American, sometimes referred to as WASP (White, Anglo-Saxon, Protestant) or European American that originates from English Puritan roots from 1607 (Price, 2003). However, the Iroquois and other Indian nations, the Africans such as the Mandinka, Kru tribes for example, the Spanish and the French cultures also influenced this dominant European American culture (Genovese, 1974; Grinde & Johansen 1991). Culture is not a person's race, though we will commonly hear people make reference to the "White culture," the "Black culture," and the "Indian culture."

Culture is what we pass down to our children every single day through our speech, stories, wisdom, dress, behaviors, and actions. Sometimes members of the dominant culture do not realize they have a culture, which is often referred to as cultural blindness (Cross, 2012). Those who share the beliefs and value systems of the dominant culture often do not think about themselves in terms of culture and believe that only people of color or people from other countries have culture.

Drawing on the work of Peggy Macintosh (1988), who used gender as a window to understand the privilege she had as a White woman, educators can learn about and examine their privileges. McIntosh realized that her White race was invisible to her and she never had to think about it. She defined white privilege ". . . .as an invisible package of unearned assets which I can count on cashing in each day, but about which I was 'meant' to remain oblivious" (pp. 1-2). She recognized that men ". . . .work from a base of unacknowledged privilege" (pp. 1-2). She created a questionnaire to assist in her reflection on the white privilege she held and educators can use it as well.

White privilege studies have sparked interest and awareness into other types of privilege, or systemic group privileges, such as gender, ability, sexual orientation, religion, and class (Case, 2013). Privilege is commonly referred to as a special right or unearned advantage held by a person or particular group of people. Table 2.1 summarizes these privileges. As a practice, educators should reflect upon how privilege informs each of those areas in their teaching.

Another layer of complexity about cultural identity is the intersection of race and culture. Because of our limited ways of knowing, people can run the risk of stereotyping people from other racial groups and homogenizing cultural groups. For example, "All Asians are good," "Blacks look alike," and "All American Indians speak the same language." However, within each of these racial groups, many cultures exist. For example, if all the White people of the world were put in a line, one would find cultural distinctions that take root in places such as Russia, England, Portugal, etc. Some cultures in the world may be in danger of becoming extinct and their languages no longer spoken, thus emphasizing the importance of culture and the need to know who we are in order to become more effective educators to all our students.

Table 2.1.   Research-based Theories and Strategies for Equity Practices

Privilege	Description
Male	"Men must begin to understand that male privilege is an invisible package of unearned assets that men can count on each day" (Carbado, 2000, p. 527). Unearned assets include higher salaries, making society's rules and laws, perspectives and beliefs valued by society or the dominant culture, being the default gender, and having power; to name a few.
Sexual Orientation-specifically heterosexual	"Heterosexual privilege includes unearned benefits afforded to those with a heterosexual orientation and defines the sexual orientation norm" (Griffin et al as cited in Case, 2013, p. 151). Benefits include health insurance, society behaviors normed by them, being able to show affection in public without harassment, not needing to be "fixed" or "cured" to name a few.
Religion- specifically Christian	"Invisible, unearned, and largely unacknowledged array of benefits given to Christians, with which they unconsciously walk through life" (Blumenfeld and Jaekel as cited in Case, 2013, p.189). Benefits include time off from work and school for religious reasons, freedom to worship and practice their religion without harassment, holidays normed to Christianity to the exclusion of other faiths/non-faith groups.
Class	"... the system of advantages that continues to ensure that wealth, power, opportunity, and privilege go hand in hand" (Rothenberg, 2000, p. 122). Benefits would include values being accepted and normed by the dominant population; ability to buy a home, get a loan, or move into a certain neighborhood; to name a few.
Ability- Able bodied	"Differently abled persons may be viewed by the more abled as possessing a multitude of deficits. People who have limited physical mobility or who are nonsighted (without sight) are often erroneously viewed as limited mentally or emotionally" (Black & Stone, 2005, p. 250). Benefits would include having proper accommodations when traveling; being able to not think about how one could enter a building or use certain facilities; to name a few.

According to UNESCO (United Nations Educational, Scientific, and Cultural Organization) there are several cultures in the world in danger as are many cultural traditions that are gifts to the world. A tenant of UNESCO is building intercultural understanding: through the protection of heritage and support for cultural diversity. UNESCO created the idea of World Heritage to protect sites of outstanding universal value. They identified 646 languages in threat of extinction (with the status of definitely endangered (UNESCO.org, 2010). Definitely endangered means that "the language is no longer being learned as the mother tongue by children in the home. The youngest speakers are thus of the parental generation. At this stage, parents may still speak their language to their children, but their children do not typically respond in the language (Moseley, 2010, p. 12). This means that the parents are the main speakers of the language and not the children.

When a language dies so does the culture (Ibid; Cote, 2015, p. 48). For example, in the United States there are 61 American Indian languages on the endangered list (UNESCO.org). Teachers who are knowledgeable about their own cultural identity and language and the cultures of their students can serve as examples to others. These teachers can work diligently in their classrooms to foster cultural pride by integrating the knowledge of the students into the classroom.

Why Should Educators Learn about Culture?

Current United States demographics call for a deeper examination of why culture is important to educator discourse and student success. The following statistics assist in the understanding of the shift in cultural

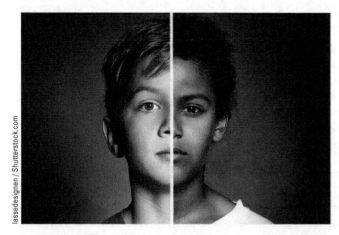

lassedesignen / Shutterstock.com

representation that is taking place in our society (macro) and its relationship to the shifts that are needed in our educational system (micro) in educating today's diverse student population. The 2014 United States Census National Projections (Colby & Ortman, 2015), predicts that by 2044 there will be a shift in majority/minority status of racial groups; meaning there will be a plurality of races not seen before. When all groups of American Indians, Blacks, Latinos, Native Hawaiians, and Asians are grouped together, they will be in the majority although the White group will be the largest single group at 44%. This means that the United States will grow from a country with 37.8% people of color in 2014 to 56% people of color in 2044. It is important to remember that this racial diversity does not reflect the numerous cultures within the United States. Because culture is not tracked in the census, it is challenging to determine actual cultural demographics.

School districts across the United States reflect these demographics in different ways depending on internal migration, immigration, employment, and the location of American Indian reservations. Some schools even reflect more diversity than the cities in which they reside. This underscores the importance of educators gaining cultural competence, especially when the cultural backgrounds of the current teaching force is much different, predominately White and culturally European American, than the diverse student population of the public school system. In lieu of this, educators must know how to effectively connect with students from these varied cultural backgrounds; know how to teach them in meaningful ways; and know how to lay the foundation for effective democratic citizenry.

Educational disparities in student achievement, student discipline, program participation rates in special education, and the representation of students of color and American Indians in gifted and talented programs are other reasons educators should learn about culture. It is also important to note that the intersection of race and culture in educational settings have marginalized certain groups of students that have been affected by these disparities. The disparities are typically related to race but will not be explored in this chapter. However, due to historical disparities in schools, scholars in the field of multicultural education, such as James Banks, Gloria Ladson-Billings, Sonia Nieto, Geneva Gay, and Paul Gorski have all called for equitable learning opportunities for all students. They have contributed greatly to explaining and creating models that advocate for an anti-bias pedagogy in Pre K through 12th grade education.

The primary foci of their work has been to advocate for the learning and validation of students' culture, building upon the cultural strengths of students, diversifying the curriculum, creating a culture of care, creating intentional spaces for critical conversations, promoting a community of social justice, and incorporating students' lives and experiences into the classroom. In order to accomplish these things, educators must first take a look at how their own personal experiences, ideologies, and biases impact the ways in which they interact and relate to students. They must:

1. Acknowledge that their cultural identity impacts how they relate to students.
2. Acknowledge that they need to re-evaluate their teaching pedagogy in order to ensure equitable learning opportunities for all students.
3. Acknowledge that they may have bought into the idea of cultural/colorblindness or monoculturalism, over cultural pluralism.

To suggest that humans are all the same based solely on the status of being human grossly over simplifies the very essence of human cognition and all but eliminates cultural diversity. It is ok to see cultural differences—we all have stories, we tell them in different ways and in different contexts, and we all have values, but they too look and feel different. Culturally blind (Cross, 2012) and racially biased classrooms, normed to the dominant culture, have been the status quo for decades (Ayers, Ladson-Billings, Michie, & Noguera, 2008; Watkins, 2001; Treuer, 2012). Educators should avoid creating spaces where students are devalued and denied freedom to embrace their own identities. Educators should create classroom communities where cultural diversity is acknowledged, respected, and validated in their student's beliefs, actions, and practices. Through these efforts, teachers can work towards creating a more culturally inclusive classroom.

Cultural Identity

Identity ". . . .is a sense of psychosocial well-being. Its most obvious concomitants are a feeling of being at home in one's body, a sense of "knowing where one is going," and an inner assuredness of anticipated recognition from those who count" (Erickson, 1968, p. 165). Identity is fluid, successive, developmental and shaped by a person's beliefs, values and norms about gender, religion, sexual orientation, profession, race, age, or something else yet undefined; identity develops from crises and the changes in one's environment (Erikson, 1994). It is presupposed that everyone already has an identity; however there are different levels of identity awareness and factors such as oppression or discrimination that can impact the forging of healthy cultural identities. According to Stuart Hall (1990) cultural identity is defined in two ways: One is the 'one true self' characterized by one shared culture, history, and language; second recognizing that cultural identity is a developmental stage of 'who we really are' based on the past but understanding the current state of 'being who we are' today due to "history intervening and . . .the colonial experience. . ."(Ibid, p. 223-225). It is important as a first step that an educator is equipped with the knowledge, appreciation, and value of their own cultural identity. This will aide them in better understanding that their students may come to the classroom with either a strong sense of cultural identity or experience identity confusion and unawareness.

The research literature on identity development includes several racial/ethnic identity models that highlight the stages that individuals encounter as their identity changes over time. The William E. Cross' Model of Psychological Nigrescence (Cross, 1991) focuses on Black identity development, White identity development is explored in Janet Helms' model (Helms 1994), Jean Phinney's Model (1990) focuses on Ethnic Identity development, the Ferdman and Gallegos Model of Latino Development (2001), Jean Kim's Asian Identity Development (1991), and Perry G. Horse's Perspective on American Indian Identity Development (2001). Table 2.2 outlines the stages of identity development in each of the aforementioned models.

Table 2.2. Various Stage Models of Identity Development

Identity Type	Researcher	Description
Human lens (not culturally specific)	Erik Erikson (1968, 1994)	Erikson lays the groundwork, from a Danish/German perspective, that humans develop their identity through stages influenced by a psychological "crisis" (1968) born of social, cultural, and family environments. His view is that identity is ever evolving.
		The stages are:
		Stage 1- Basic Trust vs Mistrust. The first year of life when a child learns whom to trust.
		Stage 2- Autonomy vs Shame and Doubt. The stage of early childhood (up to three years of age) where a child acquires interests, explores what belongs to them and others.
		Stage 3- Initiative vs Guilt. The stage from three to five years of age where a child interacts with others through play and internalizes the reactions of others.
		Stage 4- Industry vs Inferiority. The stage from five to twelve years of age when a child learns to develop skills and competence dictated by society.
		Stage 5- Identity vs Identity Diffusion (Confusion). The stage from twelve to eighteen years of age where a young person begins to learn about the roles they will take on as an adult. They explore possibilities of existence and their identity begins to develop with the end result of feeling confirmation about their identity.
		Stage 6- Intimacy vs Isolation. This stage from eighteen to forty years of age defines the development of healthy relationships with the ultimate goal of achieving love.
		Stage 7- Generativity vs Stagnation. This stage from forty years to sixty-five years of age marks the time for adults to give back to the next generation and guide them. Without this behavior adults risk stagnation and a sense of loss, boredom or a sense of impoverishment.
		Stage 8- Integrity vs Despair. This final stage from sixty-five and upwards offers an adult a chance for reflection on their life, lead a productive retirement, feel successful and accept death as a part of life.

(continued)

Table 2.2. *(continued)*

Identity Type	Researcher	Description
Black Identity	William E. Cross (1991)	Theory of Nigrescence- The process of becoming Black:
		Stage 1: Pre-encounter- A stage where a person is anti-Black (self hatred) and pro-white (assimilation).
		Stage 2: Encounter- The first time a person realizes they are Black and they want to learn more about the black experience.
		Stage 3: Immersion-emersion- A person immerses themselves in being Black. This is a stage of pro-blackness and anti-whiteness. It is a critique of white people.
		Stage 4: Internalization- A person becomes proud of being Black and love themselves. They are open to learning about other people with a strong foundation of self.
		Stage 5: Internalization- Commitment- A person believes they belong to the human race yet without relinquishing their Black identity. They are committed to working others as advocates to fight for social justice.
Latino Identity	Bernando Ferdman & Placida V. Gallegos (2001)	Five Dimensions of developing a Latino identity that are shaped by one's lens, how a person chooses to view themselves, how White people and Latinos are viewed, and how race plays into identity:
		Latino- Integrated Individuals view themselves positively in a Latino group context.
		Latino- Identified (Racial/Raza) A person identifies very positively and specifically as Latino.
		Subgroup- Identified A person has a very narrow view of being a subgroup of Latino. The subgroup is ok.
		Latino as Other The external focus of a person is not white and Latinos are viewed generically.
		Undifferentiated/Denial An individual who identifies as a person and not Latino.
		White- Identified A person's identity is White and Latinos are viewed negatively.
Asian Identity	Jean Kim (2001)	Five stages of developing an Asian identity:
		Ethnic Awareness In early childhood, the family is the primary influencer of Asian identity development. It can be neutral, positive or negative.
		White Identification Upon entering school, outside forces influence identity especially racism. This impacts self-esteem.
		Awakening to Social Political Consciousness This is a stage of a person's awakening towards new perspectives of oppression and racism. There is less identification towards White people.
		Redirection to Asian American Consciousness A person develops Asian pride and has anger for racism.
		Incorporation This is the final stage of positivity and feeling comfortable being Asian. There is respect for other groups, a person no longer identifies as being White, and holds no anger towards White people.

(continued)

Identity Type	Researcher	Description
American Indian Identity	Perry G. Horse (2005)	The development of American Indian consciousness is where American Indian identity begins. There are many issues that influence American Indian identity "…such as ethnic nomenclature, racial attitudes, legal and political status of American Indian nations and American Indian people, cultural change and one's sensibility of what it means to be a Native American in today's society" (Horse, 2005). *Ethnic Nomenclature* Who am I - Native American or American Indian? The answer is a personal preference. *Racial Attitude* Acknowledgement of White privilege as the root cause of racism, manifest destiny, and oppression. A person may take on the characteristics of the oppressor. *Legal and Political Status* The unique status of tribal sovereignty determines eligibility of citizenship in a tribal nation. *Cultural Change* American Indian cultures have changed and will continue to change. "Redefining what it means to American Indian in today's society is one of the major issues in Indian country….(It) is driven … by the response of American Indians to White privilege (Ibid, p.65) *Personal Sensibility* American Indian identity is very personal, multifaceted, and are influenced in five ways: 1. The extent to which one is grounded in one's native language and culture. 2. The validity of one's American Indian genealogy. 3. The extent to which one holds a traditional American Indian worldview. 4. One's self-concept as an American Indian. 5. One's enrollment (or lack thereof) in a tribe. (Ibid)
White Identity	Janet Helms (1994)	The development of White identity as related to race and racism occurs in two phases: Phase 1: The first is the abandonment of racism: *1. Contact* Colorblind, oblivious of oppression and racism, limited interaction with people of color. *2. Disintegration* Becomes conflicted about racism, abandons color blindness, has some relationships with people of color and their experiences influences new understandings about racism. Anxiety increases. *3. Reintegration* Regression into dominant ideology and white superiority. People of color blamed for racial problems and inequities. Guilt turned to anger. Phase 2: Defining a Non-Racist White Identity: *4. Pseudo independence* Open to learn about racism and acknowledges role of White people in racism, and their role in perpetuating it. More interaction with people of color. *5. Immersion and Emersion* Inner reflection of what it means to be White and develop a healthy identity. Begins to practice being an ally to personally address racism. Less guilt and has more hope. *6. Autonomy* Acknowledgment of whiteness with a positive and healthy White identity. Fights racism and has many friends across racial groups. Constant self reflection.
Ethnic Identity	Phinney (1993)	Three stages of developing an ethnic identity: *Stage 1: Unexamined Ethnic Identity* which depends upon a person's awareness and knowledge of ethnicity. Diffusion- No interaction or knowledge of ethnicity. Foreclosure A person has ethnic knowledge from family. *Stage 2: Ethnic Identity Search/Moratorium*- Personal encounters lead a person to seek out their ethnicity and become more aware of ethnicity. *Stage 3: Ethnic Identity Achievement* - A person has a positive identity and has positive views of other ethnicities.

Educators who are culturally knowledgeable about themselves and; acknowledge and are sensitive to cultural differences of their students will be more prepared to respond to cross-cultural conflicts that may arise in the classroom and be able to better foster inclusiveness among all students. In addition, they would be more likely to utilize strategies to build upon students' cultural strengths and validate and honor the funds of knowledge students' bring from their families and communities. The goal is to create a responsive learning environment where students from all cultures can thrive academically and socially. One example of this would be that a culturally knowledgeable teacher understands that language is the carrier of cultural ways and would not discourage, but instead enthusiastically encourage a student to speak their home language in the classroom. Research shows that students who know two or more languages have an academic advantage for problem solving, creativity, retaining working memory, learning math, and other key content knowledge (Lauchlan et al., 2013). A culturally knowledgeable teacher will know how to create positive learning environments for English Language Learners and bilingual students to use both languages to express themselves in the classroom.

Who Am I? Cultural Identity Activity

Identifying one's cultural identity can be a difficult enterprise especially if a person has never had to do it before. This activity is to aid you in determining what your cultural identity is and what has informed and shaped it. It will serve as a precursor to the creation of a critical cultural profile that is in the "Practical Encounters" section of this textbook.

Who Am I? Cultural Identity Activity ™

- Where did my ancestors come from?
- What languages did my ancestors speak?
- What traditions, beliefs, customs, and foods were practiced by my ancestors? List by the cultural groups you identified in Question 1.
- What traditions or rituals do my family and I continue to practice today from the ancestral cultures listed in Question 3. List by culture.
- What languages do I speak?
- Reflect on what you identified in the previous questions. What culture(s) has formed your identity today?
- Now that you have identified your culture, reflect on the parts of your cultural identity that make you who you are today. (i.e. your language, your beliefs, your values, your dress, your music).

Reflection Questions

Upon finishing the cultural identity activity, reflect on the following questions:

1. How does your culture impact your teaching?
2. How does your cultural identity potentially impact your interactions with students whose cultures are different from your own?

Addressing Cultural Bias Reflection Activity

Bias is ". . . reacting to a person on the basis of perceived membership in a single human category, ignoring other category memberships and other personal attributes. Bias is thus a narrow, potentially erroneous reaction, compared with individuated impressions formed from personal details" (Fiske 2002, p. 123). Memberships can include any group defined by race, gender, ability, social class, and culture to name a few examples. Having a bias is a natural occurrence of any human being and can be transmitted culturally from a family and cultural group to people without them realizing it. The tricky thing about a bias is that one is not always aware of it until they have an encounter with a person who does something different or contrary to what you perceive about that person.

Reflective questions:

1. What are my cultural biases?
2. What cultures or groups of students do I perceive I favor?
3. What cultures am I biased towards or against?
4. What do I perceive to be the reason(s) why I am biased towards the culture(s) I identified in #3?

Create a plan of action to figure out how to interrupt these patterns so students from various cultures will be validated and achieve academic success in your classroom.

Conclusion

In order for educators to effectively teach students from diverse cultures, they need to understand culture, be comfortable with their own cultural identity, and learn how to validate the cultures of their students. The cultural landscape of the United States has changed and will continue to become more racially and culturally diverse. Once you have identified your own cultural identity and biases, you can begin to better serve, understand, and work to provide a more equitable learning experience for all of your students. This is a lifelong journey of self-reflection, planning, and action.

References

Ayers, W., Ladson-Billings, G., Michie, G., & Noguera, P. A. (2008). City kids, city schools. New York, NY: The New Press.

Banks, J.A. & Banks, C. A. (2010). *Multicultural education: Issues and perspectives.* New York, NY: John Wiley & Sons.

Black, L. & Stone, D. (2005). Expanding the definition of privilege: The concept of social privilege. *Journal of Multicultural Counseling and Development, 33*(4), pp. 243–255.

Carbado, D. W. (2000). Men, feminism, and heterosexual privilege. In R. Delgado & J. Stefanic (Eds.). *Critical race theory: The cutting edge.* Philadelphia, PA: Temple University Press.

Case, K. (2013). Deconstructing privilege: teaching and learning as allies in the classroom. New York, NY: Routledge.

Cross, T. (2012). Cultural competence continuum. *Journal of Child and Youth Care Work, p. 84.*

Cross, W. E. (1991). *Shades of Black: Diversity in African-American identity.* Philadelphia, PA: Temple University Press.

Erikson, E. H. (1968). *Identity Youth and Crisis.* New York, NY: W.W. Norton & Company.

Ferdman, B. M. & Gallegos, P. I. (2001). Racial identity development and Latinos in the United States. In C. L. Wijeyesinghe & B. W. Jackson, III (Eds.). New perspectives on racial identity development: A theoretical and practical anthology (pp. 32–66). New York, NY: New York University Press.

Gay, G. (2000). Culturally responsive teaching: Theory, research, and practice, Multicultural Education Series (2nd ed.). New York, NY: Teachers College, Columbia University.

Genovese, E. D. (1974). Roll jordan roll: The world the slaves made. New York, NY: Vantage Books.

Grinde Jr, D. A. & Johansen, B. E. (1991). *Exemplar of liberty: Native America and the evolution of democracy. Native American Politics Series, 3*(3). Los Angeles, CA: AISC Publications.

Hall, S. (1990). Cultural identity and diaspora. In J. Rutherford (Ed.). *Identity: Community, culture, difference* (pp. 22–37). London, UK: Lawrence & Wishart.

Helms, J. E. (1990). Toward a model of White racial identity development. In *Black and White racial identity: Theory, research and practice* (pp. 49–66). New York, NY: Greenwood Press.

Horse, P. G. (2005). Native American identity. *New perspective for student success, 2005*(109), 61–68.

Colby, S. L. & Ortman, J. M. (2015, March). *Projections of the size and composition of the U. S. population:* 2014 to 2016. United States Census Report, March 2015. Retrieved from https://www.census.gov/content/dam/Census/library/publications/2015/demo/p25-1143.pdf

Kim, J. (1991). Asian American identity development theory. In C. L. Wijeyesinghe & B. W. Jackson, III (Eds.). New perspectives on racial identity development: A theoretical and practical

Lauchlan, F., Parsi, M. & Fadd, R. (2012). Bilingualism in Sardinia and Scotland: Exploring the cognitive benefits of speaking a minority language. *International Journal of Bilingualism, 17*(1), 43–56.

McIntosh, P. (1988). White privilege: Unpacking the invisible knapsack. *Independent School, 49,* 31–35.

Moseley, C. (Ed.). (2010). *Atlas of the world's languages in danger. Memory of peoples* (3rd ed.). Paris, France: UNESCO Publishing.

Phinney, J.S. (1993). A three-stage model ethnic identity in adolescence. In M. E. Bernal & G. P. Knight (Eds.), Ethnic identity: Formation and transmission among hispanics and other minorities (pp. 61–79). Albany, NY: State University of New York Press.

Price, D. A. (2003). Love and hate in jamestown: John Smith, Pocahontas, and the start of a new nation. New York, NY: Vantage Books.

Rothenberg, P. S. (2000). *Race, class, and gender in the United States:* An integrated study. Lawrence, KS: University Press of Kansas.

Sleeter, C. E. & Cornbleth, C. (Eds.) (2011). *Teaching with vision: Culturally responsive teaching in standards-based classrooms,* New York, NY: Teachers College Press.

Treuer, A. (2012). *Everything you wanted to know about indians but were afraid to ask.* St. Paul, VA: Minnesota Historical Society Press.

Trompenaars, F. & Hamden-Turner, Charles. (1997). *Riding the culture wave.* New York, NY: McGraw Hill Publishing.

Wallace, L. (2009). What's lost when a language dies. *The Atlantic*

Watkins, W. H. (2001). The White architects of Black education: Ideology and power in America, 1865:1954. New York, NY: Teachers College Press.

Expert Corner
Responsibilities of Schools for Providing Receptive Cultures
Carlos Diaz, Ed.D.

In order to promote an accommodating school culture, faculty and staff should attempt to meld the identities students bring from home with knowledge students need to succeed in academics and in the larger society. This is a delicate "balancing act". Educators generally do not have parental permission to do a "cultural makeover" of students in their own cultural image, no matter how tempting this may sound. The key is to respect the culture and identities students bring from home while pointing out what will be needed to succeed academically. Often, identities reinforced at home can be used as a "springboard" for academic and occupational success.

To successfully transition all U.S. schools to places where multiple identities are respected, we must first examine some school traditions which may interfere with this goal. Historically, schools did not take into account students' many identities. Quite to the contrary, historically public schools often practiced "forced assimilation". In doing so, they typically engaged in remaking students' ethnic, racial, gender, linguistic and cultural identities into a model reflective of U.S. mainstream American culture. These efforts were made with little regard for the kinds of identity conflicts this would create at the time, or later. After all, the rationale was that this was being done for the students' "own good". Historically, public schools were used as "agents of deculturalization" (Spring, 2007) that sanctioned segregation and a rejection of identities that did not fit the native English-speaking, White Anglo-Saxon Protestant norm of American society. This point is raised, not to dwell on the negative, but because it is part of the American educational tradition and it still has an influence on the culture of schools and the actions of some school officials today.

When students whose identities differ from the mainstream do not feel comfortable in a school setting, they develop a variety of coping strategies. Studies have documented these adaptations for Asian, (Lew, 2006) Latino/Latina (Barajas and Ronnkvist, 2007) and African American (Tyson and Darrity, 2005) students. Some of these coping strategies involve students of color segregating themselves during the school day in environments (such as the school cafeteria) where they control how they will use that space. Other students may withdraw from active engagement in the classroom or in school culture. Others may "act out" as a way of conveying to school authorities that they are uncomfortable in situations or a school culture which they do not control. What is abundantly clear is that when students attend school and feel comfortable in that school's culture, they can focus on their academic demands. Conversely, when students do not feel their identities are affirmed in school, this detracts from their academic performance. As one student remarked to her teacher, "I don't care how much you know, until I know how much you care". While no school environment can claim perfection, school cultures do not often conflict with the backgrounds of middle and upper-class mainstream students. Most of these students attend schools which provide an environment of cultural and identity affirmation. Other students may be trying to compete with their mainstream peers while engaging in "coping strategies" during the school day because their identities are not affirmed. At the end of twelve years of school, educators measure grade point averages, standardized test scores and other evidence of academic learning and rank order students for future academic (and eventually job) opportunities. Nowhere in this process is there a serious attempt to account for the "affective climate" or the cultural continuity/discontinuity that students experienced during their elementary and secondary schooling. Yet, there is significant research that indicates the "affective climate" and affirmation of identity which students experience affect academic performance.

If you are a current or future educator, you need to be keenly aware of what the "affective climate" in your classroom is for diverse groups of students. You cannot assume this affective climate, you must actually survey your students in an anonymous manner so if there are problems your classroom's academic climate, students are free to tell you without fear of retribution.

Individual and Societal Definitions of Identity

People arrive at their own definition of self-identity. For most people, their individual definition matches the way their society views them. For example, a White female born in the United States who identifies with a Christian religious denomination is likely to see herself as a member of the majority group in her nation. American society is very likely to view and treat her in a manner which is consistent with her self- identification.

A contrasting case would be an Afro-Cuban woman who is an immigrant to the United States and identifies with a Christian faith. She may see her primary identity as Cuban, Cuban American and Latina. American society may see her simply as a Black citizen. In this instance, self and societal identities do not match.

Most educators have self-identities which match societal perceptions of them. As a result, they have not experienced the stress felt by those in society whose self-identities and societal identities do not match. Societies look for certain "markers" in defining individuals. Some markers, such as race and gender, are readily obvious. The very presence of a person tells others what they are. Other characteristics, like native or immigrant status, are not immediately visible, but rely on other markers like accents or speech patterns. While most immigrants to the U.S who learned English as a second language after childhood carry a trace of their first language in the way they pronounce English, not all do. Those immigrants that speak English with native fluency and accent are often seen as natives unless they choose to identify otherwise. These persons can easily find themselves in the middle of conversations which insult immigrants because they don't have any visibility as immigrants. Then, they face the following dilemma: do they identify themselves as immigrants and "dampen the atmosphere" or do they simply remain silent and leave the impression they agree with the comments?

In schools, gay and lesbian students are often faced with circumstances similar to low visibility immigrants. In some cases, the sexual preference of gay and lesbian students is known by their teachers and fellow students. In other cases, these students have opted to keep their sexual preferences private. These students also face a similar dilemma as low visibility immigrants when they hear homophobic remarks in schools.

Educators should be aware that some of their students face the stress of experiencing disconnections between their individual and societal identities. If their individual identities are not valued by many in their schools, it is not unusual for these students to try to "pass" as members of another group. In South Florida high schools, there have been cases of Haitian students trying to "pass" as African American, just like some light-skinned African Americans identified themselves as White during the era of legal segregation in the United States. Trying to "pass" as anyone other than who you are is very emotionally stressful. When people do this, it is obvious that their authentic identity is not being respected in that environment.

Racial and Ethnic Identity

This type of identity is particularly salient when it involves biracial or multiracial people. American society tends to view the great golfer, Tiger Woods, as African American. However, a similar case could be made that he is the world's greatest Asian American golfer since his mother is from Thailand. When persons of biracial or multiracial backgrounds choose to identify more with that portion of their background which is less physically visible, society will often choose to identify them with the group which is more physically noticeable. Further stress is created when biracial or multiracial persons are asked by others to "choose" which aspect of their background they want to recognize. Some individuals have answered this question by saying, "You are asking me to choose between my father and my mother."

References

Barajas, H.J. & Ronnkvist, A. (2007, June) Racialized space: Framing Latino and Latina experience in public schools. *Teachers College Record, 109*(6), 1517–1538.

Lew, J. (2006, December). Burden of acting neither White Nor Black: Asian American identities and achievement in urban schools. *The Urban Review, 38*(5).

Spring, J. (2007). *Deculturalization and the struggle for equality.* New York, NY: McGrawHill.

Tyson, K. & Darity, W., Jr. (2005). It's not "a Black Thing": Understanding the burden of acting White and other dilemmas of high achievement. *American Sociological Review, 70,* 582–605.

Practical Encounter

Practical Encounter #1

Directions: Read the following Mini Case Studies and answer the questions based on the concepts presented in this chapter.

A Native Alaskan teacher speaking on what she learned in teacher education courses:

"I only learned how to teach white kids. I didn't learn one thing about teaching Native kids. It is different, you know. But I don't think they even thought about that."

An African-American woman, education graduate comments on the reason she chose not to enter the profession:

"My cooperating teacher was just [damaging] for black kids. She was [damaging] for low-achieving black kids. She had no notion of how to build self-esteem, or even that she should. In her opinion, the bright kids deserved attention, and she was there to prove that the others couldn't learn."

Questions:

1. How can teacher education programs better address the needs of pre-service teachers of color so that all voices are heard?

2. How do we assure that the pedagogy that is being taught will benefit all students in the school system?

Practical Encounter #2: Critical Dialogue on Privilege

Directions: Read the following articles and answer the critical reflection questions. The articles can be found in the Appendix of this text.

Read *An Indian's Father Plea* by Robert Lake "Medicine Grizzly Bear"

1. What did the father of Wind-Wolf not understand? Why is the father writing the letter to the teacher?

2. Contrast Western society's philosophy of early education from that of the Native Americans.

3. Provide evidence to support the importance of culture to this group of people.

4. Why did the father think the teacher thought his son was a slow-learner?

5. What did the father mean when he said that his son "is not culturally 'disadvantaged' but he is 'culturally different'?

6. What funds of knowledge did the Indian son bring to the classroom?

7. What forms of discrimination had the son experienced in school? Why?

8. What did the father mean when he stated that his son was, "caught between two worlds, torn by two distinct cultural systems."

Read *Unpacking the Invisible Knapsack* **by Peggy McIntosh**

1. Does being White put one at an advantage? Do Whites have privileges that members for other groups do not have?

2. How does the author (McIntosh) define "White privilege"? What is it?

3. Now knowing what it is...the question the author asks is.... "What will you do to lessen or end it?"

4. Does being White put one at an advantage? Do Whites have privileges that members for other groups do not have?

5. How does the author (McIntosh) define "White privilege"? What is it?

6. Now knowing what it is...the question the author asks is.... "What will you do to lessen or end it?"

7. The interlocking oppressions take active forms (those we can see) and embedded forms (those we are not taught to see).

8. According to the author, how was racism initially taught to her? How does the author now define racism?

9. "To redesign social systems we need first to acknowledge their colossal unseen dimensions...silences and denials... keep the thinking about equality or equity incomplete, protecting unearned advantage and conferred dominance by making these taboo subjects."

10. "...obliviousness about White advantage"...perpetuates the...myth that democratic choice is equally available to all."

Read the Interview with Beverly Tatum on Racial Privilege

1. Racial privileges are the benefits or the advantages that are given to members of the dominant group. What are some of the benefits that Tatum cite in her article?

2. How does a person support racist systems without being personally racist? Active racism? Passive racism?

3. What are the obstacles to an equal society? Why can't we be "colorblind"?

4. Doesn't the existence of multicultural curricula in the United States prove that we're making progress?

5. How does racism affect everyone?

6. Why do some people voluntarily separate themselves socially based on race?

7. How do cultural influences (television, media, etc.) make whiteness the norm and people of color "the other"?

8. How can we have control over racial stereotypes?

CHAPTER 3

Culture Matters: Creating Classroom Communities that *Mirror* Students' Lives

Traci P. Baxley, Ed.D. and Kalisha Waldon, Ph.D.

Ms. Jones' third grade class is comprised of mostly Black and Hispanic students at a local urban school. Unfortunately, the community is in an uproar over conflicts between several youth/ "gangs". Last evening, several gang members, according to police officers, incited further tension in the community which resulted in several deaths. The principal instructed the staff, who were predominately White, that most of the students in the school were up and in the streets throughout the night due to the hostilities that were a direct result of the community conflicts. Due to fear of aggression in the neighborhood, the school is on a soft lockdown, and cancelled breakfast, which the majority of students depend on. Ms. Jones attempts to cover the day's math lesson, ignoring the frightful glances, silent tears, and rocking bodies. While discussing the associative property of addition, a Hispanic female student jumps out of her seat, walks over to a Black female student, positions her face in front of hers, and screams "This is all your brother's fault! Your brother caused the fight!" The young girl begins to cry. All the students begin to argue; Ms. Jones does not know how to handle the situation. She attempts to continue her teaching, the situation continues to escalate and a fight ensues. Instruction is impacted because the students' attention is elsewhere. As a result, two students in the class are suspended and four students are expelled.

Questions to Ponder:
- What would you say could have been done differently by the teacher?
- What did she not know that could have transformed this experience into one that was meaningful for the students?
- What resources could she have utilized to make this a teachable yet meaningful experience?

Introduction

Being a classroom teacher is filled with joys and challenges. Teachers are constantly asked to make decisions concerning the academic, social, and emotional well-being of their students, and feel overwhelmed about making the best decisions when considering the implications they may have on student performance. The case study above represents situations that happen often in many schools across the country. Schools are often extensions of the communities in which they are located; and teachers, who often do not reside in the neighboring communities, are often ill-equipped to deal with and incorporate the community's knowledge and experiences in his or her classroom. Making this connection is paramount for optimal engagement and learning for students.

This chapter draws on the research that helps support teachers who work with diverse student populations and how to connect their students' lives outside of school to the academic learning that takes place inside the classroom. Gloria Ladson-Billings (1994) offers common key characteristics of culturally relevant pedagogy that teachers who are successful in working with marginalized students possess. Geneva Gay's (2010) theory of culturally responsive teaching centers around the notion that students of color perform better when teaching is filtered through their own cultural experiences. In order to address the needs of students, we must create classroom communities that are sensitive and relevant to the cultural background of the students we serve. The content of this chapter will provide a framework and a practical guide for addressing scenarios like the one at the beginning of this chapter along with other suggestions on meeting the needs of today's diverse learners. We will answer the questions, what is culturally responsive teaching, why is it needed, what does it look like in the classroom and what should my next steps as a pre-service teacher be? We will revisit the case studies once again at the end of the chapter.

What Is Culturally Responsive Teaching?

Ladson-Billings (1994) defined culturally relevant teaching as "a pedagogy that empowers students intellectually, socially, emotionally, and politically by using cultural referents to impart knowledge, skills, and attitudes" (pp. 17-18). Gay (2010) posits that culturally responsive practices infused within classrooms and instruction is the answer to building bridges of meaningfulness between students' home and school experiences as well as between their academic abstractions and lived sociocultural realities. It includes methods that attempt to bridge the gap between students from marginalized cultures and those of the non-Hispanic White/Caucasian culture whose values are often incongruent (Ladson-Billings, 1994).

Culturally responsive teaching teaches to and through the strengths of students; acknowledges the legitimacy of the cultural heritages of different ethnic groups…and as worthy content to be taught in the formal curriculum; uses a variety of instructional strategies that are connected to different learning styles; teaches students to know and praise their own and each other's' cultural heritage; and incorporates multicultural information, resources, and materials in all the subjects and skills routinely taught in schools (Gay, 2010). In essence, culturally responsive teaching espouses the following characteristics as discussed above and that will be elaborated on at different points in this chapter.

- Positive perspectives on families and culture
- Communicates high expectations
- Uses culture as a context for learning
- Reshapes curriculum and instruction

Why Is It Needed?

Based on the United States Department of Education's 2015 report of *The Nation's Report Card*, there is a significant (double digit) achievement gap between Caucasian and Black students, and Caucasian and Hispanic, students at all tested achievement levels. In 2013, the National Assessment of Educational Progress (NAEP) of the U.S. Department of Education published data showing that the achievement gap between Caucasian and African American eighth grade students was 31 points in math and 26 points in reading, and 26 points in both math and reading among fourth grade students (*U.S. Department of Education*, 2015). The prevalence of achievement gaps on mandated assessments does not imply the need for further "drill and kill" scripted instruction that is commonplace in schools with high numbers of students of color and students in poverty.

In addition, the Department of Education Office of Civil Rights (2014) provides snapshots of data that highlight the disproportionate number of students of color who are expelled, suspended, arrested, or referred to law enforcement above their White counterparts. According to the data,

Black students represent 16% of the student population, but 32-42% of students suspended or expelled. In comparison, white students also represent a similar range of between 31-40% of students suspended or expelled, but they are 51% of the student population (U.S. Department of Education Office of Civil Rights, 2014).

Assessment results and discipline data such as these necessitate alternative solutions, ones that are designed specifically with these students and their communities in mind. The Table 3.1 highlights these aforementioned disparities.

Table 3.1. Academic and School Discipline Disparities

	Academic Achievement	School Discipline
African American	*Gap between African American and Caucasian Students* • 4th graders Math & Reading- 26 points • 8th graders Math- 31 points Reading- 26 points	• 16% of the population but 32-42% of them were suspended or expelled compared to Caucasian, 51% of the population but 31-40% suspended or expelled
Hispanic	• Gap between Hispanic and Caucasian Students • 4th graders • Math- 19 points • Reading- 25 points • 8th graders • Math- 22 points • Reading- 25 points	• 2.4% increase in the Hispanic student population, out-of-school suspensions increased by 14%, while population of White students decreased by 2.7%, "with" 3% decrease in the number of suspensions
Native American	• *Gap between Native American and Caucasian Students* • 4th graders • Math- 23 points • Reading- 27 points • 8th graders • Math- 25 points • Reading- 26 points	

One reason for this disparity is embedded in the very design and value system of the public school system. The ways of learning and knowing of schools mirror the middle class white Western European, heterosexual, male-dominated culture, while excluding or limiting the inclusion of the voices of diverse cultures and histories. This exclusion of culture and histories results in the loss of opportunities for students to see themselves in the curriculum, thus making culturally relevant teaching necessary. The pedagogy that is most often practiced in classrooms empowers students from mainstream backgrounds, while marginalizing students whose backgrounds are different. For example, many students come from backgrounds where oral history and storytelling is the norm. Their way of making sense of the world often involves discussion, animation, and active learning. Schools should acknowledge their processing systems and the ways these students make sense of the world and recognize the assets they bring to the classroom by integrating their cultural nuances into the pedagogy of teaching. The cultural mismatch between the teacher and his/her students result in far too many occasions of students feeling uncomfortable or "othered", more disciplinary issues, referrals to special education and students less likely to graduate (Au, 2001; Gorski, 2013).

Often the ideology that governs teachers' views of marginalized students is one that espouses the characteristics of the deficit ideology. Oakes and Lipton (2006) refer to deficit thinking as assumptions that low income children, children of color, and their families are limited by cultural, situational, and individual deficits that schools cannot alter. According to this theory, these students are incapable of performing or working up to the level of their more privileged peers. This ideological framework of deficit thinking has shaped the state of education in the United States (Sleeter, 2005; Weiner, 2006) and suggests that certain groups of students fail in schools because they are lazy, not motivated, are linguistically deficient, or have parents who do not care about their education (Gorski, 2013). The "counter" to this frame of thought, or one that culturally responsive teaching embraces, is one that believes that all students can learn and should see their lives, cultures, or ways of knowing mirrored in the curriculum, regardless of their backgrounds, histories, and linguistic abilities. These families possess funds of knowledge that should be honored and highlighted in classrooms, the curriculum, and teaching practices.

Moll (1994) insisted that teachers make use of the "funds of knowledge" that students bring from their home lives. Knowing your students should influence the decisions regarding curricular content and methodology. A culturally responsive teacher is sensitive to the cultural values represented in the classroom and uses this knowledge to connect and build on the experiences the students bring to the classroom. These practices should validate and affirm the cultures of traditionally marginalized students while focusing on fundamental knowledge needed to assist them in becoming capable readers and writers (Baytops, 2003; Delpit, 1995; Tatum, 1997). Sleeter and Grant (2009) proposed teachers ask themselves two vital questions: (1) What standard/concept is being taught, and (2) what funds of knowledge do my students have that can make this standard/concept relevant? Curricula focused on the rote learning of lower level skills, where personal connection is not a goal, would not be beneficial for marginalized students seeking culturally responsive instruction (Au, 2001).

On the individual level, traditional education further aligns with White privilege through systemic inequities and through the school curriculum. McIntosh (1988) reflects,

> I have come to see white privilege as an invisible package of unearned assets that I can count on cashing in each day, but about which I was "meant" to remain oblivious. White privilege is like an invisible weightless knapsack of special provisions, maps, passports, codebooks, visas, clothes, tools, and blank checks p. 10.

In essence, these unearned assets are perks or advantages that Whites enjoy whether they are consciously aware of it or not. According to Holladay (2000) "...white privilege shapes the world in which we live — the way that we navigate and interact with one another and with the world" (np). Examples of this in schools would be for the ease of a White student to learn about and to see pictures of people who look like him or her; in the teaching of content, Whites become the standard by which other groups of people are held; and the curriculum is "white-washed." In order for White privilege to be eliminated from education, we must intentionally include diverse groups of people in the curriculum, including Whites. Harpalani (2002) asserts,

> Whites must also be included as one of these diverse groups, and their cultural practices must be examined in the same way.... the overall goal should be the transformation of all education to treat these diverse groups equally. (np)

Educators and schools should be systematically involved in prejudice reduction, the "counter." According to Banks (2004) prejudice reduction consists of the inclusion of instructional practices and lessons that assert the positive representations of diverse groups and the improvement of relationships between them. For example, Rethinking Schools, a non-profit organization focused on equity and democracy in schools, is the publisher of *Rethinking Columbus* (Bigelow, 1998), a text that presents history from the Taíno Native Americans' under-represented viewpoint. It offers instructional approaches and methods that teachers can use to help

students ponder perspectives that are often silenced in the traditional classroom curriculum. One of the objectives of materials like *Rethinking Columbus* (Bigelow, 1998) is to teach students to engage in critical literacy, challenge students to read beyond the written word, and to understand text in terms of sociopolitical consequences and structures of power.

We spoke briefly before about the achievement gap and statistics that reveal the disparities in achievement. Gorski (2013) purports that the disparities are bolstered through school reform, such as the *No Child Left Behind Act of 2001*, merit pay, and school choice that utilizes evidence such as "standardization, adequate yearly progress, accountability, and even data-driven decision-making" (p. 110). Much of the school reform effort focus on the achievement gap and the academic differences between groups of students, and is equivalent to putting a bandaid on an open wound. We need to refocus education reforms that address the opportunity gap (Ladson-Billings, 2006).

Active Learning

Before reading further, think about 2-3 opportunities more privileged students have that marginalized groups of students are not afforded?

There is a greater need for more aggressive interventions that focus less on comparing students' achievements, and more on the critical issue of opportunities to learn that is often absent from schools working with students that need more experiences. The implementation of high-quality preschools; more qualified teachers; an engaging, challenging curriculum; and access to advanced courses are strides towards more equitable learning opportunities.

Striving for equity and anti-bias education is often halted by institutional barriers, such as institutional racism. Whether implicitly or explicitly expressed, institutional racism occurs when a certain group is targeted and discriminated against based on race. An example of this would be zero tolerance school policies that often impact the rate at which marginalized students are expelled or suspended in schools compared to their counterparts, thus creating a school to prison pipeline.

Traditionally, racism has pervaded society and has thus trickled into our educational system. Institutional racism can go unnoticed as it is often normalized and can be overlooked. We must take stock of our practices in order to provide equitable learning experiences. No longer should the "traditional" be acceptable. If we are committed to creating learning opportunities to all students, transformative learning should replace what has become commonplace in our schools and classrooms. The Table 3.2 below provides a summary of what Waldon, Baxley, and Harrison (2015) discuss as the traditional education ideologies or belief systems that have become normalized in education, and offers ideologies that counter those perspectives and places equity pedagogy at the center of teacher practice.

Table 3.2. Model of Transformative Educational Ideologies

	Status Quo (Traditional)	Counter (Critical)
Ideology	*Deficit perspective*	*Funds of knowledge*
Individual	*White privilege*	*Prejudice reduction*
School-Based/Curriculum	*Achievement gap*	*Educational debt/opportunity gap*
Institutional	*Institutional racism*	*Notions of equity/social justice*

Source: Waldon, Baxley & Harrison (2015)

What does the "Counter" look like in the Classroom?

According to Paulo Freire (1998), "an intimate connection between knowledge considered basic to any school curriculum and knowledge that is the fruit of the lived experience of... students as individuals [must be established] in order to sustain the learning process" (p. 16). Using the Curriculum Connections Instructional Model™ (Boston & Baxley, 2014) we will discuss what the "counter" to the traditional classroom culture is. This model is grounded in the fundamental idea that recognizing, defining, and sustaining multiple domains of the learner is central to understanding the complexity of the personal and academic lives of our students and examining the reciprocal relationship between the school curriculum and the funds of knowledge students bring with them into the classroom. The six domains of the Curriculum Connections Instructional Model™ include: *connections, community, culture, character, content, and critical consciousness.* In the section that follows, we attempt to integrate the six domains and the theory of culturally responsive teaching to paint a more vivid picture of what the "counter" classroom looks like.

Domain 1 – Connections. It is imperative that a two-way reciprocal relationship between the teacher and student is established so that teachers and students construct knowledge together. To sincerely engross students in the learning process, it is essential that teachers connect with students in ways that are culturally and linguistically responsive and appropriate. Practicing culturally relevant pedagogy requires teachers to develop cross-cultural communication skills through the scrutinizing of their personal cultural assumptions and stereotypes, and moving beyond "color blind" teaching that may impede potential relationships with students and their families. This can be accomplished by teachers getting to know the culture of their students, their families, and the communities from which their students reside; by them developing an understanding of the uniqueness in each student; and seeing their diverse cultures as a window into each student's identity, perspectives, and values (Baxley & Boston, 2014; Ladson-Billings, 1994).

Children who develop quality relationships with their teachers have fewer behavior problems, demonstrate more engagement in learning, and research has shown the potential for these connections to alter the paths of students in high risk situations. Students also develop a sense of belonging and social acceptance (Pianta, 2001). Conversely, when teachers and students have conflicts and do not establish personal connections, there are more risks for students to demonstrate behavior outbursts, be sent out of the classroom, be retained, or drop out of school (Meehan, Hughes & Cavell, 1999).

The teacher should begin the learning process by developing a mutually respectful partnership with students as co-investigators through inquiry and dialogue. Freire (2000) believed that authentic dialogue only occurs when the preconditions of love, humility, trust and hope are present. Radical love, according to Freire, is a genuine care and commitment for life and people, and is the foundation for dialogue. Practicing dialogue in this way leads to a way of thinking, changing, and making room for new knowledge that is created as a result of listening and learning from each other. This in turn creates a new relationship, through dialogue:

> The teacher-of-the-students and the students-of-the-teacher cease to exist and a new term emerges: teacher-student with students-teachers. The teacher is no longer merely the one-who-teaches, but one who is [themself] taught in dialogue with the students, who in turn while being taught also teach. They become jointly responsible for a process in which all grow. (Freire, 2000, p. 80)

In the dialogical relationship of student-teacher and teacher-student, both participants must respectfully listen and learn from one another. This democratic positioning supports the idea that dialogue and critical questioning are not seen as a threat to the existing power structure, but rather as a necessity in successfully practicing culturally relevant teaching and critical education.

Domain 2- Community. In this framework, community is identified in two ways: 1) the culture of care that is created within the schools (Nieto, 1994) and from individual teachers (Noddings, 2002); and 2) the inclusion of families and stakeholders (e.g. local business owners, religious leaders, community activists) that live and work within the school's surrounding neighborhoods. Creating positive relationships in the classroom and in neighboring communities is an essential part of educating the whole child. Every child should "live in a home that has at least adequate material resources and attentive love…and schools should include education for home life in their curriculum" (Noddings, 2002, p. 289).

In culturally relevant schools students are free to take risks and know that they will be treated with respect and kindness. The culture in classrooms should manifest genuine respect for all students. Nieto (1994) maintained that our classrooms and schools should move beyond tolerance which is more of a superficial type of multicultural support. She states,

> It is my belief that a movement beyond tolerance is absolutely necessary if multicultural education is to become more than a superficial 'bandaid' or a 'feel-good' additive to our school curricula. I would argue that tolerance is actually a low level of multicultural support, reflecting as it does an acceptance of the status quo with but slight accommodations to difference. (p. 7)

The Table 3.3 below illustrates the types of multicultural support Nieto (1994) describes, with the last level as the goal.

Table 3.3. Nieto's Levels of Multicultural Support

Level	Description	Example
Monocultural Education	Schools that adopt a monocultural education consist of "school structures, policies, curricula, instructional materials and even pedagogical strategies that are primarily representative of only the dominant culture" (Nieto, 1994, p. 8).	Most teachers represent the dominant culture instead of a reflection of the student body. Curriculum is made up of the European Canon (no diverse representation). Teaching with a "color-blind" perspective.
Tolerance	Differences of students are endured, not necessarily embraced or celebrated. Something that is tolerated today can easily be rejected the next day.	Bulletin boards represent commonly discussed minority contributions (e.g. Martin Luther King, Jr. and Rosa Parks). Welcome sign is prominently displayed for parents, but it is written in English only. Encouraging non English speakers to speak English and use home language for emergencies only (assimilation is encouraged).
Acceptance	Schools with this type of multicultural support recognize "differences...and their importance is neither denied (n)or belittled" (Nieto, 1994, p. 8). There is movement towards multicultural education.	Seminars on different learning styles, recognizing that all students bring something special to the class (assimilation is not the goal). Bulletin boards represent various cultures and ethnicities. Bilingual education is used as a choice for students learning English as second language.
Respect	There is "admiration and high esteem for diversity. When differences are respected, they are used as the basis for much of what goes on in schools" (Nieto, 1994, p. 13).	Letters to parents and materials are written in several languages. Teachers develop curriculum around themes that are multicultural in nature. Curriculum is antiracist and honest and classrooms become a safe place to discuss controversial issues in society.
Affirmation, Solidarity and Critique	The premise of this level of multicultural support is that "the most powerful learning results when students work and struggle with one another....the many differences that students and their families possess are embraced and accepted as legitimate vehicles for learning....this level is concerned with equity and social justice..." (Nieto, 1994, p. 15).	Schools that have safe, encouraging, and inviting environment that practices cross-cultural school discipline and requires students to learn two languages across the school. Parents and community members are highly involved, respected, and have decision-making power in the school. Tracking is eliminated and teachers work together to plan for various levels within their classrooms.

Compassionate classrooms are places where students' voices, students' experiences, and students' ideas are valued. Nurturing begins with teachers cultivating an environment of respect, honesty, integrity, and empathy through daily modeling and concrete examples. Researchers (Banks, 2009; Bress, 2000) reported that when students listed characteristics of effective teachers, the lists consistently included caring as the most important quality, which supports students' increased self-esteem and self-efficacy. According to Noddings (2002), caring teachers shift from their own experiences to the experiences and well-being of their students and develop a sense of community and safety that supports both social and academic engagement of their students. Culturally responsive teachers are "demanding but facilitative, supportive and accessible, both personally and professionally" (Gay, 2010, p. 48).

Multicultural educators recognize that community is developed within classrooms guided by democratic principles and teachers with caring classroom practices. Creating mutually respectful relationships start with the climate that teachers foster and nurture in the class. Culturally relevant classrooms move away from traditional classroom management ("doing to" students) to a more democratic classroom of care (working with students). The Table 3.4 below illustrates key differences between traditional and democratic classroom communities.

Table 3.4. "Doing to" vs. "Working with" classroom practices

"Doing to" Traditional Classrooms	"Working with" Culturally Relevant Classrooms
• Focus on making students follow directions (conform)	• Students play active role in decisions
• Focus is on student behavior	• Teachers work with students (partnerships/relationships)
• Compliance is important	• Learner's interests drive curriculum
• Standards drive curriculum	• Environment support questioning, critically analyzing
• Punishments/reward systems	• Promote positive self-value and love of learning
• Order and control is paramount	• Compassion and empathy are paramount

The **Community** domain also emphasizes the need to include the students' families and local community as partners in the nurturing and development of the student. A democratic classroom stresses teamwork, collaborative decision making, and having a shared vision. Parents and the local community are a big part of this vision. More traditional teachers often blame the families to explain why students are not thriving academically. We often hear that parents "don't care" about their children or they don't "value" education. This is far from the truth. Some cultures may show that they "care" by working two jobs to provide food and shelter. Some parents may show they "care" by allowing you, as the teacher, to do your job at educating their child while staying out of your way. It is the school's responsibility to find ways to make space for parents in the school and to provide ways to meet the families' needs.

In a school practicing culturally sensitive pedagogy it is the assumption that all parents want the best for their children and the onus is on the staff of the school to examine their notions of "caring parents" and challenge the traditional ways of interacting and communicating with parents. For example, educators expect parents to attend parent-teacher conferences before or after school. Often when parents do not show up, teachers make judgments about their parenting skills. There can be many reasons why a parent does not attend a conference, including the parent's hourly wage job does not permit him/her to leave without losing pay, a parent could have more than one job and can't make it to school during those hours, parents may not have positive memories of their own educational experience, or there could be a formal education gap or language barrier and the parent feels intimidated being there. Culturally responsive teachers find creative ways to meet the needs of parents and they are persistent and consistent in connecting with them via home visits, e-mails, postcard check-ins, phone calls, texts, Skype (or similar conferencing software), or video chat. Teachers should meet the parents where they are and recognize that open dialogue is the most important part of the teacher-parent connection.

The school's responsibility is to reach out to ask community leaders to partner in decision-making and collaboration. The Table 3.5 below includes ideas to foster strong school-community partnerships.

Table 3.5. School-Community Partnership

School – Community Connections	
Interest Inventory	*Find out what the parents need from the school; how do they want to communicate with the school; what language is represented in their homes; what community events are important to them; what the teacher needs to know about their child, family and community, etc.*
Community engagement sessions	*Use the survey findings to plan events that support the needs of the community. Use these events as a time to listen to parents and cultivate trusting relationships. Think about the parents that you serve as you decide what day and time the sessions should be scheduled (think outside the box).*
Family literacy center	*Create an inviting space that parents can come and meet for coffee and get various services for themselves and their children. Offer computer classes, allow parents to use computers to apply for jobs, assist them with completing governmental paperwork (social services, food services, etc.), offer GED or ESOL programs, etc. When parents have a designated space they will feel welcome and connected.*

(continued)

School – Community Connections	
Cultural/community liaison	*Hire someone from the community who can serve as a liaison between the community happenings and the school events. This person's role can include providing language translations and bringing events from the community to the attention of school personnel. They can assist teachers with including cultural funds of knowledge in the classroom and teach parents the cultural capital of the school system.*
Consistent invitations	*Teachers should continually reach out to parents to be a part of the classroom experience. This could include field trips, class presentations, lunch dates, guest speaking, or special breakfast or dinner. Equally as important is the school faculty accepting invitations from the community. Teachers could attend religious services, sporting events, community center events, or a dedication or memorial service.*
Redefining the "school's campus"	*Schools should reach out to the community and use neighborhood places to have conferences and meetings to meet the parents where they feel comfortable. The school can have a curriculum night at the local community center or take backpack snacks to the local places of worship. Students and their families should be encouraged to view the school as a staple in the community.*

Domain 3 – Culture: Culturally relevant teaching is fueled by high expectations and supports instruction and learning through the lens of multiple perspectives and histories. It is teaching that does not view students from a deficit perspective (Gorski, 2013), rather views their funds of knowledge as assets. Students' differences are in terms of culture, race, ethnicity, social class, language, sexual orientation, etc., are celebrated and a culture of acceptance that promotes equity and affirmation is fostered. In a classroom that espouses the tenets of true multicultural education, the histories, knowledge, and lived experiences of students are recognized and celebrated in the curriculum and instructional practices. The curriculum is informed by and grounded in the lives of students. According to Au, Bigelow, and Karp (2007), students should see a clear connection between what they are learning and the world around them outside of school.

Culturally responsive pedagogy starts with the premise that students' differences matter; this is often ignored in the traditional curriculum and classroom practices. In order for teachers to effectively teach and honor their students, they must first start with questioning their own biases. For example, when a Latino male walks into your classroom with a bandana on his head, what would be your first thoughts of who he is? If a student enters with torn or dirty clothes on the first day of class, would you welcome her like you did the student who came with neatly ironed clothes and clean hygiene? How do you think those perceptions would impact your expectations for them in the classroom? Would you hold them to the same standard as other students in your class? Without questioning and acknowledging your own biases, you will not be able to ensure equity for all of your students. Teachers must be cognizant of how their perceptions or the biases they hold prevent them from teaching, understanding, and valuing students and their families' histories and knowledge.

An important, yet, admittedly, sometimes difficult step, would be for you to take action towards learning about the cultures, both surface and deep levels, of your students. Not only will this inform you of the assets each of your students bring to school, but it will also provide you with knowledge on how you can use those assets to make the learning process relevant and meaningful to each student. Exploring their culture will also provide you with information on how students learn best, including the norms or deep culture, such as what is considered respect; patterns of communication, non-verbal cues, personal space, etc.

Based on what you learned about your students, you can then use this new knowledge to inform your teaching or instruction. For example, if you learned that after analyzing a learning style inventory that the majority of your students prefer to learn through the tactile/bodily kinesthetic modality, then you should use this information to ensure that you provide hands-on-activities as an opportunity for learning in the classroom and to deepen their understanding of concepts. Not only can that knowledge be used to inform instructional practices but also to make content or curricular decisions. If students' lives, cultures, or histories are not represented in the curriculum, as a multicultural educator, you should seek out supplemental resources such as personal narratives, multicultural children's literature, parents or families from the community, websites, and/or other counternarratives to the traditional curriculum. For example, in a writing lesson on the narrative genre, one great way to incorporate students' funds of knowledge would be for them to brainstorm ideas by interviewing several of their family members to learn more about their own cultural practices, traditions, values or norms in order to prominently bring their family's history into the classroom. This activity would teach them a greater appreciation for their familial roots and the nuances of their peers' background, leading to a greater understanding of each other while building a sense of community in the classroom. Additionally, activities like this can assist in bridging any gaps between family members and foster the link between school and community.

It is important however to know your students; some may not come from traditional families, so be sure the assignment has alternative options to meet the varying needs of your students. For example, if one person was living in a foster home situation and had no contact with immediate family members. In that case, you can alter the assignment to be one where they interview members of the community to write a narrative on the assets their communities possess, or the prominent people in their community, the unsung heroes. As the facilitator of your classroom, your knowledge of your student becomes the compass for your instructional and curricular decisions.

Cultural inclusion also helps insulate students from cultural and ethnic stereotypes and biases that are disseminated in the schools, the curriculum, and the media. Culturally responsive practices teach students that differences in perspectives and value systems are to be cherished and appreciated rather than judged and feared. It teaches them to problematize knowledge or messages that are exclusionary or divisive. When students' cultures are respected, included, and honored, a classroom becomes a wonderful place for students to harmoniously thrive; students feel more comfortable being themselves and viewing others in a positive light is commonplace. Schools practicing culturally relevant practices honor the families that enter their doors, honoring families' voices, the community's histories, languages, and funds of knowledge.

Active Learning

"I believe that many diverse students fail in schools not because their teachers don't know their content, but because their teachers haven't made the connections between the content and their students' existing mental schemes, prior knowledge and cultural perspectives." - Jacqueline Jordan Irvine
   Reflecting on this quote, how does it connect with what you just learned about culture?

Domain 4 – Character. This domain fosters student character building with the outcome being greater intrinsic motivation, greater awareness of self, and students engaged in social justice education. Culturally responsive classrooms should be hopeful, joyful, kind, and visionary (Au, Bigelow, & Karp, 2007); foster empathy, and should teach students to be intrinsically motivated.

Hopeful, joyful, kind, and visionary classrooms foster respect for others and self-love. Classrooms are intentionally organized to make students feel "significant and cared for" (Au, Bigelow, & Karp, 2007, p. x). Drawing on Harris and Baxley (2016),

> A Curriculum [or classroom] of Hope's goals include: 1) developing warm, supportive, nurturing relationships between teachers, students and the community; 2) cultivating the social and ethical dimensions of the learner (developing empathy and working as a team); 3) encouraging intrinsic motivation; 4) understanding and valuing the experiences and lives of the students; and 5) drawing on these when selecting materials, setting learning goals, and planning learning activities that focus on harnessing action to make possibilities into realities.

In these classrooms, spaces are created for students to uncover and name issues and practices that disempower them. This is done by encouraging them to: critically reflect and act upon issues of racism; honor their voices, embrace and legitimize their multiple funds of knowledge; foster respect for others, and develop self-love (Waldon, Baxley, & Harrison, 2015). Teachers should seek to engage children in inquiry, critical thinking, and critical action, so that their classrooms become places of hope and promise for children. Teachers should know that they and their students cannot single-handedly transform schools; they can take small steps that will make a positive difference in their worlds.

As our classrooms begin to look more and more diverse, our students need to be taught skills on how to accept those who are not like them or who may think and behave differently. A great way to do this is by teaching empathy; empathy is the ability to put yourself in the shoes of others to envision how a situation would be for someone else. In a culturally responsive classroom, teachers must first have empathy for their students and must model this trait in the classroom; then they can assist students in developing empathy. While some students will have the innate ability to show care for their peers, some will need to be taught, nurtured, or supported to do this. Creating classrooms that are safe and nurturing is the first step to developing empathy in the classroom. There should be classroom routines or expectations on how students should demonstrate the skill of listening, how to understand both verbal and nonverbal cues, how to demonstrate respect and appreciation for our classmates and their differences, and how to handle misunderstandings. Sornson (2013) believes that students should also be taught self-regulation skills- how to manage their own behaviors or impulses in order to look beyond those things to consider the needs of others.

Intrinsic motivation is the drive to engage in an activity for the sake of completing the activity. As discussed earlier, often in traditional classrooms students are motivated by extrinsic rewards or punishments. Culturally relevant classrooms strive to provide opportunities where students begin to empower themselves through self-regulation and self-fulfillment. There are many ways to encourage students to take academic, social, and emotional risks for the sake of self-improvement or empathy for others. Teachers can help develop students' intrinsic motivation by building on the student's' strengths first. This gives students a chance to use their talents while building confidence. For example, if one student is great at math, he/she can peer-teach a friend who may struggle in the same subject. The student will begin to feel a sense of pride and begin to recognize that no physical reward is needed, but focuses instead on the feeling that comes from inside when using his/her talent to help a friend.

Teachers practicing culturally responsive teaching offer choices to help build intrinsic motivation. When a student has ownership, he or she is more likely to buy into the purpose behind the decision. They develop their decision-making skills and learn to live with the consequences that come with that decision because they took a personal part in it. Sometimes the choices that students make are not positive ones or they fail at the set goal. In a safe environment they can learn from their mistakes and feel supported. Developing intrinsic motivation for students sometimes means giving up the traditional role of authority or having the power in the classroom. When they are empowered to make choices, it teaches them to take responsibility. In other words, when things go wrong, they learn not to blame someone else but will begin to see their role in how a situation turns out.

Another great way to foster a sense of intrinsic motivation is creating more relevant assignments with authentic assessment opportunities in the classroom. Self-evaluation is a great tool to help students set high expectations and get excited about meeting those goals. Teachers can model goal setting and use "think-aloud" strategies to talk through the excitement of setting a goal and meeting it using intrinsic motivation language.

Domain 5 – Content. This domain sustains the connection between information and the student learner. Freire (2000) who coined the "banking concept" of education, posited that knowledge in the curriculum is determined by and is in the head of the elders. The role of the teacher is to deposit into the minds of students information deemed important by the teacher. The student is then expected to regurgitate this information or demonstrate their understanding of what the teacher taught, commonplace in the traditional standards-driven classroom model. Domain 5 rejects the "banking concept" and calls for a curriculum that is connected to the experiences and cultures of the students, and one that exposes them to multiple frames of knowing. It supports the transformative intellectual curriculum that honors the lives of students and their families.

Domain 5 also encourages the inclusion of varied bodies of knowledge in the curriculum (Sleeter, 2005) whereby students are provided opportunities to explore academic content from the perspectives of the hero and the villain; the dominant population and the marginalized; the privileged and the unprivileged. With the inclusion of these diverse voices, spaces are created for students to co-construct knowledge with their teachers; to think critically

about content; and to form their own judgements of what knowledge is worth knowing. This makes learning personal, meaningful, and rewarding for students of diverse backgrounds because it "makes a link between classroom experiences and the students' everyday lives" (Ladson-Billings, 1994, p. 94) and provides a curricular approach that integrates students' funds of knowledge with the mandated standards.

Your rationale for teaching the lesson or incorporating diverse funds of knowledge/perspectives should explain why you believe the lesson is important or needed. You could potentially have many rationales that operate on different levels. Your lesson could be designed to fulfill several of the following needs: a societal need, a community need, a school-based need, a subject-based need, and/or an individual needs. In the table sections that follows each of these aforementioned needs will be discussed with curricular examples to illustrate each of them.

Table 3.6. Curricular Rationales

Rationale	Description	Practical Example
Societal Need	Focuses on a broad social need for the lesson	The increase in teenage smoking and new research on its addictiveness in youth could be the rationale for a lesson on the impact of nicotine on one's respiratory system.
Community Need	Focuses on a need particular to the school community	Increased racial tension in a school's community could be the rationale for a lesson on recognizing and accepting cultural differences.
School-based Need	Focuses on a particular need of the school	At a school with an international baccalaureate program, a lesson plan on international calendars would be appropriate.
Subject-based Need	Focuses on a need that has emerged within the field	In order to address students' traditional fear of mathematics, a lesson plan based on a fractions game is presented. The lack of female inventors represented in science textbooks is the rationale for a lesson on famous and influential female scientists.
Individual Need	Focuses on the more personalized needs of the students within a class	Students' preoccupation with violent movies is the rationale for a lesson on the impact of the media on social and emotional behavior.

Teachers should use the mandated standards as a tool for active learning that is taught in tandem to the students' lives. However, the traditional approach of integrating cultural knowledge or multiple perspectives into the curriculum, termed the contributions approach to multicultural education (Banks, 2004) is insufficient. For example, teaching about the same people of color from year to year, such as Martin Luther King, Jr. and Rosa Parks during Black History Month, is problematic. This minimal exposure may give a false impression that the contributions of certain groups of citizens are far more limited than reality. On another note, when heros of color are mentioned, the narrative that is written is often water-downed or told from the dominant perspective. It often creates a one-dimensional figure and diminishes the role he/she played historically by avoiding the more controversial issues of the time period. For example, it was safer for historians to paint a picture of Rosa Parks as a secretary who was too tired to move from her seat versus the counternarrative, that demonstrates her being a political activist who was well-respected by members of the Civil Rights Movement and who volunteered to be an active participant in the movement.

Culturally responsive teachers should take the opportunity to create classrooms that culturally affirm, understand, and encourage students (Gay, 2010) that ultimately assist students in achieving academic success, maintaining cultural competence, and critically addressing injustices in the world around them (Gay, 2010; Ladson-Billings, 1994).

When considering what content teachers should ask these kinds of questions: What do I want students to be able to do as a result of this lesson? What is important for them to know? What is the most efficient and effective way to reach this goal for all students? How will I know that my students have accomplished the prescribed goal(s)? To begin to determine what your answers to these questions are, Sleeter (2005) posits that you should first brainstorm what you want students to know about the concept and then clarify these ideas according to whether the central ideas are "worth being familiar with, important to know and/to do, [and/or] essential to enduring understanding" (p. 47). Additionally, Wiggins and McTighe (2005) suggest that teachers should begin with a clear vision of the desired result. From there you can decide what you specifically want students to know with those understandings.

Sleeter (2005) posits, "...developing intellectually rich curriculum requires thinking through not just what facts and information are worth consuming, but also what the intellectual basis of knowledge is." This is one key when considering the choice of textbook, the content that will be presented, and the taught epistemological underpinnings of the lesson that is taught.or presented in a lesson. It is important for you as a teacher to examine what your beliefs and assumptions are. Do you value other diverse ways of knowing? Often, if so, the knowledge, skills, and beliefs set forth in your curricula are a testament to your appraisal of diversity in constructing ways of knowing. Teachers should interrogate their own beliefs about what it means to know and question the implications of how they appropriate intelligence in the classroom.

Below is an example of a lesson plan adapted from a lesson created by Marissa Wildrick and Stephanie Silva that takes into consideration the key concepts of creating lesson plans that include diverse funds of knowledge.

Topic:	Cell Division (Incorporating Diverse Contributors)
Subject:	Science
Grade Level:	Middle School
Duration of Unit:	(4 Days)/50 Minute Sessions
Social Justice Issue:	Questioning Textbook Bias

Rationale of the Lesson:
This topic was chosen for the following reasons:
- Science in general is a dense subject and is often considered to be "neutral."
- It is critical for students to learn basic knowledge of cells and their processes. Without the cell cycle, humans would not survive.
- School textbooks are considered accurate and unbiased. This lesson will highlight the biases of the textbook by bringing in diverse biologists and/ or scientists who have contributed to the process of cell division as well as major breakthroughs in cytology.

Goals & Objectives
Short Term Goals
By the end of the lesson, students will be able to:
- Identify the stages of cell division
- Identify the main processes involved with each stage
- Discuss the scientists from underrepresented populations that have contributed to the establishment of theories and discoveries that relate to what we know today about cells

Long Term Goals
Over a longer period of time, students will be able to:
- Question and identify bias in a variety of media (ie textbooks, movies, newspapers, etc.) textbook bias (especially in Science)
- Learn how to further research topics within their textbooks to consider multiple perspectives

Outline of Content
What is cell division?
Mitotic cell division is a process of nuclear division amongst two distinct parent cells that divide to create two genetically identical daughter cells. The reasoning and importance of mitotic cell division is essentially the genetic material (DNA) that is copied in the division process. Copies of DNA are being made. This allows for developmental growth in the human body.
Key Vocabulary & Concepts: mitosis, meiosis, spindle fibers, nucleus, centrioles, telophase, anaphase, metaphase, prophase.
Stages of Cell Division (in order)
Prophase → Metaphase → Anaphase → Telophase
What Happens When Mitosis Goes Wrong?
Mitosis results in the creation of two daughter cells, each carrying a copy of the parent cell's DNA. Errors in mitosis can result in an incorrect copy of DNA. Two types of errors may occur when DNA is not properly copied: 1) one has no impact on the DNA sequence, and 2) the other changes the DNA sequence leading to cell cycle interruption and the formation of tumor cells. Tumor cells don't stop dividing and eventually result in cancer. If, during mitosis, chromosomes fail to attach to the spindles, then the resulting daughter cell will either have an extra or missing copy of a chromosome. One common disorder that results from the chromosomal abnormality is Down Syndrome. Abnormalities in chromosomes also create a higher chance of getting Alzheimer's and leukemia.

Textbook Perspective of Cell Division (Core Scientists)
Prentice Hall: Biology by Kenneth Miller and Joseph Levine
- Robert Hooke - English physicist, who was the first to describe cells in 1665.
- Mathias Schleiden - German botanist who contributed to the development of the cell theory by recognizing the importance of the cell nucleus and connected it's key role to cell division.
- Theodor Schwann - German physiologist who also contributed, with Schleiden, to the development of the cell theory by discovering the Schwann cells in the peripheral nervous system. These cells were named in honor of his discovery.
- Walter Flemming - German biologist and founder of cytogenetics. He described chromosome behavior during mitosis.
- Rudolph Virchow - German physician, pathologist, and anthropologist who concluded that cells develop from existing cells.

Multicultural Perspective (Scientists from Diverse Cultures)
- Lynn Margulis - Female American biologist known for her theory on the origin of eukaryotic organelles
- Karl August Möbius - German zoologist who first observed the structures that would later be called "organelles"
- Ernest Just - African American biologist who recognized the fundamental role of the cell surface in the development of organisms
- Jewel Plummer Cobb - African American cell biologist who majored in cell physiology, known for her research development on chemotherapeutic drugs on cancerous cells in the body.
- Santiago Ramon y Cajal - Hispanic neuroscientist illustrated the arborization (branching out like trees) of brain cells

Textbook Bias
Bias is a prejudice in favor of or against one thing, group, or person that is usually considered unfair. Textbooks often underrepresent the contributions of certain groups of people on what we know today about science. Gender stereotyping is also seen in textbooks; the contributions of females are often excluded from textbooks. certain groups such as African Americans, Latinos, Asian Americans. Students will be invited to analyze their science textbook and explore why diverse voices are not included in the narrative.
Video: Mitosis: The Amazing Cell Process that Uses Division to Multiply!
- A walkthrough video on the reason for mitosis, mnemonics to help learn the phases, and real world examples. https://youtu.be/f-ldPgEfAHI

Day 1: Introduction to Cell Division & Key Terms (What is cell division?)	
Initiating Activity:	*Students will complete a KWL on their prior knowledge of cells and their processes. They will complete the K and then the W (what they want to know and learn about cell division).*
Core Activity:	1. Students will be introduced to key terms relating to cell division. 2. The teacher will present a PowerPoint presentation on the cell cycle of nuclear division. The presentation will include: what the cell cycle is, and a description and function of each of the following, mitosis, meiosis, prophase, metaphase, anaphase, spindle fibers, nucleus, and centrioles.
Closing Activity/ Evaluation:	Exit Slip- students will be invited to write a slip of paper one thing they have learned today about cell division and one thing they would like to explore further or have questions about.
Day 2: Textbook Perspective. (Stages of Cell Division & Core Scientists)	
Initiating Activity:	1. Students will be given an entrance ticket from the teacher with the question, "What is cell division?" 2. On the entrance ticket they will reflect on the lesson from the day before, listing off the key terms and their meaning. With their responses, they are to complete the L, what they learned, part of their KWL charts.

Core Activity:	1. The students will be shown a short video by the Amoeba Sisters titled: Mitosis: The Amazing Cell Process that Uses Division to Multiply! on YouTube.
	2. The importance of cellular division will be reviewed and the ideal of identifying abnormalities that can occur if the cells do not divide. Strategic questioning will be instructed such as:
	  a. What do you think would happen if cells did not divide properly?
	  b. Would there be negative or positive effects?
	  c. Why are cells so important to our existence?
	3. The students will then be introduced to the core scientists, found in their textbooks, who contributed to the information they just learned.

Closing Activity:	1. Each student will also summarize what they learned about the significant scientists, specific to this day, in cytology theories. 2. Students should be divided into groups to collaborate on completing the cell cycle model. 3. Students will construct cell cycle models.

Day 3: Diverse Perspective

Initiating Activity:	1. Upon entering the classroom, the teacher will direct the students to the 5 different stations located throughout the classroom. Each station consists of a different scientist/biologist who contributed to what we know about cells or cytology. 2. Students will take notes about what they learned from each station.
Core Activity:	1. After viewing the diverse scientists around the room, the students will be led to a discussion about these scientists and what they contributed to what we know about cytology. The teacher will explain that they are going to be working in groups for a project they will be presenting the following week. The teacher will then split the students into (5) heterogeneous groups of 3-4 students in each group. Each group will be assigned to a specific scientist/biologist whom they will conduct research on. They will be instructed to create a list of 7-10 details/key events on their scientist's life and works and contributions to cell theory.
Closing Activity:	1. Each group will fill out a Closure and Evaluation Form where they discuss: what they learned, what may have surprised/interested them, and what they newly discovered. 2. Each group will share out their information.

Day 4: Critical Examination of the Topic/Textbook, etc. (textbook bias discussion)

Initiating Activity:	1. Think, Pair, Share Activity- The students will reflect on the question, "Why weren't the contributors they researched yesterday included in their science textbook?" 2. After individually reflecting on the question, they will share their thoughts with a partner. 3. The class will share their thoughts collectively and the teacher will record their thoughts on chart paper.

Core Activity:	1. The students will be lead into a discussion on textbook bias and the importance of diversity. They will then become "textbook detectives" and, in groups, read excerpts from the school textbook about the core scientists they were introduced to previously. The teacher will have a list of the following questions for the students to consider, discuss, and answer: • Why do you think this textbook excluded the scientists we learned about yesterday? • Who would benefit from this lack of information? • Why is it important to tell students about diverse individuals who have contributed to cytology? • How can you ensure that you are getting all of the perspectives when learning a specific topic? • How can we identify textbook bias in the future? • What can you do to change the one-sided perspective given in your textbook?
Closing Activity:	Students will be asked, if you had the power to do something, what would you do it about the representation of diverse voices in their textbook. In groups students will discuss this question and then report out to the class. The class will then decide on one of the courses of action to implement as a class (ie. letter to the textbook publisher, discussion with social studies teachers in the school petitioning diverse voices to be incorporated in the science curriculum, etc.)

Active Learning
What is multicultural about this lesson plan?

Domain 6 – Critical Consciousness. This domain represents the primary outcome of the learning process, to provide students with an emancipatory experience that both empowers and inspires. Freire (1974) posited that critical consciousness unfolds in several phases: magical, naïve, and critical. The process moves individuals from a passive state to a position that problematizes knowledge, "and takes action against the oppressive elements of reality" (Freire, 2007, p. 35). In essence, critical consciousness is the process by which individuals become aware of internal and external practices, systems, ideologies, and powers that seek to oppress or dehumanize a person (Freire, 2007). As such, critical consciousness; (1) invites the voices of the marginalized to share their own personal narratives (Harrell & Gallardo, 2008); (2) invites them to expose the hidden processes of society, the curriculum, and their world that have either overtly or covertly oppressed them and shaped society's view of difference. Critical multicultural education that is emancipatory in nature will reposition students to actively construct their own realities and perceptions of themselves and others while unearthing the ideologies and practices of the dominant culture that promote false consciousness (Waldon, 2015).

Educators who are committed to students reaching the highest level of critical consciousness or awareness ensures that their classrooms and curriculum are inclusive of transformative intellectual knowledge which consists of "bodies of knowledge that have been historically marginalized or subjugated" (Sleeter, 2005, p. 83), a curriculum that not only highlights assumptions posited by the dominant population but challenges them to the benefit of marginalized groups of people and communities (Sleeter, 2005). The transformative approach, according to Banks (2006) allows students to view content through the lens of diverse perspectives). While this is the first step to facilitate students' critical consciousness, this should not be the end withal. Knowledge should be connected with action, which is the fourth level of Banks' levels of multicultural education. These ideals of action are espoused in classrooms that promote social justice.

Harris & Baxley (2016) provides an example of a social justice activity in a kindergarten classroom. Mrs. Philips, a veteran kindergarten teacher works at an upper-middle class public school. After overhearing several of her kindergarteners discussing a homeless panhandler that they encountered each morning on their way to school, she created space in the school schedule for the children to explore the topic of homelessness. Her goal was to move her students from a state of curiosity and confusion to empowering them through action. After discussions during morning class meetings, Mrs. Philips created inquiry groups where students came up with questions and concerns that they wanted to investigate in greater depth.

After a few weeks of discovery; which included questioning parents, exploring informational books from the library, sharing picture books during read aloud, and using technology; the students were enthusiastic about turning their critical literacy project into an action plan. Over the next 6 weeks, the kindergarten students brought in spare change and began filling up a large "Give" jar. The children asked family members for contribution--some students performed extra chores around the house, a few class members even demonstrated entrepreneurial creativity (setting up lemonade stands, selling arts and crafts projects, stationary, friendship bracelets, and cookies).

Mrs. Philips arranged an after school family field trip to the neighborhood grocery store where the students were divided into small groups (with adult supervision). Each group had a grocery list, calculator, and money. The objective was twofold: (1) to have students involved in life skills, such as counting money, finding the best bargains, budgeting); and (2) to see how their hard work and commitment really made a difference to people in need.

The students made their purchases and all of the parents drove to the local community outreach program, which feeds people who are homeless and hungry twice a day, where the students were able to put all of the purchased supplies in the outreach center. The center's director and staff members poured out gratitude and admiration for the kindergarten students' efforts to assist those in need. The children left the center feeling both empowered and encouraged...that one person *can* make a difference.

To summarize traditional and counter approaches using CCIM, the following table (Table 3.7) is set forth.

Table 3.7. Comparison of Approaches to Learning

Traditional Approach to Learning	Curriculum Connections Model™
Connection: Relationships between the teacher and student are passive and is centered on a one-way structure of power.	**Connection:** A two-way connection is established between the students and teacher as co-investigators in dialogue and learning (Freire, 2000).
Community: Emphasis is placed on individual knowledge and achievement. Students often work in isolation and there is an expectation that students will obtain knowledge at the same rate. Expertise of families and community knowledge are seldom tapped as key tools for teaching and learning.	**Community:** A collective learning community is established through democracy-centered practices in the classroom (Dewey, 1938). Emphasis is placed on personal relationships and partnerships with families, communities, local businesses and organizations. Relationships are made relevant and integrated into the learning process (Ladson-Billings, 1994).
Culture: Ethnic and racial backgrounds are often not considered during instructional delivery and/or content. Teachers' color-blind perspectives render culture irrelevant and invisible.	**Culture:** Students' ethnicity, race, class, etc. become relevant to the content and the teaching & learning process (Banks, 2004 Gorski, 2013). Cultural funds of knowledge and cross-cultural communication are encouraged and capitalized (Sleeter & Grant, 2009).
Character: Isolated character traits/values are highlighted. Students are rewarded/punished based on compliance behavior model. Emphasis is based on conformity.	**Character:** Care-theory is emphasized, producing intrinsically motivated individuals (Noddings, 2002). Emphasis is based on respecting multiple viewpoints and building empathy.
Content: Student receives content through skills-based approaches using the banking system of instruction (Freire, 2007). Emphasis is centered on mandated standards and learning isolated subject areas only.	**Content:** Content is developed with students & standards in mind, delivered through Inquiry-based and problem-posing learning approaches (Sleeter, 2005). Students are encouraged to bring diverse experiences and expertise.
Critical Consciousness: Critical consciousness is rarely reached in a traditional model. It is viewed as "extra" if time permits.	**Critical Consciousness:** Education is used to empower and to transform. Students are given space to inquire, question, and explore power structures. Critical Consciousness is at the center of the Curriculum Connections Model™ and is the ultimate goal of education.

Rawpixel.com / Shutterstock.com

Conclusion

In conclusion, culturally responsive teaching practices are important to provide equitable learning opportunities for all students. Effective instruction is anchored in students' lives. Recognizing and honoring the cultural backgrounds, families, and home experiences of your students is paramount in creating culturally responsive classrooms. The first step in implementing inclusive practices is to acknowledge your own biases; become more aware of your thinking and attitudes. How can you take a stance that supports the idea that all students can learn and are assets to the classroom if you hold on to deficit ways of viewing them and/or their families?

Getting to know your students and their families through needs assessments, surveys, home visits, etc. is the next step. It is highly recommended that you also get to know members of the community in order to know what resources are available for your use within the classroom. Every effort should be made to infuse your students' funds of knowledge into the curriculum and instruction so that students' learning experiences are relevant and authentic. Use their experiences as resources instead of obstacles to overcome. It is important for you to create experiences that will not only ensure that students are proficient on grade level learning outcomes, but also that space is created to problem-pose and to challenge systems and/or knowledge that seek to undermine the contributions and cultural knowledge of diverse and/or marginalized groups.

> ### Active Learning
> Return to the case study presented at the beginning of the chapter and respond to the questions again. As a result of your reading of this chapter, how have your responses changed?

References

Advancement of teaching. (2016). Retrieved from http://ucat.osu.edu/professional-development/teaching-portfolio/rationale/

Alda, A. F. & Zubizarreta, R. (n.d). Honoring family in the classroom. Retrieved from http://www.colorincolorado.org/article/honoring-family-classroom

Au, K. H. (2001). *Culturally responsive instruction as a dimension of new literacies.* Reading Online 5. Retrieved from http//www.readingonline.org/newliteracies/lit_index.asp?HREF=au/index. htmlBaytops

Au, W., Bigelow, B., & Karp, S. (Eds.). (2007). *Rethinking Our Classrooms: Teaching for Equity and Justice.* (Vol. 1). Milwaukee: Rethinking Schools Ltd.

J. L. (2003). Counseling African American adolescents: The impact of race, culture, and middle class status. *Professional School Counseling, 7*(1), 40–50.

Banks, J. A. (2004). Multicultural education: Historical development, dimensions, and practices. In J. A. Banks & C. A. McGee Banks (Eds.), Handbook of research on multicultural education (2nd ed., pp. 3–29). San Francisco: Jossey-Bass.

Banks, J. A. (2006). *Cultural diversity and education: Foundations, curriculum and teaching* (5th ed.). Boston, MA: Pearson, Allyn & Bacon.

Banks, R. C. (2009). Caring teachers and their impact: A phenomological study of students' perceptions. Unpublished dissertation, Washington State University.

Baxley, T. P., & Boston, G. H. (2014). *(In) Visible presence: Feminist counter-narratives of young adult literature by women of color.* Rotterdam, The Netherlands: Sense Publishers.

Bigelow, B. (Ed.) (1991). *Rethinking Columbus: Teaching about the 500th anniversary of Columbus's arrival in America.* Milwaukee, WI:

Boston, G. H. & Baxley, T. P. (2014). *Connecting readers to multiple perspectives: Using culturally relevant pedagogy in a multicultural classroom.* Bookbaby Publishers

Bress P (2000). What makes a teacher special. English Teaching Professional 14.

Delpit, L. (1995). *Other people's children: Cultural conflict in the classroom.* New York, NY: The New Press.

Dewey, J. (1938). *Experience and education.* New York: Touchstone.

Freire, P. (1974). *Education for critical consciousness.* New York, NY: Continuum.

Freire, P. (1998). *Pedagogy of Freedom: Ethics, democracy and civic courage.* New York, NY: Rowman and Littlefield Publishers.

Freire, P. (2000). *Pedagogy of the oppressed.* New York, NY: Continuum.

Freire, P. (2007). *Pedagogy of the oppressed.* New York, NY: Continuum. (Original work published 1970).

Gay, G. (2010). *Culturally responsive teaching: Theory, research, and practice.* New York, NY: Teachers College Press.

Gorski, P. C. (2013). *Reaching and teaching students in poverty: Strategies for erasing the opportunity gap.* New York: Teachers College Press.

Harpalani, V. (2002). White privilege: A challenge for multicultural education. Retrieved from http://thenotebook.org/articles/2002/09/25/white-privilege-a-challenge-for-multicultural-education

Harrell, S., & Gallardo, M. (2008). Sociopolitical and community dynamics in the development of a multicultural world-view. In J. Asamen, M. Ellis, & G. Berry (Eds.), *The Sage handbook of child development, multiculturalism, and media* (pp. 113–127). Thousand Oaks, CA: Sage Publications.

Harris, D. L. & Baxley, T. P. (2016). Hungry, homeless, and hurting: Helping novice teachers develop a curriculum of hope for today's children of poverty. *Teacher Education Yearbook XXV: The Association of Teacher Educators*

Holladay, J. R. (2000). White antiracist activism: A personal roadmap. *The Whiteness Papers, Volume 4.* Retrieved from http://www.cddbooks.com/Bookstore/DetailPage.asp?item=WP004

Ladson-Billings, G. (1994). *The dreamkeepers: Successful teachers of African American children.* San Francisco, CA: Jossey-Bass Publications.

Ladson-Billings, G. (2006). From the achievement gap to the education debt: Understanding achievement in U.S. schools. *Educational Researcher, 35*(7), 3–12.

Neito, S. (1994). Affirmation, solidarity and critique: Moving beyond tolerance in education. *Multicultural Education,* Spring, 9–12, 36–37.

Noddings, N. (2002) *Starting at Home.* Caring and social policy, Berkeley, CA: University of California Press.

Mcintosh, P. (1988). White privilege: Unpacking the invisible knapsack. Retrieved from http://www.education.monash.edu.au/indigenous-ed/docs/unpackingtheknapsack.pdf

Meehan, B. T., Hughes, J. N., & Cavell, T. A. (2003). Teacher–student relationships as compensatory resources for aggressive children. Child Development, 74(4), 1145–1157.

Moll, L. C. (1994). Literacy research in community and classrooms: A sociocultural approach. In R. B. Rudell & H. Singer (Eds.), *Theoretical models and processes of reading* (pp. 179–207). Newark, DE: International Reading Association.

Oakes, J. & Lipton, M. (2006). *Teaching to change the world.* New York: McGraw-Hill

Pianta, R. C. (2001). STRS: Student-teacher Relationship Scale: professional manual. Psychological Assessment Resources.

Sleeter, C. E. (2005). *Un-standardizing curriculum: Multicultural teaching in the standards-based classroom.* New York: Teachers College Press.

Sleeter, C. E., & Grant, C. A. (2009). *Making choices for multicultural education: Five approaches to race, class, and gender.* Hoboken, NJ: John Wiley & Sons, Inc.

Sornson, B. (2013). Developing empathy in the classroom. Retrieved from http://corwin-connect.com/2014/06/developing-empathy-classroom/

Tatum, B. D. (1997). *Why are all the Black kids sitting together in the cafeteria? And other conversations about race.* New York, NY: Basic Books.

U.S. Department of Education, Institute of Education Sciences, National Center for Education Statistics, National Assessment of Educational Progress (2015). *The Nation's Report Card.* Retrieved from http://www.nationsreportcard.gov/reading_math_2013/#/achievement-gapsU.S.

U.S. Department of Education Office of Civil Rights, Civil Rights Data Collection. (2014). Data snapshot: school discipline. Retrieved from http://ocrdata.ed.gov/Downloads/CRDC-School-Discipline-Snapshot.pdf

Waldon, K. A. (2015). *Black adolescents' critical encounters with media and the counteracting possibilities of critical media literacy.* (Doctoral Dissertation). Florida Atlantic University, Boca Raton, FL, USA.

Waldon, K., Baxley, T. P., & Harrison, C (2015). Challenging the status quo: An agenda of hope for students of color. Paper presented at the Annual Meeting of the National Association of Multicultural Education (NAME), New Orleans, LA.

Weiner, L. (2006). Challenging deficit thinking: Urban teachers must question unspoken assumptions about the sources of their students' struggles. *Educational Leadership*, 64(1), 42–45.

Wiggins, G., & McTighe, J. (2005). *Understanding by design.* Alexandria, VA: Association for Supervision & Curriculum Development.

Voice in the Field: Restorative Circles for Building Community and Breaking Down Barriers

Martha A. Brown, Ph.D.

To construct a classroom that is just, equitable, and truly inclusive or culturally relevant, educators must make building relationships with their students a priority (Brown, 2015). Although all students benefit from trusting relationships with adults in their schools, research has shown that positive connections and trusting interpersonal relationships with their classmates and teachers are particularly advantageous for African Americans, Hispanic, and/or first generation low income students (Carter, 2008; Day-Vines & Terriquez, 2008; Schademan & Thompson, 2015; Tosolt, 2010). While student-centered instruction and culturally relevant teaching practices are important (Gay, 2000), teachers must at the same time work intentionally to build trust and create a strong sense of community where every person in the room is welcomed, valued, respected, honored, and appreciated (Bryk & Schneider, 2003).

More and more, schools wishing to create healthy relational ecologies in the classroom and throughout the entire school adopt restorative justice (RJ). RJ, when implemented with fidelity across all school environments, prevents challenging behavior and provides processes for responding to harm in ways that do not exclude or stigmatize students (Riestenberg, 2012). The values of indigenous peoples form the foundation for contemporary restorative justice; these values are "about healing rather than hurting, moral learning, community participation and community caring, respectful dialogue, forgiveness, responsibility, apology, and making amends" (Morrison, 2007, p. 75). Zehr (2002) expressed the belief that underlying the values of restorative justice is the vision of interconnectedness: "We are all connected to each other and to the larger world through a web of relationships. When the web is disrupted, we are all affected" (p. 35).

When restorative justice is implemented in schools, it is called restorative justice in education (RJE). Foundational to RJE is the focus on building community and holding school community members accountable to each other for creating and maintaining a safe, respectful, and positive learning environment (Amstutz & Mullet, 2005). As Morrison and Vaandering (2012) noted, "The deeper social and emotional foundation of relational ecologies moves the application of RJ away from a disciplinary measure of control to a pedagogy and praxis of engagement, development, and integrity at both individual and institutional levels" (p. 141). RJE, then, is about meeting needs, providing accountability and support, making things right, viewing conflict as a learning opportunity, building healthy learning communities, restoring relationships, and addressing power imbalances (Evans & Lester, 2013).

This voice in the field focuses on one of the most flexible and frequently utilized restorative practices in schools today, the Circle. "Establishing a Circle practice with students in the classroom begins with the classroom teacher's commitment to create a caring and respectful classroom culture" (Boyes-Watson & Pranis, 2015, p. 45). Although there are many relational pedagogical practices that facilitate student engagement, at this time few teacher educators and pre-service teachers understand how to use Circles to provide both the space and processes for building the relational trust and sense of belonging that are so essential to fostering a truly inclusive classroom.

What follows is a description of the Circle process and examples of how real-life teachers, including myself, use restorative Circles in classrooms. I will conclude with a brief list of resources where readers can turn to learn more about restorative justice and specifically, how to use Circles in any classroom.

Description of the Circle Process

Because Circles have been used by indigenous people around the world for thousands of years, the process itself is simple even though the impacts are often quite powerful. First, students and teachers sit together either on the floor or at desks arranged in a Circle. This equalizes the power dynamics, which may take both students and teachers some getting used to. A Circle Keeper (in this case, the teacher), acts as a guide and facilitator, but not as an authoritarian director. Anyone can be the keeper, and as students learn the Circle process, they quickly become adept at "circling up" when they feel the need.

The Circle Keeper introduces a talking piece, which usually has some kind of meaning and in a classroom, should be unbreakable. I use a variety of pieces in my classroom: a small rock that I gathered on a hike, a seashell, a squishy ball, or an Ugli Doll. The talking piece really guides the conversation, as only the person holding the piece can speak, while all others listen. It is important to explain this carefully. Every person in Circle has the same opportunity to speak and be heard, and all members of the Circle are equally valuable. People may choose not to speak when the piece is passed to them as well, and never should a student be coerced into speaking if they do not want to. Because ritual is an important part of Circle, keepers often bring people physically, emotionally, and spiritually into the Circle with a meaningful poem or story, a meditative chime, or breathing exercise before offering the prompts for discussion. After bringing everyone together in Circle, the Keeper will then introduce a "round." The keeper poses a question, and may choose to answer first or last. Then, the keeper passes the piece to the left, (clockwise), so that the Circle flows in harmony with the Earth as it moves around the sun. The keeper should take care not to always start with the person on the immediate left and hand the talking piece to different people around the Circle so that the Circle starts and ends with different people. As the talking piece is passed, those who choose to speak will, and all others will listen, not responding or debating – only listening. Those who choose not to speak will simply pass the piece to the next person. When the Circle is over, the keeper honors participants for speaking their truth, and closes the Circle with breathing, a chime, or another meditative reading. Using this simple process, Circles can be used to transform conflicts, talk about the curriculum, build relationships, gain consensus, check in to see how students are feeling, and more! I now provide two real-life examples, both from my own personal experiences sitting in Circle in classrooms.

Real- Life Example #1: Community Building Circle in a 6th Grade Classroom

A sixth grade teacher in an Oakland Middle school held community building Circles in her class every Friday, in addition to harm Circles when they were needed. She and her students were adept at listening and speaking in Circle and were excited and happy to be in this community building Circle. The teacher invited me to participate in this Circle while I was visiting the school. Students decided what three prompts they could choose to talk about. With one prompt inviting participants to share something about their country of origin. As the piece was passed, I learned that there were students in this classroom from more than 6 countries! Here is just one story that was told that day:

> When one boy received the talking piece, he shared that he and his brother, who sat next to him and did not speak when he received the piece, were "from a country where there was a lot of violence and where people were kidnapped a lot." That country was Nepal. As soon as he said that, students quieted down and tuned into the petite, smiling, dark-haired boy holding the talking piece. He talked about how they lived in houses made of mud, not cement, and that they only had dirt roads and outhouses. Some students, especially those who lived in Oakland, could not imagine living in a place that did not have indoor plumbing. He explained how they lived near the jungle where there were wild animals and elephants, and how their mother was almost bitten by a green mamba. Students who lived in the high crime neighborhood near the school identified with this boy and his brother, who painted a very different picture of an unsafe environment.

Because this teacher used circles regularly, students had built trust with each other. Such trust created a safe space for this boy to be open, honest, and vulnerable and to tell his personal story to a Circle of 28 squirming sixth graders who listened to him with respect and compassion. He and his brother were part of a caring and safe classroom community, which they needed, especially considering the dangers he was exposed to as a young child in his homeland.

Real- Life Example #2: Circles for Teaching and Learning in a College Classroom

As a professor, I open and close every class that I teach in Circle. First, I open with a "check in" round where I ask students to share how they are feeling at the moment. This first round tells me if students are stressed, if something has happened in their life, or if they are ready to learn. Sometimes I even ask them to share something good that happened to them during the week; this round usually results in laughter and applause as a wave of celebration and happiness fills the room. Next, I move into the curriculum, where I conduct several more rounds asking students to either share something they learned from the readings or ask a question about something they did not understand. This Circle then becomes a formative assessment, where I can determine who has done their reading, who has not, and what students learned or did not learn. It also allows students to share what resonated with them or what confused them, and I then use this information to inform my instruction for that class. To close the class, I ask them questions like, "What is one thing you are still not sure about?" or "What is your take-away from today's class?" or "What is your personal plan to ensure you get your project done on time?" By asking this last question, students make a public commitment to themselves, to me, and to their peers to do their best work on an assignment, and become accountable to their classroom community. If it has been a particularly intense class, my final round might simply be, "Share with the group something that brings you joy." Then even with pending deadlines and exams, we all leave the class smiling.

Practical Resources to Learn More About How to Use Circles in Your Classroom

Amstutz, L., & Mullet, J. H. (2005). The little book of restorative discipline for schools. Intercourse, PA: Good Books.

Boyes-Watson, C., & Pranis, K. (2015). Circle forward: Building a restorative school community. St. Paul, MN: Living Justice Press.

Clifford, A. (n.d). Teaching Restorative Practices with Classroom Circles. Developed for the San Francisco Unified School District. Downloadable guide with lesson plans for using circles in the classroom. http://www.healthiersf.org/RestorativePractices/Resources/documents

Evans, K. & Vaandering, D. (2016). The little book of restorative justice in education. Skyhorse Publishing, Fall, 2016.

Hopkins, B. (2011). The restorative classroom: Using restorative approaches to foster effective learning. London: Optimus Education.

Oakland Unified School District. (2015). Restorative Justice. Watch videos of actual circles, download the OUSD Implementation and Impact Report. http://www.ousd.org/restorativejustice

Pranis, K. (2005). The little book of circle processes. Intercourse, PA: Good Books.

Riestenberg, N. (2012). Circle in the square: Building community and repairing harm in school. St. Paul, MN: Living Justice Press.

References

Amstutz, L., & Mullet, J. H. (2005). *The little book of restorative discipline for schools*. Intercourse, PA: Good Books.

Boyes-Watson, C., & Pranis, K. (2015). *Circle forward: Building a restorative school community*. St. Paul, MN: Living Justice Press.

Brown, M. A. (2015). *Talking in circles: A mixed methods study of school-wide restorative practices in two urban middle schools.* Unpublished dissertation.

Bryk, A. S., & Schneider, B. (2003, March). Trust in schools: A core resource for school reform. *Educational Leadership, 60*(6), 40–44.

Carter, D. (2008). Cultivating a critical race consciousness for African American school success. *Educational Foundations, 22*(1–2). 11–28.

Day-Vines, N. L., & Terriquez, V. (2008). A strengths-based approach to promoting prosocial behavior among African American and Latino students. *Professional School Counseling, 12*(2), 170–175.

Evans, K. R., & Lester, J. N. (2013). Restorative justice in education: What we know so far. *Middle School Journal, 44*(5), 57–63.

Gay, G. (2000). *Culturally responsive teaching: Theory, research & practice.* Columbia University: Teachers College Press.

Hopkins, B. (2011). *The restorative classroom: Using restorative approaches to foster effective learning.* London: Optimus Education.

Morrison, B. (2007). *Restoring safe school communities: A whole school response to bullying, violence and alienation.* Sydney, Australia: The Federation Press.

Morrison, B. E., & Vaandering, D. (2012). Restorative justice: Pedagogy, praxis, and discipline. *Journal of School Violence, 11*(2), 138–155.

Riestenberg, N. (2012). *Circle in the square: Building community and repairing harm in school.* St. Paul, MN: Living Justice Press.

Sanchez Fowler, L. T., Banks, T. I., Anhalt, K., Der, H. H., & Kalis, T. (2008). The association between externalizing behavior problems, teacher-student relationship quality, and academic performance in young urban learners. *Behavioral Disorders, 33*(3), 167–183.

Schademan, A. R., & Thompson, M. R. (2015). Are college faculty and first generation, low-income students ready for each other? *Journal of College, Student Retention, Research, Theory & Practice, 0*(0), 1–23. doi: 10.1177/1521025115584748

Tosolt, B. (2010). Gender and race differences in middle school students' perceptions of caring teacher behaviors. *Multicultural Perspectives, 12*(3), 145–151.

Zehr, H. (2002). *The little book of restorative justice.* Intercourse, PA: Good Books.

Practical Encounter #1

Directions: Read the following Case Study and answer the questions that follow.

Case Study: Make Your Voices Heard by Leila Shatara

As a Muslim and an American, it pains me to know that we are constantly being told we cannot be both or that we must choose one or the other. We are not the first to be persecuted based on religious beliefs in this great democratic country that was founded by people fleeing religious persecution. However, we should have learned some lessons from our history by now. How many groups must we vilify and demonize to propel a politically motivated agenda? How many times will we divide the country based on race, ethnicity, and religion? Do not fool yourself into thinking this is different; Muslims have brought it on themselves, look at all the terrorist attacks and wars and violence. Do not swallow every lie, every half-truth; every tale the media spins to instill fear. Remember it was not too long ago that white Americans felt that blacks did not deserve to be treated as equal human beings and justified it by using the bible. It was not long ago that Jews in America were afraid to identify themselves as such and changed their names in fear of persecution. Just as we see it as absurd now only a few decades later, so is the idea that Muslims are terrorists and enemies of democracy and the West. How many genocides, how many holocausts will it take for humanity to learn the lesson that human rights and justice is for all. We cannot wait another 50 or 60 years of increased Islamophobia until we realize how wrong this is and how detrimental it is to our fabric as a civil and just society.

Why does my 17-year-old daughter have to be subjected to "Are you happy with what your people did in Paris" a day after the Paris attacks? She had just stepped onto her college campus when a stranger approached her and angrily shouted at her. She was taken aback but was strong enough to respond, "Those are not my people." She went on to explain what the belief system in Islam and how "those people" were killing more Muslims than non-Muslims. Why does she have to sit through classes where students and even sometimes instructors repeatedly make derogatory comments about Muslims and claim they are just repeating facts? If news channels and newspapers reported on every death caused by guns, we would think the country was at war with itself with 51, 812 incidents in 2014 alone. Imagine if you saw 12, 591(this is the statistic for 2014) reports on deaths by firearms on the news in a year that would be an average of 34 reports per day!!! Imagine what you would think and how you would feel. Then everyone would be demanding a war on guns not a war on terror.

Media, politics, and a war machine that makes many people rich and powerful by merely instilling fear is hard at work. They choose how and what you see and how often and with what intensity. Most people do not stop to question because our emotions take over and it is in our nature to defend ourselves and that is what they have been feeding into for years. Fear needs an enemy and that enemy is now Muslims. Attacks on Muslim are on the rise and have increased over the past year. Recently while my 15-year-old son and I sat in a hospital waiting room for his post op exam, a stranger, a man in his late 50s began to direct some vulgar remarks towards us and became loud and more vulgar because we did not respond or react. He eventually began to shout obscenities about Islam, Allah, and Muhammad and said he was voting for Trump so he could kick all of our ____out of America. I shifted to stand up as I was going to call the security guard, and he shouted "Watch out she's got a bomb!" Eventually security escorted him away and we had to have someone checking on us the rest of day to make sure we were safe. Why did my son who was recovering from his fourth surgery in 3 ½ months have to endure the hatred, vulgarity, and demeaning comments from this absolute stranger filled with venomous hate? In a room of about 100 people, a woman did stand up and put him in his place and it is people like her who will make things right. I did not know her nor did she know us but she recognized an injustice and stood and raised her voice above that man's and shut him down with her words. It will take many more people to stand up and raise their voices, voices demanding fair treatment of others and justice for all.

Teachers can make a difference by teaching differently, teaching a curriculum that opens minds. Teach about Islam and Muslims, go to a nearby mosque and meet Muslims, read and watch things from a Muslim perspective, and understand more of the reality for Muslims. Teachers have the power to change history while it is being made. Hate comes from fear and fear is instilled based on ignorance, therefore education is the key to unlocking the hearts and minds of people who just do not know. A teacher who educates students to be analytical thinkers, to ask questions, to demand answers, and to understand what it means to be a just society. To be able to think from different perspectives, to see another person's ideas as valid even if they do not agree, to be able to solve problems while working with others, to be able to stand up with courage and speak on behalf of those who cannot speak for themselves is the truest form of education.

Based on the Case Study above, reflect on the following questions:

1. How would you respond to this mother regarding her concern for the safety and well-being of her daughter in your classroom?

2. What is your responsibility as a teacher in creating a classroom of care for Muslim students (or any other groups of students that have been marginalization)?

3. How can Muslim students and their funds of knowledge be honored in the classroom?

4. How can you create an open environment in your class where sensitive topics are shared in a constructive manner?

5. What activities or opportunities can be incorporated in the classroom that advocate for social justice and equity?

Practical Encounters #2

CCIM™ Exercise

Next to each domain, brainstorm strategies or actions that may be possible to implement in your classroom as a result of what you learned in this chapter.

6 Domains of CCIM™ Curriculum Connections Approach	Possible Classroom Practices/Strategies
Connection: establishes a two-way reciprocal relationship between the teacher and student. The teacher begins the learning process by developing a mutual, respectful partnership with students as co-investigators through dialogue and inquiry.	
Community: recognizes that community is developed within the classroom using democratic principles and caring classroom practices. This domain also emphasizes the need to include the students' families and local community as partners in the nurturing and development of the student.	
Culture: recognizes and celebrates the differences of learners (culture, race, ethnicity, social class, language, sexual orientation, etc.), thus creating a culture of acceptance that promotes respect, equity, and affirmation.	
Character: fosters student character building through an emphasis of intrinsic motivation, self-identity and awareness, and social justice education.	
Content: sustains the connection between information and student learner. Problem-posing and inquiry-based modes of learning guide instruction and curriculum. Teachers use the mandated standards as a tool for active learning that is taught in tandem to the students' lives.	
Critical Consciousness: represents the primary outcome of the learning process, is an emancipatory experience that both empowers and inspires.	

CHAPTER 4

Promoting Inclusion for Students of All Abilities

Cynthia L. Wilson, Ph.D.   Kathleen M. Randolph, MS.Ed   Brianna Joseph, M.Ed.

Ms. Smiley who is a first year teacher, just returned to her classroom after attending the first fourth grade planning meeting of the school year. She sits down at her desk with a million questions running through her head as she stares at her class roster of twenty-two students. She was informed in the planning meeting that while all of her students are fourth graders, her students' learning needs are quite diverse. She is wondering how she can meet the needs of her student who was described as gifted, while also meeting the needs of the two students with learning disabilities who are functioning at academic levels that are below fourth grade in reading and language arts, but are on or above grade level in math and science. She even has one student who is identified as "twice exceptional." She learned that means he is both gifted and has a learning disability. But, she is most concerned about the one student she will have who has autism and the student who is an English language learner. She asks herself if it is possible for one teacher to meet the needs of students who are so differently abled while providing a classroom that is nurturing and one that provides fair and equitable opportunities for all students to learn. Then she remembers, while she is only one teacher, she is a part of a team of teachers and, more importantly, a school that emphasizes the inclusion of all students in the general education classroom. While still feeling somewhat overwhelmed, she remains excited, committed and determined that her classroom will be a quality environment for all of her students, regardless of ability or disability.

Questions for discussion

1. Compare this setting to classroom settings that you have experienced either as a K-12 student, in a field-based experience as a college student, or as a classroom teacher.
2. What is the responsibility of the general education classroom teacher for addressing the needs of all the students in the classroom? Should Ms. Smiley ask for reassignment for some of her students so that she has more students that have "like" abilities? Why or why not?
3. How can Ms. Smiley ensure that she establishes high expectations for all of her students regardless of ability level or cultural background?
4. What are some inclusive practices that you have learned about that are essential in today's schools? What strategies and/or accommodations can you recommend that Ms. Smiley implement in her classroom to ensure that she meets the needs of her diverse group of students?

Defining Inclusion

The definition of the concept of *inclusion* presented in this chapter is grounded in a discussion of the federal law, the Individuals with Disabilities Education Act, Individuals with Disabilities Education Act (IDEA) 2004. In addition to identifying and defining the 13 disability categories that may entitle students to special education services, the IDEA also mandates the required involvement of general education teachers

in the education of students with disabilities as appropriate. The responsibility of general education teachers for students with disabilities is based on the concept of the requirement that students with disabilities are to be educated in the least restrictive environment, (LRE) which is also a component of IDEA. Palley (2006) notes that, "the LRE provision guarantees a student's right to be educated in the setting most like that for peers without disabilities in which the student can be successful with appropriate supports provided" (Palley, 2006 as cited in Friend & Bursuck, 2012, p. 5). For most students with disabilities, the LRE is full-time or part-time participation in the general education classroom. While the term inclusion does not actually appear in the IDEA, it is a long held belief that the LRE provision, along with the mandate of access to the general education curriculum requirements for all students (including students with disabilities) to participate in high stakes assessments, along with civil rights legislation has led state and local policymakers to stress inclusive practices. It is safe to say that inclusion is a concept that is here to stay and that general educators must be prepared to provide the necessary accommodations and instructional strategies to assist students with disabilities so that they can be successful in the general education classroom.

For students to access the general education curriculum and to be successful in the general education classroom, the concept of inclusion must go beyond the definition of inclusion as mere placement in the general education setting, where students with disabilities are often treated as temporary guests. Rather, the concept of inclusion must be expanded to encompass the notion of *inclusive practices*. The principle underlying inclusive practices acknowledges inclusion as a philosophical belief that students with disabilities should be fully integrated into their school communities and the general education classroom and that their instruction should be based on their abilities, not their disabilities (their strengths, not their weaknesses) (Friend & Bursuck, 2012). It encompasses the belief that educators' strong preference is for students with disabilities to be educated with their peers without disabilities and that general educators will embrace the following three dimensions of inclusive practices:

- *Physical Integration*: Placing students in the same classroom as nondisabled peers should be a strong priority, and removing them from that setting should be done only when absolutely necessary.
- *Social Integration*: Relationships should be nurtured between students with disabilities and their classmates and peers as well as adults.
- *Instructional Integration*: Most students should be taught in the same curriculum used for students without disabilities and helped to succeed by adjusting how teaching and learning are designed (that is, with accommodations) and measured. For some students with significant intellectual disabilities, instructional integration means anchoring instruction in the standard general curriculum but appropriately adjusting expectations that is, making modifications (Friend & Bursuck, 2012, p. 6).

Additionally, the concept of inclusive practices must embrace a responsibility to collaborate with and involve families in the education of students who have disabilities. It is essential that general education teachers maintain positive contact with parents and caregivers of students. The recommended approach for collaborating with families is referred to as family-centered practices (Dunst, 2002; Hansuvadha, 2009). Family-centered practices are based on the belief that outcomes are best for students when the culture of the families and families' perspectives are respected, the families' input is sincerely sought, and teachers view their job as helping families get the information they need to make the best decisions for their children.

Disability Categories in IDEA

There are 13 named disability categories defined in IDEA that entitle students to receive a free appropriate public education including special education and related services and/or supportive services in general education classrooms with appropriate accommodations. These federal terms guide how states define disability (although states may use different terms than those in the federal law). In order to fully meet the definition and eligibility for special education and related services, a student's educational performance must be adversely affected due to their disability. The 13 named disability categories in IDEA and brief descriptions for each disability are provided in Table 4.1.

Table 4.1.   Disability Categories

Learning Disability	A disorder related to processing information that leads to difficulties in the acquisition and use of listening, speaking, reading, writing, reasoning, and mathematical skills. Dyslexia is a specific type of learning disability which describes students who have serious problems learning to read despite normal intelligence, normal opportunities to learn to read, and an adequate home environment
Speech or Language Impairment	A disorder related to accurately producing the sounds of language or meaningfully using language to communicate, including disorders such as stuttering, impaired articulation, and language impairment
Emotional Disturbance	Significant problems in the social-emotional area that result in behavioral or emotional responses that are different from appropriate age, cultural, and ethnic norms and are not the result of temporary, stressful events in the environment
Mental Retardation	While this term remains in federal law, the recommended term is now intellectual disability which is defined as significant below average general intellectual functioning existing concurrently with deficits in adaptive behavior (i.e., the collection of conceptual, social, and practical skills that all people learn in order to function in their daily lives)
Autism	A developmental disability characterized by impairments in communication, learning, and reciprocal social interactions
Developmental Delay	Significant delay in one or more of the following areas: physical development, cognitive development, communication, social or emotional development, or adaptive/behavioral development; applicable for children ages 3-9
Hearing Impairment	A partial or complete loss of hearing that is permanent or fluctuating and may be referred to as hard of hearing or deaf
Visual Impairment	A partial or complete loss of vision such that the student cannot use vision as a primary channel for learning or has such reduced acuity or visual field that processing information visually is significantly inhibited and specialized materials or modifications are needed; the term includes blindness
Deaf-blindness	The presence of both a significant hearing loss and a significant vision loss
Orthopedic Impairment	A significant physical limitation that impairs the ability to move or complete motor activities
Other Health Impairment	Conditions resulting in limited strength, vitality, or alertness caused by chronic or acute health problems
Traumatic Brain Injury	A serious brain injury that occurs as a result of accident or injury potentially affecting learning, behavior, social skills, and language
Multiple Disabilities	The simultaneous presence of two or more disabilities such that none can be identified as primary, the most common combination being a physical and an intellectual disability.

The abovementioned disability categories are used by federal and state education agencies for counting the number of students with disabilities receiving special education services and for allocating funding to educate them. However, for those who have the responsibility to actually teach students with disabilities, the specific category of disability may not be useful in guiding teachers in determining students' strengths and weaknesses and devising appropriate teaching strategies. This is due to the heterogeneity that can exist within disabilities (e.g., one student with a learning disability may manifest their disability in difficulties with learning to read, while another student may have difficulty with mathematical computations). Additionally, students in different categories often benefit from the same instructional accommodations and strategies (e.g., both students with autism and students with emotional disturbances benefit from structured, organized classrooms).

Classroom Accommodations and Teaching Strategies for Students with Disabilities

A cross-categorical approach to teaching, which pays more attention to students' learning needs than their special education disability category or label, is likely to be more beneficial. This may be especially so in the general education inclusive classroom where teachers may have multiple students with different categorical labels in the same classroom. One such cross-categorical approach is making accommodations and implementing teaching strategies based on the severity of the disability (i.e., mild, moderate, severe) and the level of support that may be needed in the inclusive classroom. Therefore, we recommend that inclusive teachers who are serving students with disabilities in the general education classroom make accommodations and implement instructional strategies based on the severity of the student's disability (mild, moderate, severe) rather than their disability category label (learning disability, emotional disturbance, etc.). Thus, recommendations for accommodations and instructional strategies are presented in this chapter using this approach.

Students with mild disabilities

Students with mild disabilities make up 80% of all students who have disabilities (U.S. Department of Education, 2015). These students are more likely to receive resource (part-time) special education services, but spend the majority of school days in the general education inclusion classroom setting, and receive minimal consultation and support services from a special education teacher for a small part of the day. Students with mild disabilities are more like their non-disabled peers than they are different from them. In fact, they are often hard to distinguish from peers without disabilities in non-school settings. They exhibit a combination of behavioral, social, and academic problems and benefit from systematic, explicit, highly structured instructional interventions.

Accommodations for students with mild disabilities
- Provide guided notes for note-taking (e.g., lecture notes with blank spaces for students to fill in);
- Provide study guides for students to prepare for tests;
- Permit students to use calculators, reference sheets, times tables, etc.;
- Give scaffolded homework and classwork (e.g., breaking homework and classwork into mini-lessons, checking between each lesson for student understanding to move students progressively toward understanding of more difficult content);
- Use preferential seating (e.g., in the front of the room to reduce distraction, near better lighting for students with visual impairments);
- Provide large print books and/or materials for students with visual impairments;
- Provide audio books so student can listen to assignments;
- Design classroom layout to accommodate students with physical impairments, such as students who may be in wheelchairs;
- Provide extended time to complete projects, assignments, and tests (e.g., give students with disabilities 1½ times the amount of time provided to general education students);
- Administer tests in small groups so that questions may be read aloud;
- Permit use of a word processor during writing assignments;
- Clearly define expectations;
- Use verbal prompts (e.g., provide students with a spoken complete response to a question just asked) and cues (verbal clue or hint for an expected response); and
- Teach students to graph/chart behavioral and academic data so they can monitor their own progress.

Teaching strategies for students with mild disabilities
- Teach students organizational skills (e.g., write assignments daily in planner, use checklists);
- Use proximity (e.g., stand near the student) to gain student attention;

- Use modeling to expand students' language by verbalizing appropriate examples for students to imitate;
- Read, clarify, and simplify directions for understanding;
- Use daily behavior chart to track student behavior;
- Reward appropriate student behavior consistently;
- Use learning centers to differentiate instruction;
- Teach mnemonic strategies for rapid recall (e.g., PEMDAS - Please Excuse My Dear Aunt Sally [Parentheses, Exponent, Multiplication, Division, Addition, Subtraction] to remember order of operations in math); and
- Teach learning strategies (e.g., test taking skills, study skills, how to use graphic organizers, etc.).

Students with moderate disabilities

Students with moderate disabilities require additional educational support and structure. These students require smaller core academic classes that provide direct instruction, remediation, repetition, and structured classroom routines. Students with moderate disabilities may be included part of the day in academic classes, with general education teachers providing the appropriate accommodations and teaching strategies necessary for their success. These students typically have activities and assignments that differ somewhat from those of other students in the general education classroom, but their work should still be aligned with the general education curriculum.

Accommodations for students with moderate disabilities
- Provide visual and verbal prompts and cues;
- Work with tangible objects before moving on to pictured objects;
- Provide praise and tangible reinforcement in response to good attempts;
- Provide tactile prompting (e.g., tap student on shoulder);
- Use pictures and words to identify items and activities in the classroom;
- Provide a visual schedule to reinforce daily classroom activities;
- Create and provide a predictable environment; and
- Encourage appropriate social interactions.

Teaching strategies for students with moderate disabilities
- Collaborate with related service providers (e.g., special education teacher, speech pathologist, occupational therapist, physical therapist) to determine student's present level of academic, behavioral, and functional performance;
- Provide a functional curriculum, emphasizing practical skills aligned to the general education curriculum;
- Emphasize using the five senses (i.e., hearing, sight, taste, touch, smell);
- Enunciate words to ensure proper use of mouth (e.g., th, f, r, s);
- Teach blending sounds at different times (e.g., ch and sh should not be taught at the same time);
- Emphasize grammar conventions—create rules for different types of words;
- Sequence activities in the appropriate order (e.g., left to right, top to bottom, first to last, easy to difficult);
- Begin each lesson with a review, followed by individual and/or small group work;
- Task analyze and teach concepts from simple to difficult (i.e., break activities into small steps);
- Ensure mastery of each concept individually before moving forward;
- Scaffold correct responses using prompting and modeling to shape/assist with responses until correct;
- Use functional behavioral assessment to determine function of challenging behaviors and determine appropriate replacement behaviors;
- Provide a highly structured behavior support program to teach appropriate replacement behaviors;

- Implement positive behavior intervention plans as appropriate; and
- Use check-in/check-out systems for daily behavior monitoring.

Students with severe disabilities

Students with severe disabilities have intellectual and physical difficulties that impact daily access to major life activities (Developmental Disabilities Assistance and Bill of Rights Act, 2000). These students' intellectual impairments and adaptive behavior deficits are so significant and pervasive that considerable support is needed for them to learn. Students with severe disabilities have ongoing needs for support throughout the school day. These students may receive systematic instruction from a special education teacher and other individualized services in a small classroom setting that is designed to provide individual attention and adult support to allow for multiple learning and physical differences within the classroom setting. Thus, they are more likely to receive most of their services in special education and outside of the general education inclusion setting. While these students may spend the majority of their day in the special education classroom, these students can also benefit from social interactions with classmates who do not have disabilities in the general education classroom. The inclusive general education teacher should use the following accommodations and strategies to foster a nurturing and supportive environment for *all* students in the inclusive classroom.

Accommodations for students with severe disabilities
- Use assistive technology (e.g., tablets, assistive augmentative and alternative communication devices, push buttons with single button to indicate response);
- Provide frequent breaks;
- Provide one-on-one instruction from teacher or paraprofessional;
- Designate non-disabled peers to serve as peer mentors;
- Provide and support use of individualized schedules with Picture Exchange Communication Systems (PECS); and
- Set up the classroom to meet needs of students with mobility challenges.

Teaching strategies for students with severe disabilities
- Emphasize functional academics and daily living skills aligned to the general education curriculum;
- Clearly define expectations;
- Target teaching to emphasize goal-driven daily programming (i.e., based on IEP goals);
- Emphasize generalization of skills across settings (i.e., school, home, community);
- Reinforce skills learned in community-based instruction and transition programs; and
- Design activities to include students with severe disabilities in cooperative learning groups with their non-disabled peers.

Providing the appropriate services, accommodations and teaching strategies for students with disabilities within the inclusive general education classroom should be based on student ability and need. Some accommodations and strategies are helpful for all students and can be applied in every classroom to a varying degree regardless of individual disability label. Scaffolding instruction, providing additional time on task, and a structured environment with high expectations for *all* students are appropriate in every classroom including those who serve *other students with learning and behavioral needs*, who don't meet special education eligibility requirements under the IDEA. These students will be the focus of the remainder of this chapter.

Other Students with Learning and Behavioral Needs

There are students with learning and behavior needs that are different from both their typical peers and their peers with disabilities, but who don't meet eligibility requirements for special education services under the IDEA. These students may be entitled to accommodations mandated by Section 504 of the Vocational Rehabilitation

Act of 1973. Section 504 is legislation that resulted from the civil rights movement and was created to prevent discrimination against individuals with disabilities. Known as the civil rights law for persons with disabilities, Section 504, prevents discrimination against all individuals with disabilities in programs that receive federal funds, as do all public schools. For school-aged children, Section 504 ensures equal opportunity for participation in the full range of school activities (Walker, 2006; Zirkel, 2009).

Students with attention-deficit-hyperactive disorders

One particular group of students who receive accommodations in inclusive general education classrooms under Section 504 is students with attention-deficit-hyperactivity disorder (ADHD). Students with ADHD have a medical condition characterized by an inability to attend to tasks for long periods of time, excessive motor activity, and/or impulsivity. These students typically spend all of their day in the general education classroom, unless their condition is determined to be so severe that it meets requirements for being classified as a health impairment and it is determined their needs can best be met by full-time or part-time placement in a special education classroom. The accommodations provided for these students can include some of the same types of services and supports that students eligible through the IDEA receive; however, one crucial difference is that the general education teacher is responsible for making accommodations for students who qualify for services based upon Section 504. There are no mandated services required by special education personnel for students with ADHD being served under Section 504.

Accommodations for students with ADHD
- Provide a quiet workspace free of distractions;
- Decrease the number of items in assignments, emphasizing essential content;
- Provide additional time to complete assignments;
- Provide note taker as necessary;
- Create an organizational system such as the use of a list of items to include in backpack before leaving home for school and leaving school for home;
- Allow rest periods;
- Seat students nearest to where instruction takes place;
- Use timers and/or visual clues to indicate beginning and ending times for instruction and assignments;
- Use multisensory (see, hear, touch, feel, smell) presentation techniques; and
- Establish a home-school communication system for monitoring behavior.

Students who are English language learners

English language learners (ELLs) are students whose native language is not English. They are not to be confused with students who have a speech or language disability as defined in IDEA. While ELLs may experience difficulties in receptive and expressive verbal language, comprehension, and initiation and maintaining conversation with others who are native English speakers (Morales-Jones & McHugh, 2015); being an ELL is not the same thing as having a disability. ELLs have a language difference; they do not have a disability. However, they may need additional assistance in school learning.

There are varying levels of support that may be needed by ELLs so that they can be successful in the general education classroom. ELLs may receive varying supportive levels of bilingual immersion in the general education classroom. These students may also receive services outside of the general education classroom to assist with emerging English language, which is provided by an ELL certified teacher. Services outside the general education classroom allow the student to receive individualized instruction in small groups. Other services include remedial courses that are intended to clarify material from content areas and improve comprehension skills in English, and mentoring programs that pair ELLs with native English speakers to improve their conversational skills (Ariza, 2015).

Teaching approaches for ELLs

Bilingual Immersion is a method of teaching ELLs by targeting language through the curriculum and media. Bilingual immersion has three generic levels; early immersion for ages 5-6, middle immersion for ages 9-10, and late immersion for ages 11-14. Each level emphasizes the English language based on the developmental age of the student (Rivera & Collum, 2006). In partial immersion, the student receives instruction for half of the day in English and the other half in his/her native language. In two-way immersion, instruction is given in both English and the native language of the student, emphasizing one language at a time during instruction, and peer-to-peer facilitated language sharing (Ariza, 2015). In total immersion, the majority of instructional time and curriculum is in English.

Teaching approaches that are similar to bilingual immersion for ELLs include late-exit/developmental bilingual education, sheltered English, content based language learning and language experience approach (Ariza, 2015). *Late-exit/developmental bilingual education* decreases instruction by the teacher in the student's native language throughout the content areas and grade years. *Sheltered English* (also known as specially designed academic instruction in English) features ELL instruction in English by simplifying the English language specifically in core academic content areas to integrate and enforce text materials and new vocabulary. In *content based language learning,* teachers use materials, tasks, and techniques from each of the academic content areas to drive the development of the English language. The *language experience approach* is where students develop their own materials to assist them while engaging in content areas. The teacher uses these materials to teach skills in the content area. Each teaching approach contains evidence-based strategies to increase English language proficiency, provide maintenance, and assist in generalization to other settings for ELLs in schools.

Strategies for teaching students who are ELLs
- Set high but realistic expectations;
- Teach content and objectives through simplified language for better understanding;
- Consider cultural backgrounds when developing and implementing materials and content;
- Present students with challenging yet meaningful curriculum content and materials;
- Support student self-data and reporting;
- Establish peers as teaching partners;
- Progress monitor students using portfolios, data collection, and observations;
- Modify language and concepts;
- Teach using multidisciplinary thematic units;

Students who are Gifted and Talented

In addition to students who may have learning and behavioral needs including difficulty meeting typical curricular expectations, general education teachers can also expect to have students who have extraordinary abilities and skills in their inclusive classrooms. While many states provide gifted education under their special education umbrella, the federal definition for students who are gifted is not included in the IDEA (which as previously discussed mandates services for students with disabilities). The federal definition for these students is stated in the Javits Act (Jacob Javits Gifted and Talented Students Education Act of 1988). Gifted and talented students are identified as children and youth who have demonstrated or potential high-performance capability in intellectual, creative, specific academic and leadership areas, or performing and visual arts. The provision of services for students who are gifted and talented is delegated to the state education agency, and often falls on the local education agency (school district) to provide specific funding. Table 4.2 describes each of the five categories of funding and the corresponding US States (including Washington, D.C.) (*Davidson Institute for Talent Development,* 2016).

Identification of students for gifted eligibility is the responsibility of the local education agency. There is no uniform system for identifying and serving students in gifted education. Gifted students cannot be characterized into one group, nor can they be provided with the same type of instruction. Gifted children have similar characteristics and tendencies including IQ scores that are well above average (130 and above),

Table 4.2. US States According to Funding Categories for Gifted Education

Levels of Funding	States
1. Mandated (fully funded)	Georgia, Iowa, Mississippi, and Oklahoma
2. Mandated (partially funded)	Alabama, Arkansas, Colorado, Florida, Idaho, Indiana, Kansas, Kentucky, Louisiana, Maine, Minnesota, New Jersey, New Mexico, North Carolina, Ohio, South Carolina, Tennessee, Texas, Virginia, Washington, West Virginia, Wisconsin, and Wyoming
3. Mandated (not funded)	Alaska, Arizona, Connecticut, Maryland, Montana, Oregon, Pennsylvania, and Rhode Island
4. Not Mandated (funding is available)	California, Hawaii, Nebraska, Nevada, North Dakota, and Utah
5. Not Mandated (no funding available)	Delaware, Illinois, Massachusetts, Michigan, Missouri, New Hampshire, New York, South Dakota, Vermont, and Washington, D.C.

and early advanced skills in literacy, math, memory, and attention (Brighton & Jarvis, 2011 as cited in Kauffman, J. M. & Hallahan, 2011).

Students from culturally and linguistically diverse backgrounds, specifically Black and Hispanic students, are traditionally underrepresented in gifted education (Ford, 2014). This trend was noted when the national percentage of Black students in education (19%) was compared with the percentage of Black students enrolled in gifted programs (10%). The comparison for Hispanic students is slightly less dismal, with the national percentage of Hispanic students in education (25%) above that of the Hispanic students enrolled in gifted programs (16%). The inequality in gifted programming for Black and Hispanic students is attributed to several factors: social inequality, deficit thinking, white privilege, intent and response (Ford, 2014; Ford & King, 2014).

Several recommendations are made for the appropriate representation of Black and Hispanic students in gifted education. Educators must be cognizant of the barriers that exist for students from culturally and linguistically diverse backgrounds, and should keep those barriers in mind when looking at data for underrepresentation. Students should be screened in direct proportion to their representation in the school district, that is, if the district is comprised of 25% of Black students, then at least 25% of Black students should be screened for gifted education. The instruments used to evaluate students should be free of bias, and inclusive, rather than exclusive, and individual student experiences should be taken into consideration when students are referred to gifted education. Finally, educators need to be prepared to educate gifted students from all backgrounds, including culturally and linguistically diverse students (Ford, 2014).

Strategies for teaching students who are gifted and talented

- Make use of curriculum compacting (i.e., assess students' achievement of instructional goals and then eliminate instruction on goals already met)
- Provide opportunities for project-based learning;
- Base assignments on Bloom's Taxonomy;
- Provide continuous progress monitoring to advance in curriculum;
- Provide center-based independent learning opportunities;
- Assign students in-depth independent study opportunities;
- Incorporate field trips to enhance the curriculum;
- Permit students to complete research-based projects on topics of interest;
- Provide opportunities for academic competitions (brain bowls, etc.);

- Infuse technology;
- Provide tiered enrichment/differentiated opportunities (low, middle, and high);
- Provide opportunities for peer mentoring

Conclusion

As discussed in this chapter, general education teachers should expect to have students that are differently abled in their classrooms. Teachers must be prepared to provide an inclusive classroom environment that nurtures and meets the learning and behavioral needs of students including students with intellectual, social-emotional, and behavioral disabilities; English language learners, and students who are gifted and talented. It is critical that general education teachers become comfortable implementing instructional strategies that can be beneficial to different learners. They must learn to critically analyze students' learning needs and the specific demands of the classroom environment to make reasonable accommodations that will meet the needs of their students and maximize chances for students to have fair and equitable learning opportunities to access the general education curriculum and standards. Such opportunities must be available for *all* students; no matter their abilities and/or limitations.

References

Ariza, E. N. (2015). Cultural implications for refugees, immigrants and English learners in the United States. In E. N. W. Ariza, C. A. Morales, N. Yahya & H. Zainuddin (Eds.). *Fundamentals of teaching English to speakers of other languages in K-12 mainstream classrooms.* Dubuque, IA: Kendall Hunt.

Davidson Institute for Talent Development. (2016). Gifted education policies. Retrieved from: http://www.davidsongifted.org/db/StatePolicy.aspx.

Developmental Disabilities Assistance and Bill of Rights Act, P. L. 106-402. (2000).

Dunst, C.J. (2002). Family-centered practices. Birth through high school. *Journal of Special Education, 36,* 13-147.

Ford, D. Y. (2014). Segregation and underrepresentation of Blacks and Hispanics in gifted education: Social inequality and deficit paradigms. *Roeper Review, 36*(3), 143-154.

Ford, D. Y. & King, R. A. (2014). Desegregating gifted education for under-represented Black and Hispanic students: Equity promotes equality. *Teaching for High Potential, 1,* 13-16.

Friend M., & Bursuck, W. D. (2012). *Including students with special needs: A practical guide for classroom teachers.* Boston, MA: Pearson.

Hansuvadha, N. (2009). Compromise in collaborating with families: Perspectives of beginning special education teachers. *Journal of Early Childhood Teacher Education, 30,* 346-362.

Individuals with Disabilities Education Act of 2004, 20 USC§ 1400 et seq.

Jacob K. Javits Gifted and Talented Students Education Act of 1994, 20 USC§§ 8031 et seq.

Kauffman, J. M. & Hallahan, D. P. (Eds.). (2011). *Handbook of special education.* New York, NY: Routledge.

Morales-Jones, C. A. & McHugh, C. (2015). Integrating language and content. In Ariza, E. N. W., Morales-Jones, C. A., Yahya, N. & Zainuddin, H. (Eds.). *Fundamentals of teaching English to speakers of other languages in K-12 mainstream classrooms.* Dubuque, IA: Kendall Hunt.

Rivera, C. & Collum, E. (2006). *State assessment policy and practice for English language learners: A national perspective.* Mahwah, N.J: Lawrence Erlbaum Associates.

Snell, M. E., Luckasson, R., Borthwick-Duffy, W. S., Bradley, V., Buntinx, W. H., Coulter, D. L. & Schalock, R. L. (2009). Characteristics and needs of people with intellectual disability who have higher IQs. *Intellectual and Developmental Disabilities, 47*(3), 220-233.

U. S. Department of Education (2015). Office of Special Education and Rehabilitative Services, Office of Special Education Programs, 37th Annual Report to Congress on the Implementation of the Individuals with Disabilities Education Act, Washington, D.C.

Walker, C.J. (2006). Adequate access or equal treatment: Looking beyond the IDEA to Section 501 in a post-Schaffer public school. *Stanford Law Review, 58,* 1563-1622.

Zirkel, P. (2009). Section 504: Student eligibility update. *Clearing House: A Journal of Educational Strategies, Issues, and Ideas, 82,* 209-211.

Teachers often have questions about how they can best support the needs of English language learners (ELLs) in inclusive, English-medium classroom settings. Over the years, we have come across several myths related to how teachers consider the needs of and differentiate instruction for their ELL students. We present and discuss a few of these misconceptions below.

Myth #1: English Language Learners all have the same needs because they are all learning English.

Reality: ELLs are a highly diverse group of students, differing from each other in both demographic characteristics (age, education, knowledge of other languages, time in the U.S., socio-economic status, parent/guardian support, cultural background, etc.) and language proficiency levels. Their academic/linguistic needs are extremely different and are based upon these unique experiences and background factors. For example, in the table below, consider the profiles of three ELLs, all beginning a new school year in the same fifth grade classroom.

Kerline	Kerline is a new arrival from Haiti and is entering a U.S. school for the first time. She attended a public school where the language of instruction was French. She understands and speaks Haitian Creole and French; however, her literacy skills are underdeveloped due to limited resources in her previous school. She is reading at a kindergarten level and struggles with addition and subtraction.
Joao	Joao started school during January of the previous school year. Prior to his arrival in the U.S., he attended a private school in São Paulo, Brazil. He is an excellent reader and writer in his native language of Portuguese and was the top performing student in his class in math. His parents are both advanced English speakers who lived in the U.S. for several years before returning to Brazil to start a family before returning to the U.S.
Luis	Luis is a Nicaraguan-American student who was born in the U.S. His family lives in a predominantly Spanish-speaking community. After several years of English-only instruction, he has regressed in his ability to speak his native language and has trouble communicating with his Spanish-speaking parents and grandparents. He has not developed literacy in his first language, and his English literacy skills are below grade level.

Kerline is challenged to develop emergent literacy skills while also learning a new language and fifth grade academic content. Joao has a strong foundation in his native language of Portuguese but requires instruction that is appropriate for his level of language proficiency. Luis, although born in the U.S., did not have adequate support in his first language and continues to struggle academically as a result. Teachers must take the time to learn about students' linguistic backgrounds as well as their prior educational experiences in order to plan for instruction that addresses each individual's strengths and weaknesses.

Myth #2: ELLs at emerging or beginning English proficiency levels cannot participate in mainstream instruction until they have learned English.

Reality: ELLs at any level of English proficiency can interact in the classroom as long as the teacher provides appropriate scaffolding and comprehensible input (i.e., language that is understandable to listeners/readers even though students may not understand all the words and structures of the language/text) (Krashen, 1985).

Along with other scaffolds (e.g., providing visuals, adapting speech rate/articulation, repeating/rephrasing core concepts, using gestures and body language with speech), teachers can modify question stems and formatting to engage students at the appropriate level of discourse according to their linguistic capabilities (Hill & Flynn, 2008, 2013). By varying the linguistic demands of questions posed in the classroom, teachers can scaffold the learning experiences for ELLs to produce language that showcases both lower and higher order thinking. The example below illustrates how a teacher can scaffold language learning experiences for ELL students. This example, based on *Officer Buckle and Gloria* (Rathmann, 1995), illustrates how a student's emergent English skills do not compromise his/her ability to comprehend texts and engage in complex, abstract thinking.

Proficiency Levels	Level 1 Entering	Level 2 Beginning	Level 3 Developing	Level 4 Expanding	Level 5 Bridging
Tiered Questions	Show me something that changed about Officer Buckle's job during the story.	Tell me one way that Officer Buckle's job changed during the story.	What changed Officer Buckle's job during the story?	How did Officer Buckle's job change during the story?	How did Officer Buckle's job change from the beginning of the story to the end?

Source: Adapted from *WIDA Levels of Language Proficiency* and Hill & Flynn (2008).

Level 1 students can respond non-verbally, and the requirements for language production increase from Level 1 through to Level 5. Each question challenges students to consider elements such as cause and effect and to analyze how the character has changed throughout the story. As ELLs navigate the complex continuum of second language development, teachers can encourage participation and learning by utilizing a variety of scaffolding techniques, including tiered questions.

Myth #3: ELLs at emerging or intermediate levels of English proficiency cannot meet the same objectives of a lesson designed for English-speaking students.

Reality: Regardless of students' varying English proficiency levels, ELLs should be held to the same expectations for achievement and should experience instruction that prepares them to meet the same educational goals. Instead of creating multiple lesson objectives, teachers should choose content and language objectives that are appropriate for all students. Scaffolding should be differentiated for ELLs so they can demonstrate accomplishment of lesson goals- both the subject matter they should know by the end of the lesson (content objectives) and the language they must use to demonstrate that knowledge (language objectives). Being inclusive in your teaching means providing a variety of ways (e.g., adapted text, visuals, sentence frames) for ELLs at any proficiency level to showcase their achievement of objectives in activities and assessments. In the following example, a teacher infuses different scaffolds for ELLs at Levels 1-4 to ensure all students have the opportunity to accomplish the content and language objectives.

Content Objectives:	Students will be able to describe the characters Officer Buckle and Gloria and identify how their actions affect the events of the story.
Language Objectives:	Students will be able to use descriptive adjectives to describe the traits, motivations, and feelings of Officer Buckle and Gloria orally and in writing.
Assessment:	Complete a character map for Officer Buckle and Gloria. Draw a picture of each character, list three character traits, and write one sentence providing evidence from the text to support their claims.

Level 1 (Entering)	Level 2 (Beginning)	Level 3 (Developing)	Level 4 (Expanding)
- List 2 traits	- List 3 traits	- List 3 traits	- List 3 traits
- Use a bank of short phrases and key words	- Use basic adjectives/ word bank of key words	- Use a word bank of transition/conjunction words	- Use a word bank of transition words
- Explain verbally (oral, list) or nonverbally (draw)	- Match statements with correct traits and characters	- Use sentence starters & word bank to form complete sentences	- Use word bank to form complete sentences
- May refer to book illustrations	- May refer to book illustrations		
- May use native language to list traits			

References

Hill, J. D. & Flynn, K. (2008). Asking the right questions. *Journal of Staff Development, 29*(1), 46-52.

Hill, J. D. & Miller, K.B. (2013). *Classroom instruction that works with English language learners* (2nd ed.). Alexandria, VA: Association for Supervision and Curriculum Development.

Krashen, S. (1985). *The input hypothesis: Issues and implications.* Beverly Hills, CA: Laredo Publishing Company.

Rathmann, P. (1995). *Officer Buckle and Gloria.* New York, NY: Putnam's.

Practical Encounter

WebQuest: Search the following websites to fill in the chart below on IEPs and the 504 Plan.

A Guide to the Individual Education Plan:
https://ed.gov/parents/needs/speced/iepguide/index.html

Difference between the IEP and 504 Plan:
https://www.understood.org/en/school-learning/special-services/504-plan/the-difference-between-ieps-and-504-plans

	Individual Education Plan (IEP)	504 Plan
What is it?		
Student's Rights?		
Parents' Rights?		
Teacher's Role?		

CHAPTER 5

Rags to Riches: Honoring the Inherent Richness of Students in Poverty

Kalisha A. Waldon, Ph.D.   Traci P. Baxley, Ed.D.   Allyson Hall, M.A.

Annually, 5th grade students at Green Forest Elementary School are charged with the task of bringing awareness to a particular disease/disorder by conducting research. They present their findings to a wide range of students, faculty, parents, and community members. Other schools in the district participate in the same annual project, many of whom receive more funding and have more involved parents. In the past few years, Green Forest has received a consistent school grade of a 'C' or below. This year, the administration has invited the local news and District/Area directors to the school to highlight the academic strengths of the students.

In preparation for the media event, Ms. Alexandra, the 5th grade team leader, is pulled into the office of Ms. Richards, the principal, for an impromptu meeting to discuss her expectations for the important presentation. In this meeting, Ms. Richards states the following:

"Ms. Alexandra, it's mandatory that the students dress in their school uniform on the day of the presentation. Their uniforms must be washed, not dirty and wrinkled, like they are every day. Send a note home to the parents to let them know the expectations, not that most of them will read it anyways. . ." all in a very condescending tone. She continued, "I have asked to borrow some examples of projects completed by students at Merriweather Park, the district's top school. The students need to examine these projects for ideas and to set high expectations for their final products; I don't want to see the usual stuff that's up on the walls. I want to see correct spelling and a real effort." To comply Ms. Alexandra nods her head in agreement that she will relay this information to the students.

Ms. Alexandra left the office feeling defeated. She is aware of the financial plight of the students attending her school; many of their families live at or just above the poverty line. She begins to wonder how she can effectively communicate all of the principal's expectations while maintaining an authentic learning experience. She also begins to calculate how much she would have to spend out of her own pocket to make sure the students would be able to have the opportunity to create final products that looked similar to the "model" projects from Merriweather.

Questions to Ponder:

1. How could Ms. Alexandra have responded to the principal's comments regarding the students' appearance, the parents' involvement, and the perception of their capabilities?
2. Why did Ms. Alexandra respond to the principal in a passive manner?
3. Why might the principal react the way she does? What biases are clouding and guiding her judgments?
4. Educators are to set high expectations for all student learners. Is there a problem with showing the students the previously made projects from the other school to set the expectation for their own final projects? Why or Why not?
5. If you were Ms. Alexandra, how would you address the principal's requests? How would you communicate the project expectations to your students? What are the equity implications that would allow the students to produce the same quality projects they are being shown as guidelines?

Submitted by Ashlee Sullivan, Teacher

Introduction

This chapter will specifically address low-socioeconomic families that are often classified as those living in poverty. The chapter will then turn to discuss the barriers, "*rags*," to equitable learning opportunities for students living in poverty, the strengths, "*riches*", that students bring from their families and communities into the classroom, and strategies that *honor* and support families living in poverty. To review the American Psychological Association's (2016) definition of Socioeconomic status (SES), go to this website link: (http://www.apa.org/topics/socioeconomic-status/).

According to US standards, a family is considered poor if its pre-tax income is below the poverty threshold (see table 5.1). Thresholds are determined yearly by the federal government per family size and adjusted annually for inflation.

Table 5.1.   2016 Poverty Guidelines

Persons in Family/Household	2016 Poverty Guideline
1	$11,880.00
2	$16,020.00
3	$20,160.00
4	$24,300.00
5	$28,440.00

Source: https://aspe.hhs.gov/poverty-guidelines

This poverty guideline is also used in determining students' eligibility for free or reduced lunch, the status of a school, i.e., Title I, and school funding or resource allocation.

According to the National Center for Children in Poverty (2009), poverty levels across the U.S. remain high, with 45% of today's children living in low-income households. A more recent statistic from *The National Center for Education Statistics* (2014) reported approximately 20% of school age children were in families living in poverty. Figure 5.1 reveals the poverty rates by race, ethnicity, and family structure with children under the age of 18.

According to the chart, the poverty rate for Blacks, Hispanics, and American Indian/Alaska Native are higher for mother-only households, whereas Whites and Asians are below the national poverty line regardless of family structure. However, across racial or ethnic groups, the poverty levels are lower for married-couple households. It is important to recognize however that when these statistics are compared to the overall actual number of children without considering family structure (see Table 5.2), the 2014 United States Census indicates

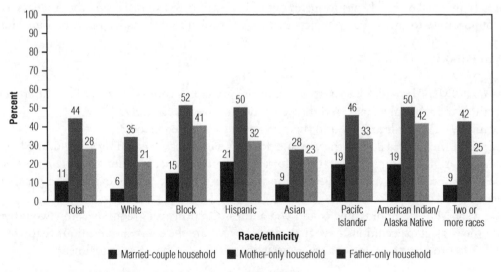

Figure 5.1.   Adapted from The National Center for Education Statistics (2014).
Source: Allyson Hall.

Table 5.2.   Number and Percentage of Children under 18 Living in Poverty by Family Structure, Race/Ethnicity, and Selected Subgroups 2014

Total	15,276	(98.6)	21.2	(0.13)	10.5	(0.11)	44.4	(0.27)	28.2	(0.36)
White	4,650	(45.7)	12.5	(0.12)	6.3	(0.9)	34.6	(0.39)	21.0	(0.44)
Black	3,725	(39.8)	38.1	(0.36)	14.9	(0.39)	51.6	(0.45)	40.5	(0.90)
Hispanic	5,559	(48.1)	31.7	(0.27)	21.3	(0.29)	50.2	(0.45)	32.3	(0.75)
Cuban	85	(5.2)	20.8	(1.10)	11.1	(0.90)	43.0	(2.69)	20.2	(3.67)
Dominican	166	(9.3)	34.0	(1.46)	20.8	(1.77)	46.4	(2.16)	29.8	(3.62)
Mexican	4,038	(45.5)	33.3	(0.34)	23.7	(0.34)	51.9	(0.61)	34.2	(0.94)
Puerto Rican	530	(13.4)	32.1	(0.70)	12.8	(0.73)	49.8	(1.10)	34.2	(2.20)
Spaniard	29	(3.5)	14.7	(1.57)	4.6	(1.03)	38.4	(4.19)	26.7	(5.76)
Central American[3]	475	(17.2)	32.6	(0.91)	23.4	(1.11)	49.6	(1.54)	28.5	(2.30)
Costa Rican	5	(1.3)	14.7	(3.46)	6.6	(2.52)	30.3	(9.07)	‡	(†)
Guatemalan	156	(7.8)	39.6	(1.54)	32.1	(2.12)	54.4	(3.24)	39.7	(3.96)
Honduran	105	(7.6)	41.6	(1.81)	26.9	(2.72)	60.4	(2.78)	34.3	(5.87)
Nicaraguan	23	(3.0)	23.8	(2.95)	9.3	(2.42)	42.7	(5.48)	30.6	(9.15)
Panamanian	6	(1.3)	14.5	(2.78)	‡	(†)	33.1	(7.09)	‡	(†)
Salvadoran	178	(10.9)	28.4	(1.33)	21.4	(1.84)	44.6	(2.02)	19.4	(2.67)
South American	126	(7.2)	17.0	(0.94)	10.0	(0.91)	36.2	(2.15)	18.5	(2.68)
Chilean	5	(1.0)	13.9	(2.84)	9.6	(2.94)	22.3	(7.75)	‡	(†)
Colombian	34	(2.9)	16.0	(1.28)	8.7	(1.41)	36.7	(3.21)	13.0 !	(4.05)
Ecuadorian	40	(4.6)	24.8	(2.27)	13.9	(2.13)	46.7	(4.53)	31.8	(5.76)
Peruvian	16	(2.4)	11.9	(1.66)	6.9	(1.84)	26.0	(4.36)	10.7 !	(4.60)
Venezuelan	11	(2.2)	14.9	(2.85)	11.3	(2.61)	29.6	(7.73)	‡	(†)
Other South American	20	(2.7)	16.1	(2.00)	10.1	(2.25)	36.5	(5.35)	‡	(†)
Other Hispanic	111	(5.7)	23.0	(0.96)	12.7	(1.15)	42.8	(1.86)	19.3	(2.99)
Asian	385	(9.6)	11.6	(0.28)	8.8	(0.28)	27.5	(1.50)	23.3	(1.91)
Chinese[4]	72	(4.4)	10.4	(0.64)	7.8	(0.62)	23.5	(2.31)	27.0	(4.84)
Filipino	27	(3.0)	6.1	(0.65)	3.7	(0.59)	16.6	(2.61)	6.8	(1.87)
Japanese	5	(1.3)	7.2	(1.87)	3.5	(1.22)	37.8	(10.14)	‡	(†)
Korean	23	(2.5)	9.9	(1.05)	7.5	(1.01)	30.9	(4.72)	23.1 !	(9.16)
South Asian[5]	98	(5.5)	9.5	(0.52)	8.6	(0.57)	21.4	(2.79)	24.6	(5.24)
Asian Indian	48	(4.3)	5.9	(0.51)	5.0	(0.52)	18.1	(2.86)	19.9	(5.18)
Bangladeshi	13	(1.8)	28.9	(3.40)	29.0	(3.70)	‡	(†)	‡	(†)
Bhutanese	4	(1.6)	51.8	(12.46)	51.4	(12.71)	‡	(†)	‡	(†)
Nepalese	8	(1.4)	24.3	(3.82)	21.8	(3.92)	‡	(†)	‡	(†)
Pakistani	25	(3.2)	21.1	(2.33)	20.1	(2.47)	24.6	(10.29)	‡	(†)
Southeast Asian	140	(6.9)	21.4	(0.88)	16.0	(0.85)	37.3	(2.81)	29.3	(4.11)
Burmese	17	(2.2)	39.2	(4.14)	39.3	(4.74)	‡	(†)	‡	(†)
Cambodian	13	(2.1)	22.7	(2.97)	13.4	(3.32)	41.1	(6.76)	27.3 !	(9.13)
Himong	35	(4.2)	33.2	(3.32)	27.5	(3.97)	37.8	(7.27)	46.2	(9.76)
Laotian	12	(2.1)	23.9	(3.54)	5.5	(2.10)	55.9	(7.33)	33.7 !	(11.05)

Total	15,276	(98.6)	21.2	(0.13)	10.5	(0.11)	44.4	(0.27)	28.2	(0.36)
Thai	6	(1.6)	24.1	(5.33)	17.7	(5.21)	57.0	(13.90)	‡	(†)
Vietnamese	53	(3.7)	15.0	(0.95)	11.4	(1.14)	30.9	(2.96)	16.1	(3.88)
Other Southeast Asian[6]	2	(1.0)	15.6	(5.44)	17.1	(5.93)	‡	(†)	‡	(†)
Other Asian	20	(2.7)	10.4	(1.24)	6.4	(0.97)	30.9	(5.46)	21.6 !	(6.78)
Pacific Islander	33	(3.4)	27.3	(2.33)	19.5	(2.66)	46.3	(4.88)	33.2	(8.18)
American Indian/ Alaska Native[7]	188	(6.2)	34.9	(0.99)	19.4	(1.34)	50.2	(1.60)	42.1	(2.39)
American Indian	165	(5.4)	36.3	(1.01)	20.6	(1.51)	51.7	(1.58)	41.7	(2.60)
Alaska Native	9	(1.4)	28.5	(3.97)	19.1	(5.54)	38.8	(8.09)	33.3	(6.93)

SOURCE: U.S. Department of Commerce, Census Bureau, American Community Survey (ACS), 2014. See *Digest of Education Statistics 2015, table 102.60.*

that there is a greater number of Whites under the age of 18 living in poverty. This supports the notion that poverty is not race-based, but touches every racial and ethnic group. This counters the master narrative that paints the picture that poverty is primarily a black and brown issue.

Active Learning

1. What trends do you see in the table?
2. How does this align with what you already know or have learned?
3. What are possible implications to your future teaching?

Economic crises such as the housing market crash, increase in unemployment rates, home foreclosures, unavailability of low-skilled jobs, and affordable housing, etc. have affected the funding of public schools and their surrounding communities. Poverty disrupts virtually every aspect of school, home, and community life; it damages the physical and emotional health of family members, and interferes with children's academic, physical, and intellectual development. With increased levels of families in poverty, more children face hunger/food insecurity, homelessness, and a host of other hardships.

Food insecurity, often a result of poverty, even on a temporary basis can have a profoundly negative impact on children's cognitive development, health, and academic performance (*National Center for Children in*

Suzanne Tucker / Shutterstock.com

Poverty, 2009; Wight, Thampi, & Briggs, 2010). Hunger can affect children's behavior and is associated with increased aggression, destruction, and dysfunctional social skills. According to the American Psychological Association (APA) (n.d.), children who are hungry exhibit 7 to 12 times as many incidences of misconduct than their non-hungry peers. Along with hunger, homelessness, and unemployment, family stress levels have increased dramatically, leading to higher substance, domestic, and child abuse issues. Many of today's children are also having to make significant transitions in their lives, often having to transfer schools due to parental employment dilemmas. This can cause anxiety which often negatively affects their classroom behavior.

As multicultural educators, it is important that we do not allow stereotypical views of children living in poverty and expectations of their academic capacities to be marred by their socioeconomic realities. Students who live in poverty are as capable of success as those that are from more affluent communities; however, they need the support and encouragement from multicultural educators who can provide opportunities that assist them in navigating the world around them. Unfortunately, many educators hold on to negative images and messages that are associated with economically-challenged students. In the following section we will explore common preconceived notions that have been traditionally held by educators.

Deficit Thinking

Deficit theory (Collins, 1998; Dudley-Marling, 2007; Gorski, 2008a), deficit ideology (Sleeter, 2004), and deficit thinking (Ford & Grantham, 2003; Pearl, 1997; Valencia, 1997; Yosso, 2005) refer to the holding of low expectations for students with demographics that do not fit the traditional context of the school system (Simone, 2012). Oakes (1995) referred to deficit thinking as assumptions that low income children, children of color, and their families are limited by cultural, situational, and individual deficits that schools cannot alter. Drawing on the work of Gorski (2008), Brandon (2003), Valencia (1997), and Yosso (2005), Gorski (2011) posits that deficit ideology essentially is:

> . . . (the) belief that inequalities result, not from unjust social conditions such as systemic racism or economic injustice, but from intellectual, moral, cultural, and behavioral deficiencies assumed to be inherent in disenfranchised individuals and communities. (p. 154)

These ideas prove harmful to students who are products of systematic oppression and discrimination and to those whose superficial differences erroneously render them academically inept or unequal.

Deficit thinking robs families and their children of opportunities to showcase the inherent value of their culture and conventional wisdom. This ideological framework of deficit thinking has shaped the state of education in the United States (Valencia, 1997) and suggests that certain groups of students fail in schools because they are unduly characterized as lazy, poor, apathetic, or without motivation. Their parents are criticized as being disinterested in their children's education, substance abusers, or having home lives that are dysfunctional and/or harmful to the well-being of their children. In short, this perspective provides teachers with the opportunity to lower the academic bar and create a barrier between student potential and the educator's ability or willingness to nurture his or her student's growth (Gorski, 2011).

These perceived deficiencies are often attributed to non-traditional or non-mainstream family structures (Valencia, 1997). It places families and children that live in poverty at the epicenter of concern and liability. This mode of thinking is so deeply infused in our educational system that those who are perceived as "different" are also often given the title of "deficient" (Gorski, 2011). As such, students may become immersed in educational environments that undermine their value (Skrl & Scheurich, 2001) and can potentially lead to the adoption of negative perceptions of self in accordance with Merton's self-fulfilling prophecy theory (1957). For example, if an instructor demonstrates higher expectations academically for a student from a more affluent family than for a student from a lower socioeconomic background, then the more affluent student will often embody the perceptions and expectations of their teacher, and mirror those expectations in their effort and grades - thus engaging in fulfilling the prophecy.

Active Learning

1. Were any of these experiences present during your K-12 experience?
2. If your answer is yes, what did these experiences do for you?
3. If your answer is no, how would things be different for you today?
4. Why do you think these equity practices are necessary in today's classroom?
5. Did the principal in the introductory case study espouse any of these perspectives? Explain.

What Does Deficit Thinking Look Like?

While deficit thinking/ideology may be an abstract concept, the realization of these ideas are often palpable and visible in political arenas and in our classrooms. An example of deficit ideology can be seen in Florida. According to the 2012 Florida State Board of Education Strategic Plan, all students were expected to be proficient in reading and math by the 2022-2023 school year. Although a plan was in place to narrow the achievement gap, the initiative was underfunded from the onset. From that time, the annual per pupil funding decreased from year to year (see Figure 5.2).

Adjusting for inflation, per pupil spending in Florida has steadily declined, reflecting a nearly 11.5% decrease since 2008. What is also problematic is that in 2012, the *Florida Department of Education* (FLDOE) approved academic benchmarks which, in effect, set lower expectations for students living in poverty. One such academic standard was that by the year 2018, the FLDOE expects that only 78% of their economically disadvantaged populations will reach reading and math grade level proficiency (*Florida Department of Education,* FLDOE, 2012). While this goal of 78% does represent a projected increase in achievement (46% and 48% were proficient in Reading and Math respectively in 2012), compared to other subgroups, this projected expectation is lower for economically disadvantaged students (low-SES). Figure 5.3 and 5.4 illustrate the performance goal targeted increase from 2012-2018 in both reading and math across student subgroups.

These goals suggest that in just five years, 78% of students from economically disparate communities are expected to achieve momentous gains on standardized assessments with less funding due to inflation (see figure 5.2). Furthermore, in 2015, Florida ranked 37th out of 50, thus earning them a grade of D+ when state spending trends per pupil were compared to those of the national average change to: (*Education Week Research Center,* 2015). What does this say about the expectations FLDOE has for students who come from low-SES backgrounds? How are limited funding patterns expected to raise achievements for students who need additional resources?

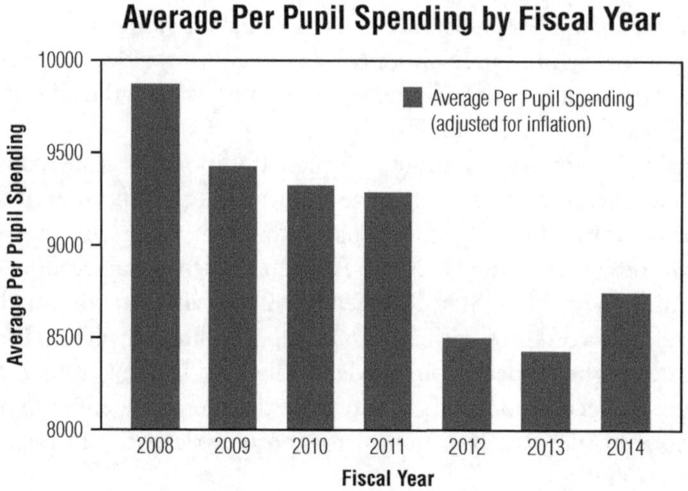

Average Per Pupil Spending by Fiscal Year

Figure 5.2.   State of Florida Average Per Pupil Spending 2008-2014

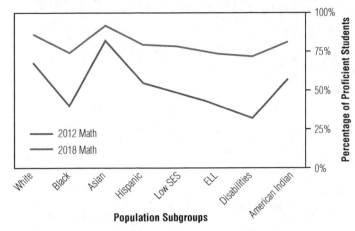

Figure 5.3. Florida Strategic Plan Performance Goals (Math)
Source: Allyson Hall. Adapted from http://www.governing.com/gov-data/education-data/state-education-spending-per-pupil-data.html

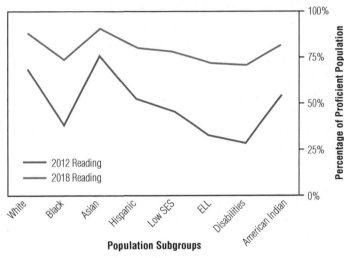

Figure 5.4. Florida Strategic Plan Performance Goals (Reading)
Source: Allyson Hall. Adapted from http://www.fldoe.org/core/fileparse.php/7734/urlt/0075039-strategicv3.pdf

Barriers to Equitable Learning Opportunities

There are several barriers to equitable learning outcomes for students in poverty. The economic gap is most evident in communities and public schools that are segregated along the lines of race and class. Darling-Hammond (2012) reported that "more than 70% of Black and Latino students attend predominantly minority schools, and nearly 40% attend intensely segregated schools, where more than 90% of students are minority and most are poor" (p. x).

The schools in these neighborhoods, as a result of poverty, lack proper funding, access to highly qualified teachers, limited advanced coursework and extracurricular activities, and poor school facilities.

There are several barriers that impact the everyday realities of providing equitable learning opportunities for low-SES students. One such barrier is the lack of proper funding. According to the United States *Department of Education* (2011), many high-poverty schools receive less state and local funding which leads to fewer resources for these schools when compared to the resources more affluent schools receive. One example of this is illustrated in a report by Filardo, Vincent, Sung and Stein (2006) who found that more affluent school districts invested more funding in school facilities ($9,361 per student) than what was invested in facilities for the least

Andrii Kondiuk / Shutterstock.com

affluent schools in the district ($4,800). While funds were invested in affluent and low-income schools, the low-income schools' funds were used to make basic repairs, such as the installation of new roofs or the removal of asbestos. Funds in the more affluent schools were used for the building of science labs or performing arts centers. The authors (Filardo, et. al., 2006) also cite that school districts invested the least dollar amount in the poorest communities ($4,140 per student) and the higher investments were made in the high-income communities ($11, 500 per student). When race was a factor, the predominately minority schools received $5,172 per student for school facilities and $7,102 per student in predominately White schools.

Another barrier to school equity is a lack of access to highly qualified educators. Teachers with the least formal training teach the most educationally vulnerable students. For example, according to Strauss (2013), high poverty secondary schools have a rate of 21.9% of classes taught by "out of field" teachers compared to more affluent schools with only 10.9% of "out of field" teachers. In addition, teachers at high poverty schools often have salaries that are lower than their colleagues who work at more affluent schools. Educators working in high poverty schools often teach classes with over 40 students compared to their peers averaging 20 students per class; often without adequate resources and supplies (Darling-Hammond, 2003). Gimber, Bol, and Wallace (2007) draw attention to the fact that a teacher's years of experience and quality of training is correlated with children's academic achievement.

According to Rothawell (2012) housing and zoning policies in communities are segregated based on income, thus making this another equity barrier. Rothawell found that "across the 100 largest metropolitan areas, housing costs an average of 2.4 times as much, or nearly $11,000 more per year, when located near a high-scoring public school than near a low-scoring public school" (p.1). Housing and zoning policies bolster academic disparities and create opportunity gaps that have the potential to compromise economic futures, especially for Blacks and Hispanics. The author goes on to note that students from middle and high-income families attend better-performing schools than low-income students.

Active Learning

Think of two schools in your surrounding area (one in an affluent neighborhood and another in a poverty-stricken neighborhood).

1. What are the similarities between the schools?
2. What are the differences?
3. How do the differences reinforce educational disparities for students?

Theories and Equity Practices for Working with Students in Poverty

It is assumed that students from poverty bring little to nothing with them to the classroom; however, these students possess valuable knowledge and experiences, and bring these strengths to the classroom. Our classrooms are full of unique and inquisitive students that bring cultural enrichment to school each day; a parent's conventional wisdom, a holistic home remedy, familial proverbs, oral histories, and other ways of knowing are all a part of funds of knowledge that students carry with them. According to Moll, Amanti, Neff, and Gonzalaez (1992) *funds of knowledge* is defined as "historically accumulated and culturally developed bodies of knowledge and skill essential for household and individual functioning and well-being" (p. 133). Students' skills, language, values, and abilities are often ignored, when these cultural gems should be used as catalysts for student success in the classroom. These cultural funds (Moll, et. al, 1992) prove valuable to educators who are keen and eager to explore and incorporate them in the classroom. Educators are challenged to consider and embed a student's standpoint into curricula as a way of accentuating the funds and mitigating traditional monolithic perceptions of what it means "to know" or what is considered "real" knowledge.

In their research, Moll et al. (1992) trained a group of educators who made home visits to observe the knowledge, dispositions, and experiences that their students and families utilized in their home settings. The teachers used what they learned about the families and incorporated the students' funds of knowledge into the curriculum. Ultimately, the more students' funds of knowledge were integrated into the curriculum; the more engaged the students were in the classroom. Ladson-Billings' (2009) research further posits that teachers of traditionally marginalized students should possess cultural competence in order to ground students in "their own culture as a prerequisite to becoming versed in what might be considered mainstream culture" (p. xi). Culturally competent teachers do not buy into the stereotypes that pervade society regarding students from poverty, such as students from poverty are lazy, they all have behavior problems, they lack the ability to achieve academically, etc. Students are viewed from a deficit perspective when teachers do not make an effort to learn about and integrate students' strengths and funds of knowledge into the classroom; they are, in essence, setting are in essence setting their students up for failure.

Without a relevant curriculum, students of poverty will continue to face obstacles in receiving equitable educational opportunities. As a multicultural educator, you are charged with helping to minimize the educational debt students are faced with in today's classrooms. The consequences of not doing so, and constantly disregarding children of poverty's funds of knowledge, are damaging. As a teacher of students who live in poverty, you will be confronted with many challenges, including lack of appropriate resources and a lack of professional development when dealing with the impact that poverty has on students' learning. In spite of these issues, a more concerted effort is needed to reach out to students and families and build personal connections between the home and school.

Active Learning

1. How can you make connections between the homes and school of your students of poverty?
2. Why is it important to incorporate their funds of knowledge into the classroom or the curriculum?
3. What resources can you draw upon to accomplish this?

Donna Beegle (2012), a presenter at the United States Department of Education's Smaller Learning Communities Program, discussed five research-based theories and strategies for equity practices used by educators working with students and families in poverty: (1) strengths perspective approach; (2) resilience theory; (3) asset theory; (4) social capital theory; and (5) faulty attribution theory. Table 5.3 summarizes each of the theories and aligns them to equity practices that can be used with students in poverty. While the strategies are presented individually, they are fluid and overlap. They represent the notion that a culture of care and mutual respect must be present in classrooms in order to create learning environments or communities that support students that build upon their knowledge and experiences.

klublu / Shutterstock.com

Table 5.3.   Research-based Theories and Strategies for Equity Practices

Theory	Equity Practices
Strengths Perspective Approach Use of this approach seeks to honor and empower individuals by focusing on their strengths and the skills and knowledge they do possess.	1. Look for ways and opportunities to validate students and their families. 2. Ask parents who may have expertise in a certain area or skill to contribute to a lesson or activity you are teaching in the classroom. 3. Find ways to celebrate and highlight individual students and families (i.e. catching students in positive situations and making an effort to acknowledge that publicly).
Resiliency Theory Using this theory, educators affirm students' abilities, knowledge, and experiences to develop self-confidence. This will lead to resiliency.	1. Practice seeing the strengths in your students and their families instead of viewing them from a deficit perspective. 2. Help students identify what they are good at and use previous experiences as building blocks for the future. 3. Show empathy towards your students and build that skill within them.
Asset Theory With this theory, educators build upon students' internal and external assets (strengths) while assisting them in developing more skills (i.e. conflict resolution, relationship building) to succeed.	1. Learn what assets students and families possess. 2. Connect students and families to resources. 3. Build partnerships in the community to assist you in meeting the needs of your students and honing in on resources you can use in the classroom. 4. Teach them how to navigate their own realities/worlds and mainstream society.
Social Capital Theory With this theory, educators help to build students' social capital (people and community network) and increase their chances to build meaningful connections with people in the community.	1. Invite successful members from the community into the classroom to speak or to mentor students. 2. Inform students and families about opportunities in the community to interact with leaders, entrepreneurs, etc. 3. Pair students and successful members of the community in mentoring relationships and partnerships based on affinities and interests.
Faulty Attribution Theory Take time to understand the 'why' behind a student's or their family's actions.	1. Understand that the way you think/ behave can be different from the way students and their families think/behave. 2. Tell yourself that people may be doing the best they can; don't cast judgment. 3. Engage in self-reflective practice on your role in facilitating your students' learning and the 'why' behind their story.

Drawing upon students' funds knowledge and interests and forging partnerships with the community and families, teachers will begin to see and uncover the unique brilliance in each of their students. In this process students will begin to feel more validated and will continue to develop more confidence. As a teacher, you begin to feel more confident in creating a learning community that is inclusive and built on trust. This confidence will lead both you and your students to more risk-taking, more critical thinking, more social inquiry and academic conviction.

Conclusion

Possessing a commitment to ensure that your classrooms are environments of care and where students of poverty feel safe and nurtured (Noddings, 2002) is paramount. Since the classroom may be the only stable place in some students' lives, as a multicultural educator, your role is to establish a consistent, predictable structure that also offers flexibility and comfort, while incorporating your students' experiences and funds of knowledge into your curriculum. As you find ways to facilitate learning that is relevant, meaningful, and worthwhile in your student's lives, you should implement classroom practices that promote engagement and joy for all students.

References

Brown. E. (2015, March 12). In 23 states, richer school districts get more local funding than poorer districts. *Washington Post*. Retrieved from: https://www.washingtonpost.com/news/local/wp/2015/03/12/in-23-states-richer-school-districts-get-more-local-funding-than-poorer-districts/#graphic

Collins, J. (1988). Language and class in minority education. *Anthropology & Education Quarterly, 19*(4), 299-326.

Darling-Hammond, L. (2012, January 11). Why is Congress redlining our schools? *The Nation*. Retrieved from https://www.thenation.com/article/why-congress-redlining-our-schools/

Darling-Hammond, L. & Sykes, G. (2003). Wanted: A national teacher supply policy for education: The right way to meet the "highly qualified teacher' challenge. *Educational Policy Analysis Archives, 11*(33). Retrieved from http://epaa.asu.edu/epaa/v11n33.

Dudley-Marling, C. (2007). Return of the deficit. *Journal of Educational Controversy, 2*(1). Retrieved from http://www.wce.wwu.edu/Resources/CEP/eJournal

Filardo, M. W., Vincent, J. M., Sung, P. & Stein, T. (2006). *Growth and disparity: A decade of U.S. public school construction.* Retrieved from http://citiesandschools.berkeley.edu/reports/BEST_GrowthandDisparity_2006.pdf

Florida Department of Education (2012). Strategic plan for the public school system and the florida college system. Tallahassee, FL.

Ford, D. Y. & Grantham, T. C. (2003). Providing access for culturally diverse gifted students: From deficit to dynamic thinking. *Theory into Practice, 42*(3), 217-225.

Gimbert, B., Bol, L. & Wallace, D. (2007). The influence of teacher preparation on student achievement and the application of national standards by teachers of mathematics in urban secondary schools. *Education and Urban Society, 40,* 91-117.

Gorski, P. C. (2008). Peddling poverty for profit: Elements of oppression in Ruby Payne's framework. *Equity & Excellence in Education, 41*(1), 130-148.

Gorski, P. (2011). Unlearning deficit ideology and the scornful gaze: Thoughts on authenticating the class discourse in education. *Counterpoints, 402,* 152-173. Retrieved from http://www.jstor.org/stable/42981081

Ladson-Billings, G. (2009). The dreamkeepers: Successful teachers of African American children (3rd ed.). San Francisco, CA: Jossey-Bass.

Merton, R. K. (Ed.). (1957). The self-fulfilling prophecy. *Social theory and social structure* (pp. 421–436). Glencoe, IL: The Free Press.

Moll, L., Amanti, C., Neff, D. & Gonzales, N. (1992). Funds of knowledge for teaching: Using a qualitative approach to connect homes and classrooms. *Theory Into Practice, 31*(2), 132–141.

National Center for Children in Poverty. (2009). Basic facts about low-income children, 2008. Retrieved from http://www.nccp.org/publications/pub_892.html

Noddings, N. (2002). *Starting at Home. Caring and social policy*, Berkeley, CA: University of California Press.

Oakes, J. (1995). Two cities tracking and within-school segregation. *Teachers College Record, 96*(4), 681-691. Retrieved from http://www.someaddress.com/full/url/

Pearl, A. (1997). Democratic education as an alternative to deficit thinking. In R. R. Valencia (Ed.). *The evolution of deficit thinking* (pp. 211–241). London, United Kingdom, Falmer.

Education Week Research Center. (2015). Florida state highlights 2015: Preparing to launch early childhood's academic countdown. A supplement of Education Week's quality counts 2015. Retrieved from http://www.edweek.org/media/ew/qc/2015/shr/16shr.fl.h34.pdf

Rothwell, J. (2012.) Housing costs, zoning and access to high-scoring schools. *Metropolitan policy program at Brookings.* Retrieved from: http://www.brookings.edu/research/papers/2012/04/19-school-inequality-rothwell

Sleeter, C. E. (2004). Context-conscious portraits and context-blind policy. *Anthropology & Education Quarterly, 35*(1), 132-136.

Strauss, V. (2013, August 27). How the public is deceived by 'qualified teachers'. *Washington Post.* Retreived from https://www.washingtonpost.com/news/answer-sheet/wp/2013/08/27/how-the-public-is-deceived-about-highly-qualified-teachers/

The Education Trust. (2015, March 25). Students who need the most continue to get the least [Press Release]. Retrieved from: https://edtrust.org/press_release/students-who-need-the-most-continue-to-get-the-least/4

United States Census Bureau. (2014). *American fact finder* [Data file]. Retrieved from http://factfinder.census.gov/faces/tableservices/jsf/pages/productview.xhtml?pid=SSF_2014_00A08&prodType=table

United States Department of Education. (2011). More than 40% of low-income schools don't get a fair share of state and local funds: Department of Education Research Finds. Retrieved from http://www.ed.gov/news/press-releases/more-40-low-income-schools-dont-get-fair-share-state-and-local-funds-department-

Valencia, R. R. (Ed.). (1997). Introduction. In *The evolution of deficit thinking* (pp. ix-xvii). London, United Kingdom, Falmer.

Yosso, T. J. (2005). Whose culture has capital? A critical race theory discussion of community cultural wealth. *Race, Ethnicity and Education, 8*(1), 69-91.

Wight, V. R., Thampi, K. & Briggs, J. (2010, August). Who are America's poor children? Examining food insecurity among children in the United States. *National Center for Children in Poverty.*

Inquiry Connector

Homelessness and Hunger in Our Community

Traci P. Baxley & Kalisha A. Waldon

Inquiry Connectors are used or created by teachers to engage their students in critical inquiry work. These are perfect opportunities for teachers to draw upon real world issues/problems, students' wonderings and their lived experiences in the classroom. Below is a connector that was created for a 2nd grade class based on students' questions surrounding what they saw on their way to school one day.

Topic: Homelessness & Hunger in Our Community
Grade Level: 2nd grade
Cross- Curricular Subjects: Social Studies, Language Arts

Introductory statement/questions: Several students from the class were having a discussion about their ride to school. They chattered about seeing the homeless people holding signs asking for food on the side of the road on their way to school. There were several questions that came from these conversations.
- Why can't the people just go to the store and get food?
- Why can't their families give them food?
- Why don't they have a house?
- What if nobody gives them money out of the car window?

Inquiry: In order to find answers to your questions, you are encouraged to do the following:
1. Explore several books that focus on people who are homeless and hungry.
2. Watch the video "Helping Hands Food Kitchen."
3. Talk with volunteers in our community, place of worship, or family members to begin to answer questions.
During your book exploration, your viewing of the video, and the interviewing of community members, jot down information in your journal that gives you an indication as to why people are homeless, why they don't have enough to eat, and how people who are homeless get food.

Critical Discussion:
(Answer the following questions based on your exploration of the topic.)
4. What did you learn about homelessness and hunger in our community?
5. What are some reasons why people have become homeless?

Action Plan:
(Answer the following questions in order to create an action plan to help members of your community who are homeless or hungry.)
6. What do you see others doing about this problem?
7. What other solutions to the problem can you think of?
8. How can our class make a difference for the homeless and the hungry in our community?
9. What individual commitments can we make to help the homeless and hunger in our community?

Literature Resources:
Gettin' through Thursday by Melrose Cooper
For André and his family, it's always a struggle to get through the week until Mom gets her paycheck on Friday. When he makes the honor roll at school on Thursday, though, his family has an extra special celebration. Grades K-2.
Uncle Willie and the Soup Kitchen by Dyanne Disalvo
A young boy learns about hunger and poverty in his community by volunteering with his Uncle Willie at the local soup kitchen. This is a useful introduction to the emergency food network and other local efforts to fight hunger. Grades K-2
A Shelter in my Car by Monica Gunning
After Papa died in Jamaica, Zettie and Mama came to America looking for a better life. They now live in the city in the backseat of their car, while Mama tries to go to school and earn enough money to rent a room for her and Zettie. Grades K-2.
Tight Times by Barbara Hazen
A young boy struggles with the frustration of wanting a dog when his father has lost his job. May be used to stimulate discussion about circumstances that cause people to go hungry. Grades K-2
The Lady in the Box by Anne McGovern
A storybook about two young children who notice a homeless woman in their neighborhood and are inspired to help by volunteering at a local soup kitchen. Grades K-2.
Sidewalk Story by Sharon Bell Mathis
 Lilly Etta is upset when her friend's family is evicted from their apartment and no one seems to care. Her determination to make someone pay attention brings about an extraordinary outcome. This book demonstrates the difference that one committed person can make. Grades 3-5

Hunger, Homelessness and Poverty

Annotated Bibliography

Additional Children's Literature on Homelessness and Hunger

Baker, J. (2004). *Home.* New York, NY: HarperCollins.
Boelts, M. (2007). *Those shoes.* Cambridge, MA: Candlewick Press.
Bunting, E. (1996). *Going home.* New York, NY: HarperCollins Publishers.
Bunting, E. (1996). *Train to somewhere.* New York, NY: Clarion Books.
Bunting, E. (1991). *Fly away home.* New York, NY: Clarion Books.
Carmi, G. (2006). *Circle of friends.* Long Island City, New York, NY: Star Bright Books.
Chin, K. (1997). *Sam and the lucky money.* New York, NY: Lee & Low.
DiSalvo, D. (2001). *A castle on Viola Street.* New York, NY: HarperCollins Publishers.
DiSalvo, D. (1994). *City green.* New York, NY: HarperCollins.
DK in association with UNICEF. (2002). *A life like mine: How children live around the world.* New York, NY: Dorling Kindersley Publishing, Inc.
Dylan, B. (1973/2008). *Forever young.* New York, NY: Atheneum Books.
Hawthorn, L. (1994). *Way home.* New York, NY: Knopf.
Hazen, B. (1983). *Tight times.* New York, NY: Puffin Books.
Hertensten, B. (1995). *Home is where we live: Life at a shelter through a young girl's eyes.* Chicago, IL: Cornerstone Press.
Hoose, P. (1993). *It's our world too! Young people who are making a difference: How they do it—how you can too!* Boston, MA: Joy Street Books.

Khan, R. (2004). *The roses in my carpets.* Markham, ON: Fitzhenry & Whiteside.

Kimmel, E. (2004). *Cactus soup.* New York, NY: Marshall Cavendish.

Kindersley, B. & Kindersley, A. (1995). *Children just like me: A unique celebration of children around the world.* New York, NY: Dorling Kindersley Publishing, Inc..

Lewis, B. (1995). *The kids guide to service projects: Over 500 service ideas for young people who want to make a difference.* Minneapolis, MN: Free Spirit Publishing.

McBrier, P. (2001). *Beatrice's Goat.* New York, NY: Athenium Books.

McGrath, J. (2006). *The Storm: Children of Biloxi, Mississippi remember Hurricane Katrina.* Watertown, MA: Charlesbridge Publishing.

McPhail, D. (2002). *The teddy bear.* New York, NY: Henry Holt & Company.

Milway, K. (2008). *One hen: How one small loan made a big difference.* Toronto, ON: Kids Can Press.

Mortenson, G. (2009). *Listen to the wind: The story of Dr. Greg and three cups of tea.* New York, NY: Dial Books.

Polacco, P. (1999). *I can hear the sun.* New York, NY: Penguin.

Rylant, C. (1992). *An angel for Solomon Singer.* New York, NY: Orchard Books.

Shoveller, H. (2006). *Ryan and Jimmy: And the well in Africa that brought them together.* Toronto,ON: Kids Can Press, Limited.

Smith, D. (2002). *If the world were a village: A book about the world's people.* Toronto, ON: Kids Can Press.

Suvanjieff, I., Engle, D. (2008). *Peacejam: A billion simple acts of peace.* New York, NY: Puffin Books.

Testa, M. (1996). *Someplace to go.* Morton Grove, IL: Albert Whitman & Company.

Tolan, S. (1992). *Sophie and the sidewalk man.* New York, NY: Simon & Schuster

Upjohn, R. (2007). *Lilly and the paper man.* Toronto, ON: Second Story Press.

Williams, V. (1984). *A chair for my mother.* New York, NY: HarperCollins

Wyeth, S. (2002). A piece of heaven. New York, NY: Yearling.

Wyeth, S. (1998). *Something beautiful.* New York, NY: Dragonfly Books.

Wyeth, S. (1998). *Always my dad.* New York, NY: Scholastic.

Youme, (2004). *Selavi, that is life: A Haitian story of hope.* El Paso, TX: Cinco Puntos Press.

Videos for Kids

(Videos available on loan from Church World Service, 1-800-297-1516, ext. 338)

Charlie Cheddar's Choice (13 min)

A friendly mouse, Charlie, introduces youngsters to some basic facts about hunger and some responses. Charlie has a series of dreams that prompt him to read, think, and take action.

Helping the Homeless: One Boy's Crusade (6 min)

The inspiring story of eight year-old Jerry Evans, who took it upon himself to help raise money for a local homeless shelter that was in danger of closing for lack of funds. Illustrates the difference one young person can make when she/he decides to take a stand against hunger and homelessness.

Shooting Back: Photography By Homeless Children (30 min)

Homeless and "at-risk" young people in Washington, DC, take part in photography workshops that give them an opportunity to shoot back. A look at life in the shelters through the eyes of children.

Practical Encounter

Practical Encounter #1

Directions: Indicate whether you agree or disagree with each of the following statements. Use evidence from the chapter to support your responses.

	Agree	Disagree	Evidence from Chapter
Class privilege is strongly embedded within the fabric of American society, including the educational system, so as to maintain the myth of meritocracy.			
Members of mainstream society are taught to view their beliefs, perspectives, and/or ways of life as "the norm.".			
As in the case of their more affluent counterparts, students of poverty are provided equitable opportunities to progress academically.			
America's public schools and neighborhoods today are segregated, much like schools before desegregation and the urban "white flight" migration.			
Our biases/assumptions or lived experiences/ backgrounds often impact how we view the achievement of our students and the expectations we have for them.			
To resolve the educational disparities that exist, more emphasis should be placed on the achievement gap versus the opportunities that students of poverty are afforded or not afforded.			
Viewing students of poverty from a deficit perspective or a perspective that focuses on their deficiencies has become a common practice within schools.			
Closing the achievement gap begins with closing the opportunity gap. This will require that school resources, talent, and funding be allocated toward schools and programs that serve disenfranchised or marginalized groups of students.			
An empathetic stance to educating students will ensure equitable learning outcomes for students of poverty.			
Culturally relevant/teaching pedagogies will hinder progress toward enculturation.			

Practical Encounter #2

Directions: Provide at least 5 bullets in each category that indicates concerns students or schools face and areas of opportunity that teachers and schools should consider in each of the following categories.

Concerns = Problems that schools, teachers, or students are faced with in ensuring equitable learning outcomes

Opportunities = Opportunities that schools, teacher, or students can make use of to ensure equitable learning outcomes.

	Concerns	Opportunities
Learning Styles		
Instruction		
Assessment		
Parental Involvement		

CHAPTER 6

Faithism in the Public School: What Educators Must Know to Avoid Religious Bias

Ilene Allgood, Ed.D.

"There are hundreds of paths up the mountain, all leading to the same place, so it doesn't matter which path you take. The only person wasting time is the one who runs around the mountain, telling everyone that his or her path is wrong."

A Hindu Proverb

Religious Biases: Faithism in the Public School

The Imperative for Religious Education

There is an imperative for educators to develop a knowledge base in religion and religious diversity in the United States, especially for those seeking to teach in this nation's public schools. Public school educators generally are not adequately prepared to handle the multifarious challenges when religion and public schooling intersect in their classrooms. Within the US macroculture an overwhelming influence of Protestant-Christianity exists which is reflected in the society's institutions (including its schools). Consequently, there is a strong potential for the marginalization of religion-minority (non-Christian[1]) and secular students in the public school.

Without a firm grounding in religious education (RE) there is a potential for educators to be unaware of their own religious ignorance and biases. When teachers remain ignorant about their students' religious beliefs, what often results is insensitivity, inequity and marginalization.[2] Unfortunately, inadequately prepared teachers are often inept or unmotivated to teach about religion and to navigate religious issues that invariably enter their classrooms. Intolerance and estrangement are fueled by religious ignorance. At a minimum, this ignorance may lead to a form of religious suppression in the classroom. Well-meaning, yet unprepared teachers can be detrimental to young religious minority students by inadvertently ostracizing them.

Regrettably, teacher education programs, even those with a robust multicultural education emphasis, do not usually include a required component dedicated to this particular diversity. With this premise that many public school educators are not adequately prepared to handle the various, complex challenges that occur when religion and public schooling intersect, curriculum with guiding critical questions, teachers' resources, and case studies designed for preparing teachers in the area of religion and public schooling are provided in this chapter.

---

[1] Even the phrasing *"non-Christian"* – is in itself a depreciating term. For example, "Whites" are usually not referred to as "non-Blacks" in the literature.

[2] E.g. some people allege that Catholics are not Christian.

Critical Questions to Guide the Curriculum

Initially, several overarching critical questions are posed to guide the preservice teachers' learning process: (1) In the United States, a nation which has arguably been built upon a Judeo-Christian[3] moral code and which demonstrates predominantly Christian perspectives,[4] how are people of different faiths and secular worldviews perceived and treated in public schools? (2) When students of minority religions and secularist (nontheist[5]) worldviews have been marginalized (either inadvertently or intentionally) in schools, what are the educators' ethical, legal, and professional responsibilities in rectifying this problematic and inequitable situation? (3) What do educators need to teach (or avoid teaching) regarding religion while keeping the Constitution's First Amendment's religious liberty clauses[6] in mind? Finally, (4) what knowledge and skills must the educator acquire in order to support authentic religious pluralism in their classrooms?

These questions are critical because there are numerous challenges that teachers grapple with in their classrooms regarding the overlapping of religion and public schooling. Educators need to develop a substantial knowledge base about key diverse religious groups in the US. They must also learn to advocate for and protect the religious liberties of their future public school students. They should develop a sense of responsibility in their role to make classrooms comfortable places for students of many religions as well as for those who subscribe to no religion.

What do teachers need to know about religion?

Religious Pluralism and Public Education

Educators must learn about the diverse religious affiliations of the people of this country. For example, a key finding of the recent Pew Study on the Religious Landscape in the US, concluded that "42% of U.S. adults do not currently belong to their childhood faiths" (*Pew Research,* 2014). Millions of people have left the faith or denomination in which they were raised in favor of another religion - or no religion at all. Moreover, the study found that almost 23% of US adults have no religious affiliation whatsoever while just over 70% of the survey's respondents identified Christianity as their faith[7]. These data point out that while the US is diverse in religion, a significant number of people claimed no religious affiliation at all. The majority religious group is comprised of various Christian faiths. While public schools are reflective of our nation's religious diversity, it is the Protestant-Christian majority that has had the most sway over public schooling in this country. Nonetheless, this country was built on a foundational principle of religious pluralism.

Educators must understand and deeply appreciate *authentic* religious pluralism and why it is vital to protect this tenet. Authentic religious pluralism is demonstrated when people have a healthy engagement with their own religious ideology (way of thinking) while at the same time are open to learning about, companionate toward and respectful of others' religious ideologies (Wuthnow, 2007). Another way to look at this concept of authentic religious pluralism is when the teachers' willing engagement with diverse religions correlate minimally with Stage 3 on Banks' (2009) Cultural Typology (Cultural Identity Clarification), but ideally a teacher functioning at Stage 5 (Multiculturalism) would be better adept at authentic/reflective religious education.

Consider how you might work toward achieving authentic religious pluralism in school knowing that attaining a state of authentic religious pluralism has often been thwarted by religious ignorance. *The American*

---

[3] This terminology (Judeo-Christian) is problematic in and of itself because, as Laura Levitt (2009) and many others argue, the phrase overgeneralizes and at the same time discounts intra- and inter-group diversity.

[4] Examples of this phenomenon include: the regular usage of Anno Domini (A.D.), meaning "in the year of our Lord" to describe the Common Era (C.E.); the swearing of oaths upon the King James Bible and the Pledge of Allegiance's 'under God' clause; Sunday being viewed as the collective Sabbath day, and Christmas being treated as a de facto national holiday.

[5] The Secular Coalition for America describes its constituency as nontheistic Americans, including those who describe themselves as "atheist, agnostic humanist, freethinker, skeptic, bright, ignostic, materialist, and naturalist," among others. See: *Secular Coalition for America*, accessed July 1, 2014 http://secular.org/constituency

[6] "Congress shall make no law respecting an establishment of religion or prohibiting the free exercise thereof..."

[7] This figure has dropped 8 percentage points since the previous survey conducted in 2008

Academy of Religion (2010) acknowledges that few teachers have taken religious studies courses before they teach and they enter the classroom illiterate in comparative religions. Religious illiteracy is highly problematic if teachers are to provide a fair and balanced curriculum that includes religious diversity.[8] Moreover, religious illiteracy can fuel prejudice and even antagonism (2010). This can result in inequitable treatment and potential exclusion of students of minority faiths or secular world views in public schools. An excellent book to start on the path of religious literacy would be Stephen Prothero's (2007) *Religious Literacy: What Every American Needs to Know and Doesn't.* (See footnote for suggested journal activity.)[9] Additionally, Richard DiPasquale's (2012) curriculum guide offers examples of a comparative religions course that is being used in high school social studies in the Darien, Connecticut public school system. (*Additional resources for acquiring a knowledge base in Religions in the US are offered at the end of the chapter.)

The Role of Religion in the K-12 Public School

In addition to starting a process of acquiring a basic religious literacy, teachers must learn the role of religion in the public school and their role regarding religion-education[10]. There has been decades of argument and scholarship on this issue. Many scholars have advocated for religious studies to take place in K-12 public schools; however, religions' context and content are debated in the literature. For example, Peggy Levitt suggested that faith groups transcend national borders and they should be seen as multi-centered and integral pieces of the larger global religious landscape (2006). Categories such as "race" and "ethnicity" do not adequately capture religious groups. James Fraser (2000) states that religious studies fit well in the public school curriculum infused within the disciplines of social, global and multicultural studies. When framed as religious pluralism it aligns well with the mission of these disciplines.

Besides the debate about the place of religion in public school, there has also been considerable debate about *how* to incorporate religious studies into public school curricula. Suzanne Rosenblith (2008) contends that a comprehensive education in religion should require an investigation of various religious ideological core tenets (i.e. evaluating the veracity and credibility of specific religious claims made by different religions) (p. 114). Emery Hyslop-Margison and Philip Peterson (2012) challenged this by arguing that religious "truth claims"

---

[8] Religious literacy is as important as racial, ethnic, gender and linguistic competence as foundations needed in teacher preparation and to attain equitable pedagogy.

[9] Activities that encourage learning about religions include providing a reading list and guiding questions to study a minority faith group in this country. A journal activity may be used to identify prior knowledge about the religion and compare it with new information gleaned from the reading. For example, a participant will be asked to choose a faith or a religion with which you yourself do not personally identify. In your journal (prior to researching), identify several key values or tenets of the faith group you selected to write about. After reading the appropriate chapter in Prothero's (2007) *Religious Literacy: What Every American Needs to Know and Doesn't,* compare your initial journal entries with what you learned.

[10] A distinction is made between "religious education" and "religion-education". The former term refers to teaching religious theology, the latter refers to teaching about religions (religious studies).

are neither measurable nor verifiable as Rosenblith suggests. Moreover, Hyslop-Margison and Peterson (2012) assert that attempts to validate religious claims can be disrespectful and may inadvertently feed a potential for conflict among people of diverse faiths or worldviews. Similar to Peterson's and Hyslop-Margison's (2012) position, this author suggests that the *validity* of religious truth claims is outside the scope of public school debate and should not be inculcated in their classrooms. However, teaching about diverse religious groups' history, cultural values and literature are necessary elements of a public school curriculum and are within the spirit of religious freedom and academic inquiry.

The Legal Parameters of Religion in Public Schools

Teachers must consider the legal mandates concerning religion in public schooling, specifically the First Amendment's religious liberty clauses. How should educators treat religion in their classrooms and what should they teach in order to avoid marginalizing minority-faith and nontheistic students? How does one teach about religion while complying with First Amendments' standards? The collective body of Supreme Court decisions indicates that the line between *Religion* and the *State* in public schools is essentially a serpentine wall. To understand the parameters of this wall, the future teacher must know the high court's decisions that established the constraints. Teacher preparation and curriculum should include a thorough discussion of the various legal conflicts regarding religion within the domain of public schools. Several of the recommended resources for teachers provide for this discussion. (See the ADL, 2012 and ACLU, 2013.)

For example, educators must learn that the landmark US Supreme Court ruling in *Lemon v. Kurtzman* (1971) requires that any curriculum employed in a public school pertaining to religion must pass a three-prong litmus test (purpose, effect, entanglement) in order for it to be considered permissible content by First Amendment standards. This Supreme Court ruling requires: (1) The content or activity must have a secular (academic) purpose[11] (i.e., the purpose prong); (2) the public school teacher (in this government capacity) may neither advance nor inhibit religion (i.e., the effect prong); and (3) the teachers'/schools' action must not result in an excessive government entanglement with religion (i.e., the entanglement prong). Simply stated, the law requires that the mission of the public school is to 'teach' not 'preach.' It is also crucial for teachers to avoid making negative value judgments about the validity of others' faiths.

Educators must be prepared to choose resources carefully to comply with *Lemon v. Kurtzman's* guidelines.[12] Their methodology must also conform to the *Lemon* standards. For example, teacher-candidates must understand that over-generalizing or teaching too superficially about any given religious group can lead to incorrect assumptions or faulty comparisons about religious principles or practices.

In addition to landmark Supreme Court rulings, recent examples of the breakdown of Church/State separation are provided (*See Table 1*)[13] to give the educator a sense of the scope of the legal issues one may encounter.[14] It is necessary to also examine actual cases concerning religion and First Amendment issues (ACLU, 2006, 2007, 2013). After a guided discovery and investigation of the laws and litigation surrounding religious liberty, teachers are more likely capable of teaching as religious pluralists (with the caveat that they also acquire the necessary religious literacy).

Safeguarding Religious Pluralism -- a Professional Responsibly

It is critical to learn how to safeguard this fundamental principle in the classroom. Public schools are State (government) institutions that are required to uphold the First Amendment's religious liberty clauses, which forbid government from establishing a national religion and prohibits it from depriving any individual of his/her right to free religious expression. Teachers (as government employees) must adapt to an unfamiliar role in

---

[11] This means the curriculum is not religiously indoctrinating and must have an academic/scholarly purpose.

[12] For further information on what constitutes permissible and impermissible content, see the Anti-Defamation League http://www.adl.org/civil-rights/religious-freedom/ and the American Civil Liberties Union https://www.aclu.org/religion-belief

[13] Supreme Court Cases involving Religion in Schools http://judiciallearningcenter.org/your-1st-amendment-rights/

[14] An example of a case involves the ACLU's objection to a Nebraska public school district's policy barring students from wearing rosaries (See Miller, 2011).

which they are required to give their students' religious freedom a higher priority than their own religious expression. It is understandable that teachers may be resistant in this unaccustomed role, so substantial discussions (and case studies) about religious pluralism and school law help in the professional development of teachers.

Moreover, even a teacher's classroom management style and choice of curricular resources may be influenced by a one's personal religious orientation (White, 2010). In the public school, teachers' confusion and ignorance may relegate students of minority faiths to the status of "outsiders," leaving them vulnerable and making them feel ostracized from the mainstream.[15] For example, Arab-Muslim students who grow up in a macroculture which disregards their cultural identities find that messages they learn in school often conflict with the values and traditions they learn at home (Wingfield & Karaman, 2001). In addition to this disconnect, Muslim students report that their peers frequently hold negative and inaccurate preconceptions about Islam which lead to deeply hurtful experiences (p. 134). In some cases, students feel compelled to hide their religious affiliations from others to avoid negativity or devaluation. In extreme cases, older students might rebel against or even sever ties with the faiths of their parents and grandparents. If religious intolerance presents itself and isn't dealt with in a professional manner, it can do severe damage to students' interpersonal relationships and self-esteem. For instance, a recent ADL poll concluded that 26% of Americans currently believe that "Jews were responsible for the death of Christ" (*Anti-Defamation League*, ADL, 2013, p. 19). This historically catastrophic accusation and other beliefs of this nature (i.e. Jews, Mormons, and Muslims are doomed to hell) sometimes cause students to say cruel things to other students (Tashman, 2011). It is both ethical and imperative that educators understand what is at stake and how to behave when negative religious messages permeate the classroom. Moreover, teachers should be cautious to never obstruct their students' religious beliefs and identities. A powerful method to reinforce these professional responsibilities and practice the skills of professional behavior are through a process involving case study analysis. A sample case study with processing questions is provided in the Practical Encounters section.

Educational Equity in Schools

Teachers in public schools have a moral and legal obligation to defend their students' religious identities and sensibilities in the same way that they would protect their racial, ethnic and linguistic identities.

It is important to note that educational inequity can be worsened by the macroculture itself, when the religious majority's tenets and values unilaterally are communicated and promoted through the schools, while non-Christian religions' tenets are generally non-existent. In the case of students with minority faiths, Christian messages may conflict with their own (and their families') religious teachings. (E.g. Monotheism is truth but polytheism is not.) Inadvertently, students may perceive the dominant group's religious perspectives as "normal" while other groups' religious beliefs (theologies) are regarded as outside the norm and thus misguided. Minority religious views are often labeled as "strange or false." Even worse, an ignorant person may label a religion and its adherents as dangerous (e.g., labeling Islam a terrorist religion) or despicable (e.g., anti-Semitism). These attitudes cast a shroud of 'otherness' on minority-faith students and their families that isolates them from the 'insiders.' For example an adult Jewish individual recounts that as a child, she distinctly remembered looks of pity from her teachers and classmates when she would inform them that she didn't celebrate Christmas and often heard condescending comments aimed at her mother for *depriving* her of Santa Claus. Another example of inter-religious misunderstanding occurring is when, for example, a Jewish person is asked to confirm what Jews believe (or don't believe) about Jesus. The problem is not the curiosity behind the question, but rather the nature of the question itself which seeks to correlate concepts that are not equivalent. The question thwarts understanding Judaism in its own terms since it has a dichotomizing consequence; i.e. one is left with trying to comprehend Jewish belief by relating it to how it is *not* Christian belief.

---

[15] Case studies are provided that show how Muslim and Jewish students may be excluded based on religious observances and dietary restrictions. For example, a teacher schedules a pizza-party during the month of Ramadan, a solemn Islamic holiday which excludes Muslim students from this communal class activity. In a similar case, a pizza party is scheduled in the Spring during Passover. This would alienate Jewish students who observe that holiday by refraining from eating leavened products such as bread.

Other Considerations for Teachers

It is vital that teachers understand the potential for damaging effects of mishandling religion in their classrooms. Moreover, it is helpful that teachers acquire an understanding of the concept of prejudice as it relates to *faithism*[16]. Gordon Allport, in his classic work on the nature of prejudice (1979) explains prejudice as the rendering of a pre-informed judgment about 'others' without engaging in any critical inquiry of the subject(s). Taking this a step further -- what alleviates prejudice is a critical analysis of the "others' (that includes viewing 'the others' from their own perspectives) thus broadening and deepening the understanding of the "other'. This is of the utmost significance to an educator. Faithism on the other hand, can be understood as a type of discrimination or diminution towards a person or group of people based on their religion or belief system. Persons engaging in faithism act as though their own faith is the exclusive, absolute truth while other faiths are misguided. When faithism and prejudice occur in the classroom, the teacher's ability to provide equitable educational opportunities is compromised. This is not to say that teachers who believe their faith is the absolute truth will not perform fairly; however, they must exhibit professional skills to make sure students of other faiths are dealt with equitably.

Methodology to Address Religious Conflicts in the Classroom

Utilizing a case studies method, teacher-candidates are asked to identify underlying problems posed in hypothetical scenarios, discuss the issues, and arrive at solutions to the problem(s). The cases describe actual classroom situations that arise, which the teacher must navigate. Educators must consider not only the legal parameters, but also the pedagogical approaches to creating a religiously pluralist climate. In other words, what do they need to teach?

Deciding on the appropriate course of action as the Christmas season approaches is a major quandary for most teachers (especially those in elementary schools) and is widely misunderstood by virtually all stakeholders. This confusion that plagues teachers has been dubbed the 'December Dilemma' (ADL, 2012). Well-intentioned teachers are frequently left in an uncomfortable predicament regarding the winter holidays. For example, a Jewish parent may volunteer to help out a teacher by conducting a Hanukah[17] lesson (ostensibly to prevent his/her own children from feeling excluded by Christmas festivities). This can become problematic, however, for several reasons. Parents are often not cognizant of school law and policy and as a result may inadvertently provide inadequate lessons. Messages that tokenize a religious holiday such as Hanukah[18] are not only marginalizing, but frequently violate the First Amendment's prohibitions. At a minimum, the *teacher* in this case should be cognizant of other significant Jewish (and other faiths') holidays and provide a fair balance of instruction that permeates the other seasons as well as winter.

The academic goal in this example would be for students to learn about the significant holidays of different cultural groups in order to broaden and deepen the scope of their knowledge base. Academic instruction *about* religion would entail a diversity of non-secular groups being represented in the curriculum and content infused at appropriate times. For example, lessons on Ramadan, Diwali, Bodhi Day, or Passover, in proximity to when they *actually* occur during the school year, would be included in an appropriate/balanced curriculum in certain grades and subjects. Teachers need to be aware that opting out (i.e., ignoring religion entirely) would not necessarily represent fair, balanced instruction (as *Lemon v. Kurtzman* requires) because that approach permits the dominant Christological ideology of the macroculture to continue influencing, while stifling all others. A dearth or absence of instruction about minority religions is tantamount to ignoring certain students.

---

[16] Faithism like other "isms" implies that one faith group sees itself as superior or as more important than other faith groups. Usually people of the majority faith group enjoy faith-privilege as well.

[17] It is interesting to note that the English spelling of the Jewish holiday is often inconsistent. This is because the name of the holiday is a Hebrew word that means "dedication". The various spellings we see in English (Chanukah, Hanukah, etc.) attempt to transliterate the initial Hebrew letter which does not have a corresponding English sound/letter.

[18] E.g. curriculum that includes content on Hanukah (a festival), but doesn't include Rosh Hashana, Yom Kippur, or Passover is problematic because it excludes these major Jewish holidays. The content in this case would be incomplete and slanted. Moreover, to teach that Hanukah is tantamount to a Jewish Christmas is also problematic since this is inaccurate.

Brian A Jackson / Shutterstock.com

Educators are required to act as advocates and defenders of students' religious freedom. In doing so, they come to recognize the distinction between teaching ***about*** religion to educate and teaching *of* religion to indoctrinate. This position has been argued eloquently by Sinensky and Samulon et al. (2002) and is an important distinction for educators to internalize, master and practice.[19]

Assessment

Assessing the educator's readiness to teach *about* religion and religious diversity in general entails the ability to analyze critical questions in a variety of ways.[20] One way to reflect is by individual journaling or essay-writing. Another effective means of exploring the critical questions and issues is in small discussion groups wherein case studies and reflections are processed and ultimately concussions (best practices) are presented to the class. The case studies discussions provide evidence of learning and practical application of the principles taught. A culminating activity that demonstrates synthesis and application of the concepts involves creating an *original* case study/scenario illustrating an issue or aspect of religion in a public school venue. By including processing questions that teachers would need to ask themselves in order to ensure compliance with the Lemon decision and other Supreme Court rulings demonstrates critical thinking skills. These original cases also provide teaching and learning opportunities when they are presented and moderated (by the author of the case) and

[19] When examining the myriad ways that religion and public education interconnect, there is potential for problems on religious, pedagogical, and legal grounds. Teachers need guidance on issues including: prayer, holidays, accommodations, displays/symbols, dress codes, dietary restrictions, and teachers' own religious expression. Acquiring this information is achieved through required readings, guided discussions and personal reflection. Resources for teachers to acquire this understanding are provided herein.

[20] Critical questions educators must consider: Explain in your own words the intent and purpose of the First Amendment's religious liberty clauses and how they preserve religious liberty in schools. What makes it challenging for teachers in public schools to teach about religion? Explain and provide examples of faithism. How are students influenced by faithism? What is the dynamic between religion and teaching and why is it important for teachers to understand this dynamic? Identify examples of overt, hidden, or null curriculum vis-à-vis religion and show how people of minority faiths (and secularists) are perceived and treated in public schools. How are students affected by null and hidden curriculum? How might you implement religious content in your classroom? What content would you need to know in order to facilitate religion-based concepts in the curriculum? Identify the gaps in your own knowledge-base and create a plan to close those gaps.

then discussed in larger groups. During any processing activity it is important to ask participants to identify the underlying issues presented in the case and provide examples of the steps a teacher might take in addressing the dilemma.

Reactions to the religious diversity component and case study method have been significantly positive. A typical comment by students having taken a multicultural course with a religious diversity unit follows: *"I now see how complicated the concept of religion as it applies to teaching is and why it is so important for teachers to learn about it. I admit – I'm overwhelmed, but the information I learned about religion opened my eyes. It was difficult at first but the case studies were great in helping me understand how to treat religion in my (future) classes. I never learned anything like this in other classes."*

It is important to reiterate that *all* teachers including those with unwavering religious beliefs need to acquire knowledge and skills to protect the religious liberty of their students.

Conclusion

It is essential for educators to be prepared to navigate religion in schools and deal with the challenges that arise. How might a teacher who recognizes that certain students are being marginalized or ostracized due to religion react? How might the educator include and validate those who hold only secular (not religious) viewpoints as well as those with minority faith perspectives? How might teachers provide a balanced curriculum that meets the standards of religious neutrality? How are teachers to implement religious concepts and still comply with First Amendment requirements? If not done correctly, what are the consequences?

Teachers must learn to appreciate that religious diversity and liberty are foundational tenets of this nation and that religion is exceedingly significant in most cultural/ethnic groups. Through religious studies, they develop a deep understanding of what divergent religious viewpoints are, not to validate their truth claims, but instead to *contrast* and *compare* them. This knowledge would avoid over-generalization and simplistic conceptualizations that might lead to marginalization of minority-faith students. Learning about diverse faith-groups entails acquiring a critical understanding of a group's deepest values in its own terms without making premature judgments as to their rightfulness, authenticity, or legitimacy.[21]

The best teachers are equipped with a knowledge base of diverse religions and are committed to building a classroom climate that is receptive and respectful beyond mere tolerance, while steadfastly maintaining religious neutrality. These teachers will resolutely advocate for, and protect, the religious liberties of all students in their charge. This display of professionalism, while demanding at times, is essential in providing an equitable educational experience for diverse students. Ultimately, it is an ethical issue that requires commitment and vigilance.

While opposition to religion in public schools has been fierce at times, Warren Nord (2011) along with Charles Haynes (1998) contend that teaching about our nation's religions in public schools is not a violation of the First Amendment to the Constitution. Instead, not teaching about religion is a violation of the public trust. There is an imperative to engage in a reflective discourse on these issues.

If schooling is to be a remedy for ignorance (and its corollary, intolerance), then what emerges is an imperative for public school educators to teach about our nation's religiously diverse people in an academic and profound way in order to mitigate the ramifications of prejudice and discrimination based on religion. There is evidence that religion has an effect on intergroup social contact/distancing of students and can be a positive influence in Peace Education (Yablona, 2010). Multiculturalism in US public schools should promote authentic religious pluralism.

Liberty, equality, and justice are the prime components of our national doctrine. When the majority of us unflinchingly internalize what these core values mean and how to work *toward that more perfect union* together, "we the people" will be better and stronger because we will be living our creed. Education holds the key to the success of this mission. As educators, when we teach others how to appreciate and safeguard our fundamental principles (and help them abandon the ignorance that destroys our national pride), we are brightening our collective future.

---

[21] DiPasquale, R. 2012. Comparative world religions curriculum guide.
http://www.darienps.org/uploaded/content/district/departments/curriculum/social-studies/curriculum_socialstudies_comparative-world-religion.pdf

References

Allport, G. (1979). *The nature of prejudice*. Cambridge, MA: Addison Wesley.

American Academy of Religion. (2010, April). Guidelines for teaching about religion in k-12 public schools in the United States. Accessed July 7, 2014. https://www.aarweb.org/sites/default/files/pdfs/Publications/epublications/AARK-12CurriculumGuidelines.pdf.

American Civil Liberties Union (ACLU). (2006, June 5). ACLU of New Jersey defends second-grader's right to sing religious song. Accessed August 23, 2016. https://www.aclu.org/religion-belief/aclu-new-jersey-defends-second-graders-right-sing-religious-song.

American Civil Liberties Union (ACLU). (2007, March 7). ACLU of New Jersey sues Newark Public Schools for holding graduation in church. Accessed August 23, 2016. https://www.aclu.org/religion-belief/aclu-new-jersey-sues-newark-public-schools-holding-graduation-church (accessed August 23, 2015)

American Civil Liberties Union (ACLU). (2013). Religion and belief. Accessed August 23, 2016. https://www.aclu.org/religion-belief (accessed August 23, 2015)

Anti-Defamation League. (2012). Religion in the public schools: Guidelines for a growing and changing phenomenon for K-12. New York: Anti-Defamation League. Accessed August 23, 2016. http://www.adl.org/assets/pdf/civil-rights/religiousfreedom/rips/ReligPubSchs-PDF.pdf

Anti-Defamation League. (2013, October 28). ADL poll: Anti-Semitic attitudes in America decline 3 percent but deep-seated anti-Semitic beliefs linger. Accessed August 23, 2016. http://www.adl.org/press-center/press-releases/anti-semitism-usa/adl-poll-anti-semitic-attitudes-america-decline-3-percent.html#.U48nfHJdXh4

Anti-Defamation League. (2013, June 5). ADL welcomes FBI proposal to separately report hate crimes directed against Sikhs, Arabs, and Hindus. Accessed August 23, 2016. http://www.adl.org/press-center/press-releases/hate-crimes/adl-welcomes-fbi-proposal-to-separately-report-hate-crimes-against-sikhs.html#.U480KnJdXh4

DiPasquale, R. (2012). *Comparative world religions curriculum guide*. Accessed December 20, 2013. http://www.darienps.org/uploaded/content/district/departments/curriculum/social-studies/curriculum_socialstudies_comparative-world-religion.pdf

Fraser, J. (2000). *Between church and state: Religion and public education in a multicultural America*. New York, NY: St. Martin's Griffin.

Hyslop-Margison, E. & P. Peterson. (2012). An exchange on evaluating religious claims in public schools. Epistemic evaluation of religious claims in public schools: A response to Suzanne Rosenblith. *Religion & Education, 39* (March), 3-12.

Lemon v. Kurtzman. 1971. 403 U.S. 602.

Levitt, L. (2009). Interrogating the Judeo-Christian tradition: Will Herberg's construction of American religion, religious pluralism, and the problem of inclusion. In S. J. Stein (Ed.). *The Cambridge history of religions in America. Cambridge histories online* (vol. 3) (pp. 283-307). Cambridge: United Kingdom, Cambridge University Press. Accessed July 7, 2015. http://dx.doi.org/10.1017/CHOL9780521871082.015.

Levitt, P. (2006). God needs no passport: Trying to define the new boundaries of belonging. *Harvard Divinity Bulletin, 34*(3). Accessed July 7, 2015. http://www.hds.harvard.edu/news-events/harvard-divinity-bulletin/articles/god-needs-no-passport.

Miller, A. (2011, Ocotber 3). That gang of nuns looks pretty dangerous. American Civil Liberties Union of Nebraska. Accessed July 7, 2014. http://www.aclunebraska.org/index.php/religious-liberty/127-that-gang-of-nuns-looks-pretty-dangerous.

Nord, W. A. (2011). Does God make a difference? Taking religion seriously in our schools and universities: An excerpt. *Religion and Education, 38*(1), 3-23.

Nord, W. & C. Haynes. (1998). *Taking religion seriously across the curriculum*. Alexandria, VA. Association for Supervision and Curriculum Development.

Peterson, P. & E. Hyslop-Margison. (2012). Epistemology or self-delusion? A final word on evaluating religious truth claims. *Religion and Education, 39*, 24-27.

Pew Research Religion in Public Life Project. (2014, May). America's changing religious landscape. Accessed August 23, 2016. http://www.pewforum.org/2015/05/12/americas-changing-religious-landscape/pr_15-05-12_rls-00/.

Pew Research Religion in Public Life Project. (2008, June). Religious landscape survey. http://www.pewforum.org/2008/06/01/u-s-religious-landscape-survey-religious-beliefs-and-practices/.

Prothero, Stephen. (2007). Religious literacy: What every american needs to know and doesn't. New York, NY: HarperCollins

Rosenblith, S. (2008). Beyond coexistence: Toward a more reflective religious pluralism. *Theory and Research in Education, 6, 107-21.*

Secular Coalition for America. Our Constituency. Accessed Dec. 20, 2013, http://secular.org/.

Sinensky, J., Samulon, D., Stein, K. & Perl, J. (2002, July). *Religion in the public schools: A primer for students, parents, teachers, and school administrators*. New York, NY: The American Jewish Committee (AJC).

Tashman, B. (2011, October 8). Jeffress: Jews, Mormons, Muslims and gays are going to hell. People for the American Way -- Right Wing Watch. Accessed July 7, 2014. http://www.rightwingwatch.org/content/jeffress-jews-mormons-muslims-and-gays-are-going-hell#.

White, K. (2010, March 9). Asking sacred questions: Understanding religion's impact on teacher belief and action. *Religion and Education, 37*(1), 40-59. Accessed July 7, 2014. DOI: 10.1080/15507390903559103.

Wingfield, M. & B. Karaman. (2001). Arab stereotypes and American educators. Accessed July 7, 2014. https://www.tanenbaum.org/sites/default/files/arab_stereotypes.pdf.

Wuthnow, R. (2007). America and the challenges of religious diversity. New Jersey, NJ: Princeton University Press.

Yablona, Y. B. 2010. Religion as a basis for dialogue in peace education programs. *Cambridge Journal of Education, 40*(4), 341-351. Accessed July 7, 2014. DOI:10.1080/0305764X.2010.526590.

Appendix 1:

Recommended Resources for Teachers

American Civil Liberties Union (ACLU). (2013). Religion and belief. Accessed August 23, 2016. https://www.aclu.org/religion-belief

Anti-Defamation League. (2012). *Religion in the public schools: Guidelines for a growing and changing phenomenon for K-12.* New York, NY: Anti-Defamation League. Accessed August 23, 2016. http://www.adl.org/assets/pdf/civil-rights/religiousfreedom/rips/ReligPubSchs-PDF.pdf

Anti-Defamation League. (n.d.). Religion in the public schools: Guidelines for growing changing phenomenon for (K-12). Retrieved from http://www.adl.org/civil-rights/religious freedom

Bordelon, Janet E. (2012, Feb). "Teaching about religions: A democratic approach for public schools" by Emile Lester [Book review]. *Religion & Education, 39,* 109-111. doi: 590 10.1080/15507394.2012.648592

DiPasquale , R. (2012). *Example of comparative religions curriculum at the high school level: Comparative world religions for the Darien Pub - 595 Public Schools in Connecticut in 2012.* Retrieved from http://www.darienps.org/uploaded/content/district/departments/curriculum/social-studies/curriculum_socialstudies_comparative-world-religion.pdf

Fisher, M.P. (Ed.). (2011). Living religions. New York, NY: Prentice Hall.

The American Academy of Religion. (2010). Guidelines for teaching about religion in K-12 Public Schools in the United States. Religion in the schools 600 task force. Retrieved from https://www.aarweb.org/sites/default/files/pdfs/Publications/epublications/AARK-12CurriculumGuidelines.pdf

Judicial Learning Center. (n.d.). First amendment rights. Accessed May 1, 2010 from http://judiciallearningcenter.org/your-1st-amendment-rights/ (accessed May 1, 2016)

Lester, E. (2011). Teaching about religions: A democratic approach for public schools. Ann Arbor, MI: University of Michigan Press.

Prothero, S. (2007). Religious literacy: What every american needs to know and doesn't. New York, NY: HarperCollins.

Tanenbaum Center for Interrigious Understanding. (2014). Combatting religious prejudice. Retrieved from https://www.tanenbaum.org/resources

Tannenbaum. (2012). Religion in my neighborhood: Teaching curiosity and respect about religious differences. Retrieved from https://tanenbaum.org/programs/education/curricula_for_educators/religions-in-my-neighborhood/

National Council for the Social Studies, Religion in Schools Committee. (1998). Position statement. Retrieved from http://www.ncss.org/positions/religion

In an atmosphere that has been poisoned by bigotry and hatred towards Muslims, it is difficult to envision a classroom, a school, or a teacher that has not been impacted by the stereotypes in the media. When asked what a teacher should know about Muslims, especially schoolchildren, it is simple to respond. Know that a Muslim child is no different than any other child you will encounter and all that is required is that they be treated kindly and fairly. As a parent and as an educator, I feel afraid for our children, not just Muslim children but all of our children. Racism, bigotry, hatred, and violence do not only impact one group or the oppressed group; this downward spiral of divisiveness impacts everyone and leads us towards a more destructive path. As educators then, we have a responsibility to be the power that moves the mind. But in order for this to happen we must be open to learn and interact with groups of people who are different and whose lives are foreign to us.

How do some Americans perceive Muslims/Islam?

According to Moore (2015), a recent survey of 1000 adults in the U.S. shows that 55% of Americans have an unfavorable view of Muslims/Islam. What was more disheartening than the numbers was reading the comments posted at the bottom of the article. The level of hate and animosity and at times vulgarity, made me feel sick. If we as adults have a difficult time dealing with what people say about us, how will Muslim children be able to survive this onslaught of negative comments and the "war on Islam". Moore (2015) presents statistics to put things into perspective about what Muslims face.

1. When over 3,000 Americans were polled by the *Pew Research Center* in 2014, Muslims scored a 40 on a scale that measured the "feeling" about a particular faith. The scale: 0 to 100 coldest to warmest.
2. 28% of respondents say they have a somewhat unfavorable opinion of Islam, while 27% say very unfavorable and 25% are unsure.
3. Only about 20% of respondents have a favorable opinion about Muslims.
4. 74% say they have never worked with anyone who is Muslim.
5. 68% say they do not happen to have any friends who are Muslim.
6. 87% have never been inside a mosque. (Moore, 2015)

It is because of this unfamiliarity with Muslims that allows the media, politicians, and hate groups to instill in the minds and hearts of people a mistrust of Muslims as the "other". According to UC Berkley's *Islamphobia Documentation and Research Project (2015)*, "Muslims have been transformed into a demonized and feared global "other," subjected to legal, social, and political discrimination. Newspaper articles, television shows, books, popular movies, political debates, and cultural conflicts over immigration and security produce ample evidence of the stigmatization of Islam within dominant culture." The good news is that if unfamiliarity is in large part the problem, then education is the solution.

What should you know about Islam?

1. "Islam" means "surrender" or "submission". "Salam" (which means "peace") is the root word of "Islam". In a religious context the word "Islam" means "the surrendering of one's will (without compulsion) to the true will of God in an effort to achieve peace". Muslim is "anyone who surrenders themselves to the will of God."
2. Islam is not a new religion; it traces its roots through Prophet Abraham and back to the first humans, Adam and Eve. Nearly a quarter of the world's population is Muslim. But while Islam is currently the world's second-largest religion (after Christianity), it is the fastest-growing major religion.
3. There are five pillars of practice in Islam and six articles of faith in Islam-the basic beliefs that one must have in order to be considered a true Muslim (see table below).

Five Pillars of Islam	Six Articles of Faith
1. Declaration of Faith-that there is only One God and Muhammad is His messenger	1. Belief in the oneness of God
2. Prayer-Praying five times a day within prescribed times ranging from dawn to night time.	2. Belief in all His Prophets; including Adam, Noah, Moses, Abraham, Isaac, Jesus, and Muhammad (plus many others)
3. Charity (tax)- required giving of customary 2.5% of wealth	3. Belief in His Books as revealed to Moses, David, Jesus, and Muhammad;
4. Fasting- abstaining from eating, drinking, and sexual relations from sunrise to sunset during the month of Rama	4. Belief in Angels
5. Pilgrimage to Mecca-an annual pilgrimage to Mecca is required at least once in a lifetime if one is able financially and physically (Kaba-the first house of worship built by Abraham is located in Mecca)	5. Belief in the Day of Judgment and the Hereafter
	6. Belief in Destiny

4. "Allah" is an Arabic word that means "God." Arab Christians call God "Allah" and the word "Allah" (in Arabic script) appears on the walls of many Arab churches and on the pages of Arabic Bibles.
5. Quran is the holy book of Islam and is the direct revelation to the Prophet Muhammad through the Angel Gabriel.
6. Islam granted women rights long before any Western society. Islam gave women rights to inherit, to be educated, to own property, and to be treated justly and equitably. Among the many teachings of Muhammad (PBUH) that protected the rights and dignity of women is his saying, "...the best among you are those who treat their wives well."
7. The hijab or the head covering for Muslim women is a fulfillment of a decree by God for righteous women, as has been a part of history for women, i.e. Mother Teresa.
8. Only 20% of the world's 1.6 billion Muslim population is Arab. Muslims are from all racial and ethnic backgrounds. Indonesia, with over 200 million Muslims, is the largest Muslim country. The Muslim population in the United States is about 3.3 million. This number will double by 2050 and Islam will be the second largest religion in the US by 2040 (Mohamed, 2016).
9. Killing innocent people is forbidden in Islam. An act of aggression against unarmed civilians is unacceptable. The Quran states in Chapter 5:32 "whoever kills a soul unless for a soul or for corruption [done] in the land – it is as if he had slain mankind entirely. And whoever saves one – it is as if he had saved mankind entirely." Any individual or group committing acts of aggression or killing against civilians are acting in contradiction to the tenets of Islam.

What now, for Muslim students?

Our children are bombarded with negative stereotypes, news about war and terror, and a world around them that says everything about Islam and being Muslim is bad. Parents protest the content about Islam in World history books and an entire school district in Augusta County, Virginia was shut down for a day when a teacher gave an assignment on Arabic calligraphy. This level of paranoia fueled by the media has led to a struggle for Muslims in the US.

"Last year, CAIR-Florida documented a 500 percent increase in anti-Muslim hate incidents in Florida -- from threats to burn down mosques and kill Muslim children to physical assaults on immigrants and gunfire and vandalism targeting Muslim homes or places of worship" (Shibley, 2015).

It will require a force of teachers, who are well armed with knowledge, understanding, and compassion to dispel the myths, misconceptions, and shear hate that has been perpetrated against Muslims in recent years. Students must be taught to challenge these myths and misconceptions that have become a part of the fabric of what we think we know about Muslims and the generalizations or stereotypes that continually haunt many Muslims and that do not speak to who they are at the core.

For more information or resources on Islam, visit the following websites:

- Discover Islam - www.discoverislam.com
- Why Islam - www.whyislam.org
- Muslim Beliefs - http://www.pbs.org/wgbh/pages/frontline/teach/muslims/beliefs.html

Works Cited

Center for Race and Gender. (2015). *Islamophobia research and documentation project.* Berkley, CA: University of California.
Islam101.com. (n.d.) Islamic theology. Retrieved from http://www.islam101.com/theology/
Lipka, M. (2015). *Muslims and Islam: Key findings in the U.S and around the world.* New York, NY: Pew Research Center.
Moore, P. (2015, March 9) Poll results: Islam. YouGov: What the world thinks. *Huffington Post.* Retrieved from https://today.yougov.com/news/2015/03/09/poll-results-islam/
Mohamed, B. (2016). *A new estimate of the US Muslim population.* New York, NY: Pew Research Center.
Shibly, H. (2016, April 27). Letter to the Editor prepared for Bradenton Herald: False portrayal of Islam sows seeds of hate, violence. *Council of American-Islamic Relations, Florida.* Retrieved from https://www.cairflorida.org/newsroom/news/91-editorial/234-false-portrayal-of-islam-sows-seeds-of-hate-violence.html

Practical Encounter

Practical Encounters by Ilene Allgood

Case studies are an excellent way for preservice educators to practice applying school case law in actual and possible scenarios that may occur in a public school setting. Case studies are best processed in small group discussions and then solutions and best practices shared with the class. Examples of case studies along with processing questions about a common dilemma appear below.

Case Study #1:

It is the last full week of school before spring break begins. Among other things, you have scheduled for your 4th grade class this week are an important science lesson on Wednesday and a science test on Thursday. On Friday you have planned an Easter egg hunt in the morning and a class pizza party for lunch in the afternoon. Your only Jewish student, Joe, reminds you on Monday that he is going to be absent from school on Wednesday and Thursday of this week because it is Passover. (His parents provided a note at the beginning of the school year about his absences for Jewish holidays.) He mentions that he will not be attending a synagogue service at all during the eight-day holiday. Joe also tells you that he and his parents are upset about the party that you planned for Friday. A couple of students overhear this conversation and complain to you that it's not fair that Joe gets to "play hooky" and gets special treatment because he's Jewish. They are also mad at Joe for complaining about the Friday activities. To make matters worse, Joseph, who wears a yarmulke to school (a head covering worn by observant Jewish males) is also teased for wearing a "beanie" to school. There is a strict dress code policy in the school that does not allow hats to be worn in school.

Questions:

1. Applying what you have learned, explain how you (as the teacher) would react in this situation above.

2. How would you handle Joe's absences from school and the exam?
   a. Is it okay that he is not going to synagogue?
   b. What about his head covering and the school dress code policy?

3. Why specifically is Joe upset about the Friday activities?

4. What do you know about the dietary restrictions associated with this holiday?

5. How do the First Amendment's religious liberty clauses apply in this case?

Case Study #2:

It was three weeks before Christmas and Ms. Jones decided to have her 5th grade students make Christmas stockings. She showed her excited students the sample stocking and told them that they would each make one after lunch. As the students lined up, she noticed that both Manuela and Sara were upset. She asked them what the problem was. Manuela responded, "I'm a Jehovah's Witness and I'm not allowed to make Christmas stockings but I don't want the other kids to make fun of me." Sara didn't say a word. The next day Sara's mother came in and complained that the teacher was insensitive to her religion.

Questions:
1. What are the underlying issues/problems in this case?

2. What is the teacher's responsibility in this situation?

3. What needs to be taught and how?

4. What case law applies in this case?

Case Study #3:

Angela and her family are devout members of a local African Methodist Episcopal Church. Angela tried out for and was given a major role in a middle school play. Miss Shepherd, the director/drama teacher scheduled Wednesday night for the final dress rehearsal. The Wednesday rehearsal conflicted with Angela's evening bible study and worship service and she told Miss Shepherd this. Miss Shepherd asked Angela to see if her parents would let her skip church for the one night and allow her to come to the rehearsal. The next day, Angela told Miss Shepherd that she was sorry but she'd have to go to the prayer service and couldn't come to the rehearsal. Miss Shepherd said "that's too bad" but she would have an understudy do Angela's part for the dress rehearsal. A few days later Angela's mother confronts Miss Shepherd for being insensitive to their religion.

Questions:
1. What are the underlying issues in this case?

2. Was the teacher, Miss Shepherd insensitive to the family's religion?

3. What is the reason that Angela's mother is upset with the teacher? Explain.

4. What is the best way for the teacher Miss Shepherd to handle the parent's complaint?

Cases 2 & 3 adapted from the Anti-Defamation League. 2012. *Religion in the public schools: Guidelines for a growing and changing phenomenon for K-12*. (See: http://www.adl.org/assets/pdf/civil-rights/religiousfreedom /rips/ReligPubSchs-PDF.pdf)

CHAPTER 7

It's Never Too Early: The (In)Visibility and Importance of an LGBTQ Inclusive Curriculum in Elementary Schools

Dominic Grasso

Introduction

One goal of multicultural education is to ensure that *all* students, including students of diverse backgrounds receive culturally relevant instruction, which in turn will help students develop positive concepts about themselves as well as improve their academic achievement. While there has been a push for multicultural education to create classrooms that provide equitable learning experiences for *all* students, there are still groups that are marginalized, silenced, or just simply "left out." Despite seeing increases in the inclusion of Native American, African American, Hispanic American, Asian American and religious relevant themes within curriculum in both schools and college level teacher preparation programs, one topic that is still significantly left out of multicultural education discourse is sexual orientation.

This chapter will consist of the following:

1. Reasoning and rationale on why sexual orientation should be examined and included within multicultural education classrooms.
2. An examination of what the current school climate is like for students or families who may identify as LGBTQ (Lesbian, Gay, Bisexual, Transgender, and Queer/Questioning).
3. Suggestions and ideas on how to successfully integrate curricula that highlights gay, lesbian, and transgender themes into your own classroom.

Sexual Orientation in Multicultural Education: Why?

When asked about the inclusion of LGBTQ themes in their classroom, many educators, especially those teaching at the elementary level, immediately question why that is relevant to students. Before exploring researched-based arguments that justify the inclusion of LGBTQ issues in the mainstream curriculum, I will begin with a personal account that has deepened my passion on this topic.

I have been teaching at the elementary level for seven years now, and have experience teaching grades 1–5. Throughout my years of teaching, I have heard *many* students use anti-gay terms when referring to something or someone they did not like. None of these situations registered quite as deeply with me as this most recent incident.

It was approximately 7:45 a.m. and I was preparing my classroom materials for the day ahead. Students were starting to file down the hallway after eating breakfast in the cafeteria. I was writing on my whiteboard when all of a sudden, I heard the door to my classroom open, and saw a familiar 5th grade student poke his head in. He looked at me, and I looked at him, knowing that he wasn't supposed to be in my room at this current time. Before I could open my mouth to direct him to go to his homeroom class, he looked at me, shouted "faggot," began laughing, closed the door, and proceeded to march merrily down the hallway to his class.

I cannot tell you what made me angrier, the fact that I had just been degradingly insulted by a fifth grader, the fact that he laughed about using the word "faggot," or the fact that I didn't feel 100% comfortable bringing up the issue of t sexuality and the word "faggot" to my administration. Although I have only had experience teaching at low-socioeconomic, high minority schools, I believe that teachers, at all schools, hear students use anti-gay remarks. I also believe that many teachers, like me, are at a loss for words the moment it happens.

In the 1990's, James Sears, one of the leading scholars in the field of queer theory, proposed the radical idea of "queering" the elementary curriculum. At the time, his reasoning behind it was simple: kids are not as innocent when it comes to issues of gender and sexuality as most adults frequently believe them to be. This leads to the first reason that LGBTQ themes and issues should be addressed as part of a well-balanced multicultural curriculum. "Childhood innocence is a veneer that we as adults impress onto children, enabling us to deny desire comfortably and silence sexuality" (Sears, 1998 p. 9).

Assumptions today about children not being aware of gender or sexuality are outdated. We are living in an age when LGBTQ issues (Pulse Nightclub shooting, Supreme Court ruling on Gay Marriage, North Carolina Bathroom Bill) and people (Michael Sam, Caitlyn Jenner, Anderson Cooper) are constantly seen on TV, written about in magazines, and discussed on the radio. Furthermore, the vast expansion of social media has seemingly expedited how and when students are exposed to people and topics revolving around gender and sexuality.

Past research projects such as the documentary *It's Elementary* (Chasnoff & Cohen, 1996), and *The No Outsiders Project* (DePalma & Atkinson, 2009) have proven that students know a great deal more about gender and sexuality than most adults might predict. In elementary school, a student typically is exposed to anti-LGBTQ remarks, and they might not know exactly what specific words mean, but what they do know is that there is a negative connotation that goes along with them. Peer enforcement or acceptance of narrow gender roles through homophobic harassment and name-calling has become common (Bickmore, 1999; Sears, 1998). Unfortunately, what tends to happen in situations revolving around anti-LGBTQ remarks, is a dangerous domino effect that can worsen as a child progresses through their academic years in school. By middle and high school, children begin to understand the meaning behind derogatory LGBTQ remarks, but by this age, they have been socialized to automatically associate anything or anyone that does not conform to the dominant heterosexual discourse as inferior or othered.

In order to stop the domino effect before it begins, it is important that teachers begin to introduce LGBTQ themes, topics, and families at an early age: in elementary school. Too often, teachers shy away from the idea of including LGBTQ themes or literature in the elementary classroom because they are under the guise that LGBTQ books might contain sexually explicit materials (Bickmore, 1999). This could not be further from the truth, as the majority of elementary level LGBTQ themed books focus on topics such as: alternative family types, gender nonconformity, bullying, and social exclusion. In fact, Bickmore (1999) writes that the vast majority of stories included in an elementary school classroom *already* quietly include sexuality in the form of normalized nuclear families, characters, and heterosexual relationships. *Ironically, he points out that often times books considered multicultural because the character is distant from the dominant culture in other ways (race, religion, etc.) tend to particularly emphasize the protagonists' heterosexuality.*

Active Learning

After reviewing some of the suggestions for integrating LGBTQ themes into the curriculum, think about your future classroom and what grade level(s) you envision yourself teaching. What suggestions, if any, do you see yourself implementing if any? If not, why not?

Debates about sexuality-related education in schools, especially elementary schools, tend to hinge on the idea that children are vulnerable and innocent, and the topic of sexuality, homosexuality in particular, is generally considered to be inappropriate. In today's society, young children in elementary school are no longer sheltered from topics of sexuality. Students in elementary school carelessly throw out anti- homosexual slurs such as "dyke," and "faggot," at disturbingly increasing rates (Kosciw, Greytak, Palmer & Boesen, 2014). Instead of teachers vainly trying to "protect" young children from the discomforts of learning about sexuality they can gently "invite students into the ongoing predicament of a world that includes troubles such as homophobia" (Ellsworth, 1997, p.24). By doing so, teachers can empower the next generation of adults to question and challenge the rigid rules and categories that have oppressed the LGBTQ community, even within multicultural education discourse.

Bennian / Shutterstock.com

School Climate

Over the past few years, school climate for LGBTQ students has improved slightly, yet there is still a need for drastic improvements in several areas. Unks (2003), identified American schools as, "the most homophobic institutions in the American society" (p. 323). Over a decade later, for students who identify as LGBTQ, school remains a hostile environment that can negatively affect academic performance and their emotional well-being (Blackburn & Pascoe, 2015; Kosciw et al., 2014; Kosciw, Greytak, Bartkiewicz, Boesen, & Palmer, 2012; Wimberly, Wilkinson & Pearson, 2015). A hostile school climate can result from factors such as feeling unsafe at school (Espelage, 2015), being exposed to anti-LGBTQ remarks at school (Davis, Saltzburg & Locke, 2009; Lugg, 2006; Watson & Russel, 2015), being harassed or assaulted at school (Espelage, 2015), and facing discriminatory school policies (Kosciw, Greytak, Diaz & Bartkiewicz, 2010).

The table below summarizes key research studies of issues LBGTQ youth are faced with that are tied to school climate.

Issue	Researcher	Findings
Abuse	D'Augelli (2003)	Out of 206 lesbian youths aged 14-21 • 30% had been threatened with a physical attack • 17% have had objects thrown at them • 13% had been physically assaulted and 12% had been sexually assaulted.
Bullying	Almeida, Johnson, Corliss, Molnar & Azrael (2008) Birkett, Espelage & Koenig (2009) Finlison et al. (2008) Warner, McKeown, Griffin, Johnson, Ramsay, Cort & King (2004)	LGBTQ adolescents are more likely than heterosexual or non-transgendered adolescents to report being bullied or physically assaulted, and much of the bullying and victimization haves strong anti-homosexual overtones Across two decades in Britain it was found that there was a significant increase in bullying of LGBTQ youth from 1981 to 2001 A study in England and Wales indicated that: • 31.6% of youth described being insulted in regards to their sexual orientation • 17.9% of youth described being bullied based on their sexual orientation.
Discrimination	Blackburn & Pascoe (2015) Poteat (2008)	LGBTQ youth are more likely to experience discrimination based upon their gender expression or sexual orientation than other identifying characteristics LGBTQ youth are subject to high levels of social exclusion, and are frequently left out of social functions (proms, dances, etc.) due to their sexual orientation or gender expression
Feelings of Being Unsafe in School	Kosciw et al., (2014) Meyer (2008)	• 56% of students who were harassed or assaulted in school did not report the incident to school staff • Over 60% of students who did report an incident indicated that school staff did nothing in response
Mixed	Williams, Connolly, Pepler & Craig (2003)	• In Canada, LGBTQ youth reported more bullying, harassment, and physical abuse over a two-month period than their heterosexual peers.

The above table points out that school is definitely not a safe environment for LGBTQ youth for a variety of reasons. The fact that bullying, harassment and discrimination towards LGBTQ youth continues to increases in schools across the country and throughout the world indicates that teachers, staff, and higher level administration are currently failing LGBTQ youth in regards to providing a safe, welcoming learning environment. By not addressing the mistreatment of LGBTQ youth at schools, teachers are strengthening the heteronormative power structures that control schools across the country (Unks, 2003).

Additionally, bullying, harassment and discrimination towards LGBTQ youth and families has now become common in elementary schools as well. This only strengthens the need for teachers to implement a more LGBTQ inclusive curriculum as well as adapt more complete bullying and anti-discrimination policies that protect LGBTQ youth and families from a young age.

Effects of Issues on LGBTQ Students

The fact that an unsafe school environment for LGBTQ youth is prevalent not only in the United States, but in other countries as well, indicates the need for an in-depth analysis of the ways that heteronormativity and homophobia can be challenged in all school settings. LGBTQ youth experience a range of negative effects that researchers believe may be a result of persistently unwelcoming and hostile school environments. GLSEN's (2014) research indicates that an overwhelming amount of LGBTQ youth in school feel unsafe because of their sexual orientation (55%), or their gender expression (37.8%). Feelings of insecurity at school are further supported by statistics showing the overwhelming amount of LGBTQ youth who are harassed, either physically or verbally at school. The graphic below provides a snapshot of reasons why youth are harassed in Florida Schools.

As you can see, the majority of assaults relate to matters of gender and sexuality. In this section we will explore some of these negative effects.

Psychological and Mental Effects

According to Espelage (2015), peer victimization and homophobic teasing can have significant psychological effects amongst LGBTQ youth. One research study that examined the emotional distress among LGBTQ youth based on discrimination found that lesbian, gay and bisexual youth have higher levels of emotional distress than their heterosexual peers (Almeida, Johnson, Corliss, Molnar, & Azrael, 2008). These researchers purport that one reason for this emotional distress or elevated risk of emotional distress among adolescents with a minority sexual orientation or transgender identity was due to the fact that these youth encounter stress with having a stigmatized identity.

Several researchers (Birkett et al., 2009; Bontempo & D'Augelli, 2002; Espelage et al., 2008; Poteat, 2008), note that LGBTQ students who experience poorer psychological well-beings also grapple with higher levels of substance abuse, depression, and rates of suicide than heterosexual students. Constant bullying, name-calling, exclusion and physical assaults can lead to LGBTQ youth committing suicide. According to Almeida et al. (2008), LGBTQ youth exposed to high levels of victimization had higher rates of suicide attempts than heterosexual youth exposed to high levels of victimization. The troubling concern is that these youths often do not report self-harm or suicide ideation (Almeida et al., 2008). Other studies have also indicated that gay males were more likely to have a major depressive disorder than heterosexual males, and lesbian adolescents were more likely to have post-traumatic stress disorder, drug abuse and alcohol use than their heterosexual counterparts (Davis, Saltzburg, & Locke, 2009).

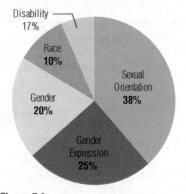

Percentage of Students Physically Harassed in Florida Schools (2013)

Disability 17%
Race 10%
Gender 20%
Gender Expression 25%
Sexual Orientation 38%

Figure 7.1.
Source: Dominic Grasso. Adapted from
GLSEN Florida State Snapshot, 2013

Academic Effects

A study conducted by the California Safe Schools Coalition (CSSC) and the 4-H Center for Youth Development (2004) examined bullying based on actual or perceived sexual orientation. They found that students who were victims to bullying, as compared to students who were not bullied, reported greater rates of absenteeism, and lower grades. According to Birkett et al. (2009) and Rivers (2000) LGBTQ youth who are victims of constant bullying at school have excessive rates of truancy or frequent absenteeism. These studies indicate that the unsafe school environments frequently experienced by LGBTQ youth can significantly affect their academic achievement. This could lead to even greater long-term effects such as non-acceptance into college, as well as a lack of employment (Birkett, 2009; Rivers, 2000).

Extension

Using one of the books selected above, create a formal lesson plan that is interdisciplinary (connects more than one content area) and reflects the Florida Standards and/or Common Core Standards. Be sure to include materials, learning objectives, and how you will assess whether the students have mastered the learning objectives or not.

"That's So Gay"

In all educational contexts, phrases such as "that's so gay," (or something similar) are used quite frequently. Usually, the educational setting in which the phrase is used can reveal a great deal about the meaning behind their word choice. For example, kindergarteners while playing at recess might refer to a boy playing with the girls in the jump rope area by exclaiming "that's so gay!" While at this age, they may not know exactly what the phrase means, but they know enough to correlate the phrase with someone or something that does not conform to the heteronormative gender and sexuality roles they have already been exposed to through socialization.

Davis et al. (2009) found that LGBTQ youth are even more likely than LGBTQ adults to be victimized by antigay prejudice or discriminatory remarks. This shows that children in schools are using anti-gay language, whether or not they know what the remarks mean. Since children in schools are already spewing anti-gay remarks, it makes sense that teachers, beginning in elementary school, should include LGBTQ themed literature in their classroom. This may help educate students as to what exactly the negative remarks they are using mean, as well as how much of an impact they can have on LGBTQ youth.

GLSEN's (2014) survey found that 71% of students heard "gay" used in a negative way frequently or often at school, and 65% of students heard homophobic remarks such as "faggot" or "dyke" frequently or often. As if homophobic remarks from peers were not bad enough, more than half of students reported hearing homophobic remarks from their teachers or other school staff on a regular basis (Kosciw et al., 2014).

As students' progress through high school and into college, they may still use the phrase "that's so gay," however at this point students are most likely so accustomed to hearing it that there is no malice or intentional discrimination behind what they are saying. It is unfortunate that a phrase that usually relates being gay with something or someone that students are seeking to verbally belittle, has become common vernacular in educational contexts. In the latest GLSEN school climate survey (2014), over 90% of Florida students reported hearing the phrase "that's so gay" frequently or often in school (Kosciw et. al, 2014).

While it may seem like a simple phrase such as, "that's so gay," couldn't possibly do much harm, I believe that it is actually how we, as educators, react to hearing this type of language in schools that makes all the difference. I remember very early on in my teaching career overhearing a group of first graders using the phrase "that's so gay." At first, I panicked and was not sure how to respond. Eventually, I responded the way I believe most teachers would respond today, by saying something to the effect of, "Please don't use that type of language," or "We shouldn't use that type of language in school." While at first I thought that I had done an admirable job of defusing the situation, I realized that I may have unintentionally done more harm than good. I realized that there was a good chance that most of those students I had disciplined did not even know what the word "gay" meant. I also realized that in the minds of students I have branded the word "gay" as something so bad, and so abhorrent, that it shouldn't be discussed in school. I left those students with the impression that whatever it meant to be gay was something that should be kept out of school dialogues just the same as other expletives, and was not

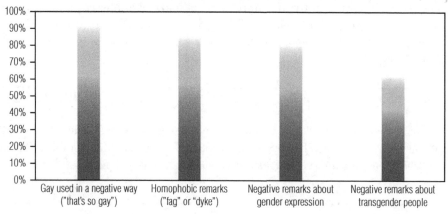

Figure 7.2.
Source: Dominic Grasso. Adapted from *GLSEN Florida State Snapshot, 2013*

appropriate to be discussed in front of other children or even teachers. By simply responding as most teachers probably would have, I may have contributed to a student's developing negative perception of people in the LGBTQ community.

Active Learning
Think about how you have, or how you believe you might react to students using the phrase "that's so gay," in your classroom. What are some possible reactions that might be better alternatives than telling students not to use language like "gay" in school?

As teachers, the natural response when we hear students discussing something that we don't feel is appropriate is to promptly instruct students to end the conversation. However, I believe that a different approach is necessary when we overhear students negatively using phrases such as "that's so gay." Below is a list of strategies and suggestions teachers can use to proactively handle classroom conversations involving the negative usage of "that's so gay" and other similar dialogue:

What Do You Say to "That's So Gay"
- Ask students to explain what the word gay means. If they do not know what gay means, explain it to them.
- Explain to students that even if they didn't mean for what they said to be hurtful, when they use the word gay to mean something bad, stupid, or weird, it is hurtful.
- Be clear with students that when they use the phrase "that's so gay" in a negative way they are being disrespectful and hurtful to other students who may identify as gay, may have parents, aunts, uncles, or neighbors who are gay.
- Do not ignore the situation! Any response is better than no response. By not responding, the teacher may be creating a classroom environment in which students feel they have no limits when it comes to discrimination and name calling.
- Do not try to judge how upset other children might be. Often times, victims of name calling and discrimination, especially in relation to phrases such as "gay," "fag," or "dyke" will be too scared to show how upset they really are. It is better to assume that the victim *is* upset, even if they don't show it.
- Don't trivialize the behavior. Using the word gay in a negative way *is* a big deal and it should be dealt with and handled as such.

Source: It's Elementary (1996) and Welcoming Schools Guide (2007).

Creating Safe Spaces

Even though some might be quick to underestimate the negative effects of an unsafe and hostile school environment for LGBTQ youth, the results of an unwelcoming and hostile school environment can be drastic, and unfortunately, lives can be at stake. The fact that these unsafe and hostile school environments can have such a tremendous impact on LGBTQ youth greatly emphasizes the need for educators to be more attentive when it comes to dealing with LGBTQ issues in their classrooms.

There are simple steps that educators can take to create safer, more inclusive classroom environments for students and families who identify as LGBTQ. The first steps educators can take is to ensure that their classroom is physically and aesthetically inviting and welcoming for all students. Educators can accomplish this by ensuring that there are posters, signs and rules that explicitly address bullying, respect, and diversity. Additionally, educators can ensure that inspirational messages throughout the classroom avoid gender roles (boys/girls) and instead include messages such as "all students" or "everyone." Creating stereotypical areas in the room such as library sections focusing on boys' or girls' interests should also be avoided, and copies of books representing a variety of different family types should be featured in classroom libraries.

When creating classroom groups, educators should avoid placing students into boy groups and girl groups and can instead use grouping strategies such as separating students by birthday months, or first letters of last names. When addressing the class, educators should avoid phrases that are often used such as "boys and girls" and instead include phrases such as "children, scholars, or students." Another idea might be to name your class after a sports team, animal, or movie character and addressing all students by their group name. For example, you might try, "Good morning, Dolphins!"

A final suggestion for educators looking to create more inclusive classrooms would be to be proactive instead of reactive. For example, if educators take the lead and incorporate LGBTQ issues into their lessons early on in the year, they will set the tone in regards to diversity, acceptance, and bullying in their own classroom. Most importantly, educators should never avoid a situation in which a student bullies, harasses, or discriminates against another student based upon their sexuality or gender expression. By doing nothing, educators may be doing more harm than good, because students will feel as if their teacher does not care that they have been victimized because of their gender expression or sexuality. By being a role model for all students in regards to students and families in the LGBTQ community, educators, even at the elementary level, can make a significant impact by helping to shape the minds of more accepting, empathetic, and diverse students.

Active Learning
After reviewing some of the suggestions for integrating LGBTQ themes into the curriculum, think about your future classroom and what grade level(s) you envision yourself teaching. What suggestions, if any, do you see yourself implementing if any? If not, why not?

Extension
Using one of the books selected below, create a formal lesson plan that is interdisciplinary (connects more than one content area) and reflects the Florida Standards and/or Common Core Standards. Be sure to include materials, learning objectives, and how you will assess whether the students have mastered the learning objectives or not.

Literature Connections: Practical Suggestions for an LGBTQ Inclusive Curriculum

Compiled by Dominic Grasso

Grade Level	Materials	Content Area/Topic/ Theme	Student Activities
K-2	*Red- A Crayon's Story* by Michael Hall *The New Girl and Me* by Jacqui Robinson	Language Arts & Social Studies: • Creating a Welcoming Classroom Environment • Treating Others with Respect • Being Yourself	1. Read the two trade books. 2. Lead a discussion of the themes of each book. 3. Have students draft a new set of class rules that set the tone for a more inclusive classroom environment for all students and encourages students to be themselves. 4. Have students create a venn-diagram chart discussing times they have felt "unwelcome" at school and times they have felt "welcomed" at school and how they can act towards others to make their classmates feel welcomed.
3-5	*And Tango Makes Three* by Justin Richardson and Peter Parnell	Language Arts/Science: • Animal Adaptations • Animals in Captivity • Different Animal Family Types • Diverse Human Families (Two Moms, Two Dads, Grandparents, Stepmom, Stepdad, etc.)	5. Read the picture books. 6. Discuss the big ideas in the story with students. 7. As a science activity, discuss animal adaptations, such as adaptations that penguins have that help them survive in the arctic environments and connect how the unique family structure presented in the book has helped the penguins to survive. 8. Students can conduct research reports on animals that have unique adaptations or unique family structures. 9. Using critical conversations, students can debate the pros and cons of keeping animals in captivity versus allowing animals to remain in their natural habitats.
K-5	*I am Jazz* by Jessica Herthel and Jazz Jennings *Jacob's New Dress* by Sarah and Ian Hoffman *The Sissy Duckling* by Harvey Fierstein	Language Arts/Social Studies: • Gender • Bullying • Expressing Yourself • Families	10. Read one or more of the trade books. 11. Using critical conversations, lead a class discussion regarding gender roles and bullying. 12. *Primary students* can compare and contrast how the characters in the book responded to the problem of not conforming to their gender. 13. *Intermediate students* can conduct character analyses of the protagonists and explain how the theme of bullying is developed and explained through the plot.
3-5	Various research articles on famous LGBTQ people including: • Elton John • Barney Frank • Frida Khalo • Melissa Etheridge • Sir Ian McKellen • John Ameachi • Michael Sam • George Takei • Walt Whitman • Oscar Wilde	Language Arts and Art, Music, Physical Education, and Drama	14. Have students conduct research on famous LGBTQ individuals who have had influential lives as artists, actors, musicians, or athletes. 15. After conducting their research, students can create a poster board, brochure or visual presentation highlighting their chosen individual's accomplishments and how they have impacted the lives of many others.

Adapted from *Welcoming Schools* by the Human Rights Campaign Foundation

Boris15 / Shutterstock.com

References

Almeida, J., Johnson, R.M., Corliss, H.L., Molnar, B.E. & Azrael, D. (2008). Emotional distress among LGBT youth: The influence of perceived discrimination based on sexual orientation. *Journal of Youth Adolescence, 38*(1), 1001–1014.

Atkinson, E. & DePalma, R. (2010). *Undoing homophobia in primary schools by the no outsiders project.* Staffordshire, UK: Trentham Books Unlimited.

Bickmore, K. (1999). Teaching conflict and conflict resolution in school: (Extra-) curricular considerations. In A. Raviv, L. Oppenheimer & D. Bar-Tal (Eds.). *How children understand war and peace* (pp. xx-xx). San Francisco, CA: Josey-Bass. San Francisco: Jossey-Bass.

Birkett, M.A., Espelage, D.L. & Koenig, B. (2009). LGB and questioning students in schools: The moderating effects of homophobic bullying and school climate on negative outcomes. *Journal of Youth and Adolescence, 38*, 989–1000.

Blackburn, M. & Pascoe, C. (2015). K-12 students in schools. In A.E. Association (Ed.). *LGBTQ issues in education: Advancing a research agenda* (pp. 89–105). Washington, D.C.: American Educational Research Association.

Bochenek, M. & Brown, A.W. (2001). *Hatred in the hallways: Violence and discrimination against lesbian, gay, bisexual, and transgender students in US schools.* New York, NY: Human Rights Watch.

Bontempo, D.E. & D'Augelli, A.R. (2002). Effects of at-school victimization and sexual orientation on lesbian, gay, or bisexual youths' health risk behavior. *Journal of Adolescent Health, 30*, 364–374.

California Safe Schools Coalition & 4-H Center for Youth Development. (2004). *A safe place to learn: Consequences of harassment based on actual or perceived sexual orientation and gender non-conformity and steps to making schools safer.* San Francisco and Davis, CA: Authors.

Chasnoff, D. & Cohen, H.S. (1995). *It's elementary: Talking about gay issues in school* [video]. San Francisco, CA: Women's Educational Media.

D'Augelli, A.R. (2003). Lesbian and bisexual female youths aged 14 to 21: Developmental challenges and victimization experiences. *Journal of Lesbian Studies, 7*(4), 9–29.

Davis, T.S., Saltzburg, S., & Locke, C.R. (2009). Supporting the emotional and psychological well being of exual minotrity youth: Youth ideas for action. *Children and Youth Services Review, 31*, 1030–1041.

DePalma, R. & Jennet, M. (2007). Deconstructing heteronormativity in primary schools in England: Cultural approaches to a cultural phenomenon. In I van Dijk & B. van Driel (Eds.). *Confronting Homophobia in Educational Practices* (19–32). Trentham, UK: Stroke on Trent.

Espelage, D.L. (2015). Bullying and K-12 students. In A.E. Association (Ed.). *LGBTQ Issues in education: Advancing a research agenda* (pp. 105–121). Washington, D.C.: American Educational Research Association.

Espelage, D.L, Aragorn, S.R., Birkett, M. & Koenig, B.W. (2008). Homophobic teasing, psychological outcomes, and sexual orientation among high school students: What influences do parents and schools have? *School Psychology Review, 37*(2), 202–216.

Finlinson, H.A., Colon, H.M., Robles, R.R. & Soto, M. (2008). An exploratory study of Puerto Rican MSM drug users: The childhood and early teen years of gay males and transsexual females. *Youth & Society*, 39, 362–384.

Kosciw, J.G. & Diaz, E.M. (2008). *Involved, invisible, ignored: The experiences of lesbian, gay, bisexual, and transgender parents and their children in our nation's K-12 schools*. New York, NY: Gay, Lesbian, and Straight Education Network.

Kosciw, J.C., Greytak, E.A., Bartkiewicz, M.J., Boesen, M.J. & Palmer, N.A. (2012). *The 2011 National School Climate Survey: The experiences of lesbian, gay, bisexual, and transgender youth in our nation's schools*. New York, NY: Gay, Lesbian & Straight Education Network.

Kosciw, J.G., Greytak, E.A., Diaz, E.M. & Bartkiewicz, M.J. (2010). *The 2009 national school climate survey: The experiences of lesbian, gay, bisexual and transgender youth in our nation's schools*. New York, NY: Gay, Lesbian, and Straight Education Network.

Kosciw, J.G., Greytak, E.A., Palmer, N.A. & Boesen, M.J. (2014). *The 2013 national school climate survey: The experiences of lesbian, gay, bisexual, and transgender youth in our nation's schools*. New York, NY: Gay, Lesbian & Straight Education Network.

Lugg, C.A. (2006). Thinking about sodomy: Public schools, panopticons, and queers. *Educational Policy*, 20(1–2), 35–58.

Meyer, E.J. (2008). Gendered harassment in secondary schools: Understanding teachers' (non) interventions. *Gender & Education*, 20(6), 555–572.

Pearson, J., Muller, C. & Wilkinson, L. (2007). Adolescent same sex attraction and academic outcomes: The role of school attachment and engagement. *Social Problems*, 54(4), 523–542.

Poteat, V. P. (2008). Contextual and moderating effects of the peer group climate on homophobic epithets. *School Psychology Review*, 37(2), 188–201.

Rivers, I. (2000). Social exclusion, absenteeism, and sexual minority youth. *Support for Learning*, 15(1), 13.

Russell, S.T., Seif, H. & Truong, N.L. (2001). School outcomes of sexual minority youth in the United States: Evidence from a national study. *Journal of Adolescence*, 24, 111–127.

Sears, J. (1998). A generational and theoretical analysis of culture and male (homo) sexuality. In W. Pinar (Ed.). *Queer Theory in Education* (pp. 73–106). Mahwah, NJ: Lawrence Erlbaum.

Unks, G. (2003). Thinking about the gay teen. In A. Darder, M. Baltodano & R.D. Torres (Eds.). *The critical pedagogy reader* (pp. 322–330). New York, NY: Routledge Falmer.

Warner, J., McKeown, E., Griffin, M., Johnson, K., Ramsay, A., Cort, C. & King, M. (2004). Rates and predictors of mental illness in gay men, lesbians, and bisexual men and women: Results from a survey based in England and Wales. *British Journal of Psychiatry*, 185, 479–485.

Watson, R.J. & Russell, S.T. (2015). Schools and children in LGBTQ families. In A. E. Association (Ed.)., *LGBTQ issues in education: Advancing a research agenda* (pp. 75–89). Washington, D.C.: American Educational Research Association.

Welcoming Schools. (n.d.). Retrieved June 23, 2016 from http://www.welcomingschools.org/

Williams, T., Connolly, J., Pepler, D. & Craig, W. (2005). Peer victimization, social support, and psychological adjustment of sexual minority adolescents. *Journal of Youth & Adolescence*, 34(5), 471–482.

Wimberly, G.L., Wilkinson, L., & Pearson, J. (2015). LGBTQ *student achievement and educational attainment*. In A. E. Association (Ed.). *LGBTQ issues in education: Advancing a research agenda* (pp. 175–219). Washington, D.C.: American Educational Research Association.

Practical Encounter

Practical Encounter #1

Case Study

Directions: Reflect on the author's personal narrative on the first page of this chapter and answer the questions that follow.

It was approximately 7:45 a.m. and I was preparing my classroom materials for the day ahead. Students were starting to file down the hallway after eating breakfast in the cafeteria. I was writing on my whiteboard when all of a sudden, I heard the door to my classroom open, and saw a familiar 5th grade student poke his head in. He looked at me, and I looked at him, knowing that he wasn't supposed to be in my room at this current time. Before I could open my mouth to direct him to go to his homeroom class, he looked at me, shouted "faggot," began laughing, closed the door, and proceeded to march merrily down the hallway to his class.

1. Where do you think the student learned this word?

2. Do you think he or she knew the negative connotation surrounding the use of the word?

3. How would you have responded as the teacher?

4. If you watched this scenario play out in the hallway, what would have been your response to your colleague or even to the student who made the comment?

5. What practices or strategies could be put in place to make the environment more culturally responsive for all students, including those within the LGBTQ Community?

Practical Encounter #2

Cultural Perceptions, Tensions, or Biases Dialogue Activity

Directions: Watch the following videos and take note of any perceptions or tensions noted by the various cultural groups represented. Also note where their perceptions are rooted.

	Video Clip	Cultural Perceptions, Tensions, or Biases
African American	http://www.youtube.com/watch?v=m1AYIxGM_2g	
Latino LGBT	http://www.youtube.com/watch?v=ntfct4veZ8c& feature=related	
Asian LGBT	http://www.youtube.com/watch?v=OJMqIEBf2lY& feature=related	

What are the similarities and differences between each cultural group and their possible stances against/or for the LGBTQ lifestyle?

_____

_____

What would be your response to a parent who feels strongly against inclusive practices of LGBTQ students in your classroom?

_____

_____

CHAPTER 8

Fundamentals of Multicultural Lesson Planning

Allyson Hall, Kalisha A. Waldon, Traci P. Baxley

Lesson Plan Contributors: Marissa Wildrick and Stephanie Silva

The objectives of this chapter are to:

- Provide an overview of the essential components of a unit plan
- Explain how a multicultural lens can be used to create units that are inclusive and representative of varying perspectives
- Demonstrate a method for successfully aligning lesson objectives, instruction, and assessment(s)
- Offer culturally responsive strategies that meet the diverse needs and learning styles of all students.

Chapter Overview

In traditional curriculum design, a unit of instruction is known as a pedagogical plan driven by specific objectives that are based on standards or desired student outcomes. A unit plan often consists of a series of individual interrelated lessons which, when taught in a predetermined sequence, aim to fulfill desired student learning outcomes (SLOs). Units vary in the depth and breadth of content and often consist of topics, which are typically subdivided into more specific lessons. These lessons consist of elements or sections that support effective instruction (See Figure 8.1).

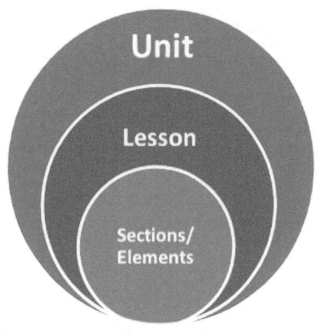

Figure 8.1. Unit Plan Overview/Components

In what follows, we offer a discussion of five sections/elements of an effective lesson plan: rationale, objectives, content, instructional activities, and evaluation. We then provide a discussion of the goals of MCE, discuss the importance of constructing a culturally responsive curriculum, and provide active learning activities and practical scenarios for personal reflection. Throughout this chapter, an example of a multicultural science lesson plan created by two pre-service teachers is used to illustrate the principles of multicultural curriculum design.

Determining Your Rationale

A lesson plan's rationale speaks to the "why" of the curriculum and helps to justify each piece of the big picture (University Center for the Advancement of Teaching, 2016). It is each unit's *"raison d'être" or, purpose for existence*. In the planning process, justifying each lesson's rationale is an important step in developing a culturally responsive unit and can be intuited through a close examination of the choice of content. Therefore, when determining a lesson's rationale, teachers are encouraged to interrogate the necessity of the lesson and the epistemological (what knowledge is valued and whose knowledge is considered valid) underpinnings of all the materials that will be included in the content of the lesson. For example, take a moment to reflect on the rationale of the traditional story of Christopher Columbus on his voyage from Spain to the Americas. Generations of school-aged children cantillate the following rhythmic recitation chronicling his audacious and courageous exploits: "In fourteen hundred ninety-two,/Columbus sailed the ocean blue./He had three ships and left from Spain./He sailed through sunshine, wind and rain" (In 1492, n.d.).

While this is just the first four lines of this poem, consider the underpinnings of including this popular piece in your classroom lesson plan. Notice the idyllic resonance of this stanza. Now, consider what you have been taught about the historical outcomes of this voyage? Ask yourself, what is the purpose served by presenting this perspective on his journey? Whose story is told, and to whose benefit? Now, conversely, consider the same opening stanza which is a recast of the 1492 poem written from a Native American's perspective: "In Fourteen Hundred and Ninety Two,/Columbus sailed the ocean blue./But everything else in the childhood rhyme,/Ignores the historic details and genocide" (Hall, 2012).

This counter-narrative tells the story of Columbus and his venturous crew from an alternate perspective and presents knowledge from a non-traditional or critical point of view. Now, reconsider what you have been taught about the outcomes of this voyage and the purpose served by presenting this perspective on their journey. Once again, think of the story being told. In either poem, each stanza embodies a set of values, espouses an objective, and supports a rationale or purpose.

Every lesson's purpose is its driving force. As such, each objective, reading, video, activity, assignment, and assessment should be aligned' with the purpose and focus of the lesson. Your rationale will explain why you believe the lesson is important and speak specifically to the purpose of its implementation. A multicultural lesson plan should espouse a rationale that teaches content in a method that represents an appreciation for diverse backgrounds, cultures, and perspectives (Nieto, 2011). The purpose of multicultural education is to serve the increasingly diverse populations in our classrooms. As such, lesson plans that speak to the culturally, ethnically, linguistically, and ideologically diverse students we teach inevitably improve instructional efficacy. Throughout the process of unit planning, you could potentially have several rationales that operate to serve different needs. The multifaceted nature of lesson planning could serve multiple functions and meet more than one purpose or need. For example, your lessons could be designed to fulfill societal, communal, school-based, subject-based, and/or individual needs. In Table 8.1, the aforementioned levels of need are discussed with curricular examples to illustrate each.

Table 8.1. Lesson Plan Needs

Rationale	Description	Practical Example
Societal need	Focuses on a broad social need for the lesson	The increase in teenage smoking and new research on its addictiveness in youth could be the rationale for a lesson on the impact of nicotine on one's respiratory system.
Community need	Focuses on a need specific to the school community	Increased racial tension in a school's community could be the rationale for a lesson on recognizing and accepting cultural differences.
School-based need	Focuses on a particular need of the school	EX 1) At a school with an international baccalaureate program, a lesson plan on international calendars would be appropriate. EX 2) In a school with high levels of teenage pregnancy, an emphasis on family planning or sexual education could be useful.
Subject-based need	Focuses on a need that has emerged within the field or specific content area	EX 1) In order to address students' traditional fear of mathematics, a lesson plan based on a fractions game is presented. EX 2) The lack of female inventors represented in science textbooks is the rationale for a lesson on famous and influential female scientists.
Individual need	Focuses on the more personalized needs of the students within a class	EX 1) For students who experience or see increasing levels of poverty in their local community, a lesson on poverty reduction or solutions to food insecurity could be of use.

Now, it is your turn. Take a moment to complete this activity:

Active Learning

Based on the information provided in the table below, what needs are addressed in the embedded science unit plan?

Topic	Cell Division (Incorporating Diverse Contributors)
Subject	Science
Grade Level	Middle School
Duration of Unit	(4 Days)/50 Minute Sessions
Social Justice Issue	Questioning Textbook Bias

Rationale of the Lesson
This topic was chosen for the following reasons:

- Science, in general, is a dense subject and is often considered to be a "neutral subject."
- It is critical for students to learn basic knowledge of cells and their processes. Without the cell cycle humans would not survive.
- School textbooks are considered accurate and unbiased. This lesson will highlight the biases of the textbook by bringing in diverse biologists and scientists who have contributed to the process of cell division as well as major breakthroughs in cytology.

In this exemplar, a subject-based need is addressed. What makes the rationale of this lesson multicultural is that it not only teaches students about cell division, but it also aims to provide opportunities for students to challenge the exclusion of scientists from diverse backgrounds. This lesson challenges students to recognize the implications of the monolithic approach so often adopted by traditional textbooks.

Goals/Objectives

Once you have determined the "why" of your lesson, the next step is to articulate the anticipated outcomes. This portion of the lesson plan is focused on the desired Student Learning Objectives (SLOs). It is important to note that in our standards-driven educational system, learning standards, as often determined by state departments of education, mandate what students are expected to know in all subject areas by the end of each school year. These standards should always be considered when designing lessons, especially as grade-level assessments are designed around these standards and high-stakes funding consequences for students, teachers, and districts are increasingly tied to student performance on these tests. It is also important to note that one critical expectation of multicultural educators is that they set high expectations of learning for all of their students. This expectation should be articulated in lesson objectives and goals.

When considering the goals and objectives of a multicultural lesson, curriculum planners ask questions like:

- What do I want students to be able to recognize/do as a result of this lesson?
- What concepts, ideas, or processes are important for them to know?
- What is the most efficient and effective way to reach this goal for ALL students?
- How will I know that my students have accomplished the prescribed goal(s)?

To begin to determine what your answers to these questions are, Sleeter (2005) suggests that you should first brainstorm on what you want students to know about the concept and then clarify these ideas according to whether the central ideas are "worth being familiar with, important to know and/to do, [and/or] essential to enduring understanding" (p. 47). In other words, what is the "so what" of your lesson. Additionally, Wiggins and McTighe (2005) suggest that all curriculum design begins with a clear vision of the desired result. From here, a decision can be made concerning the specific constructs students should grasp by the end of the lesson.

Using Bloom's to Develop Learning Objectives

Bloom's Taxonomy has been used when designing educational, training, and learning processes. The revised taxonomy, which includes meta-cognitive domains, offers promising opportunities for improved learning outcomes (Bush, Daddysman, & Charnigo, 2014). While Bloom's taxonomy offers an effective resource to begin behavioral objectives, remain mindful of the need to create lessons that are inclusive and diverse in nature.

When planning your instruction, Bloom's taxonomy can:

- Be a helpful tool in designing instruction that is scaffolded
- Promote higher-order cognition
- Offer structure and alignment in articulating lesson goals and objectives.

Figure 8.2 depicts a visual rendering of Bloom's taxonomy which represents six hierarchical levels of learning through knowledge acquisition, comprehension, application, analysis, synthesis, and evaluation. The structure of Bloom's taxonomy encourages instructors to design lessons that scaffold or build on foundational knowledge and progress to higher levels of cognitive work (Adams, 2015).

Lesson goals and objectives that employ the use of Bloom's taxonomy can target both short- and long-term pedagogical pursuits. Short-term objectives are learning outcomes that you desire students to achieve during or immediately following the lesson. An example of a short term objective is: *"By the end of the lesson, students will be able to accurately identify the process of photosynthesis."*

Long-term goals are learning outcomes you desire students to achieve over a prolonged period of time. For example, after a lesson focused on cultural sensitivity, you may hope that over a longer period of time students would refrain from telling jokes that are insensitive or derogatory toward certain social groups. This goal could be articulated as one that speaks to the third level of Bloom's: Application – *"Students will be able to recognize the effects of insensitive language and exchange, and identify ways to foster and promote inclusion and acceptance amongst peers."*

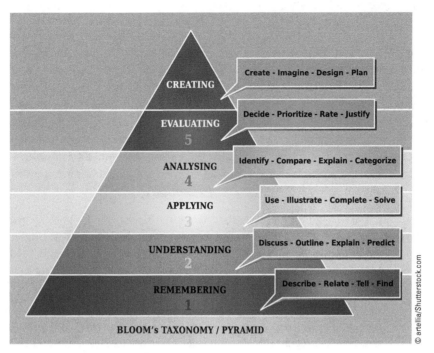

Figure 8.2. Bloom's Taxonomy

Active Learning

Based on the lesson's Goals and Objectives
Based on the following goals and objectives, what specifically does the teacher want students to know or be able to do at the end of this embedded exemplar?

Goals & Objectives
By the end of the lesson, students will be able to:

Short-Term Goals

- Identify the stages of cell division
- Identify the main processes involved with each stage
- Explain the reasoning and importance of mitotic cell division
- Discuss the scientists from underrepresented populations that have contributed to the establishment of theories and discoveries of cellular division

Long-Term Goals

- Question and identify bias in a variety of media (ie textbooks, movies, newspapers, etc.)
- Learn how to further research topics within their textbooks and consider multiple perspectives

Specifically students should be able to identify the stages and processes of cell division and explain the importance of mitotic cell division. They should also be able to discuss the contributions of underrepresented scientists to the theory of cell division. Students are introduced to textbook bias; however it is listed as a long-term goal because it is not a skill that can be fully achieved by the end of one lesson or unit.

Content

Sleeter (2005) posits, ". . . developing intellectually rich curriculum requires thinking through not just what facts and information are worth consuming, but also what the intellectual basis of knowledge is" (p. 29). It is important for you as a teacher to examine the beliefs and assumptions embedded in the curriculum and the content materials you choose. The content section of the lesson plan focuses on what you will teach, or the knowledge that is embedded in the lesson. To counter the monolithic (single-sided) and often biased manner in which content is presented to students, teachers should intentionally design lessons that are inclusive of multiple perspectives. Drawing on several multicultural educators (Sleeter, 2005; Banks, 1998; Nieto & Bode, 2008), Table 8.2 offers recommendations for countering dominant curricular narratives.

Table 8.2.   Recommendations for Countering Dominant Narratives

Ask Yourself	If Not	How To
Is the content that I intend to include representative of the population(s) that I teach?	Work to include the knowledge-base or funds of knowledge of your students in your lesson plan. Incorporate materials or ways of knowing representative of students' heritage or thought process as a springboard for learning.	This could be a good time to do inquiry-based projects that empower them as the researcher to answer their own questions by asking a parent or close family member first. This often lays the groundwork to introduce processes that assist in meaning making that will be relevant and relatable. It may also be helpful to do an initial assessment on the topic you aim to teach with your students. Find out what they know on this this subject. After this initial conversation, find ways to include representations of their knowledge in the literature you choose, the films you watch, and the assignments you provide.
Does this video, reading, assignment, etc. align with the general purpose of the lesson while including diverse ways of knowing?	Think of why it is a part of your repertoire. Is this a film mandated by county/state/federal standards? If not, speak to colleagues about their choice of content and perform a basic internet search to find other instructional materials that will help in furthering the purpose of the assessment. Be sure though, that the materials are purposefully selected and that your inclusions add value to content clarity and coherence.	Search the internet for creative commons or crowdsourcing sites that offer suggestions on how to represent the knowledge of students in course deliverables. Work with your curriculum coordinator or curriculum specialist to secure resources that speak to the diverse realities of the classroom and give voice to often marginalized or excluded populations. Research primary sources that can be used to enhance the curriculum (i.e. personal narratives, documentaries, historical archives). Review instructional materials and resources offered by the publishers of the texts you use. Often, questions from these test banks or assignments can be equitably enhanced to include more culturally competent and relevant material.
Does my content represent diverse perspectives while still maintaining the integrity of school/county/ statewide standards?	Become familiar with the standards that are expected of your class/ grade-level. Often, the language of standards are general enough to add material to your lesson that will meet the needs of diverse learners as well as the mandates of state standards.	Identify canonical or traditional historical figures and seek to find the hidden figures from diverse populations who have also contributed to ways of knowing and are often excluded from the dominant narrative. Highlighting these figures offers students opportunities to "see themselves" in the curriculum and to examine forms of knowledge construction from different cultural lenses. Field trips also become an excellent time to take a step away from direct instruction. If given the flexibility to propose and arrange field trips, suggest locations that are off the beaten path. Perhaps visiting a cultural art museum could supplement teaching about historical and culturally relevant works of art.
Have I interrogated my inherent biases and worked toward equitable pedagogy?	Develop a cultural profile of yourself. Investigate who you are as a person, a professional, a woman/ man, a parent, and an educator. Know the biases that you bring to the table so you are better able to think clearly and objectively when faced with them.	Reflect on your personal knowledge and history. Think about how this influences what you teach and how you teach it. Reflect upon your understanding of the subject matter and critically question your biases and assumptions. Think of ways to counter the inherent biases represented in the content materials. Search for instructional materials that represent perspectives which counter dominant narratives. (To begin your personal reflection, see Cultural profile on pg. ____)

Often, the knowledge, skills, and beliefs set forth in curricula are a testament of one's appraisal of diversity and the ways in which truth and meaning are negotiated. Teachers should interrogate their own beliefs about what it means to know and question the implications of how they appropriate intelligence in the classroom.

Ask yourself: Do I value diverse ways of knowing?

Active Learning
What is considered the traditional content that students would be taught in this exemplar? Whose voices are honored? What impact do you think the inclusion of the diverse scientists would have on the students?

What Is Cell Division?
Mitotic cell division is a process of nuclear division amongst two distinct parent cells that divide to create two genetically identical daughter cells. The reasoning and importance of mitotic cell division are essentially the genetic material (DNA) is copied in the division process. Copies of DNA are being made. This allows for developmental growth in the human body.

Key Vocabulary

- Mitosis: A type of cell division that results in two daughter cells that have the same number of chromosomes as the parent nucleus.
- Meiosis: A type of cell division that occurs after mitosis. It results in four daughter cells each with half the number of chromosomes as the parent nucleus.
- Spindle fibers: Form a protein structure that divides the genetic material in a cell. They are called mitotic spindles during mitosis.
- Nucleus: A membrane-enclosed organelle that contains DNA and RNA. It is also responsible for growth.
- Centrioles: A cylindrical organelle near the nucleus involved in the development of spindle fibers in cell division.
- Telophase: The final process of mitosis. The chromosomes decondense, the nuclear envelope forms, and cytokinesis is complete. Two daughter cells are created.
- Anaphase: The process when the chromosomes are split and the spindle fibers shorten pulling the sister chromatids to the opposite poles of the cell. This phase ensures that each daughter cell gets identical sets of chromosomes.
- Metaphase: The process in which the chromosomes align in the middle of the cell.
- Prophase: The first phase of mitosis that separates the duplicated genetic material carried in the nucleus of a parent cell into two identical daughter cells. The complex of DNA and chromatin condense.

Stages of Cell Division (in order)
Prophase → Metaphase → Anaphase → Telophase

What Happens When Mitosis Goes Wrong?
Mitosis results in the creation of two daughter cells, each carrying a copy of the parent cell's DNA. Errors in mitosis can result in an incorrect copy of DNA which can range anywhere from benign to deadly, depending on the severity of the error. Two types of errors may occur when DNA is not properly copied: 1) one has no impact on the DNA sequence, and 2) the other changes the DNA sequence leading to cell cycle interruption and the formation of tumor cells.

Tumor cells do not stop dividing and eventually result in cancer. If, during mitosis, chromosomes fail to attach to the spindles, then the resulting daughter cell will either have an extra or missing copy of a chromosome. One common disorder that results from the chromosomal abnormality is Down Syndrome. Abnormalities in chromosomes also create a higher chance of getting Alzheimer's and leukemia. This lesson will touch on the fact that when cells do not properly divide, the resulting daughter cells can create cancer as well as other abnormalities.

Textbook Perspective of Cell Division (Core Scientists): Prentice Hall: Biology by Kenneth Miller and Joseph Levine

- Robert Hooke – English physicist, who was the first to describe cells in 1665.
- Mathias Schleiden – German botanist who contributed to the development of the cell theory by recognizing the importance of the cell nucleus and connected its key role in cell division.
- Theodor Schwann – German physiologist who also contributed, with Schleiden, to the development of the cell theory by discovering the Schwann cells in the peripheral nervous system. These cells were named in honor of his discovery.
- Walter Flemming – German biologist and founder of cytogenetics. He described chromosome behavior during mitosis.
- Rudolph Virchow – German physician, pathologist, and anthropologist who concluded that cells develop from existing cells

Multicultural Perspective (Scientists from Diverse Cultures)

- Lynn Margulis – Female American biologist known for her theory on the origin of eukaryotic organelles
- Karl August Möbius – German zoologist who first observed the structures that would later be called "organelles"
- Ernest Just – African–American biologist who recognized the fundamental role of the cell surface in the development of organisms
- Jewel Plummer Cobb – African–American cell biologist who majored in cell physiology, known for her research development on chemotherapeutic drugs on cancerous cells in the body.
- Santiago Ramon y Cajal – Hispanic neuroscientist illustrated the arborization (branching out like trees) of brain cells

Textbook Bias

Bias is a prejudice in favor of or against one thing, group, or person that is usually considered unfair. The teacher will show students how to detect the biases in their science textbook.

Critical Questions

- What does textbook bias mean? Why does it exist?
- How is omission or marginalization a form of bias?
- How can we identify textbook bias in the future?

Outlining the content of the unit/lesson would provide teachers with an overview of the specific knowledge or salient concepts the lesson would include. An initial outline of the content will also provide an indication as to what knowledge or perspectives have been omitted or not included. This would provide teachers with the opportunity to fill in those gaps through the inclusion of knowledge that may be embedded in their students' personal and prior experiences or that of the community surrounding the school. It also affords the opportunity to seek out the voices of non-traditional writers, scientists, populations, etc. who are not included in the traditional dominant narrative but who have contributed to the focused topic, concept, event, etc. that is under study. This not only provides students with a more balanced view of what they are learning (and perhaps seeing themselves represented in the content), but also gives them the opportunity to form their own opinions and perspectives or to further develop their critical thinking skills. Thinking about ways to connect what they will learn to other concepts being taught in other subjects or to even extend what they are learning to the real world is also something that can be done when teachers analyze their curriculum more intentionally and critically.

Instructional Activities

This is the section of the lesson plan where the focus is on the "how" of content teaching? Teachers should document sequentially all of the steps, activities, and accommodations that would be used to engage students in learning the content from the beginning of the lesson to the end. In determining the how, the instructional decisions teachers make should begin with the end (what the students need to walk away knowing) in mind. It is equally as important that the needs and learning styles of the students are carefully considered. To do this, teachers should consider asking themselves the following questions:

1. What do I want my students to know at the end of this lesson?
2. What do students already know?
3. What gaps are there between the first two questions posed?
4. What strategies or activities should be incorporated to meaningfully engage students in the learning process?
5. How can I connect what they are learning in this lesson to the real world?

Table 8.3 lists a variety of instructional activities that can be used to engage students who have different learning styles/preferences.

Effective teaching should consist of the following: (1) Explicit instruction, (2) Guided Practice, and (3) Independent Practice. This scaffolding of instruction gradually moves students from dependent to independent learners. At the beginning of the lesson teachers will engage the students to pique their interests and model the skill, concept, or strategy they desire their students to learn/master. Explicit, concrete instruction is provided in this stage of the teaching process, which connects what the students already know to what they need to know in order to master the objectives of the lesson. Explicit instruction does not consist of teachers lecturing (Banking model) or giving worksheets (busy work). Explicit instruction is modeling, demonstrating, and verbalizing what students should be able to do or know by the end of the lesson.

The teacher then provides guided practice, an opportunity to practice the skill with feedback. Teachers check for understanding and provide more support for students who require it. This support could include student think alouds, student accountable talk, and completion of graphic organizers. Guided practice is not providing the same support to every student, giving independent seatwork, or even students working in groups without teacher support.

The final step in this process is for students to practice the skill independently (alone and/or in a small group). Teachers are responsible for monitoring for understanding and concept mastery. Independent practice is not doing work that is unrelated to the goal of the lesson or prior to students receiving explicit directions.

Table 8.3. Instructional Strategies

Learning Style/Preferences	Strategies/Activities
Auditory	• Think, Pair, Share • Listening to books on tape • Speaking and listening games • Debates and discussions • Oral quizzes
Visual	• Visualization games and exercises • Graphic organizers • Photo essays • Visual or illustrated logs and journals • Daily use of Planners
Bodily-Kinesthetic/Tactile	• Interactive whiteboards • Hands-on experiments • Use of math manipulatives • Engaging in brief "Brain Breaks"

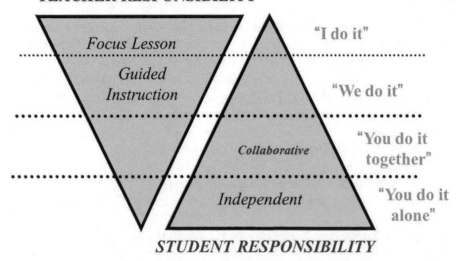

Fisher, D., & Frey, N. (2008). *Better learning through structured teaching: A framework for the gradual release of responsibility.* Alexandria, VA: Association for Supervision and Curriculum Development.

Figure 8.3.   Scaffolding Model

Figure 8.3 depicts how Fisher and Frey (2008) demonstrated the role of the teacher shifting throughout a lesson. The educator's role/responsibility changes from that of instructor to facilitator while students' independence is increased.

Scaffolding strategies such as Read Alouds, Graphic Organizers, Cooperative Groups and I Do-We Do-You Do, are excellent tools to assist students on the road to becoming more independent.

Active Learning

Identify the components of effective instruction (explicit, guided, and independent instruction) in the lesson plan below. Consider ways in which the lesson was successful in accomplishing the lesson objectives while embodying diverse funds of knowledge, the experiences of the students, and problem-posing instruction.

Day 1: Introduction to Cell Division & Key Terms (What Is Cell Division?)

Initiating Activity: Students will complete a KWL (Know, Wonder/Want to Know, and Learned) on their prior knowledge of cells and their processes. They will complete the K and then the W: what they know and want to learn about cell division.

Core Activity:
1. First I will tell the students to pull out their textbooks and paper to write notes.
2. Students will be introduced to the key terms of cell division and be asked to find the definitions within the textbook.
3. Once new vocabulary has been introduced and defined, the teacher will present a PowerPoint presentation on the cell cycle of nuclear division. The presentation will include:
   a. What the cell cycle is; mitosis and meiosis
   b. A short description on prophase and a microscope slide showing prophase
   c. A short description on metaphase and a microscope slide showing metaphase
   d. A short description on anaphase and a microscope slide showing anaphase
   e. A short description on telophase and a microscope slide showing telophase
   f. A microscopic image of spindle fibers, nucleus, and centrioles followed with detailed explanations of what they do

Closing Activity: Near the end of class, the mentioning of assigned groups will be presented to promote cooperative learning the following day in continuation of the lesson plan. Students will be responsible for putting away all the materials used. In preparation for tomorrow all the KWL charts and notes will be collected to assure they have the notes for tomorrow. Prior to dismissal, the students will be instructed to create a circle around the room where they will each quickly and verbally share one thing they learned in class. They will be tossing a ball from one to another to share. The student who possesses the ball speaks and then tosses it to the next student so that they can share their thoughts.

Evaluation: Students will turn in the notes with the vocabulary definitions. KWL charts will be collected to assess their prior knowledge on cells. The students will be completing the L portion of the chart the next class period. Evaluating the definitions will ensure that students matched the vocabulary words properly to their meaning.

Day 2: Textbook Perspective. (Stages of Cell Division & Core Scientists)

Initiating Activity: As the students enter the classroom they will be given an entrance ticket from the teacher. The ticket will instruct them to get into their assigned groups from the previous day and also ask the question "what is cell division?" Students will be asked to reflect on the lesson from the day before, listing off the key terms and their meaning. With their responses, they are to complete the L (what they learned) section of their KWL charts.

Core Activity:
1. The students will be shown a short video by the Amoeba Sisters titled: Mitosis: The Amazing Cell Process that Uses Division to Multiply! on YouTube.
2. The importance of cellular division will be reviewed and the ideal of identifying abnormalities that can occur if the cells do not divide. Strategic questioning will be instructed such as:
   a. What are some advantages of cellular division?
   b. What do you think would happen if cells did not divide properly?
   c. Would there be negative or positive effects?
   d. Why are cells so important to our existence?
3. The students will then be introduced to the core scientists, found in their textbooks, who contributed to the information they just learned.

Closing Activity: Students will be asked to gather in their assigned groups to collaborate on completing the cell cycle model; each student will also summarize what they learned about the significant scientists, specific to this day, in cytology theories. Students will be responsible for constructing and completing their own cell cycle model.

Evaluation: In evaluating their understanding, each student will demonstrate their own understanding of the lesson by constructing their own cell cycle model. They will be responsible independently to complete these diagrams but be allotted the ability to ask their peers for assistance if needed. This will build student confidence in ability and allow for individual assessment.

Day 3: Diverse Perspectives

Initiating Activity: Upon entering the classroom, the teacher will direct the students to the (5) different stations located throughout the classroom. Each station will provide information on a different scientist/biologist who contributed to cytology and mitosis. The students will spend about 2–3 minutes at each station to establish a quick observation on what each of the scientists/biologists contributed.

Core Activity: 1. After viewing the diverse scientists around the room, the students and instructor will discuss these particular scientists and why they have been placed throughout the classroom.
                    2. The teacher will explain that they are going to be working in groups for a project they will be presenting the following week. The teacher will then split the students into (5) heterogeneous groups of 3–4 students in each group.
                    3. Each group will be assigned to a specific scientist/biologist whom they will conduct research on. They will be instructed to create a list of 7–10 (can be more) details/key events on their scientist's life and works to be turned in at the end of the class period. They will need to include at least two references for information.

Closing Activity: Toward the end of the class, the students (in groups) will fill out a Closure and Evaluation Form where they discuss: what they learned, what may have surprised/interested them, what they enjoyed, and what they newly discovered. The teacher will ask each group to share one surprising fact they learned about their scientist.

Evaluation: The students will turn in their list of 7–10 details/key events (with references) about their scientist. They will receive 10 points for completion as long as the information is viable with sources cited. The information they gather will be used in their project and for the next class.

Day 4: Critical Examination of the Topic/Textbook, etc. (textbook bias discussion)

Initiating Activity: The students will be placed into the same groups from the day before to complete a data race. The students will be sent off on a 'race' to find key bits of information on their vocabulary and the scientists they have learned about. The pieces of information will be hidden within the textbooks and around the classroom. Once they have gathered five pieces of information, the students will need to write out the full detail of that piece given (i.e., if they have "recognized fundamental role of cell cycle" then they must state the scientists name "Ernest Just") onto a plain sheet of paper they are to title "Data Race Results." The students will have 10 minutes to complete their data race.

Core Activity: The students will be lead into a discussion on textbook bias and the importance of diversity. They will then become "textbook detectives" and, in groups, read excerpts from the school textbook about the core scientists they were introduced to previously. The teacher will have a list of the following questions for the students to consider, discuss, and answer in groups:
                    • Why do you think this textbook excluded the scientists we learned about yesterday?
                    • Who would benefit from this lack of information?
                    • Why is it important to tell students about diverse individuals who have contributed to cytology?
                    • How can you ensure that you are getting all of the perspectives when learning a specific topic?
                    • How can we identify textbook bias in the future?
                    • What can you do to change the one-sided perspective given in your textbook?

Closing Activity: The students will each share their response to one of the above questions. The teacher will inform the students that they must present their answers in their presentation as well as the information they gathered on their scientist/biologist.

Evaluation: The groups will turn in their "Data Race Results" sheet. The teacher will evaluate the content and ensure each piece of information was correctly completed.

Evaluation

Evaluation focuses on how you will know that the students have learned the material (i.e. fulfilled the goals/ objectives specified). As noted in the daily instructional plans above, evaluation should be embedded into instruction and on-going. It is always helpful to identify multiple evaluation strategies, or to develop an evaluation that moves beyond the traditional "test." This will be further explained in the next chapter.

References

Adams, N.E. (2015). Bloom's taxonomy of cognitive learning objectives. *Journal of the Medical Library Association*, 103(3), 152. Retrieved from http://go.galegroup.com.ezproxy.fau.edu/ps/i.do?id=GALE%7CA426999565&sid=summon& v=2.1&u=gale15691&it=r&p=AONE&sw=w&asid=68530c22dd913aa4a3393753e287b11e.

Banks, J.A. (1998). The lives and values of researchers: Implications for educating citizens in a multicultural society. *Educational Researcher*, 27(7), 4–17.

Bush, H., Daddysman, J., & Charnigo, R. (2014) Improving outcomes with bloom's taxonomy: From statistics education to research partnerships. *Journal of Biometrics and Biostatics, 5.* DOI:10.4172/2155-6180.1000e130.

Fisher, D., Frey, N., & NetLibrary, I. (2008). *Better learning through structured teaching: A framework for the gradual release of responsibility*. Alexandria, VA: Association for Supervision and Curriculum Development.

Hall, D. (2012). Fourteen hundred ninety-two: The columbus poem rewritten. *Indian Country Today*. Retrieved from: https://indiancountrymedianetwork.com/news/fourteen-hundred-ninety-two-the-columbus-poem-rewritten/.

In 1492. (n.d.) In *Hot chalk lesson plans*. Retrieved from http://lessonplanspage.com/lasscolumbusDayrhymingin1492poemk1-htm/.

lesson.[def.1] (n.d.). *Dictionary.com Unabridged*. Retrieved September 27, 2016 from http://www.dictionary.com/browse/ lesson.

Nieto, S., & Bode, P. (2008). *Affirming diversity: The sociopolitical context of multicultural education*. Boston, MA: Allyn & Bacon.

Nieto, S. (2011). Multicultural Education. In *Diversity, community, and achievement*. Retrieved from http://www.teachingasleadership.org/sites/default/files/Related-Readings/DCA_2011.pdf.

Sleeter, C. (2005). *Un-standardizing curriculum*. New York, NY: Teachers College Press.

University Center for the Advancement of Teaching. (2016). *Rationale for course materials*. Retrieved from http://ucat.osu .edu/professional-development/teaching-portfolio/rationale/.

Wiggins, G., & McTighe, J. (2005). *Understanding by design*. Alexandria, VA: Association for Supervision & Curriculum Development.

Why Should I be Thinking Backwards About my Curriculum?

As a new teacher, the number of decisions you are asked to make in a single day is overwhelming at best. However, one of the most important considerations for new teachers is often not a consideration at all. . .how is the curriculum designed and aligned with state mandates and with my students' prior experiences and cultural backgrounds in mind? Teachers are often working in schools where curriculum and assessments are prescribed and organized for them, leaving teachers to simply follow the plan as mandated. While curriculum designers and school districts have good intentions when creating curriculum for schools and teachers to follow, there are a myriad of problems that exist when teachers do not take ownership over the design of their own curriculum and assessments (Wiggins & McTighe, 2011). Backwards design, specifically a model called Understanding by Design (UbD), is based on eight key understandings (Wiggins & McTighe, 2011). UbD is a purposeful curriculum planning model in which the primary goal is student understanding and transferable learning. As a veteran teacher and curriculum designer, I have synthesized the eight key understandings below and will explain how paying attention to your curriculum is one of the most important tasks teachers may NOT be doing.

UbD is a Way of Thinking Purposefully About Curricular Planning, not a Rigid Program or Prescriptive Recipe.

Thinking purposefully about curriculum means that the cultures, abilities, and knowledge of students within your own classroom are considered before making decisions about content learning. Prescriptive curriculum programs are built with no particular student in mind. While there are likely useful resources for you to incorporate into your instruction, your responsibility is to teach your students and to take into consideration what they need. In doing so you should ask yourself the following questions: what do my students already know, what do they need, what are they interested in, and what assessments will work the best in allowing them to demonstrate their mastery of content ? These questions will help guide your planning before blindly beginning your instruction on the first page of the textbook. Instruction should develop and deepen students' understanding of key concepts so student learning can be transferred to new situations.

It is easy to see curriculum as a set of skills students need to master, for example, multiplication, grammar, historical dates, etc. However, research on knowledge retention and student learning tells us that when students develop deep understandings about content, they are more likely to use that new knowledge in varied situations and contexts. Let's think about multiplication, while students may need to know basic multiplication facts, the crux of a unit on multiplication should focus on *when* and *why* we use multiplication to solve real-world problems. Deepening their understanding of the content and making meaning of why they would need this knowledge ensures that students will transfer their learning beyond the lesson or unit being taught to other learning situations or to the real-world.

Effective Curriculum is Planned "Backward" From Long-term Desired Results Through a Three-Stage Design Process (Desired Results, Evidence, Learning Plan).

One of the reasons we refer to this method of curriculum design as "backwards" is because of the order in which we are suggesting that the curriculum be planned. Instead of thinking of the activities you would like to do with your students first and then finding a content standard that would align with the activities and assessment; UbD encourages you to think about your desired end result first. What do you want your students to know and be able to do by the end of your lesson? What learning experiences will your students walk away with when the lesson is complete? After reflecting on this important stage, you should move to creating or using an existing assessment that captures this desired end result in an engaging and authentic way. Lastly, you should design learning activities that give students rich experiences with the content and move them closer to the desired end result. *What strategies or activities should I implement that will facilitate the best learning experience for them?*

Working backwards leads to a clearer pathway to content/skill mastery, thus avoiding a curriculum that is packed with activities which may be fun but do not facilitate students' deepened understanding, or a curriculum that relies too heavily on textbooks that do not provide the depth of knowledge students need to make meaningful connections across the curriculum. In my own experiences, the greatest benefit to a curriculum that is designed backwards is the instructional time that it saves in the classroom. When there is alignment between objectives, assessments, and activities, students (and teachers) have a clear idea of where they are trying to go and what they are working towards. This results in greater success in the classroom and more time to explore the content through rich learning experiences.

Understanding is Revealed When Students Autonomously Make Sense of and Transfer Their Learning Through Authentic Performance.

As a new teacher, you will have access to a plethora of assessments use to evaluate your students, including those tied to mandated textbooks and created by school districts, high-stakes tests, and of course teacher-created evaluations. Today's students will encounter more test preparation and mandated assessments than ever before. As a teacher, your responsibility is to make certain that instructional time is maximized and can lead to valuable learning experiences.

When designing curriculum, we should think through what it is we want our students to learn. The next thing we should do is to ask ourselves the, "What will it look like when my students truly understand this concept?" Usually, the answer to that question is not that they will be able to answer a multiple choice question. Using authentic performance assessment as a means of evaluation will ask that students demonstrate their knowledge in a way that it would be relevant and meaningful. For example, if the goal is for students to understand certain basic grammatical rules in writing, an authentic assessment might be for them to use grammar rules while writing an email to a potential employer instead of giving them a multiple choice quiz on grammar rules. The idea of assessment is also to see if your students can take what you have taught them in the classroom and apply it to a setting where they can transform and transfer the knowledge gained into addressing real world situations. Authentic assessments give the teacher a deeper understanding on what students have mastered and what may need more work in the next unit of study.

Teachers are Coaches of Understanding, Not Mere Purveyors of Content or Activity.

A coach of understanding is a teacher who uses feedback, both written and oral, to help students get closer to the desired result. This may be done through thoughtful questioning in a student conference or constructive feedback on a written assignment, but like a coach, the goal is to have students achieve without you on the field.

When I first began teaching, I thought the more I talked and explained things to my students, the more they learned. Over the years, I began to realize that the less time I spent talking and explaining, the more time students spent actually engaged with the content and each other, which led to rich dialogue, a deeper understanding, and inevitably more learning. When I became a coach that facilitated and scaffolded the process, instead of the holder of the knowledge, the students took more ownership of their own learning and more frequently understood concepts and transferred knowledge to new situations. Of course, there is a time and place for direct instruction, but as a new teacher, take time to reflect on how much of the day you spend talking at students versus how much time you are actively listening and students are engaged in relevant learning experiences.

Regular Reviews of Units and Curriculum Enhance Curricular Quality and Effectiveness.

There will be times that after completing a unit you will review your students' assessments only to realize that they did not grasp key concepts. This may be frustrating but it gives you an opportunity to reflect and redesign your curriculum and instruction so students can be more successful in the future. As a reflective practitioner, an important part of your practice is to routinely ask questions and use the answers to these questions to adjust your pedagogy to be more effective, both as a learner and a teacher. It is essential to review your work and find peers who will engage in that review with you. Working with your colleagues on how to become more effective; being open to feedback from veteran educators in the field is key to being an effective teacher. You will also find that it can be rewarding professionally and personally.

There are a number of methods and models to design curriculum effectively and UbD is only one of them. What is important to understand is that teachers should be intentional about the curriculum and assessment design process. As a new teacher, the learning curve may be steep, but do not ignore the impact you can have on your students and their learning experiences when you take ownership over the curriculum in your own classroom.

References

Wiggins, G. P. & McTighe, J. (2011). *The understanding by design guide to creating high-quality units.* Alexandria, VA: ASCD.

Practical Encounter

Directions: Using the CPALMS website, go through the followings steps:

1. Go to www.cpalms.org
2. Select a grade level
3. Select a subject/area that has instructional resources or lesson plans
4. Click lesson plans on the right side of the screen
5. Choose a lesson plan to review from the list that pops up
6. Review a lesson and answer the following questions

Which principle of multicultural education does your selected lesson exemplify?

_____

_____

_____

Has knowledge been grounded in multiple points of view? Explain (Which sections and how?)

_____

_____

_____

Whose knowledge is being 'taught'? What are the tacit values of this curriculum?

_____

_____

_____

Do learning activities facilitate instructional pluralism and cultural pluralism?

_____

_____

_____

Are all five components congruent? (e.g. Does the assessment 'measure' the goals? Do content and activities facilitate goals?)

_____

_____

_____

What adjustments would you make to the lesson to make it multicultural (theory, instruction, assessment, etc.) based on what you learned this in this course/textbook?

_____

_____

_____

CHAPTER 9
Evaluation: A Multicultural Perspective

Dr. Tunjarnika L. Coleman-Ferrell and Dr. Roxanna Anderson

Case Study

Ms. Miller, an Academic Advisor at Florida Girls School was preparing her students for the upcoming Algebra I Florida Standards Assessment. They needed to pass this test in order to receive their high school diploma. Ms. Miller figured that the students would struggle more with navigating the test than the actual assessment content. During a study session, Ms. Miller presented a PowerPoint Presentation that included examples of strategies they could use while taking the assessment.

A couple days later, Ms. Miller took the students to the computer lab and provided them with reference sheets, calculators, and examples from past assessments. Before the mock test, she noticed the students' solemn, angry, frustrated faces.

"Why are we here? Are we taking another stupid test?" Sapphire moaned.

"Well, no," Ms. Miller replied. "All of you still need to pass the Algebra 1 assessment to complete your graduation requirements. Today we are going to review strategies that can help you with that."

"There's no point," Sapphire snapped back. "I've taken this test 4 times. I don't care about this dumb test. I'm just not able to do math. I'll never pass it."

"Same!" a couple of the other students chimed in.

"Well, let's at least go through this material to see what we can do to increase your chances of success," Ms. Miller continued.

After the review session Ms. Miller asked Sapphire to stay behind.

"Sapphire, you mentioned you've taken this test 4 times. Was this at your previous school?"

"Yea . . ." Sapphire sheepishly replied. "I liked math when I was younger, but when I got to middle school that changed. The material got really hard and my teachers never wanted to help me. They always ignored my questions and just put me in the back of the room. A few of my teachers talked about how girls aren't good in math and I should just do the basics to get by."

"I see. Well, thank you for staying a moment to chat. I'm committed to helping you be successful. How about we meet for a few math tutoring sessions to prepare you further for the test?"

Submitted by Staci Miller, Teacher

Questions to Ponder:

1. What were Sapphire's previous experiences with taking assessments?
2. Why did she feel that she would not achieve success on this particular test? Do you think this feeling is felt by many of today's students? Why or why not?
3. Was the challenge in how she was prepared to take the test or in the design of the test itself?
4. What could you do as a teacher to ensure assessment equity for all of your students in today's age of testing?

Introduction

In an era of accountability, schools are mandated to ensure student proficiency via student test results, high school graduation rates, and other indicators. However as multicultural educators, our goal is to ensure assessment equity in this current data-driven arena, which often includes high-stakes consequences. Multicultural educators have a greater interest in countering the systemic testing inequities that often work against marginalized groups of students. Often, when the term multicultural is used, only race or ethnicity seem to be considered, but students are diverse in various ways, including gender, learning styles, native language, culture, socio-economic background, and abilities. This millennial classroom brings a host of questions pertaining to the education of future generations of students therefore the following questions must be addressed.

- How does the classroom educator appropriately address the needs of students?
- How does the educator obtain valid and reliable data to assist in making valuable decisions in the classroom?
- What will be an appropriate process for assessing the diverse needs of students?
- What are the guidelines for appropriately selecting, implementing and administering assessments?
- What types of instruments will be used to measure students' mastery of learning objectives?
- How will the data obtained be used to properly measure student performance?
- How will the information obtained be applied to improve the individual student's performance, as well as, improve the quality of the classroom experience?

A Historical Perspective

Students enter the classroom from diverse family backgrounds, at different stages of development, and at various academic levels. No two students are alike, they each have preferences for learning and process information differently. In order for students to achieve success academically, teachers are expected to make instructional decisions - designing lessons and determining how students will be evaluated, that meet the unique learning needs of their students. The foundation and the creation of these lessons and assessments should be based on educators setting high standards for student learning; expectations that are both measurable and attainable, with the goal of improving individual educational outcomes for students. This was the goal that precipitated the need for legislations such as the No Child Left Behind Act of 2001(NCLB).

No Child Left Behind

NCLB (2001) was a collaboration between civil rights groups and politicians that was aimed at closing the "achievement gap" between groups that were privileged and those who were from minority groups or who lived in poverty. One key to the success of this initiative was the government holding schools accountable for student outcomes. NCLB replaced the Elementary and Secondary School Act (ESEA). ESEA was a product of President Lyndon B. Johnson's *Great Society* which was passed in 1965 to provide Federal Aid to school districts to cover the cost of educating poor and disadvantaged children. Since 1965, the Law has seen several reiterations. Under NCLB schools had to test students in reading and mathematics from grades 3 through 8 and once in high school. These scores had to be reported for various subgroups including English as a second language students, minority populations, and those receiving special education. A "proficiency" level was devised by each state; schools were mandated to bring their students up to this level by the 2013-2014 academic school year. What was problematic was that each state was allowed to define what proficiency meant as well as the assessment instruments.

As of early 2015, no state had been able to report their students as having reached the level of proficiency set by NCLB. However, each school had to make adequate yearly progress (AYP) or sanctions were levelled. For example, if a school did not make AYP for two or more years, for either individual students or subgroups of students, students had the option to transfer to another school within the district that demonstrated AYP. If AYP was not achieved for three consecutive years, the school was mandated to provide free tutoring. The money for tutoring had to come from Title I funds received from the federal government. The last course of action was a choice between the school being transformed into a charter school or being shut down completely.

In the wake of NCLB, the field of education has been faced with the challenge of rethinking student evaluation within the context of student diversity and the multicultural classroom. Our classrooms have become more diverse in learner demographics, ethnicities, learning preferences, intelligences, and capabilities--all impacting and changing the way we think about student performance. While our classrooms are more diverse than ever before and NCLB has presented more challenges in terms of student evaluation and equitable learning opportunities, we must have some measure of competency to determine grade level proficiency for all students.

To critics of NCLB, the reform's unintentional consequences did in fact "leave children behind." One of the major criticisms was that there was no evidence that schools actually transferred or tutored students. Standardized testing, which used valuable reading and math instruction time for administering tests and for test prep, generated concerns about the assessment's reliability. Another criticism was that federal dollars never reached the critical level to properly fund the schools (Klein, 2016) or the initiative itself. For example, federal funding was to have reached twenty-five billion by 2000, but as of 2015 only $14.5 billion had been received. Another criticism was that some states ignored the part of the law that mandated that highly qualified teachers stipulation. Teachers who were certified and demonstrated proficiency in the content areas, were to be hired to teach at both underprivileged and privileged schools. By 2010, it was clear that students were not going to achieve the level of proficiency expected.

Stipek and Lombardo (2014), citing 30 years of peer reviewed research, state that leaving children behind is counterproductive and that there are long-term negative outcomes, such as loss in earnings and a delay entering into the workforce. According to Xia and Glennie (2005) there are far greater negative effects (e.g., low self-esteem and emotional distress) than there are benefits. More troubling is the long-term effect on students' well-being, such so that a correlation was found between retention and early dropout rates and subsequent drug abuse.

President Obama's Every Student Succeeds Act (ESSA)

President Barack Obama's Every Student Succeeds Act (ESSA) was signed into law on December 10, 2015. This educational reform is intended to reauthorize the Elementary and Secondary Act (ESEA). The new ACT will:

- Ensure that states set high standards so high school graduates are college and career ready
- Maintain accountability by guaranteeing that when students fall behind, states target resources toward an effective plan to assist them and their schools to continue to improve, with a particular focus on the lowest-performing five percent of schools, high schools with high dropout rates, and schools where subgroups of students are struggling.

- Empower state and local decision-makers in developing their own strong systems for school improvement based upon evidence, rather than imposing cookie-cutter federal solutions the way NCLB, its predecessor, did.
- Preserve annual assessments and reduce the often onerous burden of unnecessary and ineffective testing on students and teachers, making sure that standardized tests do not crowd out teaching and learning without sacrificing clear, annual information parents and educators need to make sure our children are learning.
- Provide more access to high-quality preschooling, giving students the chance to get a strong start to their education.
- Establish new resources to test promising practices and replicate proven strategies that will drive opportunity and better outcomes for America's students (*US Department of Education*).

ESSA is a response to the failures and rigidity of NCLB. NCLB fell short in providing the funding and the flexibility for states to make decisions that were in the best interest of their citizens. However, NCLB was

> . . . a significant step forward for our nation's children in many respects, particularly as it shined a light on where students were making progress and where they needed additional support, regardless of race, income, zip code, disability, home language, or background. (*US Department of Education*)

Ultimately ESSA gives states the responsibility and flexibility to create academic goals and accountability measures to fully prepare students for success in college and careers. This reform is committed to advancements in equity and upholding protections for students who have been traditionally marginalized. While the goal has merit, it is too early to determine if this reform will measure up to its intent and provide success for all students.

Cultural Bias-A Matter of Perspective

How does intelligence tests (IQ) relate to other tests given as a result of accountability measures? One thing we do know is that cultural bias in testing is not a new phenomenon and can be tracked past that of intelligence tests. According to Santrock (2016), bias in testing has been documented for approximately 100 years, beginning with Cyril Burt in 1909, a British educational psychologist who conducted research on intelligence. From his research he concluded that people of color were inferior to White people. His work was found to be fraudulent five years after his death; however, uncovering the fraudulent research did not stop Burt's supporters who continued to perpetuate the false accusations of Burt's work. Jensen's theoretical orientation propelled Burt's theory into the mainstream. Jensen believed that intelligence was hereditary and that people of color were inferior to White people. Around the same time, Alfred Binet in 1904, devised the IQ test which would measure five aspects of cognitive ability: (1) fluid reasoning; (2) knowledge; (3) quantitative reasoning; (4) visual-spatial processing; and (5) working memory. The fallacy of attempting to measure disparate cognitive abilities resulted in many children being relegated to classes for special education.

Context matters when it comes to measuring intelligence or evaluating any construct. Unfortunately, standardized testing opens the door for potential biases as a result of its "one size fits all" design. An example of a standardized test that can be culturally biased is an IQ test. Santrock (2016) reported that when compared to their White counterparts, African American students scored 10 to 15 points below on intelligence tests. One test item, for example, could ask a student to identify what a zebra looks like or point to the picture of a zebra. If a student has never seen a zebra, and was asked to discern which picture resembles a zebra, does answering this question incorrectly mean they are unintelligent?

Research focused on cultural bias in testing is well documented in the literature, Reynolds, Lowe and Saenz (1999), cite seven possible categories of test bias that exist when considering testing with minorities; the ones that are most relevant to our discussion are summarized in Table 9.1. These categories of testing bias bring into question how and what we do with assessment results. Are the results used in a punitive manner when there is research that supports the notion that tests are inherently biased?

Table 9.1. Possible Categories of Test Bias

Inappropriate Content	Tests are geared to the majority or dominant population's experiences, knowledge, and values or are scored arbitrarily according to majority values.
Inappropriate Standardization Samples	Minorities' representations in norming samples is proportionate to the actual population, but there is not enough representation to allow them any significant power on testing design.
Measurement of Different Constructs	Tests that are based on the experiences and/or knowledge of the majority culture measure different characteristics or constructs than what members of minority groups would know, thus rendering them invalid for these groups.
Differential Predictive Validity	Standardized tests do not accurately predict many relevant outcomes for minority groups. The criteria that tests are designed to predict may inherently be biased against minorities.
Qualitatively Distinct Aptitude and Personality	This position seems to suggest that minority and majority ethnic groups possess characteristics of different types, so that test development must begin with different definitions for majority and minority groups

Adapted from Reynolds, et al. (1999)

Although not as overt, critics still believe that there are cultural biases that are evident in present-day evaluation measures. For example, in Florida, the Florida Comprehensive Assessment Test (FCAT) (the former state assessment), was devised as a response to improve achievement in grades 3 through 11, using a criterion-referenced approach. The FCAT measured student achievement against a predetermined set of criteria. However, the expectation was that students across the state needed to reach a preset level of proficiency. This was the expectation whether or not students were explicitly taught the information, or a deep understanding was gained. With this frame of reference, one can conclude that traditionally marginalized students are often the victims of cultural testing bias due to how tests are constructed, language bias, and embedded mainstream cultural knowledge.

Psychometricians should consider the population being tested. Large publishing companies control test design or construction which mirrors the values and knowledge of the dominant population or what they deem important enough to know (i.e. cultural literacy). For example, the Educational Testing Service hires many theoreticians to devise tests which determine the long term trajectory of a student's life. It is believed that these tests, through their design, label many low socioeconomic learners as significantly below grade level (based on test results), while promoting the upper middle class and more affluent students who have access to more resources at home and in their classrooms. Low socioeconomic children are bereft of adequate textbooks and/or are not permitted to check out school books and materials to be taken home. It is not possible to adequately provide a measure that meets the standards of both reliability and validity when the populations upon which the tests have been normed do not represent the groups being tested.

Evaluation Defined

While the terms evaluation, testing, and assessment have been used interchangeably, for the purpose of this chapter evaluation will be viewed as the term of choice to indicate both formative and summative assessment of students. Evaluation is a process that is predicated on the data outcome of the measurement that was given. The process is data focused and greatly impacts schools, curricula, policy, students and staff- all things education (Popham, 2010). Formative assessment is usually ongoing, low stakes and used on a daily basis to assess student performance. However, summative assessment is usually comprehensive and often implemented in the lesson as a midterm and/or final exam. Once a measurement tool (i.e. test) has been administered the data is obtained, reviewed, analyzed, and instructional decisions are made. For example, a math teacher administers a chapter test on combining like terms. After grading the tests, the teacher would examine them to determine which questions the students did well on overall and which questions the students had more difficulty with. Based on this information, the teacher will be able to determine which skills and/or standards needed to be reviewed and or retaught. In order to successfully articulate performance or achievement, classroom educators must consider the *Who, What, When, Where,* and *How* of evaluation as follows:

1. **Who is being evaluated?** The target population, the students who will be evaluated, is critical within the context of the student's background, prior exposure to previously learned material, and their unique learning styles. This can be especially complex in the multicultural classroom as there is usually diversity within the layers of learner preferences, race, ethnicity, socioeconomic background and culture, all of which can impact a student's performance on a test.

2. **What is being evaluated?** The learning targets are often driven by standards that are set within a federal and/or state framework or guidelines. Hence, it is important to identify the skill set that a student needs prior to the test and the expectations of performance that the students should learn.

3. **How will students be evaluated?** This question is key in selecting the right tool(s) to evaluate student mastery of learning outcomes. The tool must also be an appropriate fit for the learner and the learning outcome. The aforementioned targets must be clear with attainable outcomes that are correlated with curriculum content and learning outcomes, also known as deliverables. Ideally multiple performance indicators, such as a combination of both standardized and authentic, formative and summative, should be used to increase reliability and validity of the test results. Hence, these results directly correlate to curriculum content instruction that has been previously delivered and answers the question as to whether or not learning outcomes have been properly met. The use of multiple techniques and formats accommodates different learning styles to include auditory, visual, kinesthetic, and tactile learners. In addition, cross utilization of techniques also appeals to the multiple intelligences that we see typically exhibited and honored in a multicultural classroom setting.

4. **When will the evaluation be administered?** The timeline for administration of the assessment is essential as the tool ideally should be administered after content material is sufficiently introduced to the learner. If the evaluation is formative, it could also be implemented at different points of the learning process to check for student understanding or to monitor student progress. For example, Ms. Davis introduced her first grade math students to the skill of adding two digit numbers. After she introduced the students to the skill and modeled how to work out the problem for the students, she then gave the students a problem to try out on their own. They took out their mini dry erase boards, wrote down the problem, and began to work the problem out. Ms. Davis walked about the classroom to check to see if her students understood the concept. During this time, she was able to see which students had a clear understanding of the skill and who needed further instruction. She used this information to help her determine what her next steps of instruction would be for her students.

5. **Where will the evaluation be administered?** The environmental setting in which students are assessed can have a great impact on student success. The educational setting should be free of distractions, organized, intentional in set-up, considerate of students with exceptionalities, comfortable and practical.

6. **Why is evaluation needed?** Evaluation is needed to ensure that students are mastering learning standards and/or making progress towards content mastery. It's a form of accountability for both teachers and students.

Pros of Evaluation

There are many benefits to evaluating student achievements. Evaluations can be used to promote clarity in the expectations of learning outcomes for both the educator and the student. Assessments can also promote accountability in the implementation of quality opportunities for feedback for both the educator and the student, which is positively correlated with student achievement. When implemented effectively, evaluations can also be an indicator of whether teachers have effectively delivered instruction. If not, teachers can use the assessment results to modify or reteach the lesson/skill. Evaluations allow federal, state, districts, community partners, educators, parents and students to analyze whether certain skillsets and knowledge are being effectively delivered and/or if adequate resources have been allocated. The aforementioned benefits can greatly impact the trajectory of a student's education, life and future; as well as provide opportunities for stakeholders to have a voice in the future development of new materials, content, tools, and techniques based on test results.

Cons of Evaluation

Due to the serious nature of assessment it is important for educators to also be aware of some of the concerns surrounding student assessment. Concerns with assessment revolve around the following: *content delivery, funding disparities, inadequate infrastructure, and inequitable technology.* The first concern revolves around how content or the curriculum is being taught

and what materials are being used to teach it. Are all students exposed to the same content in the same manner? What is the likelihood that everyone would be provided access to quality instruction? There are also funding disparities between schools who have access to resources to purchase trade books and supplemental resources and those who do not. However, what is also a part of this discussion is whether the reallocation of funding to low-SES neighborhoods is the answer to leveling the playing field or are there more crucial factors to consider?

The physical environment in which students test differ across states, cities and neighborhoods. Students in affluent areas enjoy the opportunity of new schools, new classrooms, new technology, and the latest testing centers, thus providing environments that are more conducive to learning and preparing students for testing, and that nurture innovation. It is imperative that educators reflect on how these factors impact the way students perform on tests and the opportunities they have for success. Students can be evaluated in various ways and with the use of different measurement tools (Popham, 2013). Our discussion now turns to highlight some of the most frequent categories of evaluation instruments- standardized tests and authentic assessments.

Standardized Testing

Standardized testing is a form of testing that is implemented and delivered in a standard and consistent manner. Its purpose is to increase the consistency and reliability in the administration of assessment tools. Standardized tests are commonly quantitative in nature and measure student success on a predetermined set of scales. Such examples include: Scholastic Aptitude Test (SAT), American College Test (ACT), Iowa Test of Basic Skills (ITBS), and the Florida Standards Assessment (FSA).

There are two main types of tests used in educational testing. The first type is criterion-referenced tests, which are designed to measure students' knowledge on a finite set of skills or learning standards, such as the standards-based assessments at the state level (e.g. FSA in Florida). In essence, these tests are used to determine if students have mastered a specific body of knowledge at the end of a specific grade level. Criterion-referenced tests may include a combination of question types: multiple-choice, true-false, and/or "open-ended" questions. Criterion-referenced tests and scores may be used for any of the following reasons: (1) to determine whether students have learned expected knowledge and skills; (2) to determine whether there are any learning gaps or deficits; (3) to determine whether a program, course, or curriculum is effective; (4) to measure student progress towards goals and objectives; and (5) to compare the academic achievement of students across schools and districts (*The Glossary of Education Reform*, 2014a).

The second type of assessment is norms-referenced tests, which are used to compare and rank students to their peers who take the same test. Test questions are carefully designed to create a bell curve spread based on students' performance. Scores on norm-referenced tests are typically reported as percentages or percentile rankings. For example, a student who scores in the ninetieth percentile would have performed at the same level as or better than ninety percent of students who took the same test, in the same grade and only ten percent of students who took the same test, in the same grade performed at a higher level than that student. An example of a norm-referenced test would be Common Core exams. Norms-referenced tests can be used in several ways, including: 1) as a pre-screening to identify a student's readiness for school; 2) to gather baseline data before a subject area course begins; 3) identify cognitive disabilities (dyslexia, autism, processing issues, etc.); or 4) to make decisions regarding college admissions with exams like the SAT or ACT (*The Glossary of Education Reform*, 2014b).

Pros of Standardized Testing

There are several benefits to the use of standardized testing as a form of evaluation. Standardized tests claim to be "objective" in nature and allow for the comparison of individual and groups of students. The instrument usually consists of mostly closed-ended responses. Well-scripted directions are provided for large scale administration of the instrument. Another benefit of standardized testing is that the tests can be easily scored. Student responses are usually recorded on a scantron or on an answer sheet that can be scored using a machine. Analysis of the responses can be quickly and efficiently done.

Cons of Standardized Testing

One of the major problems with standardized testing has always been how tests are normed, or standardized. Typically, tests are given to a sample of the population. Assessment and measurement courses insist that in order to generalize to the population one must have a representative sample as part of the norming group. Without these codicils to standardization, the reliability and validity of these tests will continue to be extremely low. According to Suzuki, Ponterotto, and Meller (2001), "the reliability and validity of a test used with individuals of different cultural or linguistic groups who were not included in the standardization group are questionable" (p. 6). The authors go on to suggest that testing can be appropriate only if they are continually updated and culturally fair.

There is an assumption in standardized testing that all students are on equal academic, psychological, and physical levels. Norming, using a population which mirrors the population under consideration, should be the standard for all assessment instruments. This leads to another issue with standardized testing, language bias. Many cultures use idiomatic language which has no correlation with items on the test. For example, non-English speaking students who have been citizens in the US for two years, are mandated to take standardized tests. Due to their unfamiliarity with the English language, many experience difficulties with being successful on the test. Lack of attention to the verbiage that is used in test design can be a fatal test flaw when correlated with different cultural biases. For example, if a student is answering a question that addresses furniture, their exposure to the language or lack thereof may determine whether or not they respond accurately to the test item. In some cultures, a couch may be called a loveseat, sofa, settee, chaise, futon, etc. The term couch may be considered a more universal term whereas students may not be exposed to some of the other terms and thus may not select the correct response simply because they do not identify with the main term used. In this case the issue is clearly not a matter of intelligence nor capability. This is a case that hinges solely based on exposure, language, and environment.

Active Learning

1. What can we do as educators to avoid biases of this nature in test design?
2. How can we avoid this pitfall when we create classroom-based assessments or when we administer textbook based assessments?

If provided with an opportunity to take the test in their native tongue, the tests could serve as a better indicator or measurement of their academic achievement. What makes this issue more complex for second language learners is that the written word can mean something different from region to region and place to place. If the language used in the home is not standard-English, then the children might be unable to determine the meaning of the paragraphs they are reading. In testing, reading passages provide cues to the answers allowing for retrieval of information from long-term memory (Caccioppo & Freberg, 2016). What happens when the words within the passage are unfamiliar? Can the child make educated guesses based on the other words in the paragraph?

One of the authors (Roxanna Anderson) served on the board of a charter school that served primarily low socioeconomic children whose parents worked more than one job, some with limited English abilities, and others with behavioral challenges. The neighborhood school was shut down because of successive failing grades on the former FCAT (Florida Comprehensive Achievement Test), thus giving parents the option to send their children to other schools in the area that had a passing school grade. Many of the students however were not accepted into these schools with higher school grades because the schools felt that they would have a negative effect on the school grade or assessment results. Those students ended up attending the charter school. During the academic year, Saturday mornings were reserved for instructional time to prepare students for the state assessment in an attempt to raise scores. From a parent's' perspective, these students were being denied time for recreational activities, like playing outside, sports, etc., rather than spending Saturday mornings preparing for the mandated test. The students, and their families, were victims of high-stakes testing.

High Stakes Testing

According to Suzuki, Ponterotto, and Meller (2001) five million children are improperly assessed each year which results in negative circumstances and outcomes. Wilson (2007) defines high stakes testing as measurements in which the outcomes are used to make decisions which could have dire consequences, such as teachers' salaries or bonuses being based on how students perform on an assessment. Another consequence of high stakes testing is the retention of students based solely on the outcome of the test. Other unintended consequences of high stakes testing include the following: (1) school districts mandating that schools close their doors who have not met AYP; (2) the housing market around the neighborhoods of low-performing schools affecting property taxes; which in turn (3) impact school funding and resources schools receive. High-stakes testing has played a role in teachers and administrators changing student answers on tests so the school could receive a passing score or grade (Erskine, 2014). It also has resulted in teachers teaching to the test, thus narrowing the scope of what is being taught in classrooms.

According to Campbell's Law, the greater the consequences that are associated with a quantitative measure, the more likely the indicator will be used for purposes they were not intended for (Nichols & Berliner, 2007). The quality of assessment used in the classroom directly impacts important decisions that will be made regarding student achievement and accountability measures that are set and considered at the local, state and federal levels in education. There are paradoxical implications that if evaluation measures are not carefully implemented within the context of the classroom setting, an adverse environment breeding cultural bias and other consequences can become evident.

Authentic Assessment

As educators, we must make great efforts to assess children's progress through the use of multiple measurements (*American Educational Research Association*, 1999). Standardized tests should not be the only instrument determining whether a student has met grade level proficiency by the end of the school year or mastered grade level learning outcomes. Students learn differently; some are auditory learners, while others may be visual, and still others kinesthetic. An effective teacher will teach and evaluate students using a variety of modalities and assessments in order for students to have adequate opportunities to demonstrate content mastery.

Authentic assessment is a form of student evaluation that engages the student's voice via real world examples and applications, as well as includes collaborative decision-making regarding students' achievement of learning outcomes. Authentic forms of assessment usually engage students in higher-order thinking and often highlight a student's progress, accomplishments, and progressive knowledge. It requires students to produce high quality products and/or a compilation of materials that reflect their mastery of content. Such examples include: discipline specific portfolios, cumulative portfolios, and progressive portfolios. Table 9.2 provides an overview of various types of authentic assessment and practical examples of each.

Table 9.2. Types of Authentic Assessment and Practical Examples

Type of Assessment	Description	Practical Example
Journals	Writing about an experience	To demonstrate their writing development and their use of writing skills taught, students could be assigned a weekly journal topic where they have to integrate what they have been taught in their weekly writers' workshops.
Peer and Self-Assessments	Using a rubric or assignment guidelines, students can rate the performance of their peers or themselves	Before students submit an assignment, they can exchange papers with their peers to give and receive feedback to make improvement based on assignment guidelines.
Portfolios	Over time students can archive projects and assignments that demonstrate their mastery of learning outcomes and/or that reflect their accomplishments	Students can be asked to keep an art portfolio where they store art projects that are completed throughout the year that demonstrate their mastery of several art skills or concepts taught. At the end of the semester they can select artwork from their portfolio to showcase in the school's art gallery.
Oral Interviews	Students can be asked questions about readings, content, etc.	As part of a formative math assessment, students can be interviewed by the teacher or another peer on the rules of divisibility.
Projects	Cumulative assignments or presentations that are assigned and that correlate with different concepts through milestones/benchmarks	To end a social studies unit on the Vietnam War, students can be assigned a project to create a mind map illustrating the causes and effects of the War, citing key information learned from the unit.

Pros of Authentic Assessment

This form of evaluation is not imposed by an external agency (i.e. school district, department of education, etc.); rather there is a focus on the broader knowledge and skills that students should know. There are several benefits to using authentic assessment in the classroom. Authentic assessment takes into account the multiple ways students learn (i.e. attitude to learning, social context of learning, external factors) and their interest levels. Students are provided with opportunities to demonstrate their knowledge in multiple ways. For example, after teaching a math unit on probability, a teacher might ask students, as one of the final assessment options, to demonstrate their understanding of the math concept by creating a carnival math game. In this math game students would be given the task to design a school carnival that reflects their understanding of probability. The criteria could include that the game must give a player a 25% to 40% probability of winning the game, and the project must include a written report that describes how to play the game, describes the design of the model game, and discusses both the theoretical and experimental probability of the game (Weigel, 2010). With an assessment of this nature, the evaluation is more authentic and requires students to apply what they have learned rather than regurgitate a series of steps to solve probability math problems. Another benefit of authentic assessment is that students are allowed to be involved in the creation of the test or assessment tasks.

Cons of Authentic Assessment

While there are benefits to using authentic assessments to evaluate student learning, there are also several drawbacks. One of the cons is that authentic assessment is time-consuming. Teachers are also not traditionally trained in test and measurement courses to construct authentic assessments or performance tasks and/or to properly construct rubrics to grade them. Also, parents and other stakeholders may not understand the value in these alternate evaluations. Some lack confidence in them because they believe that authentic assessments are subjective in nature and makes it difficult to compare students to other students and against predetermined criteria like a standardized test can.

The use of multiple techniques to include authentic assessments, standardized testing, and other forms of assessment increase the probability of students being fairly assessed. Table 9.3 provides a summary of the two main types of evaluation discussed in this chapter.

Active Learning

- How would each of these forms of evaluation be used in a multicultural classroom?
- Which one aligns more with the goals of multicultural education and in what ways?

Table 9.3. Characteristics of Standardized Testing and Authentic Assessment

Standardized Testing	Authentic Assessment
Involves quantification	More "authentic"

Enables comparisons
  ▪ Between individuals and groups
  ▪ Used to "sort"/ rank students
	▪ Evaluation not "imposed" by an external agency
	▪ Linked to authentic achievement

Claims to be "Objective"
  ▪ Same test given to everyone
  ▪ Only one right answer
  ▪ The only determinant of success is a raw score
	Personalized/individualized
	  ▪ Adapts the evaluation strategy to the individual interests of the student

Efficient
  ▪ Can be administered to large numbers
  ▪ Quick: usually a few hours (often graded by computer)
	Holistic knowledge is evaluated
	  ▪ Focus on broader and interrelated knowledge bases (not fragmented "facts")

Professional judgment is restrained
  ▪ Teacher cannot "favor" a student
	Evaluation type:
	  ▪ Takes into account multiple facets of the students' performance (i.e. attitude to learning, social context of learning, external factors)

	Formative and recursive ▪ Opportunities for feedback and improvement in performance (esp. through class-based observation)

	Non-traditional power dynamics
	  ▪ Evaluations are not something "done to" students; students actively participate in them; might even create the evaluation
	  ▪ Non-threatening

Adapted from Baxley & Waldon (2015)

Testing and the New Multicultural Classroom

Testing and evaluation drive curriculum choices and decisions about student learning. How we evaluate students and how we use assessment results are critical factors in ensuring that equity pedagogy is present (Aviles, 2000). The new multicultural classroom can be viewed from the perspective of viewing those cute little yellow Minions of *Despicable Me*. They all outwardly look alike, they seem to work in concert, but there are individual differences that must be taken into account when evaluating each of their skills and abilities. The Minions

ImageFlow / Shutterstock.com

would never have found the most evil, which is the premise of the movie, if it hadn't been for the courage, and skills of a few of them, namely, Bob and Kevin. They stepped up and demonstrated their abilities. If the teacher had relied on one standardized assessment, their unique abilities might never have been demonstrated, or worse yet, lost forever.

In classrooms, students are traditionally assessed using a score which supposedly has merit in determining how skillful the students have become or what learning standards they have mastered. What we must remember is that a score earned on a test does not determine readiness neither a student's' ability with 100% accuracy. We must be inventive in designing tools to determine students' academic, psychological, and physical readiness to learn. Evaluating students is more complex than administering a test at the end of the year or even throughout the school year. The following questions can provide you with a snapshot of reflective questioning to consider when preparing to evaluate your students.

1. What psychological or physical issues have my students undergone in their lives that may impact their academic performance? Life is a series of events, both positive and negative, and resilience in our students is idiosyncratic. Some blossom under adversity, while others succumb to the horrors of their situation.

2. How much time is needed to engage in culturally responsive evaluation for each of my students? I (Tunjarnika Coleman-Ferrell) am fond of having students tell me at the beginning of the academic year what events occurred during the summer. I can use this subjective evaluation of positive and/or negative experiences to devise tentative plans on how to engage my students throughout the year.

3. How can I assure that my assessments are aligned with learning outcomes? The answer to this question is quite complex, as learning outcomes are determined by federal and state standards. The teacher must use learning standards as benchmarks to formulating classroom activities and assessments that are meaningful for all students.

4. How well-versed am I about the various ethnicities in my classroom? Have I considered ethnicity, culture, learning styles, ability levels, etc. when selecting evaluation techniques? What evaluative tools can I employ to meet the diverse needs of my students?

Considering the diverse abilities of our students, we can develop and utilize a variety of diverse tools to encourage our students to demonstrate their knowledge in multiple ways. Your students are more than a score on a test, a standard to teach, or a benchmark to reach, they each bring a reservoir of knowledge with them to each learning situation. Evaluations, when used properly can be tools to understanding your students better and to designing lessons that are data-driven and purposeful.

References

American Educational Research Association, American Psychological Association, and National Council on Measurement in Education. (1999). Standards for educational and psychological testing. Washington, DC: American Educational Research Association.

Aviles, C. B. (2000). Teaching and testing for critical thinking with Bloom's Taxonomy of educational objectives. Retrieved from http://www.eric.ed.gov/PDFS/ED446023.pdf

Baxley, T. P. & Waldon, K. (2015). Evaluation: Testing and authentic assessment [PowerPoint slide]. Retrieved from course documents.

Caccioppo, J.T., & Freberg, L. A. (2016). *Discovering psychology: The science of mind.* (2ⁿᵈ ed.) Belmont, CA: Wadsworth Publishing Company.

Klein, A. (2015). No Child left behind: An overview. Retrieved from http://www.edweek.org/ew/section/multimedia/no-child-left-behind-overview-definition-summary.html

Erskine, J. L. (2014). It changes how teachers teach: How testing is corrupting our classrooms and student learning. *Multicultural Education 21*(2), 38-40.

Xia, N., & Glennie, E. (2005). *Grade retention: A flawed education strategy.* Center for Child and Family Policy, Duke University. Retrieved from https://childandfamilypolicy.duke.edu/pdfs/pubpres/FlawedStrategy_PartOne.pdf

Nichols, S. L., & Berliner, D. C. (2007). *Collateral damage: How high-stakes testing corrupts America's schools* (2ⁿᵈ ed.). Cambridge, MA: Harvard Education Press

Popham, W. J. (2010). *Everything School Leaders Need to Know About Assessment.* Thousand Oaks, CA: Corwin.

Popham, W. J. (2013). *Classroom Assessment: What teachers need to know (7ᵇ edition).* Boston MA: Pearson Education Inc.

Reynolds, C. R., Lowe, P. A., & Saenz, A. (1999). The problem of bias in psychological assessment. In T. B. Gutkin & C. R. Reynolds (Eds.), *The handbook of school psychology* (3rd ed., 549–595). New York, NY: Wiley.

Santrock, J. W. (2016). *Children* (13ᵗʰ ed.). New York, NY: McGraw-Hill.

Stipeck, D., & Lombardo, M. (2014). Holding kids back doesn't help them. *Education Week.* Retrieved from http://www.edweek.org/ew/articles/2014/05/21/32stipek.h33.html

Suzuki L. A., Ponterotto, J. G., & Meller, P. J. (2001). *Handbook of multicultural assessment: Clinical, psychological, and educational applications.* San Francisco, CA: Wiley.

The Glossary of Education Reform. (2014a). Criterion-referenced tests. Retrieved from http://edglossary.org/criterion-referenced-test/

The Glossary of Education Reform (2014b). Norms-referenced tests. Retrieved from http://edglossary.org/norm-referenced-test/

United States Department of Education (2015). Every Student Succeed Act. Retrieved from http://www.ed.gov/ESSA

Weigel, J. (2010). *Carnival Game.* Retrieved from http://jfmueller.faculty.noctrl.edu/toolbox/examples/weigel03/carnivalgame.pdf

Wilson, L. D. (2007). High stakes testing in mathematics. In F. J. Lester Jr. (Ed.). *Second handbook of research on mathematics teaching and learning.* Charlotte, NC: Information Age Publishing

Voice in the Field: Leveling the Testing Playing Field

Mirynne O'Connor Igualada, Ph.D.

The Florida Department of Education and the College Board have worked in partnership for sixteen years through the "One Florida: Equity in Education" program and the Florida Partnership for Minority and Under-represented Student Achievement Act (F.S. 1007.35). The purpose of the Florida Partnership is to promote success and to provide access to college for all students, through access to rigorous academics and national assessments. As a member of the Partnership team, I work to provide College Board programs and services to low-performing schools to ensure that traditionally marginalized groups of students (those who come from ethnic, racial, and socioeconomic groups who have been traditionally underrepresented) have access to Advanced Placement (AP) courses, the PSAT 8/9, the PSAT/NMSQT (Preliminary Scholastic Assessment Test/National Merit Scholarship Qualifying Test) and the SAT (Scholastic Assessment Test).

It is well documented within the research literature that national standardized assessments and standardized curriculum are not equally accessed by traditionally marginalized students (Contreras, 2011; Kewal Ramini, Gilbertson, Fox & Provasnik, 2007; Solorzano & Ornelas, 2004). In an effort to address this unequal access, the College Board has partnered with Khan Academy (Corcoran & Madda, 2016) to provide free personalized test preparation.

Khan Academy's world-class practice tools are free for all students and provides resources that enhances classroom learning as well as official SAT practice that result in personalized recommendations for instruction and practice, and has worked to address the opportunity gap (Corcoran & Madda, 2016) . The digital divide has, however, potentially impacted students' ability to access Khan Academy and the personalized learning tools. Therefore, the College Board in collaboration with the Boys & Girls Club of America and other community-based organizations have worked to try to combat this issue of student access.

Once the partnership with Khan Academy was announced and the 2016 March SAT was taken, the College Board (Corcoran & Madda, 2016) shared data that over one million unique users have accessed the Official SAT Practice feature of Khan Academy, which is more than four times the total population of students who take commercial test prep classes in a year. Also, according to the data released by the College Board, nearly half of all March SAT 2016 examinees used Khan Academy to prepare for the test. As a result there was a drop in the number of students who paid for SAT prep resources. Of those students who took the March 2016 SAT, over 60% of Asian Americans, African-Americans, Hispanic, and White test-takers indicated that they used Khan Academy to prepare. These statistics are particularly powerful in my work and within the broader realm of education, as it shows that ethnic groups are accessing and utilizing this powerful free resource with a degree of equity across the sub-groups.

Therefore, it is important for educators to be familiar with this resource, beginning in middle school, and the potential it holds for leveling the playing field for students entering the college-and-career-readiness arena and who have gaps in their foundational knowledge. This is also important because the standardized curriculum dominates their school experiences and perpetuates inequalities in the classroom, and promoting inequitable learning opportunities. Simply providing access to programs and services is not enough; student support mechanisms need to be in place that will help to provide a clear path to increasing participation and performance in rigorous courses and improved performance on national assessments. With the increased focus on standards and the corresponding assessments as required for graduation, Khan Academy helps teachers differentiate instruction through formative, rather than summative, assessments. Given the immense amount of responsibilities teachers face in today's classroom, it is difficult to find the time to utilize formative assessments to pin-point personalized learning recommendations and prescriptions for individual student success. Khan Academy however can be leveraged to help lift this burden while also providing increased support in implementing instructional interventions that will help students succeed in accessing post-secondary opportunities.

Practical Encounter

Practical Encounter #1

Directions: Answer the following questions based on the chapter reading.

What is the major differences between testing and assessment?

_____

_____

What are the pros and cons of each?

_____

_____

In your opinion, do they both have a place in the classroom? Why or why not?

_____

_____

How are standardized tests mis-used?

_____

_____

List two arguments for and against standardized testing.

_____

_____

Discuss alternatives to the over-reliance on standardized testing.

_____

_____

Practical Encounters #2

What Would You Do? Public Language, Public Lives

Sing Li does not participate in class discussions and prefers not to present her final research project. She performs well on objective tests and written assignments. Class participation is 20% of students' final grades.

1. Should she be required to present her final research project or receive a failing grade?

2. What criteria would you consider when performing a final evaluation for Sing Li and other students like her?

3. What culturally responsive practices could you implement in a scenario like the one presented here?

4. How would you justify, to a parent or administrator, your choice to use authentic instruction (differentiated instruction) with Sing Li?

CHAPTER 10

Choice, Voice, and Critical Discourse in the Language Arts Classroom

Traci P. Baxley, Ed.D.   Kalisha A. Waldon, Ph.D.

Kimberly Rhoden, M.Ed.

Case Study

Ms. Parker is teaching a unit on fairy tales to her second grade class. They are reading the well known fairy tale Cinderella. During their discussion of the key elements of the story a student raises her hand and asks, "Ms. Parker, are only White girls allowed to be Cinderella and live happily ever after? Can a girl like me with darker skin be a Cinderella?" Another student raised her hand and added, "Yeah, I haven't read any fairy tales where a girl like me is a queen or has an important role in the story? Are there any stories out there that I can read like that?" Ms. Parker told the girls that she needed to finish her lesson and would get back with them regarding their questions after the class completed the story element graphic organizer on Cinderella. The students completed the graphic organizer with the teacher but their questions were never really answered.

Questions to Ponder:

1. What opportunity did the teacher miss? How could Ms. Parker have created a lesson that was more inclusive or multicultural in nature?
2. Whose voices were missing in the lesson? What message does this send to students? Could there have been a better response to the students' questions?
3. How would you have answered the students' questions if you were the teacher?

Submitted by Kalisha A. Waldon In a multicultural language arts classroom, the role of the teacher is to create spaces where there is a reciprocal partnership, where the teacher is a learner and where students can be teachers. The traditional role of the teacher as the one who holds the knowledge and the responsibility to "deposit" their wisdom into the minds of students, coined the "banking concept" by Freire (2007), is usurped in a true multicultural language arts classroom. This chapter advocates for providing students with opportunities of choice, voice, and spaces for critical discourse, in an effort to bring about personal liberation and societal transformation. We will also explore how language arts can be taught through a multiculturally inclusive lens and encourage students to read texts from the perspectives of marginalized groups as well as empower them to re-create narratives from the standpoint of these groups. An inclusive language arts classroom can be fostered through the implementation of specific, intentional multicultural practices (Banks, 2016; Baxley & Boston, 2014; Gay, 2010; Ladson-Billings, 2001, 2009; Nieto & Bode, 2011; Waldon, 2015), some of which will be explored further in this chapter.

Samuel Borges Photography / Shutterstock.com

Types of Literacies

Functional Literacy

Functional literacy is the ability to read well enough to function in a complex society. The term is used to characterize one's ability to read, write and comprehend material critical for one's job or everyday survival. First introduced by William S. Gray (The Teaching of Reading and Writing, 1956), functional literacy was sought as an end goal of adult training and preparatory programs. The passing of the Adult Education Act of 1966 created a 12 year education system that would serve as a standard for basic literacy. According to White & McCloskey (n.d.), there are seven skills sets that are related to functional literacy: (1) *text search skills-* the ability to search text effectively; (2) *basic reading skills-* the ability to decode and fluently recognize words; (3) *language skills-* the ability to understand how language is structured, the meaning and relationships among sentences; (4) *inferential skills-* the ability to draw inferences from texts; (5) *computation identification skills-* knowing how to solve quantitative problems; (6) *computation performance skills-* the ability to work out or compute problems; and (7) *application skills-* using all the key skills to accomplish a variety of goals. Other literacies have evolved since then that are inclusive of skills necessary to live and function in the 21st century, such as computer and other digital literacies. Computer literacy consists of the knowledge of basic computer skills such as searching the internet, checking email, and using basic word processing programs that are all necessary in today's ever changing, technologically advanced society. As set forth by Kellner & Share (2007), "Computer and multimedia technologies demand novel skills and competencies, and if education is to be relevant to the problems and challenges of contemporary life, engaged teachers must expand the concept of literacy and develop new curricula and pedagogies" (p. 5).

Traditional language arts instruction is characterized as teacher-driven, standards-based classrooms in which the curriculum is mainly centered on the study of literature from a European canon with an occasional lecture on cultural diversity, such as how culture impacts an author's writing of a short story or whenever a specific topic lends itself best to the required text, and limited literary contributions from multicultural authors. According to Oakes and Lipton (2002), the traditional teaching of language arts can be problematic for teachers and the students and communities that they serve for several reasons. One reason is that traditional language arts instruction is focused on extracting meaning from texts and not on students interacting with texts to form personalized meanings or to critically reflect upon or challenge what they are reading. Instruction is inclusive of information that is decontextualized and often irrelevant rather than meaningful and relevant to the lives of the students. Traditionally, there is limited cultural representations in books and content in the language arts classroom and the subject matter is usually dominated by the western canon. Finally, teachers have limited input on curriculum design and the materials that should be used in their classrooms.

Cultural Literacy

Cultural Literacy can be defined in multiple ways depending on the personal stance in which you view the purpose and goals of education. Scholars from a traditional, mainstream perspective define cultural literacy as possessing the basic information that is needed to thrive in contemporary society. Hirsch's publication of *Cultural Literacy (1987)* sparked a debate on what students should learn in school, what constitutes "education" and whose knowledge was considered "real" knowledge or important enough to know. Hirsh, and other essentialists (i.e. Sizer and Bagley), emphasized that students should possess working knowledge that was inclusive of people, places, and events that have shaped American society. They argue in favor of the need for the U.S. to have a common cultural vocabulary, for example, core content that "every American needs to know." They believed that the role of the public school was to teach the "basic skills" in order to prepare students for the workforce; this required schools to focus primarily on reading, writing, and arithmetic (at the expense of subjects like cultural studies, theatre, music, etc.) (Cohen, 1999).

More liberal educators found Hirsh's content to be monocultural and elitist due to the number of European male names that were included in the canon of important people that American children should be familiar with, and the limited representation of more diverse groups, including women. Today the debate surrounding the question of whose knowledge should be included in the core curriculum continue. Considering the diverse demographics of our schools and the current policies, school reforms, and curricular mandates that often support the mainstream perspective (Gorski, 2013), it is imperative, now more than ever, that we redefine how the term cultural literacy is used in the educational context.

While Hirsh purports that "the basic goal of education is acculturation" (1987, xvi), critical scholars believe the purpose of education is to liberate and transform society (Freire, 2007; Kincheloe & McLaren, 2003). This liberation and transformation speaks to the connection between our current lived experiences and the socio-historical events of our society and how the juxtaposition of the two plays out in educational systems. Critical multiculturalists (Banks, 2006; Schoorman & Bogotch, 2010; Sleeter & Grant, 1999) suggest that cultural literacy could be seen as a structural reform of principles and philosophy that promote social justice and equality and supports,

> ... habits of thought, reading, writing, and speaking which go beneath surface meaning ... and mere opinions, to understand the deep meaning, root causes, social context, ideology, and personal consequences of any action ... experience, text, subject matter ... .mass media, or discourse. (Shor, 1992, p. 129)

Fostering cultural literacy in a classroom involves the ability to make conscious and informed decisions about how to approach materials that may indirectly lead to the negative or biased portrayal of a particular group of people. For example, a teacher who only shares images and stories depicting Native Americans "who provoked combat with peaceful European settlers" is doing a great disservice to his/her students. Likewise, a teacher who reserves showing interest in books about famous Hispanic Americans for only a specific month in the school year is subtly undermining the significance of the many contributions of this cultural group. Therefore, teachers and more importantly, district curriculum leaders should ensure that the year- long instructional map is inclusive of materials that encourage teachers (of all levels and subjects) to include books and materials that will highlight the significance of all cultures.

To accomplish such a feat, however, requires strategic attentiveness and advisory from all stakeholders. It is recommended that educators, parents, and students take part in an ongoing effort to provide recommendations and reviews of literature for inclusion within the mandated curriculum with knowledge that is reflective of the diversity that is represented within the school district, community, and beyond. Language arts materials that depict the interests and influence of cultural groups prevalent in other parts of the United States and that aim to project positive messages about all members of society should be visible in school media centers and classroom literacy stations and included within the curriculum.

Critical and Media Literacy

As mentioned previously, literacy, from a critical perspective, is not a set of strategies to be taught or skills to master but rather is the instrument for promoting social change. Freire and Macedo (1987) identified critical literacy as a continual process of reading the word and the world within the framework of a greater commitment to democratic practices and opportunities for all. Literacy should be viewed as a sociocultural artifact that mirrors the values and belief systems of our society. Critical literacy supports a student's understanding of the role history plays in their current lives and substantiates their existence in society, while assisting them in navigating the political, social, and cultural changes that may affect their lives and the lives of others (Tatum, 2001). Critical literacy is a system of pedagogical practices used to analyze the social construction of ourselves and the world around us.

Lewison, Flint, and Sluys (2002) in their review of 30 years of critical literacy literature found that there were four dimensions of critical literacy that emerged from their synthesis of the literature: (1) disrupting the commonplace; (2) interrogating multiple points of view; (3) focusing on sociopolitical issues; and (4) taking action and promoting social justice. The first dimension, disrupting the commonplace, focuses on practices that problematize or question texts and focus on the study of language and how it shapes identities, discourse, and disrupts the status quo. According to the authors, work within this first dimension is seen as radical when compared to the traditional role of teachers as "transmitters of knowledge." The second dimension, interrogating multiple points of view, advocates for students standing in the shoes of others in an attempt to understand their perspective and to ask questions regarding whose voices were missing and why, and working to allow those marginalized voices to be heard. This too is anti-traditional in that it called for teachers to step out of their comfort zones, both personally and in their teaching. The third dimension, focusing on sociopolitical issues, advocates for the examination of power relations, unequal balance of power and those who are affected by it. It redefines literacy as an opportunity to engage in society "as an ongoing act of consciousness and resistance" (p. 383). Taking action and promoting social justice, the fourth dimension, is the accepted definition for critical literacy, however one cannot take action without exploring issues within the other dimensions as well. Literacy within this fourth dimension is seen as engaging in praxis- critical reflection and action to question power and injustices. The main goals of critical literacy, as set forth in this chapter, are in essence a form of literacy that challenges and deconstructs oppressive structures (i.e. education) in society; supports the notion that all texts (i.e. textbooks, internet, social media, newspaper) are forms of political practice; and considers the power of texts to transform or liberate one's self and society.

Critical media literacy (CML) draws upon similar premises as the ones stated above for critical literacy. According to Kellner & Share (2007),

Critical media literacy expands the notion of literacy to include different forms of mass communication and popular culture as well as deepens the potential of education to critically analyze relationships between media and audiences, information and power. It involves cultivating skills in analyzing media codes and conventions, abilities to criticize stereotypes, dominant values, and ideologies, and competencies to interpret the multiple-meanings and messages generated by media texts. (p. 4)

A student's engagement with text is vastly impacted by their prior experiences, cultural background, and views of the world. The influence of media and the burgeoning consumption of it makes it the primary means for the construction of knowledge, including the construction of self-identities and knowledge about other groups of people (Alvermann, Moon, & Hagood, 1999; Cortes, 2001; Waldon, 2015). This is one of the primary reasons why educators must actively teach students to be critical consumers of media. The Center for Media Literacy's Framework below can be used to assist students in media analysis.

Table 10.1.   CML's Core Concepts and Questions

Five core concepts	Five key questions, deconstruction
All media messages are constructed.	Who created the message?
Media messages are constructed using a creative language with its own rules.	What creative techniques are used to attract my attention?
Different people experience the same media message differently.	How might different people understand this message differently?
Media have embedded values and points of view.	What values, lifestyles, and points of view are represented in, or omitted from, this message?
Most media messages are organized to gain profit/power.	Why is this message being sent?

Adapted from DeAbreu (2007) and Share, Jolls, & Thoman (2007)

Figure 10.1. CEU Student Counter narrative
Taken from Waldon, 2015

An example of how the tenets can be used in the classroom follows with the description of a curriculum that was taught to a group of high school students (Waldon, 2015). The curriculum, the Critical Encounters Unit (CEU), was designed to facilitate students' critical interrogation of the media. The CEU consisted of lessons that: (a) introduced students to critical media literacy concepts and questions, and (b) provided them with opportunities to analyze media texts and talk back to the master narrative through discourse and opportunities to act and create their own counter texts. The students were encouraged to critique various media portrayals of Blacks and to use their voice to seek answers to real problems they identified. Through various pedagogic opportunities, students were also encouraged to to act, question, or resist the messages promulgated through the media, and invited to view issues through the eyes or the perspectives of others outside of their cultural group. As their critical media literacy knowledge increased, the more abled they became to critique the media. Figure 10.1 is an example of a counter narrative created by one of the students as a result of what was learned in the unit.

In this example, the student challenged the notion that audiences do not have the power to control what is shown in the media through her creation of a public service announcement. The countertext encouraged audiences not to support media whose embedded messages did not align with what they believed and suggested that if audiences desired something better, the better started with them demanding something better (Waldon, 2015).

Students can be taught to analyze or critically examine all forms of text using the CML Framework; however there are also 10 quick ways students'/ children's literature can be examined for racism and sexism (*The Council on Interracial Books for Children*, 2007). These guidelines are a starting point for evaluating children's literature, including cartoons, books, etc. The table below discusses each of them and details what the author suggests we should examine in order to determine if the literature in our classrooms are perpetuating biases, stereotypes, or messages of inferiority.

Several practical examples can be found of teachers teaching students how to uncover these, sometimes overt, messages in texts and media. One such example is an activity Christensen's (2016) completed with her middle school students. She first showed them several old cartoons that have embedded stereotypes that were more blatant than the stereotypes embedded in cartoons today. While watching the cartoons, students paid attention to the roles of men, women, and people of color as well as who had the leading parts. The teacher also asked them to look at how overweight people were portrayed and who possessed the money or power, along with other things. The students easily were able to recognize and write down the stereotypes they saw; however not without some resistance.

Table 10.2. 10 Quick Ways to Analyze Children's Literature for Racism and Sexism

Guidelines	What should you look for?
1. Check the illustrations	• *Look for stereotypes* in how people are portrayed, such as the Black woman as a mammy or fat; Native Americans as savage or primitive; Puerto Ricans as gang members. • *Look for tokenism.* Do the characters have the features of a White person but are tinted darker? Are the features of minority characters stereotypical or do they have distinct features? • *Look for who's doing what.* Do minority characters appear in servant roles? Who has the power? Who is the leader or the person in authority?

2. Check the story lines	• Look for subtle forms of bias.
	  ▪ *Standards for success-* Does it take "white" behavior for a minority person to "get ahead"? In friendships between white and non-white children, is it the child of color who does most of the understanding and forgiving?
	  ▪ *Resolution of problems-* Are minority people considered to be "the problem"? Are the oppressions faced by minorities and women represented as related to social injustice? Are the reasons for poverty and oppression explained, or are they accepted as inevitable?
	  ▪ *The role of women-* Are the achievements of girls and women based on their own initiative and intelligence, or are they due to their good looks or to their relationship with boys? Are sex roles incidental or critical to characterization and plot? Could the same story be told if the sex roles were reversed?

3. Look at the lifestyles	• *Look for how minority people are depicted.* Are minorities depicted exclusively in ghettos, barrios, or migrant camps? If the minority group in question is depicted as "different", are negative value judgments implied?
4. Weigh the relationships between people.	• *Look for the power relationships.* Do whites in the story possess the power, take the leadership, etc.? How are family relationships depicted? In Black families, is the mother always dominant? In Hispanic families, are there always lots of children?
5. Note the heroes.	• *Look for who are the heros.* Are minority heroes admired for the same qualities *that* have made white heroes famous? Whose interest is a particular hero really serving?
6. Consider the effects on a child's self-image.	• *Look for instances in which a child's self-image may be negatively impacted.* Are norms established which limit the child's aspirations and self-concepts? What effect can it have on images of the color white as the ultimate in beauty, cleanliness, virtue, etc., and the color black as evil, dirty, menacing, etc.? Does the book counteract or reinforce this positive association with the color white and negative association with black?
7. Consider the author's or illustrator's background.	• *Look to see what qualifies the author to write the book or the illustrator to draw the pictures.* If the author and illustrator are not members of the minority being written about, is there anything in their background that would specifically recommend them as the creators of this book?
8. Check out the author's perspective.	• *Look for the direction of the author's perspective.* Does it weaken or strengthen the value of the written work? Is the perspective patriarchal or feminist? Is it solely eurocentric or do minority cultural perspectives also appear?
9. Watch for loaded words.	• *Look for loaded words.* A word is loaded when it has insulting overtones. Examples of loaded adjectives (usually racist) are "savage," "primitive," "lazy," "superstitious," "treacherous," "wily," "crafty," "inscrutable," "docile," and "backward"." Loaded words can also be sexist.
10. Look at the copyright date.	• *Look for when the book was written or published.* Pre-1970 books may well be biased. The copyright dates can be a clue as to how likely the book is to be overtly racist or sexist, although a recent copyright date is no guarantee of a book's relevance or sensitivity.

Adapted From: *The Council on Interracial Books for Children,* 2007

The media viewing sparked critical conversations about the cartoons and the meanings or messages that were embedded. At the end of the unit, the students wrote essays critiquing the cartoons. As a result of the unit, "students saw themselves as actors in the world; they were fueled by the opportunity to convince some parents of the long-lasting effects cartoons impose on their children, or to enlighten their peers about the roots of some of their insecurities" (Christensen, 2016, p. 185).

Literature Connections

Teachers on all levels will find that the use of literature is a powerful tool in extrapolating the attitudes, beliefs and behaviors of students. For instance, a primary teacher who reads *Corduroy* by Don Freeman will likely engage students in discussions about bravery, loneliness, and friendship. An intermediate class reading *Number the Stars* by Lois Lowry will gain insight into students' views about tolerance and determination. The integration of meaningful and research-based reading strategies could also assist teachers in connecting texts to student. For example, Fountas and Pinell (2011) note the importance of teacher engagement during interactive read alouds. This engagement can effectively support students' thinking within, beyond and about a text. The teacher's careful evaluation of literary selections can lead to the identification of important lessons that will help shape students' positive perceptions of themselves and others.

Draper (2010) explored strategies that can aid students in making more meaningful connections with text. He purports that without the application of such strategies, students can experience challenges "making meaning" of what they were are reading. Harvey and Goudis (2000) noted that struggling readers are often guilty of moving readily through a text (from beginning to end) without ever pausing to reflect on how their own knowledge, attitudes and experiences are aligned to those presented in the text. Furthermore, struggling readers do not know how to make use of their reflections in order to enhance comprehension. Therefore, teachers should guide students' reading by establishing a purpose for the text; this involves connecting students' old or current knowledge to what they will learn. Keene and Zimmerman (1997) revealed three types of connections that are essential to students understanding of a text, text to self, text to text, and text to world.

Children's literature and critical literacy are effective tools to navigating the often-controversial social issues that are relevant to the lives of students. Students can view characters as extensions of themselves, and these characters can assist them in their search for identity and social understanding within their own lives. Botelho and Rudman (2009) describe children's literature as mirrors, reflecting the lives of the reader; windows, viewing other cultures or experiences; or doors, looking at society differently and taking action. All students need to see reflections of themselves and their culture in the curriculum. Authentic literature adds to their understanding of how they view themselves and how others view and value them (Baxley & Boston, 2014; Gates & Hall Mark, 2006).

Students who see evidence of their lives and learning experiences mirrored in the books they read gain an affirmation of themselves and their identities. Conversely, students who do not see themselves reflected in books may begin to believe that they have no value or worth in the classroom or society. Multicultural literature is grounded in the inclusion of groups who have been marginalized in American society due to race, ethnicity, gender, religion, sexual orientation, social class, age, and/or ability. Teachers should carefully determine the relevancy of the themes and the characters of the literature that they introduce to their class because these texts become vital sources of self and social realization, particularly with multicultural texts. By exposing all students to selected multicultural literature through language arts instruction, students are given the opportunity to increase their knowledge of the lives, behaviors, and challenges of cultures around them. Multicultural literature allows students to experience a culture through the eyes of characters different from them and facilitates awareness, empathy, and understanding.

Table 10.3.   Text Connections

	Definition	What readers might be thinking . . .	What Teachers Can Do to Support . . .
Text to Self	Connections are highly personal; May remind students of an experience they once had or something that is very familiar to them	I remember a time when . . . I know a person who . . . I once lived in a place like . . . This reminds me of . . . This is different to me because . . .	Engage students in discussions BEFORE reading to activate prior knowledge Build Background Knowledge with students BEFORE reading to discuss events, people or challenging vocabulary Have students take notes WHILE reading to share what they may already know about a particular topic AFTER reading, guide students in a discussion about how their thoughts might have changed based on the information presented in the text.
Text to Text	Connections are made to other characters, events or problems that are from another story or text Connections are made to other nonfiction text-including some multi-media sources like online newspapers and websites	A character this reminds me of is . . . I read a story like this . . . This book is different from . . . The information in this text is similar/different from . . . The person who wrote this book shares a different/similar opinion from . . .	Expose students to a variety of literature reflecting a common theme/topic Help students get familiar with various authors to learn about different styles and techniques used in writing. Have students regularly compare and contrast information found in nonfiction sources
Text to World	Connections are made to people, places, things and events that occur in "the world around me"	I saw this person/place on television when . . . This person/place is well known because . . . When this happened it made me think about . . . . When this happened it made me feel . . . I know a lot about this because . . . This reminds me of . . .	Use journals to have students write reflectively about events that take place Use content area books and graphic aids to relate real world texts to topics being studied Periodically, have students write letters or other compositions to people they hear about in the news

Additionally, multicultural literature helps students to recognize stereotypes, make intercultural connections, and possibly change the way they see themselves (Darby & Pryne, 2002; Gates & Hall Mark, 2006). According to Taylor (2000), "We risk miseducating all of our students if we allow them to use their own cultural attitudes and values as the sole measuring stick for 'normal human nature'" (p. 25). Using multicultural literature in a critical classroom can create spaces for students to begin unlearning stereotypes and to dispel cultural myths and assumptions. "[R]egardless of their backgrounds and experiences, all students need to recognize the diversity that defines and strengthens our society" (Taylor, 2000, p. 25). When students are exposed to literature that offers various viewpoints, it increases their ability to analyze, evaluate, and make judgments (Darby & Pryne, 2002).

On the other hand, utilizing culturally relevant texts in language arts instruction can be difficult because the positionality of the educator can pose challenges, and on some occasions silence students of different backgrounds from that of the educator. "Many teachers who feel confident selecting literature on the basis of curricular goals or literary criteria lose

that confidence when it comes to selecting multicultural literature. Aware of past controversies over specific books and general charges of stereotyping or racism, they fear being accused of insensitivity or worse" (Bishop, 1992, p. 39). Despite these challenges, multicultural texts examining issues that marginalize groups should not be avoided, there should be greater emphasis placed on teachers to insist that these texts are integrated into instruction. By avoiding multicultural literature and other controversial texts, educators, in fact, avoid groups of students possibly further marginalize them and miss opportunities to facilitate critical discourse surrounding relevant issues that are often ignored.

Multicultural literature offers readers, especially ones whose race/ethnicity is commonly underrepresented, an opportunity to understand cultural differences and how the stories are significant to both personal and social development. Students should not have to choose between cultural elements of his or her home and the information and material introduced at school (e.g. language). When this level of conflict surfaces, the self-esteem of students can potentially suffer. For students of color, multicultural literature can be an instrument for personal and social validation within the classroom.

In order to motivate students and assist them in dealing with taboo subject matters like race or sexual orientation, educators must first remove personal barriers or challenge their own biases in an effort to objectively introduce, teach, and critically explore the presence of the controversial issues in books. Your role as an educator

Table 10.4.   Social Action Books for Children

Social Action Books for Children			
Primary Grades (PreK-2)			
Title	Author	Summary	Themes
Malala Yousafzai: Warrior with Word	Karen Leggett Abouraya	Malala is a young girl in Pakistan who stood up for education for girls in her village against the Taliban	Global rights for girls Bravery
Henry's Freedom Box: A True Story from the Underground Railroad	Ellen Levine	The true story of Henry Brown, a slave who mailed himself to freedom.	Slavery Underground Railroad Bravery Perseverance
A is for Activism	Innosanto Nagara	An alphabet book that encourages readers to take a stand for social action	Social Justice Activism
Wangari's Trees of Peace: A True Story from Africa	Jeannette Winter	Kenyan environmentalist Wangari Maathai, winner of the 2004 Nobel Peace Prize, planted trees in her homeland and encouraged other women to do the same. These trees profoundly improved her country's health and economy.	Environmental education Peace
Nelson Mandela	Kadir Nelson	Tells the story of Nelson Mandela from his tribal childhood, his work as a young lawyer, through his leadership against apartheid, his long imprisonment, to presidency of his country.	Positive leaders Perseverance
Intermediate Grades (3rd-5th)			
Harvesting Hope: The Story of Cesar Chavez	Kathleen Krull	The story of civil rights leader Cesar Chavez's 340-mile march to protest the working conditions of migrant farmworkers in California.	Positive leader Migrant workers
One Hen: How One Small Loan Made a Big Difference	Katie Smith Milway	Inspired by true events, Kojo, a boy from Ghana turned a small loan into a thriving farm and a livelihood for many.	Courage Imagination Poverty
Frederick's Journey: The Life of Frederick Douglass	Doreen Rappaport	Frederick's life is recounted beginning from his life in slavery to his fight for freedom as an international renown writer, lecturer and abolitionist.	Freedom Black history Hope

Social Action Books for Children			
Primary Grades (PreK-2)			
Title	**Author**	**Summary**	**Themes**
Grandfather Gandhi	Arun Gandhi	Gandhi's grandson shares a valuable lesson of love and light that he learned from spending time with his grandfather.	Peace Positive leader Change agents
Amelia to Zora: Twenty-Six Women Who Changed the World	Cynthia Chin-Lee	Details the lives of women who changed the world.	Heros Women's rights
Middle School Grades (6th - 8th)			
I Am Malala: How One Girl Stood Up for Education and Changed the World (Young Readers Edition)	Malala Yousafzai	Ten year old, Malala was taught to stand up for what she believed in and fought for her right to be educated during a time when the Taliban did not agree. Malala was shot in the face while riding a school bus for using her voice. She survived and continued to speak out for girls' rights to education.	Bravery Upstanders Human Rights Girl's rights Power of Education
Speak	Laurie Halse Anderson	This is a story about a girl, Melinda, who faced traumatic events during and after a party. Melinda chooses not to speak rather than to give voice to what really happened. Ultimately she triumphs through her own voice.	Social and family issues
The Hundred Dresses	Eleanor Estes	A young Polish girl living in America is made fun of by her classmates because she wears the same dress every day. Her classmates later feel bad about ridiculing her after she was pulled out of the school. One student in particular made a vow that she was "never going to stand by and say nothing again."	Social issues, bullying
High School Grades (9th -12th)			
Letter from a Birmingham Jail	Martin Luther King, Jr.	While Martin Luther King, Jr. was confined to the Birmingham jail, serving a sentence for participating in civil rights demonstrations, he wrote a letter that advocated for the need of nonviolent demonstrations to end social discrimination.	Civil rights, discrimination
The New Jim Crow: Mass Incarceration in the Age of Colorblindness	Michelle Alexander	Alexander makes the case with this critique of the systematic targeting of Black men in the criminal justice system and how this practice serves as a contemporary Jim Crow system against basic civil rights	Civil Rights School-to-Prison Pipeline Discrimination
Never Fall Down	Patricia McCormick	Story of a Cambodian boy, Arn Chorn Pond, who was separated from his family and assigned to a labor camp. In order to survive, he learned quickly to master the strange revolutionary songs the soldiers demanded-and how to steal food to keep the other kids in the labor camp alive. He became a human activist who vowed to "Never Fall Down."	Asian History Asian and Asian American Wars and Military Survival
The Freedom Writers Diary: How a Teacher and 150 Teens Used Writing to Change Themselves and the World Around Them	The Freedom Writers & Erin Gruwell	The students that were labeled the "unteachables" find a connection between their lives and Ann Frank and begin to journal about their experiences. This book is the culmination of those journal entries.	Tolerance Understanding Empathy

will require you to engage in continuous professional development in order to broaden your awareness on the availability and utilization of multicultural texts with diverse groups of students (Au, 2001; Ladson-Billings, 2009). While all of these social issues are equally important when choosing literature for your language arts class, the method of pedagogical infusion should also be carefully considered. Below are a list of books that can be used to foster social action that will provide opportunities to you and your students to explore themes tied to social justice matters.

A second method of pedagogical infusion is the use of literacy triads to reinforce social issues, integrate various cultural perspectives, and encourage student engagement with various genres all through the teaching of subject-based content knowledge. Literary triads are formed by combining three genres of literature (informational, historical fiction, and biography) that engage students in the critical examination of multiple points of view on a topic, social issue, or time period in history (Baxley, 2005). Using a combination of genres to teach controversial topics can be beneficial to students in several ways. Literary Triads assist in: 1) learning and retaining content knowledge that is reinforced throughout the genres; 2) interacting with text that requires open-mindedness and empathy to counterstories; 3) highlighting and encouraging student interest, experiences, and love for reading; and 4) facilitating critical inquiry and dialogue. Below is an example of a Literacy Triad centered around minorities of the revolution (Baxley, 2005).

Rosenblatt (1978) believed it was important for students to have practice using two types of reading stances: efferent (learning information) and aesthetic (reading for the love of reading). Historical fiction is an excellent genre to allow students to encounter experiences with aesthetic reading and use unique personal experiences to connect with the characters and enjoy the storyline of the text. With informational tradebooks, students experience efferent reading by looking for and acquiring information and knowledge about the social issue or historical time period. Biographies offer a unique experience; they allow the reader to experience both stances, reading for new knowledge and connecting emotionally to the characters and the subject of the text.

Table 10.5. Literacy Triads

"Minorities of the Revolution"
Bruchac, Joseph (1998). The Arrow over the Door. New York: Dial. (Historical Fiction)
In the backdrop of the American Revolution, two young men convey their differing perspectives on the war. Samuel Russell, a Quaker, wrestles with his faith's pacifism, which subjects him to colonist's criticism for refusing to fight for independence. Stands Straight is an Abenaki Indian whose family was killed by colonists. The Abenaki grapple with the decision of which side to support. The boys share a valuable learning experience when they exchange their different perspectives at the meetinghouse where the Quakers are worshipping.
McGovern, Ann (1975). Secret Soldier: The Story of Deborah Sampson. New York: Scholastic. (Biography)
A biography of the woman, because she was not ready to settle down and get married and had aspirations to see the world. She disguises herself as a man and joins the Continental Army during the Revolutionary War.
Cox, Clinton (2002). Come All You Brave Soldiers: Blacks in the Revolutionary War. New York: Scholastic (Nonfiction Text)
Thousands of African American soldiers fought for independence during the American Revolutionary War. This informational tradebook begins with the Boston Massacre and goes through the Battle of Yorktown. The story reveals the unfair treatment of Black soldiers as well as the fact that Native Americans, women, and slaves, were not part of the "all men" who were "created equal." Additional noteworthy passages touch on the Southern colonies not enlisting Black soldiers because they feared slave revolts. Jefferson's and Washington's views are critiqued, while other leaders who lauded freedom for all are referenced. Cox mentions several African Americans by name including Crispus Attucks, a Black man, who was the first to die in America's fight for independence.

Taken from Baxley (2005)

Conclusion

Our last words of admonition to you would be:

1. Examine your personal attitudes and biases towards various cultures or ethnic groups.
2. Acknowledge the prevalence of stereotypes that will impede your ability to engage all students objectively.
3. Participate in activities (i.e. visit a cultural museum, read a magazine, speak with community leaders) that will deepen students' and your own s perspective of different cultures.
4. Feature books that portray various people and cultures in a positive light and texts that highlight the voices that have been excluded or omitted from the traditional language arts curriculum.
5. Model your own metacognitive thinking by sharing think alouds and making personal connections to what you are teaching. Encourage your students to make and discuss their own personal connections as well.
6. Do not restrict the inclusion of books/topics about a particular culture to only specified months. While some districts may provide a yearly multicultural calendar and curriculum that coincides with many international celebrations, you should engage students in books/topics on broader, more universal themes (e.g. characteristics of effective leaders) that can be transferred and integrated into other subjects.
7. Display posters on the walls and include books in the classroom library of children from all over the world. Make certain that your students and their families are represented.
8. Communicate with your students' parents on a consistent basis. Speak with parents to discuss how various cultural norms, values or funds of knowledge is approached at home and can be included in the classroom community.
9. Be supportive of the students and the knowledge and experiences they bring with them, while striving to promote a learning environment that is collaborative and team-oriented at all times.
10. Provide spaces for students to critically discuss, reflect, and act upon injustices or media that are often considered taboo issues in the classroom, i.e. race, discrimination, and matters that are relevant to their personal lives.

By embracing these strategies and providing opportunities for students to have a choice in the literature they read; a voice in instructional decision-making, topics discussed, and activities that are both meaningful and engaging; and have the space to critically reflect upon and discuss issues that are anchored in their lived experiences and knowledge, you will be fostering a multicultural language arts classroom. While the strategies and information presented in this chapter will assist you in creating and maintaining a multicultural language arts classroom, they do not represent all the methods you have at your fingertips, and should be used as a springboard to encourage students to continue to learn, grow, and challenge injustices through your language arts instruction.

References

Alvermann, D., Moon, J., & Hagood, M. (1999). *Popular culture in the classroom: Teaching and researching critical media literacy.* Newark, DE: International Reading Association.

Au, K. H. (2001). *Culturally responsive instruction as a dimension of new literacies.* Reading Online 5. Retrieved from http//www.readingonline.org/newliteracies/lit_index.asp?HREF=au/index. htmlBaytops,

J. L. (2003). Counseling African American adolescents: The impact of race, culture, and middle class status. *Professional School Counseling, 7*(1), 40–50.

Banks, J. A. (2016) *Cultural diversity and education: Foundations, curriculum and teaching*(6th ed.). Boston, Massachusetts: Pearson.

Baxley, T. P. (2005). *Quality children's literature that supports fifth-grade state standards in United States history: A content analysis of historical fiction, biography, and informational tradebooks.* (Unpublished Doctoral dissertation). Florida Atlantic University, Boca Raton, FL, USA.

Baxley, T. P., & Boston, G. H. (2014). *(In)Visible presence: Feminist counter-narratives of young adult literature by women of color.* Netherlands: Sense Publishers.

Bishop, R. S. (1992). Multicultural literature for children: Making informed choices. In V. J. Harris (Ed.), *Teaching multicultural literature in grades K-8* (pp. 37–53). Norwood, MA: Christopher-Gordon Publishers, Inc.

Botelho, M., & Rudman, M. (2009). *Critical multicultural analysis of children's literature: Mirrors, windows and doors (Language, Culture and Teaching Series)*. New York, NY: Routledge.

Christensen, L. (2016). Unlearning the myth that bind us: Critiquing fairy tales and cartoons. In E. Marshall & O. Sensory (Eds.). *Rethinking popular culture and media* (2nd ed., pp. 175-186). Milwaukee, WI: Rethinking Schools Publication.

Cohen, L. (1999). Philosophical perspectives in education. Retrieved June 14, 2005, from http://oregonstate.edu/instruct/ed416/PP3.html

Cortes, C. E. (2001). Knowledge construction and popular culture: The media as multicultural educator. In J. Banks (Ed.), *Handbook of research on multicultural education* (pp. 169–183). San Francisco, CA: Jossey-Bass.

DeAbreu, B. S. (2007). *Teaching media literacy: A how-to-do-it manual and cd-rom*. New York, NY: Neal-Schuman Publishers.

Darby, M. A., & Pryne, M. (2002). *Hearing all the voices: Multicultural books for adolescents*. Lanham, MD: The Scarecrow Press, Inc.

Draper, D. (2010). Comprehension strategies: Making connections. Retrieved from http://fractions45.edublogs.org/files/2010/07/MakingConnectionsStrategy.pdf

Fountas, G. S., & Pinnell, I. (2011). *The continuum of literacy learning*. Portsmouth, NH: Heinemann.

Freire, P. (2007). *Pedagogy of the oppressed*. New York, NY: Continuum. (Original work published 1970)

Freire, P., & Macedo, D. (1987). *Literacy: Reading the word and the world*. South Hadley, MA: Bergin & Garvey.

Gates, P. S., & Hall Mark, D. L. (2006). *Cultural journeys: Multicultural literature for children and young adults*. Lanham, MD: The Scarecrow Press, Inc.

Gay, G. (2010). *Culturally responsive teaching: Theory, practice, & research*. New York, NY: Teachers College Press.

Gray, W. (1956). *The teaching of reading and writing*. Paris, France: UNESCO.

Harvey, S., & Goudvis, A. (2000). *Strategies that work: Teaching comprehension to enhance understanding*. Portland, ME: Stenhouse Publishers.

Keene, E. & Zimmerman, S. (1997). *Mosaic of thought*. Portsmouth, NH: Heinemann.

Kellner, D., & Share, J. (2007). Critical media literacy, democracy, and the reconstruction of education. In D. Macedo & S. R. Steinberg (Eds.), *Media literacy: A reader* (pp. 3-23). New York: NY: Peter Lang Publishing.

Kincheloe, J., & McLaren, P. (2003). Rethinking critical theory and qualitative research. In N. Denzin & S. Lincoln (Eds.), *The handbook of qualitative research* (pp. 279–313). Thousand Oaks, CA: Sage.

Ladson-Billings, G. (2009). *The Dreamkeepers: Successful teachers of African American children* (2nd ed.). San Francisco: Jossey-Bass.

Ladson-Billings, G. (2001). *Crossing over to canaan: The Journey of new teachers in diverse classrooms*. San Francisco, CA: Jossey-Bass.

Lewison, M., Flint, A. S., & Van Sluys, K. (2002). Taking on critical literacy: The journey of newcomers and novices. *Language Arts, 79*(5), 382-392.

Nieto, S., & Bode, P. (2011). *Affirming diversity: The sociopolitical context of multicultural education* (6th ed). Boston, MA: Pearson.

Oakes, J. & Lipton, M. (2002). *Teaching to change the world*. Blacklick, OH: McGraw-Hill.

The Council on Interracial Books for Children. (2007). 10 Quick ways to analyze children's books for children. In W. Au, B. Bigelow, & S. Karp (Eds.), *Rethinking our classrooms: Teaching for equity and justice, (Vol. 1, 2nd ed., pp. 10–11)*. Milwaukee, WI: Rethinking Schools Publications.

Share, J., Jolls, T., & Thoman, E. (2007). *Five key questions that can change the world: Lesson plans for media literacy*. Malibu, CA: Center for Media Literacy.

Tatum, A. (2001). Nesting grounds. *Principal Leadership, 2*(2), 26–32.

Taylor, S. V. (2000). Multicultural is who we are: Literature as a reflection of ourselves. *Teaching Exceptional Children, 32*(3), 24–29.

Waldon, K. A. (2015). *Black adolescents' critical encounters with media and the counteracting possibilities of critical media literacy*. (Unpublished Doctoral dissertation). Florida Atlantic University, Boca Raton, FL, USA.

White, S., & McCloskey, M. (nd). *Framework for the 2003 national assessment of adult literacy* (NCES 2005-531). U.S. Department of Education. Washington, DC: National Center for Education Statistics. Retrieved from http://nces.ed.gov/NAAL/fr_skills.asp.

"You will not engage me as a student, until you embrace me as a human."

Kimberly Rhoden, Educator

As a 4th grade teacher during Florida's impactful *Florida Writes!* and later FCAT Writing eras, I (like many of my colleagues) underwent transformational professional growth in the area of writing instruction. For almost two decades, an annual statewide assessment called on students to respond to a writing prompt for which they received a holistic score representing their performance in four key areas: Focus, Organization, Support, and Conventions. Later, education reform standards called on students' writing to exemplify analytical traits that included - ideas, sentence fluency and even voice. While some aspects of my daily Writing Block were devoted to assessment preparation, it was not the focus nor the core. In my classroom, writing instruction became a way for me to creatively tap into unique personal interests and experiences of my students. In a classroom often filled with rigid academic and curricular expectations, my Writing Block became a time where students from "all walks of life" could exercise freedom and self-expression in a way that no other discipline could allow them to experience.

"Write from the Heart" became a vessel of teaching that was designed to inspire and motivate all of my students-far beyond the purpose of mastering a statewide assessment and satisfying grade level expectations. "Write from the Heart" actively engaged students as critical readers, thinkers and writers and all but required them to seek value in their own personal journeys-no matter how mundane or complex they appeared. Students as young as elementary learned to capture the enjoyment of eating a popsicle on a warm summer afternoon or convey tense emotions while escorting a grandparent to a dreaded dialysis clinic. They relished in the notion that their very own thoughts, feelings, and words could be transformed into powerful depictions as they swirled through the minds of active readers and listeners. With an emphasis on coaching and mentoring (not just instruction), "Write from the Heart" moved students to actively seek out new ways of interpreting past and present experiences and to creatively and collaboratively explore pathways for resolving challenges. "Write from the Heart" allowed me to incorporate literature featuring characters whose lives could have easily intertwined with those of my students and to strategically apply mini lessons to enhance vocabulary, grammar and mechanics. The "Write from the Heart" classroom was a reflection of the world where my students resided and bulletin boards commonly featured writing samples about favorite people, places and events.

Moreover, it has been my constant belief that a true student centered classroom will naturally reflect sensitivity towards all learners. Great teachers know that before students can be reached as learners, they must be acknowledged and celebrated as individuals. Over time, I came to realize that my quest to evoke my students as writers hinged greatly on my ability to awaken them as individuals. I found this to remain consistent even as state expectations gradually shifted towards more formal standards of writing and called on students to cite specific text evidence from unfamiliar authors. While instruction shifted slightly to ensure mastery of this expectation, the focus of our daily Writing Block continued to place emphasis on the need for students to express themselves as individuals. Without a clear regard for the thoughts, ideas and experiences of my students, guiding them to seek out critical information from an unfamiliar source would not be beneficial. "Write from the Heart" allows students to actively appreciate their own worth and contributions, so that they can fully embrace those of others.

10 Components of a "Write from the Heart" classroom:

1. Student Writing Folders
   Obtain writing folders with pockets and prongs for all students. Most students will be willing to secure this for themselves. Folders should be used to store personal writing samples and/or handouts from the teacher. Permit students to decorate their folder with words and drawings that tell more about their personality, interests and experiences. This writing folder must be central to daily writing lessons and activities.

2. Daily Journal Writing
   Daily journal writing must engage students in the practice of writing. Topics should be general, yet relative to the interests of students. Prodding students to write about such matters as their favorite food, a family member or an after school activity are likely to generate a response from everyone. From time to time, teachers should include current event topics to allow for the natural desire of students to share knowledge and feelings about the world around them.

   Daily Journal writing will be meaningless without some form of feedback or opportunities to share. A brief response that is non critical or non-judgemental and written by the teacher can go a long way in motivating students. Stickers or stamps can come in handy as well to denote a student's participation. "Turn and Share" can be utilized to provide students with a 5 minute period where they can share a journal entry with a partner. As much as possible, teachers should provide a safe place and time to discuss or share students' journal entries.

   It is important to note that from time to time, a student may reveal something in his/her notebook that will be deemed personal or private. The student can inform the teacher of this by folding the page of the designated entry. Nonetheless, the teacher should speak with the student individually about the matter in order to ensure that no danger or threat to the student or anyone else is present.

3. All about Me
   The necessity of getting to know one's students (especially at the beginning of the school year) can be quickly satisfied in a "Getting to Know Me" exercise where students write or share quick thoughts about a series of topics. Teachers can easily find a grade level appropriate activity on the internet or create their own list of topics like the one on page 175. This completed document can be the focus of a small group or paired conference where students identify similarities and differences and can be used as a reference for topics to include in a writing piece.

   Similar "All about Me" exercises can be completed or updated throughout the year. Students love the idea that their teacher really wants to know all about them!

4. Modeling
   Seeing is believing! The value of writing in front of your students is priceless and while many teachers will admit to experiencing struggles in this area, working to overcome them will be worth it for your students! Teachers can start by composing short journal entries in front of students and "Thinking Aloud" about their thoughts. This process should be repeated as often as possible so that students can witness first-hand how ideas and thoughts and even struggles can be transformed into a writing piece.

5. Shared Writing
   A group or class working together to compose a piece of writing is known as Shared Writing. In this experience, a teacher may choose to focus on a particular writing strategy (i.e. identifying a main idea, adding meaningful details) and requesting feedback and/or responses from students as the piece is written collaboratively. Shared Writing is an excellent way to guide students in practicing a difficult strategy

6. Mini-lessons
   Rome was not built in a day and students' writing will not flourish overnight. Using a curriculum map or pacing guide, teachers should identify important skills (i.e. using commas correctly, selecting precise nouns) that will need to be taught and in what order. During mini lessons, teachers can devote time to introducing and teaching the skill, providing clear examples of how the skill is applied (using classroom literature, textbooks, and writing samples) and working with students through a Shared Writing or small group experience.

7. Writing Process

The acts of *Brainstorming, Drafting, Conferencing, Revising, Editing,* and *Publishing* are key steps in what is known as the Writing Process. Hint: Even the most successful writers do not instantly produce a "published" work. It is important to note that not all writing pieces will need to undergo all of the steps of this writing process, but allowing your students to experience conferencing and revising as much as possible is recommended.

8. Conferencing

Never underestimate the power of conferencing with students about their writing. Always allow the student to do most of the talking, however, be careful to share only constructive feedback. Asking thought provoking questions like the ones on page 176 will guide students into identifying their own opportunities for improvement.

9. Read Alouds

Teachers should seek out their favorite, high interest literature to share with students. Reading aloud from various text will allow students to "hear" what good writing sounds like. This is important as students must understand that appealing to his/her audience will be a major purpose for writing.

Displaying interest and enthusiasm about books that feature children from various cultures is especially important. Children will readily observe a teacher's body language and facial expressions as literature is being shared. Even the slightest display of disinterest or negativity relating to a character's physical features, social or cultural experiences can do great harm to a child's psyche and productivity in the classroom. A teacher's sincere respect and appreciation of all children and people can be reflected in his/her choice of pictures and posters displayed around the room as well as the varied selection of literature shared aloud or in classroom libraries.

10. Publishing

This is celebration time for students and teachers! At least once per quarter, each student-with as much help from the teacher as needed- should produce a published writing piece. If possible, the published writing should be bound and contain at least a title page and an About the Author section. Illustrations, maps, charts and other helpful features should also be included as necessary. In addition, encouraging classmates to become illustrators for their peer's published work is a great way to foster collaboration and teamwork.

Finally, providing an opportunity for students to share published works with other classes and families will make this moment extra special! Publishing allows students to experience themselves as "real" authors whose thoughts, ideas and experiences can add value to the lives of others!

All about Me

Name: _____ Date: _____

Directions: Read the phrase in each box. Complete as many boxes as you can with as many words or pictures!

My full name is	Places I have lived or visited . . .	My family always . . .
I wish that I could . . .	People that I admire . . .	I like to eat . . ..
My favorite time in school . . .	A time I could not stop laughing . . .	One day I would like to . . .
At home I always . . .	I am special because . . .	I would like to learn more about . . .
My favorite hobby is . . .	Sometimes I wonder . . .	I feel my best when . . .

Write *from* the Heart, 2016

Conferencing about Writing for the Busy Classroom Teacher

Classroom teachers can and must include conferencing as an integral part of the writing experience for all students-that is not time consuming or exhaustive.

Here are tips to ensure an effective Conferencing writing classroom:

*Schedule writing conferences with individual students using a rotation schedule. Teachers should only plan to meet with 3-5 students per day.

*Do not require or expect all students to have a completed draft in order to conference. Meet all students wherever they are in the Writing Process.

*Be prepared to engage in a Shared Writing/Conference experience to assist struggling writers.

*Always allow students to read their writing out loud. This will help them maintain true ownership of their work and control (through their own voice) of how thoughts and ideas should be conveyed.

*Keep the focus of conferencing on the revision of thoughts and ideas rather than editing for grammar or mechanics. Conferencing about revision might sound like:
  • What made you decide to write about that topic?
  • Do you think your opening will hook your readers?
  • Is there any part of your writing that speaks to your audience?
  • How will readers know that you are an expert on this topic?
  • How will readers know that you care a lot about this idea?
  • How will readers know that your information is based on evidence?
  • Can you identify 3 sentences that can help to prove your point?
  • Which statements show that you have researched your topic?
  • Will the words you have used paint a vivid picture in the minds of your readers?
  • How do you want your readers to feel when they read this section?
  • Which words or phrases did you use to make them feel that way?
  • Are there any parts of your writing that might be confusing to your readers?
  • What value will your writing add to the lives of your readers?

*Model conferencing expectations for students throughout the year.

*Provide time for students to practice conferencing with partners and eventually include *Student-Led Writing Conferences* as part of the Writing Block.

-Write from the Heart, 2016

Practical Encounter

Practical Encounter #1

What Would You Do: Reading the word. . . . Reading the World

Directions: Read the scenario and answer the questions that follow.

A group of girls are sharing books in a classroom. Abby selects one and announces, "I'm reading When Sophie Gets Angry because Sophie looks just like me!" Blanca picks up on the game. She grabs another book and says, "I'm reading A Chair for My Mother because Rosa looks like me." Both girls turn to face Lauren, who is flipping through a basket of books. She sighs, stands, and walks away, saying, "I'm tired of reading." Lauren is multiracial. None of the books feature characters that look like her.

Questions:
1. Why is it important for students to see themselves in books and other materials in the classroom?

2. How might a teacher respond to empower this student?

3. What resources would you implement in a diverse classroom as the one discussed above?

4. How might a teacher use this scenario to engage students in critical literacy?

Practical Encounter #2: Children's Books Analysis

Directions: Use the chart below to analyze a children's book. Following your analysis discuss whether or not the book is appropriate to use in the classroom and note how you can counter any racist or sexist messages embedded in the text.

Guidelines	Children's Book Title
1. Check the illustrations	
2. Check the story lines	
3. Look at the life styles	
4. Weigh the relationships of the people	
5. Note the heroes	
6. Consider the effects on a child's self-image	
7. Consider the author's or illustrator's background	
8. Check out the author's perspective	
9. Watch for loaded words	
10. Look at the copyright date	

CHAPTER 11

Social Studies and Multicultural Education:
Partners Teaching 21ˢᵗ Century Students Actively to Uphold Human Dignity for All

Rosanna M. Gatens, Ph.D.

Case Study

Mr. Johnson is wrapping up the last lesson on World War II in his American History class at James Madison High. He summarizes the unit by reviewing the top 5 events that happened during the war. One of the Japanese American students in the class raised his hand and said, "Mr. Johnson what about the internment camps? Weren't they also important to what transpired during the war? Why did you not mention that in your summary of the top 5 events? Some of my family members were held in camps like prisoners during that war. Even though they were Americans and fought in previous wars, they were treated like second class citizens and no one ever really talks about that." Mr. Johnson replies, "It was an event during WWII, but the government did what they thought was best. It was a good decision at the time to figure out who our friends were and who were the enemies. There was no other way to do that." Well my family members were Americans and not spies." Another student raised her hand and asked, "Did the American government ever apologize for their actions or show appreciation to the Japanese for fighting in the war?" "If they did not, they need to" retorted a third student. Mr. Johnson did not have an adequate response to give his students so he simply said, "What you need to know for the test are the five events I summarized."

Submitted by Traci P. Baxley, Educator

Questions to Ponder

1. What conclusions did you draw from this case study? What do your conclusions say about how we traditionally teach social studies?
2. Whose voices were omitted from American history in the lesson? What impact does this have on various groups of students?
3. How could Mr. Johnson have responded to the students' inquiries in a way that honored the history of the Japanese American student and his family in the classroom?

Traditional American Narrative

Among historians, the 1980 publication of Howard Zinn's *A People's History of the United States* heralded a transformation in the narrative of United States history. The "new history" focused on people, events, and processes that the story of heroic European Conquest of the "New World" ignored (Arnove, 2015). Zinn and the historians who followed him critically deconstructed this history of conflict between the conquerors and the conquered, between those who owned the land and the slaves and indentured servants who worked the land, between factory owners and workers, and between descendants of the founders of the United States and immigrants from the rest of the world. As a result, the traditional American narrative gave way to a more complex story of the shared struggle between oppressors and the oppressed to establish a more perfect union that could achieve the goals set forth in the nation's motto, *e pluribus unum* (out of many one), and the founding documents, *The Declaration of Independence* and *the Preamble to the Constitution of the United States*. When read as a story of conflict over power, status, and wealth, the contemporary American narrative sheds light on the many ways in which the traditional story of a superior people, destined to become the most powerful force in the world, discounts the human suffering that resulted from this very trajectory of power.

This traditional American narrative pays only minimal attention to the significance of social movements that wove the lives of the marginalized into the fabric of the American story, often portraying protestors as rabble rousers who destabilized the country. Only recently have these movements for progressive change become a positive part of the American story: the abolitionist movement, the civil rights movement, the labor movement, the women's suffrage movement, the feminist movement, and the LGBT equality movement. As Zinn pointed out, the people who were part of these movements shaped American history as much, if not more, by challenging the beneficiaries of American power to live up to the values and freedoms recorded in the founding documents of which they are so proud.

A decade and half after the appearance of Zinn's "bottom up" history, social studies educators formulated a new definition of the field and developed a comprehensive set of content and pedagogical standards that reflected the emerging significance of political and cultural diversity. These documents intentionally challenged traditional views of the purposes of social studies education. But this complex story has not yet become our story. Regardless of the fact that the heroic narrative forms a mythology about how America became a world power, educators continue to use the heroic American narrative to assimilate immigrants and refugees. The myth of America as a melting pot continues to shape our popular view that becoming American necessarily requires the destruction of one's previous language and culture. For, after all, isn't the United States "superior" to all other nations and societies? Alternative images such as the salad bowl and the quilt that describe processes of acculturation are not yet widely used. Many of the resources presently used by social studies teachers do not yet reflect the results of the last twenty years of scholarly research that informs the contemporary, multicultural narrative of the United States.

> ## Active Learning
> Think about your experiences in the PreK-12 Social Studies settings. How much of your instructional time focused on the roles of men, especially Anglo-European men, in shaping United States history? What messages did this traditional instruction in social studies send to you regarding your place in American history?

Reframing the Traditional American Narrative

Since the mid-1990s leaders in the field of social studies have been laying the groundwork necessary to reframe the American narrative at the classroom level based on the most current research findings. In 1994, the National Council for the Social Studies (NCSS) published new guidelines for social studies education (NCSS, 1994). Revised periodically to reflect accumulation of new knowledge, the document is built on an understanding of the United States as a culturally diverse nation made up of citizens who coexist based on shared respect and responsibility for its founding principles. It is clear in its statement of mission, that social studies learning goals and methodology acknowledge the multicultural nature of the United States. It is also clear that NCSS national standards incorporate the critical methods of multiculturalism in the delivery of content, in the choice of pedagogy, and with a more inclusive understanding of democracy. According to NCSS "the primary purpose of social studies is to help young people develop the ability to make informed and reasoned decisions for the public good as citizens of a culturally diverse, democratic society in an interdependent world (NCSS, 1994)." The National Association of Multicultural Education (NAME) employs similar terms in describing multiculturalism as a way of knowing and learning "built on the ideals of freedom, justice, equality, equity and human dignity as acknowledged in . . . the U.S. Declaration of Independence, the constitutions of the United States and South Africa, and the Universal Declaration of Human Rights." This disposition shapes the way we "prepare students for their responsibilities in an interdependent world. It affirms the roles that schools can play in developing the attitudes and values necessary for a democratic society. It values cultural differences and affirms the pluralism" [that students see reflected in their communities]. "It challenges all forms of discrimination in schools and society through the promotion of democratic principles of social justice" (NAME, n.d.).

This disposition emphasizes a way of learning and knowing that parallels the 2010 NCSS formulation of standards for social studies teachers which emphasize constructivist learning and five principles for teaching what the document calls "powerful social studies" (NCSS, 2010). Indeed, the methodological and pedagogical frameworks for teaching the social studies–history, economics, government, sociology, psychology—derive from the analytical principles of critical theory[1] that seek to uncover abuses of power that silence marginalized voices and impede the achievement of human equality. NCSS standards and NAME standards start from an assumption that effective learning takes place when students' own life histories and experiences lie at the center of the teaching and learning process. The following chart demonstrates these parallels.

Moving from the Ideal to the Real: Teaching social studies through a multicultural lens

It should be clear by now that both NCSS and NAME advocate social studies instruction that prepares students to become active citizens who recognize the need to uphold the dignity of all persons and who possess a skill set that enables them to take effective, meaningful action on behalf of all. Both organizations acknowledge that democracy requires an acceptance of pluralism. But from the demands of national and state government all the way down to the school district level it is often difficult to put these ideal standards into practice. In fact, the obstacles to implementing this kind of social studies instruction are great. Implementing these standards requires a critical mass of well-educated, creative social studies instructors to teach required subject matter from the perspective of the NCSS and NAME standards.

Teaching Social Studies from a Multicultural Perspective

An effective social studies teacher is one who has the knowledge, confidence and courage to guide students through contested terrain in meaningful ways. Of course, social studies instructors must master the content field which they teach. Content mastery is the basis upon which an effective teacher can choose resources, frame questions and activities that transform more traditional accounts and approaches. Social studies instructors need to be thoroughly familiar with the standards, pedagogies, learning goals and outcomes advocated by NCSS and NAME in order to apply them to more traditional required materials and pedagogies. Social studies teachers must also become thoroughly aware of state instructional standards, content scope and sequence and expected outcomes of the state standardized testing regime in order to align these to the NCSS and NAME standards while still meeting the professional requirements of a school, a school district, and a state department of education. Social studies teachers must be thoroughly familiar with instructional technologies and resources advancing a multicultural perspective in order to choose alternative sources that can assist them in accomplishing state and school district goals. Finally, the content of social studies instruction is often controversial and subject to the demands of legislators, school board members and the lay public who comprise textbook adoption committees. To sustain one's own instructional goals in the face of external opposition, social studies instructors must become actively aware of the political and social context in which they teach, well beyond salary and workload issues.

---

[1] Critical Theory is a framework of analysis that aims to critique society, social structures, and systems of power, in order to foster egalitarian social change. Adapted from Ashely Crossman, "Critical Theory: A Brief History and Highlights." Located at http://sociology. about.com/od/Sociological-Theory/a/Critical-Theory.htm

School districts throughout the United States have invested significant time and financial resources to develop matrices and lesson plans that align with state Department of Education Standards. Often these prepackaged lesson plans contain some elements of Banks' Level 1 (Banks, 1989) multicultural practices such as identifying and understanding the contributions of various groups to United States history. Often though, these lesson plans are conventionally structured from the perspective of the majority culture rather than taught as a dynamic interaction between and among groups, including the group(s) who hold social, political and economic power. From these lessons, students usually acquire a predominantly Eurocentric understanding of the social studies disciplines.

Sometimes prepackaged lesson plans reach Banks' Level 2 (Banks, 1989) by adding content about diverse ethnic groups and cultures. But this information is added into a structure that teaches students to evaluate this diversity from the perspective of the majority culture without teaching conflicts or the interpretation of the fact that the majority culture is in a dynamic relationship with other diverse cultures that change the majority culture in specific ways, such as the United States Civil Rights Movement. It remains the task of individual social studies teachers to transform the structure of conventional curricula to "view concepts, issues, events, and themes from perspectives of diverse ethnic and cultural groups" (Banks, 1989).

Transformation, Banks' level 3 (Banks, 1989) requires time, knowledge and commitment in order to replace a modernist curriculum with a postmodernist/critical multicultural alternative. The real-world example that follows illustrates this point. At the conclusion of a professional development workshop focused on implementing Florida's mandate for Holocaust education at the elementary level, a teacher returned to her school with the goal of bringing together both her social studies and language arts teams from kindergarten to grade 5 to develop a week long, school-wide study of human rights, the Holocaust, refugees, and immigrants. While a central component of the curriculum, which the school has adopted and revised annually since the spring of 2006, is guiding students to understand the nature of prejudice and its harmful effects, the curriculum had two action components. First students learned to recognize when a harm has occurred and how to take responsibility to repair the hurt. Second, teachers actively involved their students in the value and the practice of philanthropy. They learned how to organize, to gather and to distribute resources to people in need. They raised $500.00 in pennies to help the children of Darfur. Also, after learning that Afghan children living in remote areas learned to read and write by drawing in the dirt, the students gathered pencils, paper and backpacks to contribute

Table 11.1. NCSS and NAME Principles Guiding Instruction

"Powerful" Social Studies Principles[2]	Characteristics[3]	Multicultural Learning Components	Characteristics
Meaningfulness	• Students learn connected networks of knowledge, skills, beliefs, attitudes useful in and out of school • Instruction emphasizes deep development of important ideas, in context of broad topics so that students may understand, appreciate and apply ideas to life. • Presentation of content is developed through activities	Positive academic identities	• Students of color achieve academic excellence when Instructors provide students with curricula and pedagogy that builds on students' experiences and cultural frames of reference outside school • Students of color achieve academic excellence and positive self-esteem when they can apply these academic skills to develop social justice in school and community
Integrative	• Subject matter is taught topically across disciplines • Subject matter cuts across time and space • Instruction interconnects knowledge, skills, beliefs, values and attitudes with effective social/political action • Instruction makes effective use of technology • Teaching/learning is connected to other subjects	Positive social identities	• Students can learn to express pride, confidence and healthy self-esteem without denying the value and dignity of other people through a curriculum, pedagogy and classroom relationships that affirm their ethnic, racial, gender and other identities.
Values-Based	• Instructor guides students to consider ethical dimensions of topics, address controversial issues in a space that allows for a reflective development of concern for the common good and application of social values. • Students become aware of potential social policy implications, are taught to think critically, to make values-based decisions related to social issues • Instructors enable students to become aware of the values, complexities, and dilemmas involved in an issue • Consider the costs and benefits to various groups of people that are embedded in potential courses of action • Develop well-reasoned positions consistent with basic democratic social and political values • Instructors encourage acknowledgement of opposing points of view, respect for well-supported positions, • Sensitivity to cultural similarities and differences • Commitment to social responsibility	Respectful engagement with diverse people	• When teachers use curricula and interactive pedagogies that engage students across differences, students can learn, especially through student-led discussions, to examine diverse experiences and perspectives in their social, political and historical contexts, exchange ideas and beliefs in an open-minded way, and build empathy, understanding and respect.

---

[2] NCSS, National Standards for Social Studies Teachers "Thematic Strands," 2010 retrieved fromhttp://www.socialstudies.org/standards/strands

[3] NAME, "Multicultural Learning," retrieved fromhttp://nameorg.org/learn/

Table 11.1. *(continued)*

"Powerful" Social Studies Principles[2]	Characteristics[3]	Multicultural Learning Components	Characteristics
Challenging	• Expecting all students to accomplish learning goals • Modeling seriousness of purpose and thoughtful approach in inquiry • Using instructional strategies that elicit and support similar qualities from all students • Showing interest and respect for students' thinking • Demanding well-reasoned arguments rather that uninformed opinions	Social Justice Consciousness	• Students can learn to analyze individual unfairness and systemic injustice when students learn how to deconstruct their own views, through curricula that focus on these issues and when teachers use a pedagogy that supports students as they struggle with difficult, controversial, painful issues.
Active Learning	• Teachers/students engage in reflective thinking/decision-making as events unfold during instruction • Developing new understanding through active construction of knowledge • Facilitating interactive discourse so that students construct knowledge necessary to develop important social understanding • Teachers gradually move toward a less directive role in order to encourage students to become independent and self-regulated learners. • Instruction emphasizes authentic activities that call for real-life applications using the skills and content of the field [of knowledge]	Social Justice Action	• Students of color can learn to recognize their own responsibility to resist injustice in everyday life through community-based projects, curricula or pedagogy that engages students in learning how to plan strategies of participatory democratic activism.

to the education of Afghan children. Many of the students who attend this school are Haitian-Creole or of Haitian-Creole descent. Most of their families were directly affected by the Haiti earthquake in 2010. During that year, students raised funds, gathered clothing, soap and school supplies that were sent to Haiti combined with shipments of contributions from people throughout southeastern Florida.

The development of this elementary level human rights curriculum required teachers to bring all their skills and knowledge to the table. They also brought with them an abiding commitment to prepare their very diverse students to achieve academic excellence in all grades. From the perspective of multicultural education and social studies instruction, the curriculum was constructed within a multicultural framework, from the selected texts and supplementary resources, to specific teaching strategies and activities. One example, in particular, illustrates how a conventional curriculum about immigration was transformed into a curriculum unit from which students learned to understand the phenomenon of immigration through the voices and experiences of immigrants. (*Center for Holocaust and Human Rights Education at Florida Atlantic University,* 2007). Below is an outline of the lesson plan followed by a detailed discussion of the embedded instructional activities.

This grade 3 curriculum was built around two picture books, *One Green Apple* and *Molly's Pilgrim*. Both stories introduced girls whose families had immigrated to the United States, one at the turn of the 19th Century and the other just after 9/11. In each story the girls described the loneliness, isolation and worry that they faced as immigrants. Both girls experienced the overt and covert hostility of the other students in their classes. Both girls were grateful to compassionate teachers who guided their students to value the two new students.

Table 11.2. Immigration Lesson Plan

Grade Level	3rd Grade
Literature	*One Green Apple* by E. Bunting *Molly's Pilgrim* by Barbara Cohen
Social Studies Standards	The students will be able to: 1. Describe what it's like to be different from others from the points of view of Farrah and Molly. 2. Identify a time in their own lives when they have felt different. 3. Explore what it takes to reach out to someone who is different. 4. Explore what they can do to make all students feel accepted in their group, class. 5. Describe what it feels like to be isolated from other students. 6. Identify a time in their own lives when they felt isolated from others. 7. Explore ways to break their own isolation. 8. Explore ways to help others break their isolation. (Source: CHHRE K5 Curriculum)
Social Studies Content	What is immigration? Who are immigrants? How they feel about leaving what they know and coming to a new place? Historical Context (i.e. in the case of Molly, immigration because of religious persecution in her homeland) Geography- locating Farrah's, Molly's and classmates' country or culture of origin Compare and Contrast the histories and experiences of the immigrants to their own lives Cooperation in the creation and completion of a common task Drawing conclusions based on evidence—using evidence to construct their own understanding of the lesson.
Instruction	Learning Activities- One Green Apple Pre-reading: The teacher will ask students to look at the picture on the book's cover. What do you notice about the picture? What do you think this book is about? What genre is this book? Read Aloud The teacher will ask students to form a circle together. The teacher will then read the book. Activity 1: Critical Thinking a) Who is Farah? b) How can you tell that Farah is from a different county? c) Why do you think Farah was sad when she went to school? d) How was Farah like the other children? How was she different from the others? e) What factors change Farah's perspective about being in a new country? Activity 2: Writing a) Students will write a summary of the story including the main idea and important story details. b) Students will write a narrative about a time in their own lives when they felt different or alone. Learning Activities- Molly's Pilgrim Pre-reading The teacher will model a "think aloud" as s/he looks at cover, reads the back and picks out several illustrations from the story. S/He will then ask students to complete a written response to the following questions: a) What did you notice about the picture on the cover? b) What do you think this book is about? c) What genre is this book? Read Aloud The teacher asks the students to form a circle together. The teacher then reads the story aloud. While reading Molly's Pilgrim, display, *One Green Apple* and AC's of lessons learned from that book on wall so that students may compare the two stories. Activity 1: Critical Thinking a) What is the FIRST thing we learn about Molly in the beginning of this story? b) How is that similar to Farah in One Green Apple? Is what we learn about these c) Which character's the biggest problem in the story? d) Who is Molly? e) How can you tell she is from a different country?

(continued)

Table 11.2. *(continued)*

Grade Level	3rd Grade

f) How are Farah and Molly's feelings about going to school SIMILAR?

g) What was the theme or the author's message? What events helped you figure out the message?

h) How are you ALIKE or DIFFERENT from Farah and Molly? How are Farah and Molly like someone you might know?

i) How does Farah change throughout the story? How does Molly change throughout the story?

Reflecting

a) If you had been Molly, would you have acted differently? Explain why and how.

b) How would the story be different if it had happened somewhere else (or in another time period)?

Activity 2: Group Work (Writing and Illustrating)

Skill: Compare & Contrast: Instructions

1. Students will pick an index card out of a hat. On that index card is a different event that happened to Molly in the story. They will draw the event as a comic strip, breaking the event into the sequence of actions leading to that event, the climax and what the outcome was. The student will include thought bubbles of what the character thinks, revealing how the character feels, and how she interacts with the other characters.

2. The students will share their comics as if retelling that part of the story, with the rest of the members in their group providing two compliments and one tip to help presenter make project clearer.

3. Group will then take two hula-hoops to create a Venn Diagram. One group will compare Farah and Molly. Another will compare themselves to Molly & Farah.

4. Students will write a two paragraph essay explaining how immigrants feel about coming to a new country and describe what he/she can do to help newcomers who come to community feel accepted and valued.

Adapted From: http://www.coe.fau.edu/centersandprograms/chhre/curr_documents/ElementarySchoolCurriculum.pdf

The lesson's learning goals demonstrate the intentionality of the social studies lesson in facilitating students' understanding of immigration from the perspectives of immigrants themselves. The lesson incorporates several multicultural standards together with several social studies standards to guide students to an understanding of how immigrants are a valued part of our society, as well as what immigration is, who immigrants are, and the barriers they face in gaining acceptance in their new countries. The stories in the selected texts are told in the voices of the immigrants and, the lesson design incorporates students' own experiences with the feelings that the immigrant girls describe. As the lesson progresses, the students' experiences are incorporated into the learning activities.

When teaching this lesson, it is imperative that ELL students are engaged as well as native speakers of English with various learning styles. Their learning of the story and the concepts can be facilitate through the use of visual and auditory components. In small groups students work together to both draw and write their understanding of the two stories. Lastly the lesson takes into account the anxiety that some students may feel when working with others and presenting their work to a group by asking each student in a group to make two compliments and one suggestion for improvement for each presenter. This embedded practice has the effect of encouraging students' self-esteem both individually and as a member of a group.

In part two of the lesson, students are introduced to *Molly's Pilgrim*, a story about a young Russian girl who immigrated to the United States at the beginning of the twentieth century. Students learn Molly's story while building on what they learned from Farah's experience and the paragraphs they wrote about their own experiences. The framework for this set of discussion questions consists of a critical analysis of the stories based on comparing and contrasting the experiences of the two girls and students in the

michaeljung / Shutterstock.com

class. During this second discussion, students are able to refer to their conclusions from Farah's story in order to talk about Molly's experiences.

The accomplishment of the larger project of which this lesson was a part depended on teachers whose commitment to academic excellence drove them to find ways to build on the knowledge base and experience of all their students, as well as their use of multicultural principles in the selection of materials and teaching strategies. They also understood that to succeed they needed to understand how to align multicultural standards with state and local standards for measuring student achievement.

Active Learning

How did this lesson plan counter the traditional American history narrative? How will the perspectives presented impact the students in your classroom? What are the potential benefits to including multicultural literature in your social studies units?

Multicultural Social Studies Resources

In this chapter we have discussed a number of resources that teachers used to construct their Holocaust and Human Rights Curriculum for elementary schools. They used the NCSS and NAME standards that are found in Table 11.1. They also consulted the State of Florida Social Studies Standards for kindergarten through fifth grade. These standards may be found on the Florida Department of Education Website, C-Palms. Social Studies standards for the elementary grades are located at http://www.cpalms.org/Public/search/Course#0. This link consists of the general standards with hyperlinks to the specific standards for each grade level. The specific web pages for each grade contain more detailed information about course content, related courses, specific social studies standards for each grade and lesson plans. Teachers aligned the content and teaching strategies for their human rights curriculum with these standards while also perusing lesson plans for possible adaptation to the human rights curriculum goals.

To choose the books *One Green Apple* and *Molly's Pilgrim*, teachers consulted the curriculum page and lending library link of the **Center for Holocaust and Human Rights Education at Florida Atlantic University** (http://www.coe.fau.edu/centersandprograms/chhre/index.php). The following websites contain up-to-date lists of children's multicultural social studies literature. Each site gives brief descriptions of the books. Some contain lesson plans. The Teaching Tolerance website contains a wide range of multicultural literature and teaching resources as well.

Resource	Website	Description
Teaching Tolerance	http://www.tolerance.org/magazine/archives	For children's literature recommendations, consult the magazine's "What We're Reading" department.
Teaching for Change Books	http://www.tfcbooks.org/best-recommended/booklist	This website contains many other multicultural classroom resources that are appropriate for social studies instruction.
Facing History and Ourselves	https://www.facinghistory.org/educator-resources	These resources including books, educator resource books, and lesson plans are more suitable for secondary level students. The site requires individuals to set up an account to gain free access to all its resources.

Resource	Website	Description
Syracuse Cultural Workers	https://www.syracuseculturalworkers.com/.	Click on the "books" link for a list of all their available books.
Cooperative Children's Book Center, School of Education, University of Wisconsin-Madison:	https://ccbc.education.wisc.edu/books/detailListBooks.asp?idBookLists=42	A list of 50 multicultural books every child should know.
Cooperative Children's Book Center, School of Education, University of Wisconsin-Madison:	http://ccbc.education.wisc.edu/books/detailListBooks.asp?idBookLists=253	A list of thirty multicultural books every teen should know.
Cooperative Children's Book Center, School of Education, University of Wisconsin-Madison:	http://ccbc.education.wisc.edu/books/multicultural.asp.	Resources for teaching multicultural children's literature.
Diversity Book Lists and Activities for Teachers and Parents:	http://multiculturalchildrensbookday.com/multicultural-reading-resources/diversity-book-lists-for-kids/	Books and other resources for multicultural education.
Amazon: Best Sellers in Multicultural Children's Literature Books:	http://www.amazon.com/Best-Sellers-Books-Childrens-Multicultural-Story/zgbs/books/3094	
Lesson Plan Development:	The lessons in the unit described in this chapter are based on "Understanding by Design." For more information, see https://cft.vanderbilt.edu/guides-sub-pages/understanding-by-design/. An overview of Understanding by design and lesson plan template may be found at http://www.grantwiggins.org/documents/UbDQuikvue1005.pdf.	

References

Arnove, A. (2015). Introduction. In H. Zinn (Ed.), *A people's history of the United States 1492 - present* (pp. xii - xxii). New York, NN, HarperCollins.

Banks, J. A. (1989) Approaches to multicultural curriculum reform. *Trotter Review, 3*(3), Retrieved from http://scholarworks.umb.edu/trotter_review/vol3/iss3/5

Center for Holocaust and Human Rights Education at Florida Atlantic University. (n.d.). K5 school curriculum plan. Retrieved from http://www.coe.fau.edu/centersandprograms/chhre/curr_documents/ElementarySchoolCurriculum.pdf

National Association of Multicultural Educators. (n.d.). mission statement. Retrieved from http://www.socialstudies.org/standards/introduction

National Council for the Social Studies. (1994). *Executive Summary. Expectations of excellence: Curriculum standards for Social Studies.* Retrieved from http://www.socialstudies.org/standards/introduction

National Council for the Social Studies (2010). *National curriculum standards for Social Studies: A framework for teaching, learning, and assessment.* Retrieved from http://www.proteacher.com/redirect.php?goto=1539

Voices in the Field

Facilitating Students' Journey towards Empathy and Advocacy

Rachayita Shah, Ph.D.   Julie Hector, M.Ed.

Each year, thousands of immigrants come to the United States for varying reasons, ranging from travel, to work, to education, to seeking refuge. Our response to immigration – historically and socially – is often influenced by xenophobia and ethnocentrism. Consequently, prejudice against newly arrived immigrants is not a new phenomenon. In recent years an attitude of suspicion towards new immigrants has been on the rise (Pottie, K., Dahal, G., Georgiades, K., Premji, K., & Hassan, G., 2015). According to a 2009 report by the Migration Policy Institute, since 2006, policies directly targeting undocumented immigrants and their employers have increased dramatically.

A major concern among educators is the increase in immigrant bullying which has resulted from the perpetuation of dehumanizing views of groups of people. According to Pottie et al. (2015), immigrant bullying, especially among non-native speakers, has been on the rise internationally. They also reported that many immigrant students experience psychosocial stress, and are victims of bullying, sexual harassment, and violence. Our goal as researchers and educators is to assist students in developing compassion for all immigrants and to be able to better identify with their struggles. The activity that we discuss below is to help students reflect on their choices in terms of their interaction or lack of interaction with immigrant students, develop empathy for their peers; and become advocates by creating a safe environment for all.

Multicultural educators advocate that, "The more empathy students have for each other, the less likely they are to bully or abuse each other . . . there are many instances where the bullying of refugee or immigrant students is reduced simply by teaching American-born students about their foreign-born peers" (*Building Refuge Youth and Children's Services Toolkit, 2016*). We, at the Center for Holocaust and Human Rights Education, work with K-12 educators and pre-service teachers to implement lessons on human rights and genocide education. We conduct the following "Ladder of Prejudice" activity in our professional development workshops at the Center as a model of practice that teachers can use in their classrooms to promote prejudice reduction, empathy, respect, and advocacy. This activity, designed for students in grades 6-12, is an adaption from an activity designed by the Teaching Tolerance organization (n.d.; Retrieved from http://www.tolerance.org/exchange/ladder-prejudice) to help participants understand how seemingly naïve acts of indifference and apathy could lead to or contribute to extremely violent situations. Once the participants understand the role of each rung of the ladder, we engage them in a discussion of a case study, where they recognize and apply these concepts to analyze a particular situation. What follows are the steps to conduct the activity:

Step 1: We divide the participants in five groups, and give each group, a poster with one of the words from the five rungs of the ladder-speech, avoidance, discrimination, physical attack, and extermination. This is followed by giving a discussion question to each group for that particular word.

1. Speech: How could speech be hurtful? Give examples of words/statements that are used to hurt a group or a community.
2. Avoidance: When is avoidance a good or a bad thing? How is it used in society to harm people?
3. Discrimination: Can discrimination ever be a good thing? How is it used in society today?
4. Physical Attack: What are the reasons for physical attack? Could it ever be justified?
5. Extermination: What leads people to buy the idea of exterminating another group of people? OR What convinces people to exterminate another group of people?

Step 2: Each group is given a few minutes to share their thoughts within the group for their respective discussion questions.

Step 3: Once the group discussion is over, each group is asked to select a spokesperson and share key ideas of their questions with the whole group. This whole group discussion gives participants the overall picture of the ladder of prejudice, and how each step contributes to violence.

Step 4: This is followed by each group representative coming to a designated wall and placing these words in terms of their intensity. What participants interpret as the least harmful word would be put at the bottom rung of the ladder, and the most harmful word would be put at the top rung of the ladder.

Step 5: The following terms are introduced to the group: Victim, Perpetrator, Bystander, and Rescuer. Participants are asked to share their perceptions of the terms, and compare them with the formal definitions.

Step 6: Finally, participants are separated into small groups in which they are given approximately 10 minutes to complete the following activity. First, they are asked to read the newspaper article on Guatemalan teen's murder (Sarcasa, 2015), which provides a report about a hate crime which occurred in our community. The fact that the incident occurred within participants' own community is intended to encourage empathy among them and to help them see that their community is not immune to hate crimes of extremely violent proportions. Another goal is to provide students with a better understanding of the safety issues that immigrants in the United States face.

Step 7: Small Group Activity: Read the Case Study: "Guat Hunting" news-story" followed by a discussion of the following questions:

    i. What level of prejudice does this event represent?
    ii. Who do you identify as perpetrators, victims, bystanders, and upstanders in this story?
    iii. What could be the motivators for this act?
    iv. How could this story be relevant to any of you?
    v. What could we do at individual, school, and community level to instill the values of respect, human dignity, and solidarity with fellow human beings?

Students in small groups then share the answers they discussed within their group for the rest of the class. This lesson equips educators with tools to help students navigate the subtle messages that reflect prejudicial attitudes among different groups in our multicultural society, as well as recognize the impact of dehumanizing practices on the community as a whole. More importantly, this lesson encourages students to adopt an empathetic approach towards the tragedy, and consider its implications from a human perspective.

References

Building Refugee Youth and Children's Services (2016-Living document). "Refugee children in U.S. schools: A toolkit for teachers and School Personnel." Retrieved from http://www.brycs.org/publications/schools-toolkit.cfm.

Hanson, G. H., & Migration Policy Institute. (2009). *The economics and policy of illegal immigration in the United States.* Washington, D.C: Migration Policy Institute

Teachingtolerance.org. (n.d.). Ladder of prejudice activity. Retrieved from http://www.tolerance.org/exchange/ladder-prejudice

Pottie, K., Dahal, G., Georgiades, K., Premji, K., & Hassan, G. (2015). Do first generation immigrant adolescents face higher rates of bullying, violence and suicidal behaviours than do third generation and native born?. *Journal of Immigrant and Minority Health, 17(5),* 1557-1566.

Sacasa, A. (2015, October 9). Guatemalan teen's killing spurs coalition to spread message of unity. *Sun-Sentinel.* Retrieved from http://www.sun-sentinel.com/local/palm-beach/fl-hate-crime-killing-folo-20151008-story.html

Voice in the Field

Women in Curriculum: The Good, the Bad, and the Nonexistent

Jillian Berson, M.Ed.

In the 1970s and 1980s, publishers and professional associations issued guidelines for non-racist and non-sexist books. As a result, textbooks within the last twenty years have significantly improved, however they are not bias-free. While we often discuss the predominant "whiteness" of our history textbooks and we acknowledge that traditionally marginalized populations are not well-represented, something we have not spent as much time looking at is the representation of half of the population: women. This notion is supported by Rae Lesser Blumberg's point that, "Gender bias in textbooks is not a burning education issue. . ." (2008, page numbers). With this issue in mind I began to explore the following two questions through a content analysis of social studies textbooks: (1) How are female figures represented in middle school U.S. History textbooks and (2) To what extent does this representation of female figures perpetuate and/or challenge gender stereotypes?

I conducted a content analysis of Glencoe/McGraw-Hill's *The American Journey* (2005), the former Broward County, Florida, 8th Grade Social Studies textbook. A priori coding was completed through the use of Sadker and Sadker's *Seven Forms of Bias in Curriculum* framework. The first form of bias that I noted was that of invisibility. One example of this was that of the 32 chapters and 122 subtitles, there were only two subtitles within chapters that featured women. The textbook began with America's prehistory through 1492. The first mention of women is in Chapter 14.3-The Women's Movement (1820-1860), page 425.

The second form of bias was stereotyping. An example of this was the "People in History" section of the text. Of the thirty-three people highlighted, only ten of them were women. Most of the women chosen were wives of presidents and the topics discussed were who they married and how many children they had.

The next form of bias was imbalance and selectivity, which shows only one interpretation of an issue, situation, or group of people. In Chapter 21.2-Women and Progressives, the only "women's issues" addressed were motherhood, childbirth, and women's right to vote. No other facets of the women's movement are mentioned.

Fragmentation and isolation bias may seem less damaging than other forms of bias, they present non-dominant groups as peripherals of society. This was evident through the subsections addressing women or women's interests being reserved for the end of chapters, and often lumped in with "other groups" which included African Americans, Latinos, and Native Americans.

Linguistic bias can be both blatant and subtle. The foundational written pieces of American History, The Declaration of Independence and the U.S. Constitution, are written entirely with male pronouns. Both texts are heavily analyzed, but with no mention of the choice of masculine language used.

The last form of bias is cosmetic bias. The illusion of equity was used as a marketing strategy, suggesting that the text was free from bias beyond the attractive covers and photos. This was evident in the fact that the pictures in the text predominantly depicted women as mothers, religious-type figures, ethnic minorities, and in domestic scenes as homemakers.

Once an awareness is made of the abundant gender bias in our curriculum, it is our job as teachers to make that transformation for a more inclusive curriculum. Elizabeth Higginbotham (1990) offers insight on how that transformation may possibly be achieved. She says that content knowledge is key—it may take some work on your part as a teacher however you should gain information about the diversity of the female experience. The next step is to decide how to teach the new material. This is where critical pedagogy comes in—it is essential to know your students and work *with* them in order to see what works *for* them. The last piece Higginbotham points out is to structure the classroom dynamics to ensure a safe atmosphere is there to support learning for all students. A feeling of safety and trust is essential to promoting self-awareness and exploration. As educators, it is our job to promote and foster empowerment and equity. As Mahatma Gandhi so eloquently laid out we must, "Be the change you want to see in the world."

References

Abraham, J. (1989). Teacher ideology and sex roles in curriculum texts. *British Journal of Sociology of Education, 10*(1), 33-51.

Blumberg, R. L. (2008, September). The invisible obstacle to educational equality: Gender bias in textbooks. *Prospects,* 38(3), 345-361.

Bordelon, K. W. (1985, April). Sexism in reading materials. *The Reading Teacher,* 38(8), 792-797.

Britton, G. E., & Lumpkin, M. C. (1977, October). For sale: Subliminal bias in textbooks. *The Reading Teacher,* 31(1), 40-45.

Harro, B. (2008). Updated version of "The Cycle of Socialization" (2000).

Higginbotham, E. (1997, Spring/Summer). Designing an inclusive curriculum: Bringing all women into the core. *Women's Studies Quarterly,* 25 (1/2), 237-253.

McLaren, P. (2003). *Life in schools: An introduction to critical pedagogy in the foundations of education* (4th ed.). Boston, MA: Allyn & Bacon.

Sadker, M., & Sadker, D. (1995). Failing at fairness: How America's schools cheat girls. New York: Touchstone Press.

The Southern Natal Gender Committee. (1994). Gender and curriculum. *Agenda,* (21), 59-64.

Trecker, J. L. (1973, October). Sex stereotyping in the secondary school curriculum. *The Phi Delta Kappan,* 55(2), 110-112.

Young, I. M. (1990). "Five Faces of Oppression." In *Justice and the Politics of Difference.* Princeton, NJ: Princeton University Press. pp. 39-65.

Practical Encounter

Practical Encounters

Directions: Write down the names of 20 people that you think are important enough for children should learn about in school? Don't overthink, just list the names as they come to you.

After writing the names of the 20 people, answer the following questions:

- How many of the individuals are dead? Alive?

- How many male? Female?

- How many were Caucasian? African-Americans? Hispanic and/or Latino? Asian-American? Native American? Multirace/nationality? Other race/ethnicity?

- How many religions were represented? What were they?

- Do you have anyone that would be gay, lesbian, bisexual, transgender, etc.?

- What were the occupations that they individuals have? What area was she/he famous for?

Questions to Ponder

1. What big "ahas" or ideas did you discover in your 20 people?

2. How does this list reflect your Pre-K through 12th grade experiences?

3. In what ways does your list highlight your personal interests, background, and passions?

4. Why is this self-reflection important for informing your pedagogical practices?

5. Why should students be taught to critically discuss history?

6. What are some characteristics of multicultural social studies instruction?

7. How can you ensure that myths that students have been taught through social studies and/or history instruction or even what they were taught in the home or media are challenged in the classroom? Why is this important?

CHAPTER 12

Reaching our Diverse Learners through STEM

Science Contributor	Chasity O'Malley
Technology Contributor	Allyson Copeland
Engineering Contributor	Iris Minor
Math Contributor	Dana Hamadeh
STEAM Curriculum Designers	Traci Baxley, Kalisha Waldon, Allyson Copeland, Iris Minor, Ramonia Rochester
Voice in the Field (Math)	Kyla Williams

Introduction

[Science] is more than a school subject, or the periodic table, or the properties of waves. It is an approach to the world, a critical way to understand and explore and engage with the world, and then have the capacity to change that world. . . .

— President Barack Obama, March 23, 2015

The United States Department of Education embraces former President Barack Obama's call for preparing today's students to be equipped with the skills and knowledge to live and work in a global society that is experiencing growth in Science, Technology, Engineering, and Mathematics (STEM) fields. According to the 2014 United States Civil Rights Data on College and Career Readiness, the call to better prepare our students in these career fields, especially those from marginalized populations, is one that educators can no longer ignore. Below are a few highlights from that report:

- Nationwide, only 50% of high schools offer calculus, and only 63% offer physics.
- Nationwide, between 10 and 25% of high schools do not offer more than one of the core courses in the typical sequence of high school math and science education – such as Algebra I and II, Geometry, Biology, and Chemistry.
- A quarter of high schools with the highest percentage of Black and Latino students do not offer Algebra II; a third of these schools do not offer Chemistry. Fewer than half of American Indian and Native-Alaskan high school students have access to the full range of math and science courses in their high school.
- While 69% of students without disabilities have access to the full range of math and science courses, only 63% of students with disabilities served by IDEA attend schools offering Algebra I, Geometry, Algebra II, Calculus, Biology, Chemistry and Physics. For English learners, a difference in access still exists but on a smaller scale; 65% of English learners attend schools that offer the full range of courses, compared to 69% of their English-speaking peers.

Taken from: (U.S. Department of Education Office for Civil Rights, 2014)

With the increasing focus on STEM-related education and career paths, one must ask, are we preparing students in an equitable manner? Or is the opportunity gap widening for traditionally marginalized groups of students?

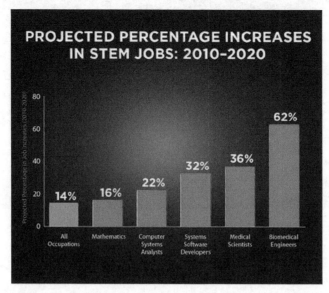

Projected Job Increase Careers in the STEM field

Figure 12.1 illustrates the field-specific projected STEM job growth over the next few years.
Taken from US Department of Education: http://www.ed.gov/stem

With this data in mind, the education community is tasked with preparing and creating access to curricula that serve diverse groups of students, specifically underserved populations, in careers related to STEM fields. Traditionally, the STEM curriculum has not been designed to include the voices, experiences, and knowledge of marginalized groups. Students are taught both explicitly and implicitly, to avoid certain subjects or topics rather than explore and embrace courses that may challenge them academically. If we want to increase the likelihood of students choosing STEM coursework or having interests in STEM careers, administrators and educators must strive to create environments, programs, and curricula geared toward fostering interest in these areas. In addition, there needs to be a concerted effort to meet the needs of students beginning in the elementary grades through post-secondary education. These programs and curricula should be inclusive of all students, including those students traditionally marginalized (i.e. Blacks, Hispanics, and Women), so their talents and genuine interests in those fields are discovered and developed.

STEM programs are and will continue to be significant catalysts for technological innovation, creativity, breakthroughs, discoveries, and transformations in our daily lives and throughout the world. When classroom instruction is driven by high-stakes testing, inflexible curriculum and/or scripted instruction, educators are faced with the challenge of balancing how best to engage and nurture students' interests and upholding the mandated standards and school district directives. However, overcoming this obstacle is what will lead to the future success and effective inclusiveness of STEM teaching for all students.

The goal of this chapter is to explore the following questions as it relates to STEM: (a) how is the subject/field viewed, perceived, or taught from a monolithic (traditional) perspective; (b) whose voices and histories are excluded from the STEM curricula; (c) how can educators use the unique voices and histories of our diverse student populations so they can become skillful and fully investigate and engage on a global scale. A practical application for designing and implementing STEM curricula with a multicultural focus will end the chapter.

Science

An experiment is a question which science poses to Nature, and a measurement is the recording of Nature's answer.

– Max Planck, 1858–1947, Theoretical Physicist

For most, science is associated with inquiry, the process of observing and asking questions that lead to more questions regarding the world around us. Science is both intellectual and practical; it is the systematic study of the structure and behavior of the physical and natural world through observation and experiment; it is a way of knowing. Science seeks to encourage students to: (1) know; (2) to know how; and (3) and to know why. The chain of "whys" and "hows" lead to a more widely accepted truth or a better understanding of the world. A person's curiosity and natural proclivity toward questioning and seeking answers are not guaranteed to remain pure and unfiltered. It changes and adapts according to present authority and the environment.

The traditional approach to teaching science does not provide learners with an opportunity to truly generate questions that are formed or rooted in their lived experiences, histories, or knowledge. Monolithic teaching is instructor-centered and requires students to perform or "regurgitate" information that is taught unidirectionally and from the perspective of the dominant population. In monolithic classrooms, students are expected to listen, understand, and apply information without opportunities to connect what they are learning to their lives or the world around them; they are often devoid of student-centered activities. This model, often referred to as the "banking concept" (Freire, 2006) or transmission model of education, makes teachers the subject while students passively learn the information being presented. In these classrooms, students' lived or real-world experiences rarely drive the curriculum or inform instructional decisions.

A more successful approach to teaching science is inquiry-based learning. There has been a rather passionate ongoing debate for several decades as to whether inquiry-based learning is an effective approach for teaching science. As a means to provide students with the best of both worlds, many educators choose to use traditional approaches with inquiry-based activities. The inclusion of inquiry-based activities in the science classroom also promotes active learning and greater student success (Freeman et al, 2014). Through the inclusion of inquiry-based methods in the classroom, Eddy and Hogan (2014) found that marginalized student populations showed a marked increase in their academic performance when compared to the performance of their peers.

For example, a traditional lecture may be paired with online homework to be completed before the lecture, where the lecture covers about 2/3 of class time, and a critical thinking exercise, experiment, or practical exercise covers the remaining 1/3 of the time. Students are encouraged to ask questions and urged to design theoretical experiments as the inquiry-based approach suggests. In this way, explicit instruction of the content or concept under study is still provided along with more authentic learning opportunities.

Structured discussion with peers is another method used in science classrooms to help encourage critical thinking. When students are given the opportunity to grapple with novel constructs, argue ideas or interpretations, and collaborate with peers, the results are often more productive conversations and improved learning (Sampson & Clark, 2009).

Ways to Incorporate Multicultural Experiences in Science

When asked about the discovery of the structure of DNA, overwhelmingly most people quickly recall the work of James Watson and Sir Francis Crick. Only a fraction of the population would include Rosalind Franklin as one who has contributed to what we know today; however, without her contribution, Watson and Crick may have never known the answer to their question about the structure of DNA. Franklin was responsible for the X-Ray crystallography that allowed for the physical structure of DNA to be seen for the first time, confirming the hypothesis of Watson and Crick. Her work was monumental and crucial for the discovery, yet her name is missing from the traditional science narrative. With this one example of a well-known topic, an open dialog can be initiated in the classroom to help generate more examples of women in science, and to expand on this topic even further to include contributions or scientific discoveries made by members of minority groups.

Active Learning
Why would it be important to discuss the contribution of Rosalind Franklin?

One way to offer students the opportunity to hear multicultural voices in science, voices that are not included in the traditional curriculum, is for teachers to intentionally provide students with meaningful exposure to scientists or theorists who are like them – ranging from race and nationality to personality and domestic similarities. Students can relate to scientists being the only child, the eldest child, overcoming adversity, or just being of the same gender or ethnicity. We are, by nature, drawn to whom and what we are most familiar. For young girls to see more than Western representations of scientific exploration in their textbook is extremely meaningful. Conversely, African–American students should be exposed to knowledge centered on the contributions of Black scientists or inventors. While reflections on the contributions of Madam Curie and George Washington Carver are notable, their history in science does not represent the spectrum of diversity in multicultural science education. For a student who lives in a low-SES neighborhood, learning about Michael Faraday, whose family was not financially well off and who became one of the most influential scientists, is meaningful.

The science classroom should provide the students with information relevant to the curriculum, while exposing them to important contributions made by the experts in the field from various cultural backgrounds. The STEM program is dedicated to the scientific process and equipping students with tools needed to discover the world. Designated time should be devoted to exposing students to people like them who dared to ask, who were tenacious to seek, and were obligated to share with the world what they knew. There will never be a shortage of needs that science must meet the challenge to create. The greater the exposure to the gamut of science fields, the fuller, more available science will become to students. Essentially, a multicultural educator must connect science content to students' funds of knowledge, history, and experiences. This will allow them to "own" the information and facilitate the application and evolution of their thinking, hopefully leading to more inquiries and explorations.

This requires the educator to be prepared with fresh examples and real-world connections to the science curriculum; this will convey to students why science is important. Table 12.1 lists a few strategies/approaches that can foster meaningful science experiences for students.

While it is important for students to see themselves in the curriculum, a multicultural science classroom and instruction should not only benefit marginalized student groups but also mainstreamed students as well. It transforms their perceptions of a curriculum that has traditionally been "white-washed." Below are examples of several scientists who counter the stereotype of scientists in the traditional curriculum, White males. One class activity could be to assign an individual student or small group to either create a presentation or write a paper on the scientist, their history, and important contributions they made to the field (See Table 12.2). By expanding their understanding of other scientists in the world, it helps to open their eyes to see how diverse the field of science truly is.

Table 12.1. Strategies for Meaningful Science Experiences

Suggestions	Practical Examples
Promote student inquiry by letting students' questions drive the curriculum and instruction	Invite students to write down any questions they wish to solve in their communities. Use these questions as the basis for scientific exploration. For example: How can we create a system in our neighborhood to keep our parks clean? Students could speak to people in the community to generate ideas and put those plans into action.
Introduce students science contributors who have diverse backgrounds	Create a list of things we use in our daily lives that were discovered or invented by scientists with diverse backgrounds. Invite students to research these individuals and integrate this knowledge into a classroom project.
Provide meaningful sensory experiences both within the classroom and beyond	When possible, go on field trips. Visit the local aquarium or zoo, check out the health department, and/or have a health fair at school. Virtual field trips are also great ways to expose students to things beyond the walls of the classroom. Several great resources to connect science to the outside world include: • www.sciencedaily.com – provides interpretations of published works of science • www.edutopia.org – provides support for all K-12 educators and has a wealth of information on multicultural education • www.NASA.gov – provides the novel science experiences that can engage students • www.NPR.org – provides interviews with teachers using innovative ways to introduce STEM to their students and has an education podcast • CDC &P (hands-on summer program for science teachers)
Provide an environment that promotes meaningful conversations that allow them to connect academically and socially	Model critical conversations and questioning techniques in class (asking questions that challenge status quo or traditional thinking). Holding debates on scientific principles and its impact on society or groups of people can be powerful for learning. The students may not agree, but seeing some talking points from other viewpoints can be very eye opening.
Equip your classroom with resources that support multicultural science learning	In your classroom libraries, include biographies and autobiographies of multiethnic scientists. Include daily or weekly "Did you know?" activities where they are introduced to facts about scientists from diverse backgrounds.

Table 12.2.   List of Science Contributors from Diverse Backgrounds

Rosalind Franklin (1920–1958)

English chemist involved with x-ray crystallography of DNA

George Washington Carver (1863–1943)

American botanist and inventor who fostered the growth of the peanut and sweet potato industry. Carver was born into slavery.

Percy Lavon Julian (1899–1975)

African–American research chemist important for the research leading to mass production of human hormones such as testosterone and progesterone. His work laid the groundwork for cortisone therapy and birth control.

Ynes Mexia (1870–1938)

Mexican American botanist who collected over 150,000 specimens, with 500 being novel species and 2 novel genera.

Technology

Technology is a powerful force in education. The era of productivity we live in has bountifully yielded a plethora of digital tools, particularly for K-12 teachers, learners, and others eager to implement new strategies and models when designing curriculum and instruction. Today, the current epoch compels learners to effectively mine exponential amounts of information, discriminately decide on the usefulness of information they are learning, and be able to use this information to solve complex problems and to make complicated decisions (An & Reigeluth, 2011). From early advances in technology, to virtual synchronous conferences, many of today's learners now have ubiquitous systems of communication and information (Rainie & Wellman, 2012). As new classroom models continue to surface (e.g. flipped, hybrid, blended, hyflex), these technologies become linchpins of our education system. As student's everyday life is infused with technology, so should their education be. Educators must model effective strategies to connect what students do outside the classroom to what they are learning inside of the classroom.

How Has Technology Marginalized Student Populations?

The growth of web-based communication, interaction, and collaboration has been described as "meteoric" (Snelson & Perkins, 2009). Consequently, the use and demand of technology in the classroom are steadily increasing and the need for educational resources to help instructors make sense of how best to use these tools with diverse populations is essential. Unfortunately, the rapid growth of technology integration continues to marginalize underrepresented groups who find it difficult to access, navigate, manipulate, and master the use of these tools.

Today, nearly 5-million American families with school-age children lack access to a steady home internet connection (Horrigan, 2015). This disparity is seen most commonly amongst low-income, minority families who would often benefit exponentially from these connections as they are expected to play "catch up" to their counterparts who have access to technology in the home. These gaps pose a great threat to students' potential for independent learning. It also serves to further marginalize groups of students as technology becomes a dialect of power, or as Bourdieu (1991) described an "official language" which represents and forms a kind of common wealth amongst members of a community.

If the Internet and its accompanying technological tools can be used as an agent of democracy, as opposed to a stratifying mechanism, educators are first in the line of duty to make sense of how to disseminate valuable information to diverse groups of students. Educators can also help to facilitate the use of these resources to imbue cultural relevance in classrooms and advocate for the inclusion of these 21st century tools and skills in curricula. Technology should help to fill the gaps that maintain inequalities, not widen them.

These technology-infused models, liked flipped classrooms, are the wave of our future, but with nearly 30% of low-income families with school-age children without internet access. How do these groups compete to remain relevant in classrooms where a great deal of the learning is dependent upon students' ability to access resources outside of the traditional learning environment?

Active Learning

Imagine the 21st century classroom, fully equipped with the latest technological bells and whistles. Now visualize this imaginary classroom as flipped – which means the instructor offers much of the lecture and learning material through streaming video, podcasts, and other web 2.0 tools, and the in-classroom instructional time is used for hands-on activities, experiments, projects, and inquiry work.

Questions to Ponder:

1. What would be the expectation of the learner in a flipped classroom?
2. How do these expectations marginalize students?

Monolithic Approach to the Infusion of Technology into the Classroom

If, as Dewey (1938) suggests, learning is indeed experiential, then the call of the 21st century educator is to connect the use of technology to students' diverse experiences. The monolithic approach of direct instruction is often ineffective when students do not recognize the role that this knowledge may play in everyday life. Educators are charged to consider context in all lessons and are challenged to infuse standard curriculum with culturally competent and relevant examples, historical figures, problems, organizations, and solutions.

Research studies in education validate the implementation of computer-based technology for all students. Studies show that the use of technology can help to improve students standardized test scores, help to enhance their inventive thinking, and help to strengthen student self-concept and individual motivation (Hew & Brush, 2007). These benefits however are not fully realized when great portions of our learner populations are affected by the inability to access the Internet and are disenfranchised because of their lack of instant and constant use of cutting-edge digital tools. The populations that often suffer here are low-income, often in urban and rural settings. Often these communities are heavily saturated with non-native English speakers, first and second-generation immigrants, and African–American and Hispanic/Latino families.

As school districts continue to encourage the integration of computers, tablets, and mobile digital devices into classrooms, concerned educators are encouraged to seek technology's relevance amongst the students they serve. The benefits of the integration of technology is realized fully when it is used to enhance and expand students' subject knowledge or content delivery. Increasingly, the responsibility of the 21st Century multicultural educator is to integrate technology into classrooms in ways that help to reshape the educational landscape by providing balance to whitewashed curricula and gender-biased textbooks (Gay, 2000).

While some educators believe that computers can be used to merely assist students with classroom assignments, innovative thought should be focused on how teachers can use digital tools to pique students' interests and expand their desire for inquiry. Educators should consider how content could be paired with technology resources to provide students tools to solve real-life problems and perpetuate a culture of competence and resourcefulness. Educators employing equity pedagogy (Banks & Banks, 1995) are often first in recognizing the power that the knowledge of technology affords our 21st century learners and should facilitate imaginative technology integration and exploration in classrooms.

Practical Examples on Using Technology to Teach from a Multicultural Perspective

Technology used in curricula this way can help give voice and agency to groups that are rarely pictured in textbooks and whose stories are seldom told. In considering this context, equity pedagogists consider their student population in relation to their world (Gay, 2000) and highlight the diverse funds of knowledge and histories of their students when planning instruction. Technology can enhance or expand traditional curriculum and teach them to problematize the social and economic issues that students face in their daily lives. Table 12.3 lists a few examples of how technology can be used to teach content from a multicultural perspective.

Table 12.3. Practical Ways Technology Can Be Used

Subject-Area	Example
Math	Students can be challenged to solve a real-world problem through the creation of a technology program. Students can be given the task of "planning an urban city" in their community. Each student could assume a role and be responsible for mathematically planning a fully functional, fiscally responsible city, accounting for educational, political, and infrastructural obligations. Students can use culturally relevant public databases and statistics to practice foundational mathematics functions. Using data relevant to their lives will make the practice of arithmetic more meaningful.
Social Studies	Students can use online primary documents and virtual tours of museums around the world- slave narratives, newspaper clippings, etc. to learn about the role of African–American soldiers in the war. Students can use social media forums to post and respond to current local and national events on a classroom page. Instructors can provide guidelines, but students choose the topic. These discussion boards serve as informal ways to infuse education, technology, and culture into lessons that promote media literacy.
Science	Students can connect with university biology labs to take part in science experiments, like dissections and DNA testing. Students can use web applications that model the human body in 3D to explain functions of the human body and pinpoint anomalies in case studies. Like medical students, if students are given a hypothetical patient profile to examine, they can use these virtual models to diagnose potential problems in the human body and practice anatomy simultaneously.
Language Arts	Students can play online games to improve their grammar, spelling, syntax, and vocabulary. Conversely, free word processing software can be used as an open-source note-taking forum for students to openly write and be reviewed by their peers in real time. Students can be asked to bring in a transcript of personal text messages exchanged between friends/family and find ways to improve the grammar, spelling, and colloquialism to turn texting-speech into works of literary art or poetic prose.
Geography/Sociology	Students can use geospatial mapping technology software, i.e. Google Maps, Google Earth, etc. to pinpoint their country or community of origin and take virtual field trips. Students can use these activities to compare developed and developing nations. These tools can serve as an impetus for conversations about colonialism, industrialization, and the influence of industry and politics domestically and abroad.
Foreign Language	Students can use mobile-based applications like Duolingo to become familiar with foreign language. Students can connect with foreign students in varying countries through linguistic exchange programs to practice the acquisition of a new language through Skype, Zoom, or other virtual conferencing software.

Engineering

Engineering is a field of science that involves problem-solving and developing new ways to help society meet its ever-changing needs through math, science, and technical content. As the national demand shifts toward the increase of STEM professions, more attention should be given to creating a diverse engineering pipeline (Morrison, McDuffie & French, 2015; Tawfik, Trueman & Lorz, 2014). Students should be introduced to diversity within the field of engineering and the impact this field has on local and global community building.

The design process used in the field of engineering is an effective way to help students solve problems in their daily lives, in their communities, and eventually in their professional careers. The engineering design process is much like that of the scientific method; however, the scientific method is usually used as a process by which scientists test explanations and predictions by using experiments to find answers to their questions. Engineers on the other hand use the engineering design process to solve problems that address specific needs. They are concerned with "**Who** need(s) **what** because **why**? And then, the engineer creates a solution that meets the need" (Science Buddies, 2002-2017). Drawing on engineering design (Acar & Rother, 2011; Science Buddies, 2002-2017), the work of Freire (2006), and Gorski & Pothini (2014); we, Waldon & Baxley (2017) offer that the classroom engineering process should consist of 7 steps and could be used across the curriculum to engage students in solving problems within their own world (See Figure 12.2). It can also become a springboard to transforming them into change agents in their own communities:

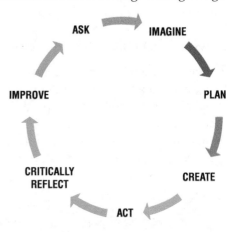

1. Defining the problem (**ASK**)
2. Research and brainstorm to find possible solutions (**IMAGINE**)
3. Develop a plan of action based on your research and the people that will be impacted (**PLAN**)
4. Design a product, good, or service (**CREATE**)
5. Test (**ACT**)
6. Evaluate from multiple perspectives (**CRITICALLY REFLECT**)
7. Make changes to prototype and redesign (**IMPROVE**)

In order to define the problem, one must first ask what the problem is and imagine the possible solutions that can be offered to solve the problem through brainstorming and research. The next step invites students to make a plan of action that is in harmony with the unique needs of the individuals who will be impacted by the implementation of the action. From there, they develop or create a product or service that would solve the problem(s) under investigation. Students are then encouraged to act, presenting their finished draft to their desired audience, and critically reflect upon their product or service to see if it meets the needs of those involved or solves the original problem. From there they further develop or tweak their product or service to better serve or answer the problem. This could lead them to asking more questions. The STEAM Curriculum at the end of this chapter is a curriculum that was created to facilitate the problem-solving processes that we offer above.

Currently there is a movement toward interdisciplinary, collaborative problem-solving in intentional spaces designed for the purpose of design. Makerspaces, a gathering place commonly used in the fields of engineering, computer science, and graphic design, provide spaces for people to come together to share resources and knowledge to solve problems. It is an ideal space where multidisciplinary and collaborative projects come to life. Makerspaces foster self-directed learning and hands-on opportunities that allow participants to view a goal from various perspectives and learn from one another. Makerspaces can be great additions to a critical multicultural classroom where students are involved in inquiry, problem-posing situations focused on issues in their everyday lives. This design-thinking, taken from the engineering profession, can lead to more critical interactions with the world (Acar & Rother, 2011).

Table 12.4. Major Branches of Engineering

Major Branches of Engineering	Description	Occupations
Chemical	Chemical engineers use chemistry and other branches of science to solve problems relating to the production and use of chemicals. They can work in areas such as chemical manufacturing, electronics, pollution control, and even medicine and food processing.	• Agricultural engineers • Product safety engineers • Soil and water conservationists • Foresters
Mechanical	Mechanical engineers have designed products from several different industries that we use every day, such as, spoons, flip-top caps on the toothpaste tube, cars, chairs, and pens.	• Marine architects • Petroleum engineers • Civil drafters • Electronic drafters • Mechanical drafters • Civil engineering technicians
Civil Engineering	Civil engineers design and build public spaces, work to improve travel and commerce, provide people with safe drinking water and sanitation, and protect communities from earthquakes and floods.	• Landscape architects • Aerospace engineers • Industrial safety and health engineers • Marine architects • Mining safety engineers • Petroleum engineers
Electrical	Electrical and electronics engineers gather and shape electricity and use it to make products that transmit power or information.	• Engineering managers • Electronics engineers, except computer • Sales engineers • Nuclear engineers • Electricians

There are four major branches of engineering- chemical, mechanical, civil, electrical; however a fifth branch, interdisciplinary engineering, has derived from a combination of disciplines and subjects. Each of the major branches of engineering has sub-branches or categories. Table 12.4, although not exhaustive, provides a brief description of the various types of engineering.

Based on the above discussion, one could then ask, does the engineering curriculum in classrooms today include issues or problems that lead to the marginalization of specific groups of students? Do minority students see themselves as successful engineers? The answers to each of these questions present new concerns in terms of equity pedagogy.

Today, top universities confer degrees to hundreds of Black and Hispanic/Latino engineering students. While degree conferral plays an important role in the field, job acquisition is often difficult for marginalized or non-mainstreamed groups. On the average, only half of Black and Hispanic graduates with degrees in computer engineering and related fields from leading universities are hired by major technology companies (Weise, 2014). Additionally, while the number of engineering degrees conferred by universities in the United States has increased, the percentage of African–American students earning those degrees has decreased from 4.3% in 2013 to 3.5% in 2014 (Learmonth, 2015). According to Nevarez (2015), the corporate vice president of Microsoft, Horacio Gutierrez, stated that the underrepresentation of Latinos in STEM fields, like engineering, has been referred to as "severe." This dearth of minority representation in the job and collegial market offers its own set of challenges that lead to the marginalization of specific groups of students.

The invisibility of diverse representations in engineering-focused curriculum has possible implications for minority students. It also serves to diminish the importance of this role in marginalized communities and limit the aspirations of youth. Table 12.5 lists individuals from traditional marginalized groups who are working in the field of engineering or who have contributed to the field. The incorporation of this and many of diverse voices in the curriculum could allow marginalized groups to see themselves in the curriculum and envision themselves working in engineering careers.

Table 12.5.   Engineers from Marginalized Groups

Aprille J. Ericsson-Jackson, Ph.D.

The first African Woman to receive an engineering degree

Elijah McCoy

A 19th century African–American inventor with over 90 patents. He is known best for his invention of lubrication devices that make train travel more efficient.

Emily Roebling

The first woman field engineer and technical leader of the Brooklyn Bridge.

Eva Saravia

Vice president of global programs at Bohemia Interactive Simulations. This company uses simulation software train soldiers for combat.

Jessica Rannow

A Senior industrial engineer and engineering project manager of at AmerisourceBergen

Ursula Burns

Chairwomen of Xerox and CEO of the company until 2009. She was the first Black woman to head a Fortune 500 Company.

Walter Braithwaite

He was named President of Boeing Africa in 2000. He contributed to the development of the CAD/CAM systems that made it possible for computers to design airplanes.

There are several factors that impact the rate at which students pursue degrees in STEM. One example is gender stereotype endorsement; this has been proven to negatively impact the performance levels of both, male and female students (Jones et al., 2013; Rice, Lopez, Richardson & Stinson, 2013) and has fueled the gender gap and has perpetuated inequities in engineering. Men are more likely to receive encouragement to aspire toward STEM goals as well as self-identify with the STEM leadership within their chosen institution (Xu, 2008).

Likewise, academic programs and instructional practices in schools today can perpetrate a cycle that marginalizes students and can produce performance anxiety (Beasley & Fischer, 2012) and beliefs that they cannot be successful in the engineering or other STEM-related fields. To better understand the instructional practices that increase STEM resiliency in underrepresented populations, Morrison, Roth, and French (2015) studied three prime principles that are perceived to be key components to successful STEM programs and have raised students' interest in STEM: problem-solving and inquiry approaches, strong social interactions, and collaborative work. This resiliency and interest can also be the result of the inclusion of curricular resources and experiences that are meaningful and relevant to students and that foster interdisciplinary skills that are imperative to the field of engineering. Table 12.6 provides a list of resources/websites that can be used in the classroom to engage students.

Table 12.6.   Real-World Examples of Relevant Engineering Curriculum/ Resources

Resource	Website
Engineering Everywhere Curriculum Units	http://www.eie.org/engineering-everywhere/curriculum-units
Curriculum for K-12 Teachers	https://www.teachengineering.org/
The Road to the STEM Professoriate for Underrepresented Minorities	http://www.air.org/sites/default/files/downloads/report/AGEP_Lit_Review_10-26-09_0.pdf
Dreambox Learning	http://www.dreambox.com/blog/world-changing-african-americans-infographic
Engineering for Change	https://www.engineeringforchange.org/
Science Buddies- Careers in STEM	http://www.sciencebuddies.org/science-engineering-careers#engineering

Math

I firmly believe that there exists a powerful light that burns within each and every one of us. We have unique and special heritages, languages, cultures, and traditions. Ethnomathematics allows us to tap into these treasures and find a connection between wisdom grounded in the past and hope for a bright and beautiful future.

– Linda Furuto as quoted in Ernst (2010)

Education should be free from discrimination. Regardless of the color, race, gender, or socioeconomic status of our students, all students deserve equitable learning opportunities where teachers have high expectations for them. As a country, we are responsible for exposing all students to career paths in STEM fields. It is vital to encourage students to follow their hearts and minds, and to change negative perceptions of STEM, particularly in mathematics, that are developed and reinforced at a young age, especially in girls.

Schools need to intentionally validate and celebrate math through the lens of various cultures. In mathematics, the notion of culturally responsive teaching has been conceptualized as ethnomathematics (D'Ambrosio, 1997), which is defined as the study of mathematics that considers and integrates the culture in which math arises or how different cultures "go about the tasks of classifying, ordering, counting, measuring or mathematizing their environment" (Oritz-Franco, 2005). Through ethnomathematics, teachers introduce mathematics by deriving it from real-life scenarios. The linking of math to students' culture makes the content matter more meaningful, thus bringing value and relevance to students' current and future lives. Preparing students to be purposeful in a competitive, global society, while teaching them to admire and appreciate their heritage and history are essential aspects of effective teaching. Ethnomathematics instruction can be conceptualized through Banks (1994) dimensions of multicultural education:

1. **Content integration:** the illumination of key points of instruction with content reflecting diversity;
2. **Knowledge construction:** helping students understand how perspectives of people within a discipline influence the conclusions reached within that discipline;
3. **Prejudice reduction:** efforts to develop positive attitudes toward different groups;
4. **Equitable pedagogy:** ways to modify teaching to facilitate academic achievement among students from diverse groups; and
5. **Empowering school culture and social** structure: ensuring educational equality and cultural empowerment for students from diverse groups (pp. 4-5).

The National Council of Teachers of Mathematics (2000) recognizes the role and importance of culture and learning as a socio-cultural process. Consequently, the organization has developed standards that include teachers' understanding of how students' cultural, linguistic, ethnic, racial, gender, and socioeconomic background influence their learning of mathematics, particularly, the role of mathematics in society and culture, and the contribution of various cultures to the advancement of mathematics. Additionally, the NCTM standards suggest pedagogical practices that include the use of inquiry-based and cooperative learning, which are aspects of culturally responsive teaching.

Given these research groundings and organizational policy statements, studies have begun to examine the application and success of the theory of culturally responsive teaching in mathematics. For example, Schoenfield (2000) examined some school districts that have reformed their curricula based on the NCTM standards. The results of this research revealed a significant improvement in students' achievement. With the new curriculum, 50% of the minority students met or exceeded the standard and the proportion of minority students performing well doubled. Schoenfield concludes that a culturally responsive curriculum helps minority students to make sense of the world.

A relevant and applicable example of how this can be done is by connecting music to mathematics. Creating the connection between the two has always been a powerful tool to help students gain a better understanding of the discipline. Using the rhythm of musical notes can provide both an auditory and visual example to explain fractions. By taking the students' culture into consideration, utilizing a culturally relevant teaching strategy can transform the learning of the concept it into a more meaningful experience.

There are many reasons why students shy away from mathematics. Some of these reasons include: (1) students underestimating themselves and their academic capabilities, (2) negative prior experiences with STEM content, which appears to be strongly linked to what they were taught in the third grade, (3) students being told they are bad at math, or (4) having had teachers who dislike math and transmit the "hatred" of it onto their students. Just as love is contagious, so is the love for math. A teacher's attitude toward the discipline plays a vital role in shaping his or her students' feelings toward and interest in the subject. It is generally agreed that mathematics makes an essential contribution to a well-rounded education; it plays a vital role in our culture and civilization (Advisory Committee on Mathematical Education, 2011; Vorderman et al., 2011). Without a solid comprehensive foundation in mathematics, the appreciation of a range of other educational disciplines such as music, the sciences, geography, and economics can be compromised (Vorderman et al., 2011).

Active Learning
Do you consider math to be a universal language? Why or why not?

It is believed that mathematics is only universal to those who share a particular historical and cultural perspective or background. Educators should help students understand that even though there are certain elements of mathematics that are ubiquitous – such as counting, locating, measuring, designing, playing, and explaining (Bishop, 1988) – there are variations in the ways diverse cultural groups view major aspects of mathematics and there are various approaches to solving the same problem. For example, Indians and Chinese believe that a result (answer to a mathematical expression) in mathematics can be validated by any method, including a visual demonstration, whereas Europeans expect a conjecture to be proven step-by-step, starting with self-evident axioms (Strutchens, 1995). Another example is proofs of the Pythagorean Theorem that have been discovered in many countries as Babylonia, China, and India (Joseph, 1987). Students should be encouraged to explore these various methods and share ideas with one another. Discussing such proofs can help students see that there are many ways to arrive at the same answers. This notion of multiple perspectives aligns with the goals of multicultural education.

Positive encounters toward different cultural groups can be encouraged by using mathematics to study social or cultural issues. Statistical data can reveal and dispel stereotypes and myths that affect cultural groups. A critical understanding of numerical data prompts individuals to question taken-for-granted assumptions about how society is structured and enables them to act from a more informed position on societal structures and processes (Frankenstein, 1990). Effective teaching recognizes, acknowledges, and embraces the individual cultures of students. Providing meaningful learning opportunities should not be tailored only to the majority. Zevenbergen, Dole, and Wright (2004) suggest that learning environments which match the learning needs, backgrounds, and interests of the students have high expectations for student success, and encourage deep learning about and through mathematics ensure all students can learn math. Groundwater-Smith, Ewing, and Le Cornu (2007) recognize the importance of providing opportunities for learning in everyday situations. Connecting to student backgrounds and practices can help to build their self-esteem, develop cultural pride, make meaning through building on prior knowledge, and identify connections between cultural and mathematical content. Awareness of these items allows students to strengthen their understanding of social and mathematical concepts in today's global and technology-infused world.

Women in Mathematics Activity

To assist teachers in creating an engaging and informative homework activity, below is a table of a few important women in mathematics who come from various cultures and deserve notable recognition for their valuable contributions to the field. This can be used as an assignment for students to create a PowerPoint, poster, or write a one-page paper related to the mathematician's biographical information. Students can also include three to five pieces of information regarding the mathematician's influences. One of the contributions can focus on how their work and/or discoveries relate to what we learn or do today.

Table 12.7. Important Women in Mathematics

Margaret H. Hamilton

1936 –

Nationality: American

A mathematician and computer scientist who started her own software company.

Led the team that created the on-board flight software for NASA'ss Apollo command modules and lunar modules.

President Obama's recipient of the Presidential Medal of Freedom in 2016.

Martha Euphemia Lofton Haynes

1890–1980

Nationality: American

First African–American Woman to earn Ph.D. in Mathematics.

Her dissertation was "The Determination of Sets of Independent Conditions Characterizing Certain Special Cases of Symmetric Correspondences."

Katherine G. Johnson

1918 –

Nationality: American

African–American NASA mathematician selected for her contributions to the space program.

Johnson's computations have influenced every major space program from Mercury through the Shuttle program.

President Obama's recipient of the Presidential Medal of Freedom in 2015.

Maryam Mirzakhani

1977 –

Nationality: Iranian

First female mathematician to receive the Fields Medal, described as a Nobel prize for mathematics.

Currently a mathematics Professor at Stanford University and is considered one of the greatest living female mathematicians.

Antonia Ferrín Moreiras

1914–2009

Nationality: Spanish

Mathematician, professor, and the first Galician woman astronomer.

She obtained degrees in Chemistry, Pharmacy, and Mathematics.

Florence Nightingale

1820–1910

Nationality: British

Nurse who was full of compassion and the founder of modern nursing.

Statistician who helped to show government why soldiers were dying and helped reduce mortality rates in both the army and at home.

STEM Curriculum Exemplar

Below is a curriculum that was created for an experiential field trip at Florida Atlantic University. The name of the curriculum is *S.T.E.A.M. for Social Justice: Using Inquiry Skills to Create Changes in Your World*. The curriculum challenged the students who were a part of the experience to think of two issues or problems that they would like to improve in their community. The students identified food insecurity and abuse as pertinent problems they wished to address. The curriculum was centered on their concerns and was infused with culturally relevant practices.

Curriculum Title	S.T.E.A.M. for Social Justice: Using Inquiry Skills to Create Changes In Your World
Curriculum Grade Adaptation:	K - 5
Curriculum Developer:	Traci P. Baxley, Ed.D.; Kalisha Waldon, Ph.D.; Allyson Copeland; Iris Minor; Ramonia Rochester

Course-Level Objectives

ISTE Standards
Students will:
1. Demonstrate creative thinking, construct knowledge, and develop innovative products and processes using online technology.
2. Apply digital tools to gather, evaluate, and use information.
3. Use digital media and environments to communicate and work collaboratively, including at a distance, to support individual learning and contribute to the learning of others.

Next Generation Science Standards
Students will:
1. Use prior knowledge to describe problems that can be solved.
2. Analyze and interpret data to make sense of phenomena, using logical reasoning, mathematics, and/or computation.
3. Compare and contrast data collected by different groups in order to discuss similarities and differences in their findings.
4. Read and comprehend grade-appropriate complex texts and/or reliable media to summarize and obtain scientific and technical ideas and describe how they are supported by evidence.

Florida STEM Common Core
Students will:
1. Use problem-solving discovery and participate in exploration in order to create artistic designs using math concepts.
2. Build upon the processing concepts presented to create new codes.
3. Use group collaboration to build a sense of community while offering assistance to peers as needed.
4. Gain a sense of academic integrity in their abilities to independently utilize math concepts throughout the course.

English Language Arts Common Core
Students will:
1. Prepare for and participate effectively in a range of conversations and collaborations with diverse partners, building on others' ideas and expressing their own clearly and persuasively.
2. Integrate and evaluate information presented in diverse media and formats, including visually, quantitatively, and orally.
3. Present information, findings, and supporting evidence such that listeners can follow the line of reasoning and the organization, development, and style are appropriate to task, purpose, and audience.
4. Make strategic use of digital media and visual displays of data to express information and enhance understanding of presentations.

Florida English Language Arts Standards:
Students will:
1. Determine the meaning of general academic and domain-specific words and phrases in a text relevant to a relevant subject areas.
2. Summarize a written text or information presented in diverse media and formats, including visually, quantitatively, and orally.
3. Write informative/explanatory texts to examine a topic and convey ideas and information clearly.

Session #	Module/Unit Topic	Module/Unit Objective(s)	Assessment(s)	Lesson Content	Material(s) Needed
1	Orientation/ Community Circles	1. Participate in the community circles each morning (ISTE-3);(STEM-3);(ELACC-1) 2. Describe something new or an interesting idea or fact that they learned about the social problem they are attempting to solve (FELAS-3); (ELACC-1,3);(NGSS-2)(ISTE-1)	• Reflection Journal (1.2) • Community discussion (1.1)	• Community Circle protocol (1.1) • Journal prompt (1.2)	• Journal (1.2) • Writing tool (1.2)
2	Research Library	1. Conduct guided research using library resources (ISTE-1-3); (NGSS-2,4) (STEM-3)(ELACC-1-2) 2. Perform web quest to find valuable resources that inform the social entrepreneurship goal (ISTE-1-3); (NGSS-2,4) (STEM-3)(ELACC-1,2,4)	• Research worksheet (2.1, 2.2) • Discuss examples of inspiring social entrepreneurship (2.2)	• Webquest guidelines (2.1; 2.2) • Tailored webquest worksheet (2.1, 2.2)	• Age appropriate library databases and libguides (2.1, 2.2) • Writing tools (2.1,2.2) • Journals (2.1,2.2)
3	Business Planning	1. Design business plan and explain its use in developing a new service or product (NGSS-1,2,4) (FELAS-1,3) 2. Explain the role of social justice organizations in alleviating community issues (FELAS-3) (NGSS-1) 3. Discuss how a business can be used to aid the selected social justice issue or cause (NGSS -1-4)	• Group Business Plan Discussion (3.2, 3.3) • Journal/ Researcher Notes(3.2) • Design a Business Plan (3.1) • Researcher Notes	• Business plan instructions (3.1) • Discussion focus (3.3) • Journal prompt (3.2)	• Writing tools (3.2, 3.3) • Business Plan template (3.1) • Journal (3.2)
4	Budget/ Financial Literacy	1. Define and explain the importance of finance and financial literacy (STEM-4) (ELACC-1) 2. Discuss how effective financial management can aid their social justice issue (ELACC-3) (FELAS-1) 3. Practice financial management principles during session (STEM-3-4)	• Business Budget Plan (4.3) • Budget discussion (4.1, 4.2)	• Budgeting worksheet (4.3) • Budgeting plan instructions (4.3) • Discussion prompt (4.2) • Explanation of Budget (4.1)	• Writing tool (4.1,4.2,4.3) • Example budgets (4.3)
5	Marketing	1. Explain the purpose and importance of marketing to a business (ISTE-2-3) (NGSS-4) 2. Discuss how effective marketing can aid the selected social justice issue or cause (ELACC-1,2,4) (FELAS-3) 3. Create a simple marketing plan (FELAS-3) (ELACC-1-4) (ISTE-1-3) (NGSS-1-4)	• Group Marketing Plan (5.3) • Journal/Researcher Notes(5.1) • Discussion (5.2)	• Marketing plan instructions (5.3) • Journal prompt (5.1) • Discussion Prompt (5.2) • Marketing plan template (5.3) • Example marketing plan (5.3)	• Writing tool (5.1,5.2) • Journal (5.1) • Computer (5.3) • Collaborative working area (5.3)

(Continued)

Session #	Module/Unit Topic	Module/Unit Objective(s)	Assessment(s)	Lesson Content	Material(s) Needed
6	Snap Circuit Kits/Lab Demonstrations	1. Explain what engineers do and how they solve social problems (ISTE-2) (NGSS-2) (STEM-3,4) (FELAS-3) 2. Discuss how engineering concepts can aid in solving the selected social justice issue or cause(ISTE-2) (NGSS-2) (STEM-3,4) (FELAS-3) 3. Model or demonstrate aspects and applications from the field (STEM-1,3,4) (NGSS-1,2,3)	• Snap Circuit Kits (6.3) • Journal/Researcher Notes (6.1) • Group Discussion (6.2)	• Engineering fact sheet (6.1,6.2) • Examples of engineering for social justice (6.1,6.2) Discussion prompt (6.1, 6.2, 6.3) • Prompt for journal (6.1)	• Snap circuit kits (6.3) • Journal (6.1) • Writing tool (6.1)
7	Graphic Design	1. Discuss the role of a graphic designer and the importance of appropriate design (ISTE-1,3) (NGSS-4) (STEM-1,3) (ELACC-4) 2. Develop a business logo (ISTE-1-3) (NGSS-1) (ELACC-2-4) (FELAS-4) 3. Discuss how the selected logo design represents their social justice issue or cause (FELAS-2) (ELACC-1-4) (ISTE-1-3)	• Design and select potential business logo(7.2) • Discussion (7.1, 7.3)	• Graphic design quick tips (7.1,7.2,7.3) • Discussion prompt (7.3) • Researcher Journal (7.2,7.3)	• Resources for personal design (7.2, 7.1) • Grid lined paper (7.2) • Coloring and shading pencils (7.2) • Computer (7.1,7.2,7.3)
8	Public Speaking	1. Explain the purpose and importance of communication in business (ISTE-3) (NGSS-4) (ELACC-1-4) (FELAS-3) 2. Discuss how effective communication can aid the selected social justice issue or cause (relas(2-3) 3. Model or demonstrate effective communication (FELAS 1-3) (ELACC-1-4)	• Prepare group presentation (8.3) • Create group business pitch (8.3, 8.2) • Journal/Researcher notes (8.1, 8.2)	• Presentation guidelines (8.23) • Presentation rubric (8.3) • Tips for successful presentation (8.1,8.2,8.3) • Presentation timeline (8.3)	• Exemplars of successful communication (8.1, 8.2, 8.3) • Computer (8.3) • Writing tool (8.1) • Journal (8.1, 8.2, 8.3)
9	Social Justice Statistics	1. Define statistics and recognize their use in social entrepreneurship (ISTE 2-3) (NGSS-2-3) (STEM - 1,3,4) (FELAS-1,3) (ELACC–1-4) 2. Identify ways statistics have been used to inform fields that mitigate effects of hunger and abuse the selected social justice issue (ISTE 2-3) (NGSS-2-3) (STEM - 1,3,4) (FELAS-1,3) (ELACC–1-4) 3. Practice statistical analysis with using web-based tools (ISTE 2-3) (NGSS-2-3) (STEM - 1,3,4) (FELAS-1,3) (ELACC–1-4)	• Journal (9.1) • Practice using real-life statistics to strengthen your argument (9.2,9.3) • Discussion (9.1)	• Statistics worksheet (9.2, 9.3) • Discussion Prompt (9.1, 9.2, 9.3) • Journal Prompt (9.1, 9.2)	• Statistics websites (9.2, 9.3) • Examples of age-appropriate statistical data (9.2, 9.3) • Journal (9.1) • Writing tool (9.1, 9.2) • Computer (9.1,9.2,9.3)

10	Web Design/ Coding	1. Demonstrate how to use algorithms to create a source code that presents various shapes, colors, and designs on the processing platform (ISTE-1-3) (NGSS-2,4) (STEM -1-4) (ELACC-1-4) (FELAS-1-3) 2. Explain how code works or might not work using processing (ISTE-1-3) (NGSS-2,4) (STEM -1-4) (ELACC-1-4) (FELAS-1-3) 3. Design and manually execute code to create basic diagrams(ISTE-1-3) (NGSS-2,4) (STEM -1-4) (ELACC-1-4) (FELAS-1-3) 4. Verbally articulate the connection between math, geometry, the number system, and its purpose during information processing(ISTE-1-3) (NGSS-2,4) (STEM -1-4) (ELACC-1-4) (FELAS-1-3)	• Activity on designing and manually executing a code (10.1, 10.2, 10.3) • Discussion (10.2, 10.4)	• Lecture on how to use algorithms to create a source code (10.1)	• Basic Coding Handouts (10.1, 10.4) • Video (10.3)
11	Critical Media Literacy	1. Define critical media literacy and understand its application in everyday media consumption and production. For example, via television and the internet (FELAS-1-2) (ELACC-1) (ISTE-1) 2. Analyze television advertisements and film clips, and discuss the obvious and latent messaging strategies used to persuade persons to buy a product or service or to hook the audience (ISTE-1,3) (NGSS-2,4) (STEM-3) (ELACC-1,2,4) 3. Document, in writing, the various strategies used in advertising 4. Practice designing or producing a media artifact based on the principles of persuasion and critical media production 5. Reflect on the importance of being critically aware of media messages via an individually produced media artifact, such as a blog or public service announcement	• Media artifact activity (11.1, 11.2) • Written reflection (11.5)	• Media Artifact worksheet (11.4) • Group discussion prompt (11.3) • Reflection prompt (11.5)	• Television commercials (11.1, 11.2) • Films clips (11.1, 11.2) • Still advertisements (11.1, 11.2)

(Continued)

Session #	Module/Unit Topic	Module/Unit Objective(s)	Assessment(s)	Lesson Content	Material(s) Needed
12	Inquiry Shop Talk (occurs throughout the unit)	1. Reflect on what they learned about their social justice issue from each session and how their group's product or service could help to solve the social issue in their world (ISTE-1,2) (NGSS-1,2,4) (STEM-3,4) (ELASS-1-4) (FELAS-1-2) 2. Visibly represent what they learned about their social justice issue(ISTE-1,2) (NGSS-1,2,4) (STEM-3,4) (ELASS-1-4) (FELAS-1-2) 3. Present their knowledge artifacts to the class(ISTE-1,2) (NGSS-1,2,4) (STEM-3,4) (ELASS-1-4) (FELAS-1-2) 4. Collaboratively discuss ideas they will use to make their product or service better as they prepare to design a website tomorrow in the upcoming days and learn how to "sell" (public speaking) their product or service(ISTE-1,2) (NGSS-1,2,4) (STEM-3,4) (ELASS-1-4) (FELAS-1-2) 5. Write personal commitment statements on what they would commit to doing today to solve social justice issues abuse/hunger in the future(ISTE-1,2) (NGSS-1,2,4) (STEM-3,4) (ELASS-1-4) (FELAS-1-3)	• Reflection Journal (12.1, 12.2, 12.3) • Artifact Presentations (12.3) • Discussions (12.4)	• Personal commitment statements (12.5)	• Personal commitment worksheet (12.5) • Journals (12.1, 12.2, 12.3)
13	"Shark Tank"	1. Present a comprehensive business plan to a group of community affiliates and potential "donors" (ISTE-1,2) (NGSS-1,2,4) (STEM-3,4) (ELASS-1-4) (FELAS-1-2) 2. Advocate for the interest of your organization(ISTE-1,2) (NGSS-1,2,4) (STEM-3,4) (ELASS-1-4) (FELAS-1-2) 3. Showcase business products and services to garner support(ISTE-1,2) (NGSS-1,2,4) (STEM-3,4) (ELASS-1-4) (FELAS-1-2)	• Presentation to community affiliates (13.1 – 13.3)	• Presentation Guidelines	• Shark Tank Panel (13.1, 13.2) • Grading Rubric (13.1-13.3)

References

Advisory Committee on Mathematical Education. (2011). *Mathematical needs in the workplace and in Higher Education.* Retrieved from http://www.acme-uk.org/media/7624/acme_theme_a_final%20(2).pdf.

An, Y.-J., & Reigeluth, C. (2011). Creating technology-enhanced, learner-centered classrooms: K-12 teachers' beliefs, perceptions, barriers, and support needs. *Journal of Digital Learning in Teacher Education*, 28(2).

Acar, A. E. & Rother, D. (2011). Design thinking in engineering education and its adoption in technology-driven startups. Retrieved from https://www.researchgate.net/publication/227127787_Design_Thinking_in_Engineering_Education_and_its_Adoption_in_Technology-driven_Startups.

Banks, C. A. M. & Banks, J. A. (1995). Equity pedagogy: An essential component of multicultural education. *Theory into Practice*, 34(3), 152-158.

Banks, J. A. (1994). Transforming the mainstream curriculum. *Educational Leadership*, 51(8), 4-8.

Beasley, M. A., & Fischer, M. J. (2012). Why they leave: The impact of stereotype threat on the attrition of women and minorities from science, math and engineering majors. *Social Psychology of Education,* 15(4), 427-448.

Bishop, A. (1988). Mathematics education in its cultural context. *Educational Studies in Mathematics*, 19(2), 179-191.

Bourdieu, P. (1991) *Language and Symbolic Power.* Ed. J.B Thompson. Translated from French by G. Raymond and M. Adamson. Cambridge, MA: Harvard University Press.

Nevarez, G. (2015). More Latinos with stem degrees needed, here are the top schools doing it. Retrieved from http://www.nbcnews.com/news/latino/more-latino-stem-degrees-needed-here-are-top-schools-doing-n376961.

D'Ambrosio, U. (1997). Ethnomathematics and its place in the history and pedagogy of mathematics. In A. B. Powell & M. Frankenstein (Eds.), *Ethnomathematics: Challenging Eurocentrism in mathematics education* (pp. 13-24). Albany, NY: State University of New York Press.

Dewey, J. (1938). *Experience and education.* Indianapolis, IN: Kappa Delta Pi.

Ernst, C. (2010). Ethnomathematics makes difficult subject relevant. Retrieved from http://www.hawaii.edu/malamalama/2010/07/ethnomathematics/.

Eddy, S. L. & Hogan, K. A. (2014). Getting under the hood: How and for whom does increasing course structure work? *CBE Life Science Education*, 13, 3453-468. DOI: 10.1187/cbe.14-03-0050.

Frankenstein, M. (1990). Incorporating race, class, and gender issues into a critical mathematical literacy curriculum. *The Journal of Negro Education*, 59(3), 336-347.

Freeman, S., Eddy, S., McDonough, M., Smith, M., Okoroafor, N. Jordt, H. Wenderoth, M. (2014). Active learning increases student performance in science, engineering, and mathematics. *Proceedings of the National Academy of Sciences of the United States of America*, 111:8410-8415.

Freire, P. (2006). *Pedagogy of the oppressed.* (Revised). New York, NY: Continuum International Publishing Group.

Gay, G., (2000). *Culturally responsive teaching: Theory, research, and practice.* New York, NY: Teachers College Press.

Groundwater-Smith, S., Ewing, R., & Le Cornu, R. (2007). *Teaching: challenges and dilemmas.* (3rd ed.). Melbourne: Thomson.

Gorski, P. & Pothini, S. (2014). Case studies on diversity and social justice education. New York, NY: Routledge.

Hew, K.F., & Brush, T. (2007). Integrating Technology into K-12 Teaching and Learning: Current Knowledge Gaps and Recommendations for Future Research. *Educational Technology Research and Development*, 55(3), 223-252.

Horrigan, J. (2015, April). *The numbers behind the broadband 'homework gap'.* Retrieved from: http://www.pewresearch.org/about/use-policy/.

Joseph, G. G. (1987). Foundations of Eurocentrism in mathematics. *Race and Class,* 28(3), 13-28.

Jones, B., Ruff, C., & Paretti, M. (2013). The impact of engineering identification and stereotypes on undergraduate women's achievement and persistence in engineering. *Social Psychology of Education,* 16(3), 471-493. DOI:10.1007/s11218-013-9222-x.

Learmonth, Michael. (2015 November 11). Tech diversity's big problem: how to find 10,000 black engineers. Retrieved from http://www.ibtimes.com/tech-diversitys-big-problem-how-find-10000-black-engineers-2183885.

National Council of Teachers of Mathematics. (2000). *Principles and standards for school mathematics.* Reston, VA: Author

Morrison, J., Roth McDuffie, A., & French, B. (2015). Identifying key components of teaching and learning in a STEM school. *School Science and Mathematics*, 115(5), 244-255.

Oritz-Franco, L. (2005). Chicanos have math in their blood: Precolumbian mathematics. In E. Gustein & B. Peterson (Eds.), *Rethinking mathematics: Teaching for social justice by the numbers* (70-73). Milwaukee, WI: Rethinking Schools Publication.

Rainie, H. & Wellman, B. (2012). *Networked: The new social operating system.* Cambridge, MA: The MIT Press

Rice, K. G., Lopez, F. G., Richardson, C. M., & Stinson, J. M. (2013). Perfectionism moderates stereotype threat effects on STEM majors' academic performance. *Journal of Counseling Psychology, 60*(2), 287.

Sampson, V., & Clark, D. (2009). The impact of collaboration on the outcomes of scientific argumentation. *Science Education, 93*(3), 448-484.

Schoenfield, A. (2000). Making mathematics work for all children: Issues of standards, testing and equity. *Educational Researcher, 31*(1), 13-25.

Science Buddies (2002-2017). Comparing the Engineering Design Process and the Scientific Method. Retrieved from http://www.sciencebuddies.org/engineering-design-process/engineering-design-compare-scientific-method.shtml.

Snelson, C., & Perkins, R. A. (2009). From silent film to YouTube[TM]: tracing the historical roots of motion picture technologies in education. *Journal of Visual Literacy, 28*(1).

Strutchens, M. (1995). Multicultural Mathematics: A More Inclusive Mathematics. ERIC Digest.

Tawfik, A., Trueman, R. J., & Lorz, M. M. (2014). Engaging non-scientists in STEM through problem-based learning and service learning. *Interdisciplinary Journal of Problem-Based Learning, 8*(2), 4. doi:10.7771/1541-5015.1417.

Vorderman, C., Porkess, R., Budd, C., Dunne, R., & Rahman-hart, P. (2011). *A world-class mathematics education for all our young people.* Retrieved from http://www.tsm-resources.com/pdf/VordermanMathsReport.pdf.

United States Department of Education Office for Civil Rights (2014). Civil rights data collection: Data snapshot (College and Career Readiness). Retrieved from http://ocrdata.ed.gov/Downloads/CRDC-College-and-Career-Readiness-Snapshot.pdf.

Waldon, K.A. & Baxley, T. P. (2017). *Creating social activist in the classroom: Using a problem-solving cycle across the curriculum.* Manuscript in Preparation.

Weise, E. (2014, October 14). Tech jobs: Minorities have degrees, but don't get hired. Retrieved from http://www.usatoday.com/story/tech/2014/10/12/silicon-valley-diversity-tech-hiring-computer-science-graduates-african-american-hispanic/14684211/.

Xu, Y.J. (2008). Gender disparity in STEM disciplines: A study of faculty attrition and turnover intentions. *Research in Higher Education* 49, 607-624.

Zevenbergen, R., Dole, S., & Wright, R.J. (2004). *Teaching mathematics in primary school.* Crows Nest, NSW: Allen & Unwin.

Mathematics uses a series of algorithms for deriving conclusions, increasing logical structures, or merely a language that enhances knowledge about numbers and space. Tate (1994) argues that traditional mathematics curricula have failed to optimize student success in mathematics courses by not promoting relevance of mathematics to students' everyday lives. With this lack of relevance, students often wonder how alphabets, known as variables in mathematics, are used in mathematics. They also wonder how a mathematical concept of solving for a variable, that represents an unknown number, is used to find a solution to a mathematical problem.

Students should acknowledge the diversity of their students and to incorporate their backgrounds and cultures into the learning experiences and classroom milieu. Instruction must connect the lives and experiences of students to what they are learning; they must see how math is relevant to their daily lives. This will enable them to fully participate in the mathematics classroom; facilitate a better understanding of mathematical content/concepts; and therefore impact their success.

Ladson-Billings (1995), Irvine (1991), Hilliard (2001), and Noguera (1997) contend that marginalized students will continue to suffer academically as long as the United States-based epistemologies that take root in deficit thinking and educational curricula and pedagogies that do not respond to students' lived experiences and knowledge. According to Duncan (2002), "The first step toward changing the conditions that undermine the achievement of minority students is listening to what they have to say about their academic and social experiences in schools" (p. 141). Allow your students to voice how their attitudes and perspectives toward mathematics have influenced their success or lack thereof. This could lead to students aiding their teacher in the development of a mathematics curriculum that mirrors their lived experiences and incorporates their funds of knowledge.

In the context of math, the wording of mathematical concepts could impact students' understanding of what is being asked of them. For example, a common mathematics word problem involving distance, rate, and time, usually is worded: The Lazy River has a current of 2 miles per hour. A motorboat can travel 15 miles down the river in the same amount of time it takes to travel 9 miles up the river. What is the speed of the boat in still water? The first issue with this type of problem is that many students may have not experienced a lazy river or a motorboat to understand what this problem is asking. Word problems should be linked to students lived experiences in an effort for students to understand mathematical concepts. Another alternative would be to provide the students with the opportunity to see what a motorboat is or to even travel on a motorboat down and up the river, and then present the math problem to them.

The idea of incorporating culturally relevant pedagogy, according to Ladson-Billings (1995), is also to promote student success while engaging students in larger social or societal issues. There should be a connection between what is transpiring beyond the classroom walls and what is transpiring within the walls of the classroom and curriculum. Instead of developing word problems just to teach a mathematical concept, create word problems that would require students to research, engage in interdisciplinary content, and identify connections between the mathematics problems and how the solutions could help in real-world situations.

RadicalMath (2007) is an excellent resource that can be used to assist teachers in facilitating the inclusion of societal and economic issues in the classroom. One example of a social justice topic that can be taught through math is that of racial profiling. Students can use math skills or content such as ratios, percentages, and probability to determine the number of minorities that fall prey to racial profiling in their local community.

According to the RadicalMath (2007) Founders, there are several benefits to teaching math from a social justice perspective such as increasing students' abilities to:

- Recognize the power of mathematics as an essential analytical tool to understand and potentially change the world, rather than merely regard math as a collection of disconnected rules to be memorized and regurgitated.
- Engage in high-level thinking about big mathematical ideas
- Deepen their understanding of social and economic issues on local and global scales
- Understand their own power as active citizens in building a democratic society and become equipped to play a more active role in this society
- Become more motivated to learn math
- Participate in actual (not just theoretical) community problem-solving projects; and
- Answer this question for themselves: "Why do I have to know this?" (Radical Math Website).

References

Duncan, G. A. (2002). Beyond love: A critical race ethnography of the schooling of adolescent Black males. *Equity & Excellence in Education*, 35(2), 131-143.

Hilliard, A. G. (2001). Race, identity, hegemony, and education: What do we need to know now? In W. H. Watkins, J. H. Lewis, & V. Chou (Eds.), *Race and education: The roles of history and society in educating African American students* (pp. 7-25). Needham Heights, MA: Allyn & Bacon.

Irvine, J. J. (1991). *Black student and school failure: Policies, practices, and prescriptions*. Westport, CT: Greenwood Press.

Ladson-Billings, G. (1995). "But that's just good teaching! The case for culturally relevant pedagogy." *Theory into practice* 34:3, pp. 159-165.

Noguera, P. (1997). *Responding to the crisis confronting Black youth: Providing support without marginalization*. Retrieved from *In Motion Magazine* website: http://www.inmotionmagazine.com/pncc1.html

Radical Math (2007). Retrieved from http://www.radicalmath.org

Tate, W. F. (1994). Race, retrenchment, and the reform of school mathematics. *Phi Delta Kappan, 75*, 477-484.

Practical Encounter: Multiple Voices Activity

Directions: Including multiple voices in the curriculum is key to empowering students from various groups. In the chart below, you are charged with identifying individuals from each of the groups listed and across the STEM curriculum that you can include in your teaching. Go beyond the ones that were mentioned in the chapter and also indicate what you learned about each one of them.

	Science	Technology	Engineering	Math
Women				
Latinos/Hispanics				
African-Americans				
Asian				
Other				

CHAPTER 13

Safe and Accessible: Creating New Spaces for "Arts Education"

Gail Burnaford, Aquil Charlton, Susan Gay Hyatt & Jeanette McCune

with Adjoa Burrowes, Sharmaine Chamberlain, Cheryl Foster, Kari Ratka & Terry Thomas

It should be a safe place. If it's not a safe place, shame on us.

Cheryl Foster, Teaching Artist

Through arts partnerships and grants that are federally funded, community art professionals or licensed arts specialists, have the opportunity to work with children in urban settings. Typically, these artists interact with young learners where they are – in their communities, in their own language and ethnic cultural context, and they develop projects that build on the cultural strengths and assets students bring to school. Geneva Gay's concept of culturally responsive teaching (2010) is an incredibly consistent framework for arts education through the lens of artist teachers in schools. "Arts-based culturally responsive pedagogy" (Lai, 2012, p. 18) invites students and teachers to rap, create hip-hop, participate in poetry slams, and experiment with digital storytelling. Expert community teaching artists are uniquely positioned to work directly with students, but also to plan and design curriculum with classroom teachers and arts specialists so that the standards-based content learning is not only integrated with arts learning, but deepened and reinforced by it.

This chapter introduces the reader to approaches, strategies, and belief systems that teaching artists and committed arts specialists have identified as successful when they work with children in schools. We do not intend to suggest that these approaches are not or cannot be seen in classes all over the country nor taught by certified arts specialists and general education teachers. Teaching artists and arts specialists have sparked new attention to artistic approaches consistent with problem-based learning, teaching through inquiry, integrating cross-curricular themes and big ideas, and making thinking visible – all familiar strategies used among teachers and teacher educators. Contemporary artist educators who Laura Reeder (2012) calls "hyphenated artists" (p. 160), invite us to think beyond borders and titles and look more seriously and collaboratively at teaching and learning. As Reeder notes, if we do so, "pedagogies for inventive social change emerge" (p. 160). She further explains:

> With the subtle shift of a metaphorical fencepost, I become a teaching-artist because I am not on the district payroll anymore. . . .I now have "other" membership, and there is a tangible distance between teaching-artist and art teacher defined by perceived or practiced agency. (p. 163)

It is precisely this sense of agency that *all* teachers can adopt. This chapter is intended to heighten awareness of the potential value added from watching and learning about artists who teach, and then enhancing our pedagogical toolbox in three typically teaching artist ways:

1. Teaching artists typically learn about students' cultures and background and build curricular bridges to engage learning
2. Teaching artists open up maker spaces within and across content areas for students to communicate in their own voices
3. Teaching artists make things with students and then invite nontraditional communities as audiences.

The federal government, under the auspices of the United States Department of Education's Arts Education grants, supports public/private partnerships between schools and arts organizations. In part, the emergence of arts partnerships is responsible for the term 'teaching artist' in the arts education lexicon. Eric Booth (2010) describes the birth of this field, noting that there is no one accepted definition of a teaching artist, nor is there a basic set of tools, approaches or practices that teaching artists are obligated to use. Booth offers a working definition which serves us well: "A teaching artist is a practicing professional artist with the complementary skills, curiosities and habits of mind of an educator, who can effectively engage a wide range of people in learning experiences in, through, and about the arts" (Booth, 2010, np). Booth's history of the movement is important for this chapter because the roles, training, certification and presence of teaching artists as they relate to certified arts specialists (i.e., music, art drama, and dance teachers) in schools continue to be points of debate.

Booth presented at the 2006 first World Conference on Arts Education sponsored by UNESCO in Lisbon, Portugal. Here he asserted: "It became clear to me that the U.S. is far below most other UNESCO nations in arts education commitment—U.S. public school students average less than one third the number of in-school arts education hours than the average in other UNESCO countries" (2010, np). With the advent of highly visible standardized test scores serving as the litmus test for effective schools, arts education has been subject to constant budget cuts, redesigns, and sometimes the arts fields have been challenged to "prove" their value too by contributing to increased math and reading achievement. But the arts education community persists.

It was not until the 1960's that there was more intentional engagement of artists, often still as one-shot performers, but increasingly in residencies and longer-term teaching episodes or projects with schools. In the 1980's, more training programs emerged, often in conjunction with arts organizations and higher education institutions in communities. Shortly after, when the federal government began funding partnerships, arts organizations began to systematically develop programs and approaches to engaging teaching artists, sometimes solely with children and young people, and sometimes with teachers in professional development. In the 21st century, it seems clear that teaching artists are inevitably a part of the pedagogical landscape, particularly for children in low-income, rural and urban schools.

It is important to note research that indicates students of low socioeconomic status (SES) who participate in the arts have better social and academic outcomes than those who do not (Catterall, Dumais & Hampden-Thompson, 2012). And, significantly, low SES, particularly students of color, have access to fewer arts education opportunities in general. Let us consider music education as an example, which is appropriate in that, if students are to have any access to the arts in schools, it is likely to be in the area of music.

Jennifer Lee Doyle (2014) synthesized selected literature on urban music education relevant to this discussion. Doyle notes that access to music education is largely universal at the elementary level in U.S. public schools (Doyle, 2014). But at the secondary level, when schools cut arts programs, urban students lose the benefits more frequently than their suburban counterparts (Doyle, 2014). Ester (2009) studied low SES students' access to musical instruments and found that, though these students were likely to join the band in the first place, they were less likely to persist, regardless of whether the school provided them with instruments. Why might that be?

Preservice music teachers are usually trained in Western classical traditions and tend to, not surprisingly, create music programs similar to what they know (Doyle, 2014). Some researchers raise the question of whether classical music is the "most culturally relevant vehicle to incite musical interest and participation for all populations" (Doyle, p. 47). Conversely, it seems that teachers who do integrate multicultural musical styles and offer nontraditional ensembles (steel drums as well as string quartets) increase participation and give more students opportunities in music (Abril, 2009; Albert, 2006).

Given this scenario, which we may assume is far more dire for other less privileged art forms in schools such as drama and dance, what possible contributions might contemporary arts professionals bring to the arts education scene in schools? Today, teaching artistry is a viable career choice for emerging art school or conservatory graduates. Teaching artists are often community artists with acknowledged bodies of work locally and sometimes nationally. They perform on community stages, conduct master classes, teach as adjuncts in teacher education and fine arts programs at universities, and, perhaps most importantly for teachers and the world of schools, teaching artists and their peer arts specialists in schools enable children and young people to produce art, perform, and gain audiences for their culturally unique voices in and beyond the school walls.

We will see clear pedagogical stances in the three vignettes below. They challenge preservice and experienced teachers to reflect and imagine classrooms in which *cultural relevance*, *creation of authentic products and performances for real audiences*, and *personal and collective voice*, and are absolute priorities and guide teaching for all students. We invite readers to consider these questions when reading these vignettes:

1. What matters to these teachers and artists?
2. How does what matters affect their pedagogy?
3. What are the takeaway equity pedagogies in their stories?

wavebreakmedia / Shutterstock.com

Point of View: Aquil Charlton, John F. Kennedy Center for the Performing Arts Citizen Artist Fellow 2016

Culture as a Container

Hip hop is part of my cultural identity because it provided rites of passage during my adolescent formative years. Early in their marriage, my parents were progressive cultural organizers, involved with the Nation of Islam, Association for the Advancement of Creative Musicians (AACM), and the New Concept Development Center. During the 1980's, when I was born, our family struggled with poverty, along with many of the associated social symptoms in communities of color. The neighborhoods where we lived were culturally rich, but financially poor, and ravaged by the "War on Drugs" in the 1990's. Hip hop provided an artistic outlet, as well as a community of other young people from similar backgrounds, that allowed me to heal from the trauma I experienced at home, in my neighborhood, and at school.

Music, dancing, and visual art were forms of celebration and healing in my home and community. However, as a result of limited access to art programs during my early school years, I did not have consistent practice or mentoring in any artistic discipline. Hip hop however provided a cultural base during adolescence from which I continued to practice visual art, music, writing, and improvisation as intuitive forms of expression and bonding in a community outside of my home. My tag, my style, and my raps were all ritual forms of communication between my peers throughout my teenage years and early twenties.

In my practice I leverage culture to provide access to intuitive and engaging music, visual art, dance, and other forms of expression. My talent in percussion comes from beat-boxing for the other rappers in my high school crew, but I learned it from scatting along with my father to his favorite jazz tunes. I validate these types of music education experiences in my practice; and replicate them through activities designed for students who may not fall into traditional categories, but who have experienced art making through more colloquial means.

My practice: ALT-City and the Mobile Music Box

The ALT-City new music ensemble and the Mobile Music Box best exemplify my approach to creating greater access to the arts. Through directing ALT-City I have negotiated space for students' influences, compositions, improvisations, and interdisciplinary collaborations in the otherwise didactic culture of Chicago Public Schools and the eighty-year-old All City Performing Arts program. As creator of the Mobile Music Box, I teach others how to make music intuitively, and instruments cheaply; as well as engage the public in improvised music production and performance.

ALT-City is purposefully inclusive of self-taught and intuitive musicians, new and diverse genres, non-traditional techniques, and unconventional equipment. We have featured an electronic mini-ensemble, including several smartphone and tablet musicians playing music through apps. ALT-City is also the only ensemble in All-City that performs student-written compositions. In 2013, "Music Sets Me Free," written by the inaugural ALT-City ensemble, was arranged for orchestra and performed by the entire cast as the finale of the spring showcase. Each year more students perform original works at auditions demonstrating how eager students are to have their ideas validated. This year, high school freshman, McKennan Campbell, served as student musical director for ALT-City, writing and arranging music for the spring show.

Chicago ALT-City 2015 Student Electronic Mini-Ensemble led by Aquil Charlton

The idea for the Mobile Music Box came from a strong desire to make music as accessible to communities in Chicago as possible; which is why I decided to incorporate making simple music instruments from recycled materials and public music production as the primary activities. I also used call-and-response songs, rhythm exercises, and rhyming games to engage the audience's intuitive capacity for music and employ culturally relevant activities. Through the "Street Studio" public music production activities I also hope to create positive interventions in neighborhoods where violent activity often detracts from the residents' sense of safety.

Is art safe and accessible to everyone?

The issues of safety and accessibility are not as clear-cut as they may seem, but are critical factors in a child's ability to fully engage in the creative process. Accessibility is not simply a matter of the number of art classes available in schools, which are already unevenly distributed in most school districts; but of how those classes and schools embrace diverse populations. Children's creative expression must be validated by others, and supported both in and outside of school.

Children and youth already struggle with feeling validated because of systemic ageism. But poor and/or queer children of color face additional systemic oppressions, resulting in even less support than their more privileged counterparts. In order to create access to the arts for all children we must acknowledge and counteract the systemic issues that interfere with the creative process.

There are many examples of how social barriers like poverty and racism affect children's engagement in the arts. Those who cannot afford private lessons or instruments do not have access to training or practice. Youth from cultures that are marginalized in society will not feel safe to produce art that is authentic. Students who do not find security in their immediate environment, or who have limited sustainable options ahead of them, will have difficulty fully engaging in an artistic practice because that requires support on all levels. Unfortunately, many students attend schools where the culture reflects the barriers they face in society. Arts and cultural activities provide important healing spaces for these and many other young people, which is why I believe they should be as accessible as possible, especially in neighborhoods and schools where there are existing gaps in opportunities to learn and practice art.

Point of View: Working for Equity Pedagogy Among Immigrant Children

A Teacher Embraces Arts Integration

Susan Gay Hyatt and Kari Ratka

What makes up a person's identity? Is it our physical make-up? Our stories? Our family, culture, or heritage? How can we explore who we are and what makes us a community as well as unique individuals? At *The Conservatory School* in North Palm Beach, Florida, Kari Ratka teaches visual art to a diverse population of K-8 students. The Conservatory School is part of the School District of Palm Beach County, which is "the 11th largest in the continental US and the 5th largest in the state of Florida with 185 schools, serving 176,724 (Total K-12) students who speak 150 languages/dialects" (*School District of Palm Beach County*, 2016). As a way to engage students and honor their diverse backgrounds, Ratka uses arts integration as a pedagogical approach to teaching the students to write original stories about their culture, identity, and heritage and then incorporate those stories into the creation of a piece of visual art.

The *Kennedy Center for the Performing Arts date?* defines arts integration as "an approach to teaching in which students construct and demonstrate understanding through an art form. Students engage in a creative process which connects an art form and another subject area and meets evolving objectives in both" (Silverstein & Layne, 2010). Ratka's use of arts integration enables her to teach both literacy and a visual art skill while honoring students' individuality; this approach is uniquely suited to teaching in a multicultural classroom, as students are able to bring their own narratives into a creative environment and share them with peers in a way that honors who they are and where they came from.

In addition to a dedication to arts integration as pedagogy, *The Conservatory School at North Palm Beach* also embraces an *inquiry-based approach* as an entry point for a unit of study. According to Ratka, this involves exploring universal human themes, such as *identity, home, love, dark vs. light, nature*, and *innovation*, and then "stepping back to allow the students to collaboratively make meaning." Ratka further notes, "looking for that authentic spark" to engage the students in a topic they find intrinsically motivating gives the students "voice and choice," as it is the students who lead the lesson by asking questions, conducting research, and framing their knowledge. In a multicultural classroom, allowing the students to lead through an inquiry-based approach opens the classroom into a dynamic environment in which the students have agency: their perspectives are important and reflected in the communal body of knowledge. According to Ratka, her students work together to plan, create, share, and discuss classroom projects in a "safe, creative environment where students are hearing the ideas of others and are encouraged to share their own." reference? (personal communication, Month, day, year)

The *Conservatory School at North Palm Beach* uses the students' artwork to reach into the community by displaying work in spaces outside the classroom; they use Twitter and other social media to share with other educators, community members, and parents, and they also host a monthly "farmers' market" in which the students sell their artwork and vegetables they've grown in their school's community garden to the public. By

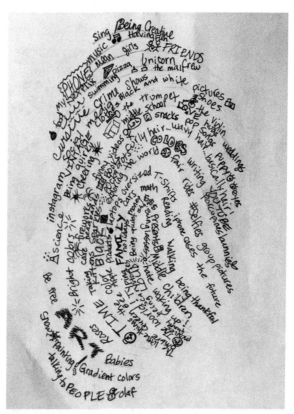

"Fingerprint Portrait" from a 7th grader
The Conservatory School @ North Palm Beach
Student work reprinted by permission.

displaying the students' work in forums outside the classroom, the school is honoring the unique contributions from each of their students.

"You Be You" Project. "At TCS we celebrate the differences that make us unique individuals – the way we each look, act, and think isn't like anyone else in our school! That's what makes us even more beautiful as we 'swim together.' In the Art Lab, TCS students fell in love with the story of Adri, the fish from Linda Kranz's book, 'You Be You.' They took the challenge to design a fish that was different and special, just like them, Our sandbox contains nearly 350 one-of-a-kind painted rock fish that are amazing alone, and even better TOGETHER!" (Kari Ratka, Visual Art Teacher)

Implications for Teachers

Equity pedagogy is an approach to teaching that draws on students' real life experiences and reflects their understanding of the world around them (Chin, 2013). By letting students decide what is important to them and what they want to know, the teacher develops "buy-in" from the class at the outset of the lesson unit. A student-led, rather than teacher-led, learning environment can open opportunities for students to bring their own experiences into the classroom, creating space for students with diverse backgrounds to present their ideas and shape a project in ways that might be overlooked in a teacher-led environment.

In an arts-integrated classroom, the students' narratives and experiences are wound into the work of art. By using the artworks as "sites of knowledge, the texts for deconstruction," teachers and students can challenge "preconceived assumptions and stereotypes about categories of art and what is considered art" (Chin, 2013). In this way, the students become the teachers, validating their cultural identity, challenging the norm, and gaining agency in the classroom as they make meaning of the world around them.

By presenting student artwork in forums outside the classroom, the school becomes an agent in creating a dialogue with the community. In sharing and honoring students' artwork, the students' views of themselves and

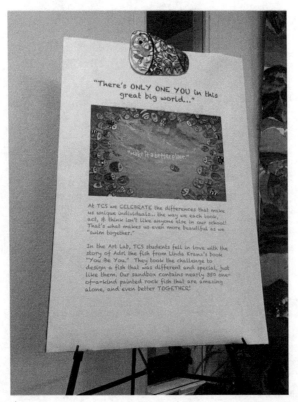

The Conservatory School @ North Palm Beach
Student work reprinted with permission.

The Conservatory School @ North Palm Beach
Student work reprinted with permission.

the world around them become part of a larger conversation about what is the norm, challenging assumptions and opening space for better understanding of those around us.

Point of View: Community Teachers in Action

Jeanette McCune, Adjoa Burrowes, Sharmaine Chamberlain, Cheryl Foster, Terry Thomas

Two arts specialists and two teaching artists were brought together by the John F. Kennedy Center for the Performing Arts Director of District of Columbia School and Community Initiatives, Jeanette S. McCune to discuss their work. Because personal voice and expression is an essential element of powerful arts education, they tell their stories in their own words. There are three pedagogical themes that become clear from this conversation. The first is the notion of **maker spaces** for young people to explore, create, and speak up. If we envision classrooms as such spaces, we are teaching children to be citizens in a democracy in an intentional and deliberate way. Second, the group responded to the notion of **audiences** for students' work beyond the classroom coupled with authentic art making that contributes to positive change in the world. Pedagogy built around real projects that move beyond the teacher as sole arbiter transforms learning. Finally, these educators offer their advice for **teachers in communities** who want to make a difference. First, they introduce themselves.

My name is Terry Thomas and I'm a visual arts teacher at Seaton Elementary. This school helps define who I am as a teacher. Seaton is a very diverse school and I'm proud to be a teacher here because I learn as much from my students as my students learn from me. I like working with teaching artists because it allows me to bring someone with different expertise than what I have. Art is a way to reach all students and there are some students who perform so well academically, but art gives the students who may not perform as well a chance to be heard and to be heard through their art. Art levels the playing field.

I am Sharmaine Chamberlain and I am the music teacher here at Seaton, native Washingtonian and a mom myself with a first grader who attends Seaton, so a lot of what I do when I'm teaching, I think about him. What sort of music education do I want him to have? I want him to have the best so I definitely try to give the best to my students as well. I have worked with teaching artists over the years and it's such a wonderful experience. A lot of times they're used to working with just the classroom teachers but they enjoy working with another music teacher too and that collaboration is so great. I learn so much from them.

I am Adjoa Burrowes and I am a practicing artist and an educator. I have worked as a teaching artist with the John F. Kennedy Center for the Performing Arts for the past 8 years. I come to my teaching through the lens of a visual artist as well as a writer and illustrator. I think that everybody has a story they can tell – it's about creating stories, narratives – sometimes visual and sometimes written. It's so powerful – giving them that space to express themselves.

I am Cheryl Foster, an artist and art educator from the United States. I design and implement visual arts workshops for children of all ages through the John F. Kennedy Center for the Performing Arts. For the past five years, I have tried to concentrate on designing programs that build character and force children to think about the hardships of others and what small things they might do to make someone's life path a little smoother.

Maker Spaces: Where Students Show the World Who They Are

What are the new ways of envisioning teaching in and through the arts? These teachers and artists describe the importance of **maker spaces** for students to explore traditional arts media as well as digital arenas for creating. The new focus on "maker spaces" (Peppler & Bender, 2013) for adults in the workplace is also a compelling and vibrant concept for artists, teachers and children. Cheryl Foster, Teaching Artist: *We are looking for spaces to display the work of our children. We can have a corner, but we deserve more than a corner. If they have exposure to that technology, this will make them workplace-ready. And yes, I love the finger painting and getting my hands dirty, but we need maker spaces; when they graduate, they should be able to slip right into those jobs.* The Reggio Emilia early childhood notion of an *atelier*, or artists' studio (Edwards, Gandini, & Forman, 1993) at the center of a school is not far from the contemporary maker spaces in which children see artists do what they do and work right alongside them. Cheryl continues: *We need spaces for children to meet real artists and learn that, "Hey, you can buy your groceries, your toothpaste and a car with a career as a professional artist." But how else would they know if they weren't part of our programs? We need artists to come in and tell them, "This is what I do."*

Cutting-edge maker spaces do not negate the value of traditional instruments, media, and arts experiences that arts specialists and artists bring to learning. Sharmaine Chamberlain, Music Teacher: *We need artists coming in and doing the traditional arts too . . .people singing opera, playing the piano. Our kids are just not used to that. Kids are more used to the digital music, hearing things on their computers. They are not used to hearing a piano or a violin.*

The idea of Space is not just a physical concept for these teacher artists. It is also a framework for conversation that grounds their practice. Accessible learning spaces in and through the arts also include plenty of opportunity for talk. Perhaps surprisingly, these artist teachers all confirmed the power of making art collaboratively and then talking about it. Terry Thomas, Visual Arts Teacher explains: *It is important for us to start children collaborating at a very young age. When they collaborate, they learn how to work together, how to listen and respect one another's views and then they take that from school to home, from home out into the community and from the community out into the world. They are actually learning to be global citizens when they start here at age 3.*

There is an agency about this conversation that focuses on giving students voice and choice, not only in the language arts or social studies classes, but in the art room: Terry asserts, *These children are citizens and they learn at a very early age whether what they have to say is important or not. . . whether what they have to say is respected or not. When they realize that what they have to say is important, then they say more.*

The pedagogy of arts education that incorporates collaboration, discourse and consciously giving students voice requires teachers to be aware of who their students are and how the arts can be a safe space to help them build enough confidence to speak and listen to each other.

Arts teachers, as these educators explain, can help young people move beyond one-word answers: Terry Thomas, Visual Arts Teacher: *We as educators have to build children's confidence from a very early age. Confidence in talking about art making, the synthesis of art making. We do a lot of the Thinking Routines* (Harvard Project Zero, 2007*). When children are first introduced to those thinking routines, they may not see a lot, but as this becomes a routine, those one-word answers become sentences.*

Cheryl Foster, Teaching Artist: *We have one-word young people, we have soft-spoken young people, and we have young people who will just not say anything at all . . . just won't. If you refuse to accept a one-word answer, then they have to move forward and eventually they will, but it takes practice. Sometimes it's about confidence and sometimes it's about discipline. Some children have been taught to be quiet.*

With an art project, it's not only doing the project, but it's also about talking about it. How did you arrive at these decisions? Make it your own, as they say on American Idol. You can give them lines and patterns and then you say, "So now what are you going to do? Take . . . it that next step." "I saw what this artist did. Now what are you going to do?" "The swirls go this way, but how else can swirls go?" You have to just keep on, keep on, and in the end, they will talk.

Kennedy Center Arts Administrator, Jeanette McCune says it all: *The arts classrooms are the one place where it can be truly a democratic education – the one place where you can contribute. The word 'citizen' is really powerful – children being able to understand and articulate what their process is in learning and making justifications on their own. It's not about being right or wrong; it's about being critical enough and being given the space to do that kind of work.*

Audiences and Agency for Community Connection

Arts should be about inclusion. They should be about connections, to the community, to each other, connecting even to other countries. It's the reach that's important. Art is power. You are starting with nothing and you're creating something. You don't get that everywhere (Adjoa Burrowes, Teaching Artist).

Building confidence in students' sense of self is part of what it means to be a teacher. Performance spaces afford children amazing opportunities to get applause and feel somehow affirmed: *Maybe you won't get "Good job!" from your teacher, but you stand in front of an audience and perform and those people don't have a nickel in that dime and they still say, "Good job!" You can physically see the impact – shoulders back, chin high, stepping a bit lighter. You can just see it. If I'm not getting it at home or in school, if I can find a place to shine, I will shine. But if there's no reason to shine, I will just stay in my corner* (Cheryl Foster, Teaching Artist).

Beyond providing those opportunities to perform, what do good teachers do? Cheryl Foster, Teaching Artist, offers one idea: *I try to remind them, "How do you feel right now? Think about what you did to get that feeling. And you can get it again. You deserve that for the rest of your life." If they can remember how special it felt, then they'll look for more opportunities to be special.* Good teachers help students remember what it feels like to be special.

We as educators have to search for those special experiences for our children. If I had to tell a preservice teacher one thing that would be it. You have to go out into the community and seek out these special experiences (Terry Thomas, Visual Art Teacher).

Teaching artists and their artist teacher colleagues in schools provide a lens on being a community teacher (Murrell, 2001) who is engaged, not just with a class of students, but with the school, neighborhood and community. *Teachers first need to know their community; my job is to get my children engaged with their community, whatever my discipline* (Terry Thomas, Visual Art Teacher).

Audience for students' work then becomes redefined to include unlikely candidates who are more like participants in the learning than passive recipients. Teaching Artist Adjoa Burrowes speaks to the importance of making learning relevant for children and designing learning around issues that students can relate to in their community and their world. *There are so many issues – what are the things that are important to **them?** Arts principles and techniques are not enough especially in today's world. You have to deal with things that they can feel.*

Teaching Artist Cheryl Foster describes three projects in which her students connected with communities and their world. Students wrote a script and filmed a video under her guidance about bullying. As they were working on the project, they realized that they themselves were being bullied. *When someone shakes you down in the lunch line, you are being bullied!* That was an unexpected outcome for the project as students realized the ways in which bullying was happening right under their noses. The video representation heightened their awareness as well as the knowledge of their peers who viewed the end product.

Foster led a project after the major Haiti earthquake in 2010. When the students saw the aftermath on TV, they noticed that there were children their age who were walking around in Port-au-Prince on concrete and steel with no shoes. She bought $7 shoes and the children painted Haitian voodoo, flags and other cultural imagery on the shoes and sent them to Haiti. *You know, they can be little Einsteins and not feel,* she observed.

In another project, fifteen and sixteen year olds researched the abandoned baby problem in seven countries (India, Malaysia, Canada, Australia, the United States and South Africa). They wrote poems, rap songs, and lullabies to babies who had succumbed to or survived abandonment. The students then painted international symbols on infant onesies. They sent the onesies to organizations that cared for abandoned babies in the seven countries. *It was the students' way of showing compassion for the babies and offering thanks to those who hold them close,* Foster noted.

Walk a Mile in My Shoes
Seaton Elementary School Haiti Earthquake Science
Cheryl Foster, Teaching Artist, Terry Thomas Visual Art Teacher

Onesies: For Abandoned Babies around the World
Wilson Elementary School
Cheryl Foster, Teaching Artist

As our conversation came to a close, these arts teachers offered some pieces of advice for teachers, beginning and experienced. These tidbits speak to a pedagogy that is grounded in human connection as well as engaged intellectual learning.

- *Books are good, but you have to have heart too. You have to be able to connect with the kids on a human level* (Sharmaine Chamberlain, Music Teacher).
- *Think about the baggage that they bring with them every day. I have children in my class who are the caretakers of the family. Teachers need to be sensitive to that. They need to know that they have to look for those things* (Cheryl Foster, Teaching Artist).
- *Look for artists in the community. There is a tendency for art teachers to just look at the textbook artists. But it's important to allow the students to make a connection with someone who is right in their neighborhood* (Adjoa Burrowes, Teaching Artist).
- *Art is a connector. Look for those connectors that can be made with the students and with their parents. Here at this school, we serve breakfast, lunch, and dinner. So we have big connections with the children. But we also have the chance to make strong alliances with the parents. They trust us with their children* (Terry Thomas, Visual Art Teacher).

Conclusions

The stories of these arts educators and teaching artists suggest that quality teaching in dance, drama, music, visual art is closely connected to the notion of community and making curricular and interpersonal connections. Their work with young people also challenges our thinking about access and voice as an integral part of the learning process. Equity pedagogy at its best pushes our expectations of what it means to learn and then express understanding. Duncom writes, "The products of most art education remain within the classroom or the hallway display cabinets, for which there are powerful reasons, including the expectations of parents, fellow teachers, and school administrators, as well as the students themselves, that art is an innocuous subject without a social agenda" (pp. 359-360). These educators suggest that art making, choreography, original digital plays by children and young people are much more than that. They teach us that curriculum content, albeit art or any other content area, is not separate from culture, but rather substantively embedded in it.

But how do we learn to teach and continue to teach in these ways? First, our chapter contributors underscore the need to experience this pedagogy first hand. Visual art teachers, Terry Thomas: *They (preservice teachers) need to see this work. They have to see what this work looks like. Young teachers need to see arts teachers and teaching artists in action. If they see it, they can do it.* Field experiences and classroom observations, provided by university programs, sought individually by prospective teachers, or arranged as cross-school exchanges, expose teachers to partnership programs and teaching artist residencies. Arts Administrator Jeanette McCune claims that leaders in a school need to provide the environment and support for such work with children, their families, and communities. Teachers, particularly collectively in teams or grade levels, can educate administrators by documenting the powerful work that students do when encouraged to express their skills and their points of view through art works. Principals and their administrative teams also need to see the work that their young charges can do.

A final thought. Arts education, and indeed all learning, is also about play. Artist teachers introduce the casual observer to all kinds of playful pedagogies that "engage directly with young people's emotional investments . . . and with their sense of agency" (Buckingham, 2003, p. 314). Maxine Greene (2010) echoes this notion when she calls for a "pedagogy of imagination" (p. 30). Because when children play, they are engaging, emotional, imagining, investing and enacting. Such learning environments are joyful spaces in which everyone listens, speaks, practices, and participates.

References

Abril, C.R. (2009). Responding to culture in the instrumental music programme: A teacher's journey. *Music Education Research, 11(*1), 77-91.

Albert, D.J. (2006). Socioeconomic satus and instrumental music: What does the research say about the relationship and its implications? *Update: Applications of Research in Music Education, 25*(1), 39-45.

Booth, E. (2010). *The history of teaching artistry.* Retrieved May 31, 2016 from http://ericbooth.net/the-history-of-teaching-artistry/.

Catterall, J., Dumais, S. & Hampden-Thompson, G. (2012). *The arts and achievement in at-risk youth: Findings from four longitudinal studies* (Research Report No. 55). Washington, DC: National Endowment for the Arts.

Chin, C. (2013). Key dimensions of a multicultural art education curriculum. *International Journal of Education & the Arts, 14*(14). Retrieved May 22, 2016 from http://www.ijea.org/v14n14/.

Doyle, J.L. (2014) Cultural relevance in urban music education: A synthesis of the literature. *National Association for Music Education, 32*(2), 44-51.

Duncom, P. (2011). Engaging public space: Art education pedagogies for social justice.
Equity and Excellence in Education, 44(3), 348-363.

Edwards, C., Gandini, L., Forman, G. (Eds). (1993). *The hundred languages of children: The Reggio Emilia Approach to early childhood education.* New York, NY: Praeger.

Ester, D. (2009). The impact of a school loaner-insrument program on the attitudes and achievement of low-income music students. *Contributions to Music Education, 36*(1), 53-71.

Gay, G. (2010). *Culturally response teaching: Theory, research, and practice* (2nd ed.). New York, NY: Teachers College Press.

Greene, M. (1995). *Releasing the imagination: Essays on education, the arts, and social change.* San Francisco, CA: Jossey-Bass.

Harvard Project Zero. (2007). Thinking routines. Retrieved June 2, 2016, from http://www.visiblethinkingpz.org/Visible-Thinking_html_files/03_ThinkingRoutin es/03a_ThinkingRoutines.html

Lai, A. (2012). Culturally responsive art education in a global era. *Art Education, 65*(5), 18-23.

Murrell, P.C. (2001). *The community teacher: A new framework for effective urban teaching.* New York, NY: Teachers College Press.

Peppler, K., & Bender, S. (2013). Maker movement spread innovation: On project at a time. *Phi Delta Kappan 95*(3), 22-27.

Reeder, L. (2012). Hyphenated artists: A body of potential. *The Journal of Social Theory in Art Education, 32*, 160-175.

School District of Palm Beach County. (2016). About us. Retrieved May 30, 2016, from http://www.palmbeachschools.org/Community/AboutUs.asp

Silverstein, L., & Layne, S. (2010). *Defining arts integration.* The John F. Kennedy Center for the Performing Arts. Retrieved May 22, 2016 from http://education.kennedy-center.org/education/ceta/

Practical Encounter

Google Culture & Art Website - www.googlecultureandarts.com

Directions: Google Arts & Culture features content from over 1200 leading museums and archives who have partnered with the Google Cultural Institute to bring the world's treasures online. This resource provides a wealth of resources (i.e. artwork, experiments, virtual field trips, etc.) for teachers to incorporate into the classroom.

In this activity, we want you to peruse this resource to discover resources you can use to teach various topics in your classroom

Topic	Google Culture & Art Resources	Objectives/Outcomes
Equity/Equality	Jackie Robinson's letter to President Eisenhower on the call for Negroes to have freedom under the constitution https://www.google.com/culturalinstitute/beta/asset/letter-from-jackie-robinson-to-president-eisenhower/jQHS7TKiqrIEAA Pictures and narrative about of the elite Blacks (Talented Tenth) who were educated during the New Deal in spite of poverty, segregation, and disfranchisement. https://www.google.com/culturalinstitute/beta/exhibit/QQV_IP01	To expose students to the non-traditional activist's and their role and contributions to the fight for equality. To explore the nation's first Black institutions of higher education To examine the lives of the privileged elite Black students during the New Deal Era.
Women in Art		
Cuban Culture		
Holocaust		

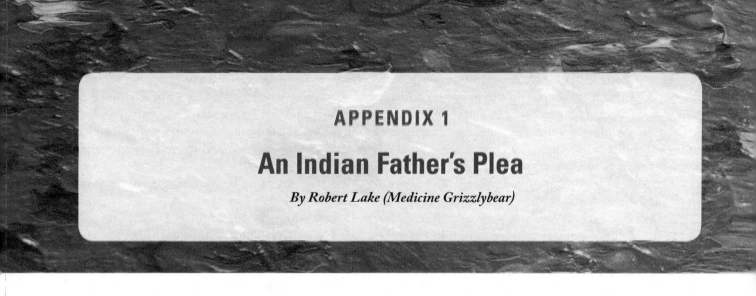

APPENDIX 1

An Indian Father's Plea

By Robert Lake (Medicine Grizzlybear)

Dear teacher, I would like to introduce you to my son, Wind-Wolf. He is probably what you would consider a typical Indian kid. He was born and raised on the reservation. He has black hair, dark brown eyes, and an olive complexion. And like so many Indian children his age, he is shy and quiet in the classroom. He is 5 years old, in kindergarten, and I can't understand why you have already labeled him a "slow learner."

At the age of 5, he has already been through quite an education compared with his peers in Western society. As his first introduction into this world, he was bonded to his mother and to the Mother Earth in a traditional native childbirth ceremony. And he has been continuously cared for by his mother, father, sisters, cousins, aunts, uncles, grandparents, and extended tribal family since this ceremony.

From his mother's warm and loving arms, WindWolf was placed in a secure and specially designed Indian baby basket. His father and the medicine elders conducted another ceremony with him that served to bond him with the essence of his genetic father, the Great Spirit, the Grandfather Sun, and the Grandmother Moon. This was all done in order to introduce him properly into the new and natural world, not the world of artificiality, and to protect his sensitive and delicate soul. It is our people's way of showing the newborn respect, ensuring that he starts his life on the path of spirituality.

The traditional Indian baby basket became his "turtle's shell" and served as the first seat for his classroom. He was strapped in for safety, protected from injury by the willow roots and hazel wood construction. The basket was made by a tribal elder who had gathered her materials with prayer and in a ceremonial way. It is the same kind of basket that our people have used for thousands of years. It is specially designed to provide the child with the kind of knowledge and experience he will need in order to survive in his culture and environment.

Wind-Wolf was strapped in snugly with a deliberate restriction upon his arms and legs. Although you in Western society may argue that such a method serves to hinder motor-skill development and abstract reasoning, we believe it forces the child to first develop his intuitive faculties, rational intellect, symbolic thinking, and five senses. Wind-Wolf was with his mother constantly, closely bonded physically, as she carried him on her back or held him in front while breast-feeding. She carried him everywhere she went, and every night he slept with both parents. Because of this, Wind-Wolf's educational setting was not only a "secure" environment, but it was also very colorful, complicated, sensitive, and diverse. He has been with his mother at the ocean at daybreak when she made her prayers and gathered fresh seaweed from the rocks, he has sat with his uncles in a rowboat on the river while they fished with gill nets, and he has watched and listened to elders as they told creation stories and animal legends and sang songs around the campfires.

He has attended the sacred and ancient White Deerskin Dance of his people and is well-acquainted with the cultures and languages of other tribes. He has been with his mother when she gathered herbs for healing and watched his tribal aunts and grandmothers gather and prepare traditional foods such as acorn, smoked salmon, eel, and deer meat. He has played with abalone shells, pine nuts, iris grass string, and leather while watching the women make beaded jewelry and traditional native regalia. He has had many opportunities to watch his father, uncles, and ceremonial leaders use different kinds of colorful feathers and sing different kinds of songs while preparing for the sacred dances and rituals.

As he grew older, Wind-Wolf began to crawl out of the baby basket, develop his motor skills, and explore the world around him. When frightened or sleepy, he could always return to the basket, as a turtle withdraws into its shell. Such an inward journey allows one to reflect in privacy on what he has learned and to carry the new knowledge deeply into the unconscious and the soul. Shapes, sizes, colors, texture, sound, smell, feeling, taste, and the learning process are therefore functionally integrated—the physical and spiritual, matter and energy, conscious and unconscious, individual and social.

This kind of learning goes beyond the basics of distinguishing the difference between rough and smooth, square and round, hard and soft, black and white, similarities and extremes.

For example, Wind-Wolf was with his mother in South Dakota while she danced for seven days straight in the hot sun, fasting, and piercing herself in the sacred Sun Dance Ceremony of a distant tribe. He has been doctored in a number of different healing ceremonies by medicine men and women from diverse places ranging from Alaska and Arizona to New York and California. He has been in more than 20 different sacred sweat-lodge rituals—used by native tribes to purify mind, body, and soul—since he was 3 years old, and he has already been exposed to many different religions of his racial brothers: Protestant, Catholic, Asian Buddhist, and Tibetan Lamaist.

It takes a long time to absorb and reflect on these kinds of experiences, so maybe that is why you think my Indian child is a slow learner. His aunts and grandmothers taught him to count and know his numbers while they sorted out the complex materials used to make the abstract designs in the native baskets. He listened to his mother count each and every bead and sort out numerically according to color while she painstakingly made complex beaded belts and necklaces. He learned his basic numbers by helping his father count and sort the rocks to be used in the sweat lodge–seven rocks for a medicine sweat, say, or 13 for the summer solstice ceremony. (The rocks are later heated and doused with water to create purifying steam.) And he was taught to learn mathematics by counting the sticks we use in our traditional native hand game. So I realize he may be slow in grasping the methods and tools that you are now using in your classroom, ones quite familiar to his white peers, but I hope you will be patient with him. It takes time to adjust to a new cultural system and learn new things.

He is not culturally "disadvantaged," but he is culturally "different." If you ask him how many months there are in a year, he will probably tell you 13. He will respond this way not because he doesn't know how to count properly, but because he has been taught by our traditional people that there are 13 full moons in a year according to the native tribal calendar and that there are really 13 planets in our solar system and 13 tail feathers on a perfectly balanced eagle, the most powerful kind of bird to use in ceremony and healing.

But he also knows that some eagles may only have 12 tail feathers, or seven, that they do not all have the same number. He knows that the flicker has exactly 10 tail feathers; that they are red and black, representing the directions of east and west, life and death; and that this bird is considered a "fire" bird, a power used in native doctoring and healing. He can probably count more than 40 different kinds of birds, tell you and his peers what kind of bird each is and where it lives, the seasons in which it appears, and how it is used in a sacred ceremony. He may have trouble writing his name on a piece of paper, but he knows how to say it and many other things in several different Indian languages. He is not fluent yet because he is only 5 years old and required by law to attend your educational system, learn your language, your values, your ways of thinking, and your methods of teaching and learning.

So you see, all of these influences together make him somewhat shy and quiet—and perhaps "slow" according to your standards. But if Wind-Wolf was not prepared for his first tentative foray into your world, neither were you appreciative of his culture. On the first day of class, you had difficulty with his name. You wanted to call him Wind, insisting that Wolf somehow must be his middle name. The students in the class laughed at him, causing further embarrassment.

While you are trying to teach him your new methods, helping him learn new tools for selfdiscovery and adapt to his new learning environment, he may be looking out the window as if daydreaming. Why? Because he has been taught to watch and study the changes in nature. It is hard for him to make the appropriate psychic switch from the right to the left hemisphere of the brain when he sees the leaves turning bright colors, the geese heading south, and the squirrels scurrying around for nuts to get ready for a harsh winter. In his heart, in his young mind, and almost by instinct, he knows that this is the time of year he is supposed to be with his people gathering and preparing fish, deer meat, and native plants and herbs, and learning his assigned tasks in this role. He is caught between two worlds, torn by two distinct cultural systems.

Yesterday, for the third time in two weeks, he came home crying and said he wanted to have his hair cut. He said he doesn't have any friends at school because they make fun of his long hair. I tried to explain to him that in our culture, long hair is a sign of masculinity and balance and is a source of power. But he remained adamant in his position.

To make matters worse, he recently encountered his first harsh case of racism. WindWolf had managed to adopt at least one good school friend. On the way home from school one day, he asked his new pal if he wanted to come home to play with him until supper. That was OK with WindWolf's mother, who was walking with them. When they all got to the little friend's house, the two boys ran inside to ask permission while Wind-Wolf's mother waited. But the other boy's mother lashed out: "It is OK if you have to play with him at school, but we don't allow those kind of people in our house!" When my wife asked why not, the other boy's mother answered, "Because you are Indians and we are white, and I don't want my kids growing up with your kind of people."

So now my young Indian child does not want to go to school anymore (even though we cut his hair). He feels that he does not belong. He is the only Indian child in your class, and he is well-aware of this fact. Instead of being proud of his race, heritage, and culture, he feels ashamed. When he watches television, he asks why the white people hate us so much and always kill our people in the movies and why they take everything away from us. He asks why the other kids in school are not taught about the power, beauty, and essence of nature or provided with an opportunity to experience the world around them firsthand. He says he hates living in the city and that he misses his Indian cousins and friends. He asks why one young white girl at school who is his friend always tells him, "I like you, Wind-Wolf, because you are a good Indian."

Now he refuses to sing his native songs, play with his Indian artifacts, learn his language, or participate in his sacred ceremonies. When I ask him to go to an urban powwow or help me with a sacred sweat-lodge ritual, he says no because "that's weird" and he doesn't want his friends at school to think he doesn't believe in God.

So, dear teacher, I want to introduce you to my son, Wind-Wolf, who is not really a "typical" little Indian kid after all. He stems from a long line of hereditary chiefs, medicine men and women, and ceremonial leaders whose accomplishments and unique forms of knowledge are still being studied and recorded in contemporary books. He has seven different tribal systems flowing through his blood; he is even part white. I want my child to succeed in school and in life. I don't want him to be a dropout or juvenile delinquent or to end up on drugs and alcohol because he is made to feel inferior or because of discrimination. I want him to be proud of his rich heritage and culture, and I would like him to develop the necessary capabilities to adapt to, and succeed in, both cultures. But I need your help.

What you say and what you do in the classroom, what you teach and how you teach it, and what you don't say and don't teach will have a significant effect on the potential success or failure of my child. Please remember that this is the primary year of his education and development. All I ask is that you work with me, not against me, to help educate my child in the best way. If you don't have the knowledge, preparation, experience, or training to effectively deal with culturally different children, I am willing to help you with the few resources I have available or direct you to such resources.

Millions of dollars have been appropriated by Congress and are being spent each year for "Indian Education." All you have to do is take advantage of it and encourage your school to make an effort to use it in the name of "equal education." My Indian child has a constitutional right to learn, retain, and maintain his heritage and culture. By the same token, I strongly believe that non-Indian children also have a constitutional right to learn about our Native American heritage and culture, because Indians play a significant part in the history of Western society. Until this reality is equally understood and applied in education as a whole, there will be a lot more schoolchildren in grades K-2 identified as "slow learners."

My son, Wind-Wolf, is not an empty glass coming into your class to be filled. He is a full basket coming into a different environment and society with something special to share. Please let him share his knowledge, heritage, and culture with you and his peers.

White Privilege: Unpacking the Invisible Backpack

Peggy McIntosh

Through the work to bring materials from Women's Studies into the rest of the curriculum, I have often noticed men's unwillingness to grant that they are overprivileged, even though they may grant that women are disadvantaged. They may say they will work to improve women's status, in the society, the university, or the curriculum, but they can't or won't support the idea of lessening men's. Denials which amount to taboos surround the subject of advantages which men gain from women's disadvantages. These denials protect male privilege from being fully acknowledged, lessened or ended. Thinking through unacknowledged male privilege as a phenomenon, I realized that since hierarchies in our society are interlocking, there was most likely a phenomenon of white privilege which was similarly denied and protected. As a white person, I realized I had been taught about racism as something which puts others at a disadvantage, but had been taught not to see one of its corollary aspects, white privilege, which puts me at an advantage. I think whites are carefully taught not to recognize white privilege, as males are taught not to recognize male privilege. So I have begun in an untutored way to ask what it is like to have white privilege. I have come to se white privilege as an invisible package of unearned assets which I can count on cashing in each day, but about which I was 'meant' to remain oblivious. White privilege is like an invisible weightless backpack of special provisions, maps, passports, codebooks, visas, clothes, tools and blank checks. Describing white privilege makes one newly accountable. As we in Women's Studies work to reveal male privilege and ask men to give up some of their power, so one who writes about having white privilege must ask, "Having described it, what will I do to lessen or end it?" After I realized the extent to which men work from a base of unacknowledged privilege, I understood that much of their oppressiveness was unconscious. Then I remembered the frequent charges from women of color that white women whom they encounter are oppressive. I began to understand why we are justly seen as oppressive, even when we don't see ourselves that way. I began to count the ways in which I enjoy unearned skin privilege and have been conditioned into oblivion about its existence. My schooling gave me no training in seeing myself as an oppressor, as an unfairly advantaged person, or as a participant in a damaged culture. I was taught to see myself as an individual whose moral state depended on her individual moral will. My schooling followed the pattern my colleague Elizabeth Minnich has pointed out: whites are taught to think of their lives as a morally neutral, normative, and average, also ideal, so that when we work to benefit others, this is seen as work which will allow "them" to be more like "us." I decided to try to work on myself at least by identifying some of the daily effects of white privilege in my life. I have chosen those conditions which I think in my case attack some what more to skin-color privilege that to class, religion, ethnic status, or geographical location, though of course all these other factors are intricately intertwined. As far as I can see, my African American co-worker, friends and acquaintances with whom I come into daily or frequent contact in this particular time, place, and line of work cannot count on most of these conditions.

1. I can if I wish arrange to be in the company of people of my race most of the time.
2. If I should need to move, I can be pretty sure of renting or purchasing housing in an area which I canafford and in which I would want to live.

3. I can be pretty sure that my neighbors in such a location will be neutral or pleasant to me.
4. I can go shopping alone most of the time, pretty well assured that I will not be followed or harassed.
5. I can turn on the television or open to the front page of the paper and see people of my race widely represented.
6. When I am told about our national heritage or about "civilization," I am shown that people of my color made it what it is.
7. I can be sure that my children will be given curricular materials that testify to the existence of their race.
8. If I want to, I can be pretty sure of finding a publisher for this piece on white privilege.
9. I can go into a music shop and count on finding the music of my race represented, into a supermarket and find the staple foods which fit with my cultural traditions, into a hairdresser's shop and find someone who can cut my hair.
10. Whether I checks, credit cards, or cash, I can count on my skin color not to work against the appearance of financial reliability.
11. I can arrange to protect my children most of the time from people who might not like them.
12. I can swear, or dress in second hand clothes, or not answer letters, without having people attribute these choices to the bad morals, the poverty, or the illiteracy of my race.
13. I can speak in public to a powerful male group without putting my race on trial.
14. I can do well in a challenging situation without being called a credit to my race.
15. I am never asked to speak for all the people of my racial group.
16. I can remain oblivious of the language and customs of persons of color who constitute the world's majority without feeling in my culture any penalty for such oblivion.
17. I can criticize our government and talk about how much I fear its policies and behavior without being seen as a cultural outsider.
18. I can be pretty sure that if I ask to talk to "the person in charge," I will be facing a person of my race.
19. If a traffic cop pulls me over or if the IRS audits my tax return, I can be sure I haven't been singled out because of my race.
20. I can easily buy posters, postcards, picture books, greeting cards, dolls, toys, and children's magazine featuring people of my race.
21. I can go home from most meetings of organizations I belong to feeling somewhat tied in, rather than isolated, out-of-place, outnumbered, unheard, held at a distance, or feared.
22. I can take a job with an affirmative action employer without having co-workers on the job suspect that I got it because of race.
23. I can choose public accommodation without fearing that people of my race cannot get in or will be mistreated in the places I have chosen.
24. I can be sure that if I need legal or medical help, my race will not work against me.
25. If my day, week, or year is going badly, I need not ask of each negative episode or situation whether it has racial overtones.
26. I can choose blemish cover or bandages in "flesh" color and have them more or less match my skin.

I repeatedly forgot each of the realization on this list until I wrote it down. For me white privilege has turned out to be an elusive and fugitive subject. The pressure to avoid it is great, for in facing it I must give up the myth of meritocracy. If these things are true, this is not such a free country; one's life is not what one makes it; many doors open for certain people through no virtues of their own. In unpacking this invisible backpack of white privilege, I have listed conditions of daily experience which I once took for granted. Nor did I think of any of these perquisites as bad for the holder. I now think that we need a more finely differentiated taxonomy of privilege, for some of these varieties are only what one would want for everyone in a just society, and others give license to be ignorant, oblivious, arrogant and destructive. I see a pattern running through the matrix of white privilege, a pattern of assumptions which were passed on to me as a white person. There was one main piece of cultural turf; it was my own turf, and I was among those who could control the turf. My skin color was an asset for any move I was educated to want to make. I could think of myself as belonging in major ways, and of making social systems work for me. I could freely disparage, fear, neglect, or be oblivious to anything outside of the dominant cultural forms. Being of the main culture, I could also criticize it fairly free. In proportion as my racial group was being make confident, comfortable, and oblivious, other groups were likely being made confident, uncomfortable, and alienated. Whiteness protected me from many kinds of hostility, distress, and violence, which I was being subtly trained to visit in turn upon people of color. For this reason, the word "privilege" now seems to me misleading. We usually think of privilege as being a favored state, whether earned or conferred by birth or luck. Yet some of the conditions I have described here work to systematically overempower certain groups. Such privilege simply confers dominance because of one's race or sex. I want, then, to distinguish between earned strength and unearned power conferred systematically. Power from unearned privilege can look like strength when it is in fact permission to escape or to dominate. But not all of the privileges on my list are inevitably damaging. Some, like the expectation that neighbors will be decent to you, or that your race will not count against you in court, should be the norm in a just society. Others, like the privilege to ignore less powerful people, distort the humanity of the holders as well as the ignored groups. We might at least start by distinguishing between positive advantages which we can work to spread, and negative types of advantages which unless rejected will always reinforce our present hierarchies. For example, the feeling that one belongs within the human circle, as Native Americans say, should not be seen as privilege of a few. Ideally it is an unearned advantage and conferred dominance. I have met very few men who are truly distressed about systemic, unearned male advantage and conferred dominance. And so one question for me and others like is whether we will get truly distressed, even outraged, about unearned race advantage and conferred dominance and it so, what we will do to lessen them. In any case, we need to do more work in identifying how they actually affect our daily lives. Many, perhaps most, of our white students in the US think that racism doesn't affect them because they are not people of color; they do not see "whiteness" as a racial identity. In addition, since race and sex are not the only advantaging systems at work, we need similarly to examine the daily experience of having age advantage, or ethnic advantage, or physical ability, or advantage related to nationality, religion or sexual orientation. Difficulties and dangers surrounding the task of finding parallels are many. Since racism, sexism, and heterosexism are not the same, the advantaging associated with them should not be seen as the same. In addition, it is hard to disentangle aspects of unearned advantage which rest more on social class, economic class, race, religion, sex and ethnic identity than on other factors. Still, all of the oppressions are interlocking, as the Combahee River Collective Statement of 1977 continues to remind us eloquently. One factor seems clear about all of the interlocking oppressions. They take both active forms which we can see and embedded forms which as a member of the dominant group one is taught not to see. In my class and place, I did not see myself as a racist because I was taught to recognize racism only in individual acts of meanness by members of my group, never in invisible systems conferring unsought racial dominance on my group from birth. Disapproving of the systems won't be enough to change them. I was taught to think that racism could end if white individuals changed their attitudes. [But] a "white" skin in the United States opens many doors for whites whether or not we approve of the way dominance has been conferred on us. Individual acts can palliate, but cannot end, these problems. To redesign social systems we need first to acknowledge their colossal unseen dimensions. The silences and denials surrounding privilege are the key political tool here. They keep the thinking about equality or equity incomplete, protecting unearned advantage and conferred dominance by making these taboo subjects. Most talk by whites about equal opportunity seems to me now to be about equal opportunity to try to get into a position of dominance while denying that systems of dominance exist. It seems to me that obliviousness about white advantage, like obliviousness about male advantage, is kept strongly inculturated in the United States so as to maintain the myth of meritocracy the myth that democratic choice is equally available to all. Keeping most people unaware that freedom of confident action is there for just a small number of people props up those in power, and serves to keep power in the hands of the same groups that have most of it already. Though systematic change takes many decades, there are pressing questions for me and I imagine for some others like me if we raise our daily consciousness on the perquisites of being light-skinned. What well we do with such knowledge? As we know from watching me, it is an open question whether we will choose to use unearned advantage to weaken hidden systems of advantage, and whether we will use any of our arbitrarily-awarded power to try to reconstruct power systems on a broader base. [1989]

APPENDIX 3

Interview With Beverly Daniel Tatum

Beverly Daniel Tatum, is a clinical psychologist, professor and President of Spelman College. She is an expert on race relations and author of Why Are All The Black Kids Sitting Together in the Cafeteria? *and* Assimilation Blues: Black Families in a White Community.

What is White Privilege?

White people, who also have a race but don't always think about what it means to be white in a largely white-dominated society, sometimes struggle with the concept of white privilege. What are the benefits or the advantages to being white in a society that has historically given benefits and advantages to members of the dominant group? If you are a person who has that privilege, you don't necessarily notice it. It is sometimes taken for granted. Let's use the example of racial profiling. If you're driving on the highway and you are not randomly stopped, you don't get to the end of your drive and say, "Gee, I wasn't randomly stopped today." You just take for granted that you got in your car, drove to your destination, without incident, like you do most days. It's not something that you think of as a function of being a white person in this society, you know?

If you go looking for an apartment and you find the apartment you like, and you rent it without difficulty, you don't say, "Gee, I benefited from being white today. I got that apartment I wanted." If you go shopping in the grocery store and find hair care products and make-up that work for you, you don't think, "Gee, I'm benefiting from being white today. The hair care products I need and the make-up I want were readily available for me."

Can I find opportunities to express my culture if I'm of Asian or Latino descent? How often during the course of a day will I be asked if I speak English, or how long I've been in this country? Will the physical symbol of my face always mark me as a foreigner? These are not things that white people think about on a day-to-day basis - they just take it for granted.

In one of my courses at Holyoke, "The Psychology of Racism," I ask students on the first day of class to get in small groups and talk about themselves in terms of their own racial or ethnic backgrounds. In one of my sessions, that there was a young white woman in a small group talking about these issues, and she was struggling with how to describe herself in terms of her race or ethnicity. Finally she said, "I'm just normal."

When asked what did she mean in that context, she said, "You know, I lived in an all-white neighborhood. I grew up with people a lot like myself, and I was just like everybody else - I was just the norm."

What I think is so significant about her choice of words - to say "I'm just normal" - is that it implies that those around you, who weren't from that background, are "abnormal." She never would have said that, but it is embedded in how we think.

How Does a Person Support Racist Systems Without Being Personally Racist?

Many people say "But I'm not racist. I don't have prejudiced beliefs. As a white person, am I racist, simply because I live in a society in which I'm systematically advantaged?"

For me the relevant issue is not, "Are you racist?" but are you actively working against that system of advantage? Active racism is what I think many people would stereotypically think of as "racist behavior": name-calling, acts of racial violence, intentional discrimination, cross burning, etc.

But there is a lot of behavior that also supports a system of advantage that we might describe as passively racist. For example, in education - if I am teaching a course in which I exclude the contributions of people of color, only talk about white people's contributions and only talk about white literature. And I never introduce my students to the work of African Americans, Latinos or Native Americans. I may not be doing that with the intention of promoting a sense of cultural superiority, but in fact the outcome of leaving those contributions out is to reinforce the idea that only white people have made positive cultural contributions.

I know a young woman who went to her English professor and asked, "Why is it that there are only white writers on our list? This is a 20th Century American Literature course. How come there aren't any writers of color?" Her professor, to his credit, was quite honest and said I'm teaching the authors I studied in graduate school. It wasn't malice on his part. He didn't wake up one day and say, "Over my dead body will there be writers of color on my syllabus." He was simply teaching the authors with whom he was most familiar.

Another example of individuals supporting racist systems can be found in our lending institutions. I might be an individual loan officer who considers herself to be quite progressive, very open minded; a person with limited, if any, prejudice. And yet I might work for a bank that has the practice of charging higher percentage rates to people who live in particular neighborhoods - specifically neighborhoods that have been redlined. So when a person of color from that neighborhood comes to see me, my own inclination might be to give that person a favorable loan. But if the policy of the bank is to give loans at a particular rate in a particular neighborhood, I might enact that policy, apart from my individual attitude, and in my decision-making reinforce the institutional racism embedded in that practice.

If we want to interrupt these cycles, we have to be quite intentional about it. Even without any malicious intents, such passive acts of giving into certain institutions or traditions will perpetuate systems of advantage based on race.

What are the Obstacles to an Equal Society? Why Can't We be "Colorblind"?

Does creating more equitable environments mean loss for some people? That's what the controversy around issues like affirmative action is about. It feels like a loss, people feel like opportunities are being taken away from them. They don't necessarily see that there is a gain for the whole society, and perhaps even for them, by creating opportunities for everybody to contribute more fairly. It's not just about taking things away, it's about creating a better environment for everyone. A safer environment - a more just environment is a more peaceful environment. Martin Luther King said there is no peace without justice. We live in a world that is increasingly torn by violence, not always described as racially motivated violence, but violence which is very much related to systems of oppression. And to the extent that we're able to interrupt those systems, we're able to create a better quality of life for everyone.

Part of the problem is that people often struggle with the concept of meritocracy. They grow up with this notion that we live in a meritocracy, that people get what they deserve. It is an idea that has been part of their socialization. And to understand racism, or sexism or classism, or other isms as systems of advantage based on race or social group membership - these really fly in the face of that notion of meritocracy.

Think about the government assistance in home financing that took place for the World War II generation in the 1950's. Who got access to those loans? Where were those new houses being built? In the suburbs. And what resulted from the racially-restrictive covenants that blocked access to that new housing for people of color? If you got a government loan with your GI Bill and bought a house in an all-white area and that house appreciated in value - that was all made more available to you as consequence of racist policies and practices. To the child of that parent, it looks like my father worked hard, bought a house, passed his wealth on to me, made it possible for me to go to school, mortgaged that house so I could have a relatively debt-free college experience, and has financed my college education. How come your father didn't do that? Well, there are some good reasons why maybe your father might have had a harder time doing that if you're African American or Latino or Native American, or even Asian American.

The best response to the colorblind notion I have ever heard came to me from an African American father who I was interviewing for a study I was doing on the experiences of black youth in predominantly white communities.

He was talking about his experiences with his children in school. They were often the only black children in a mostly white class. And he talked about the teachers who would say something like, "I'm color blind. I treat all the kids the same, all the children the same."

And his response was, "The same as what? The same as if they were all white? My children, as the only black children in the class, are not having the same experience as the white children in that class. The white children are seeing themselves reflected in the schoolbooks, in the classroom teacher. My children are sometimes called names that white children don't hear themselves being called. Their experience is not the same. So for you to say you're colorblind, that you're treating the children all the same, is to say that you're not acknowledging the reality of my child's day-to-day experience, and that feels very invalidating."

Doesn't the Existence of Multicultural Curricula in the United States Prove that We're Making Progress?

We use diversity as an umbrella term to describe the differences among people - whether those differences are cultural, religious, socioeconomic, gender, sexual orientation, age, ability, etc. When we think about the benefits of diversity, I think we have to think about the fact that we are not interested in bringing people together just so we can say, "I know somebody who is different from me." It's not just about getting to know people as friends, though certainly there can be very important and useful friendships that emerge in diverse environments. But when I think about diversity and the value of it, I think about really different approaches to problem solving, different approaches to thinking about our society that might lead us to more equitable systems, the various talents that people bring.

In some schools they try to address diversity through what we might describe as a celebration of heroes and holidays. We are going to talk about Martin Luther King in January or February. We are going to have this day where we are celebrating holidays and people are going to bring in foods from different backgrounds, and it's a fairly superficial discussion of diversity, without really engaging in the meaning of that diversity in people's lives.

So for example, as an African American, I might come to school and talk about the holiday Kwaanza as part of diversity celebrations in the school. I happen to be in a family where we do celebrate Kwaanza as well as Christmas. However, if that is all we talk about in terms of my heritage, then I would feel like we had missed the boat. We have to be clear that it's not just understanding that he eats beans and rice, and she eats egg rolls and this person celebrates Kwanza. It's not about that. It is also about understanding the history of the way those groups have been treated in our society, and what we need to do to interrupt that history; to interrupt that current situation in terms of making sure that everybody has equal access.

So it's not just understanding somebody's heroes and holidays, but it's also understanding issues of social justice and how the society operates in ways that systematically advantages some members of our community, and systematically disadvantages other members of our community.

And if we can use our understanding of diversity in those terms and can connect with one another as allies working towards a more socially just environment, then I think we have really maximized the benefit of diversity.

How does Racism Affect Everyone?

When I speak to audiences about this topic of race and racism, one of the questions that I often ask is for them to reflect on their own earliest race-related memory. In general, you can say that people of color tend to have earlier memories - particularly if they grew up in the United States - than those who are white. Having said that, when you ask them what emotion is associated with this early memory, almost everyone, both people of color and white people, will talk about things like fear, anger, sadness, shame, embarrassment, sometimes guilt.

What's really striking to me about this is not only do so many people have this experience, but when asked if they had discussed their experience with an adult or a parent or a teacher at the time, many people said they did not. They already knew that it was a topic you weren't supposed to talk about. Somehow the adults in the environment had communicated to them that this is something we don't discuss. Sometimes the people of color will say I was upset by what happened to me, and I was too embarrassed to tell anybody else about it. Sometime white adults will say that it was a trusted adult who was the source of the confusion. One of the things that makes the process so insidious is that it comes from people we know, love and trust. It's your mother who rented the videotape that was full of stereotypical images. It's your favorite uncle who tells the jokes at Thanksgiving. It's your next door neighbor who makes the casual comments that imbeds. It's your favorite English teacher who leaves writers of color off the syllabus.

What's really significant to me about this is not only that people have these negative experiences, but they've also internalized the idea that we shouldn't talk about it. And that, I think, is really problematic if we are ever going to get beyond the issue of racism as an impediment to social justice in our society because we have to be able to talk about it order to move beyond it.

Why do Some People Voluntarily Separate Themselves Socially Based on Race?

People are naturally drawn to people who they see as being familiar. However, if you want to connect with somebody who is different from yourself, you have to be able to understand where is that person coming from. And one of the things that I've observed when we talk about, for example, racial group differences, is that students of color often come already thinking about themselves as members of particular groups. Whereas white students don't necessarily come to college thinking of themselves as quote white.

That, I think, is important in terms of how young people are coming together. Because if I'm coming to school thinking about myself as African American, or Latina, or African American, and I'm interacting with white students — many of whom may have grown up thinking that the thing to do is to be colorblind. And that white student, in her effort to connect with me, says something like, "Gee, I don't think of you as a black person." Or, "Why do you put so much emphasis on being a Latina?" Or, "Why is being African American so important to you?"

And if that is a very important part of my adolescent identity development process, just asking me that question is going to signal to me that you don't get it, that you don't understand where I'm coming from. Then I have to decide do I want to explain myself to you, or not? I might be willing to explain, once or twice. But if I find that everybody I meet outside of my group needs an explanation, that might get a little old. I might get tired of that.

So I might choose to hang around with people to whom I don't have to explain why I wear my hair the way I do, or why I like to listen to this kind of music as opposed to that kind of music. Or why I speak Spanish on the phone to my mother. That if I don't want to explain certain parts of myself frequently, I might choose to hang around with people who are similar to me. And that's an understandable response.

Generally speaking, identity questions really start to come to the surface during adolescence. That's when young people really start to think, "Who am I? What do I want to be when I grow up? How do I want to interact with other people in the world? Who do I want to connect with?" All of these are questions about identity.

But when you talk to young people of color, many of their identity questions are linked to their sense of themselves as members of a particular racial or ethnic group; not only who am I, but who am I as an African American woman? Who am I as an African American male? Who am I as a Latina? Who am I as a Cherokee?

When you talk to young white people, they may be thinking about who they are and who they want to relate to, and how they want to think about themselves in the world. But it may not necessarily be linked to their sense of what it means to be white - particularly if they've grown up in a predominantly white community, or gone to predominantly white schools.

Now you might ask why do so many young people of color think about their racial group membership? If white kids aren't thinking about it, why are kids of color thinking about it? And one of the reasons they're thinking about it is because other people bring it to their attention.

How do Cultural Influences (Television, Media, etc.) make Whiteness the Norm and People of Color "the Other"?

Certainly if we're talking about white people living in predominantly white communities, it is certainly true that many people will grow up without having direct contact with people of color. And because they don't have that direct contact, the information that they have is coming to them largely from second hand sources; maybe from the television they've watched, the movies they've seen, the jokes they hear people tell, the casual comments they hear relatives making. So that the information is coming in stereotyped packages, typically.

One of the problems with stereotyping and the self-fulfilling nature of it, is that if you've heard these things, and then you meet somebody, you are likely to look for those characteristics.

Certainly if we think about how young children begin to understand race and the images that they are exposed to, we can say that white children receive many images in which they see themselves reflected. Their parents go to the library, they check out library books, and they see white children in them. They watch television, they see white children playing. Which is not to say they never see messages or images of people of color, but they're seeing lots of white images — not only on television but in their homes, in their families, in their neighborhoods. So as a consequence of that, they will tend to think of white as the norm.

One of the things that we know about white children is that they often express curiosity about that which they perceive as different. You know, the white child in the grocery store who might see a dark-skinned person for the first time saying, "Mommy, mommy, why is that person so dark?" They're not asking, "Mommy, mommy, why are we so light?" The question is framed in terms of the other.

On the other hand, young children of color growing up, even if they live in environments that are fairly homogenous - black kids growing up in black neighborhoods, Latino children in Latino neighborhoods, etc. - are going to also be bombarded with images of white people in the media, in the books they get from the library, in the television they watch. So that even though they may be surrounded by a community in which they see themselves reflected, in terms of the bigger society, they, too, are also watching the same television programs, reading the same children's books, exposed to the same curricula in school, etc. So children of color don't necessarily start out asking why do white people look the way they do, but why do I look the way I do? Young children come to understand the wider world in terms as one that is dominated by white people.

How can we have Control Over Racial Stereotypes?

"The Lion King" was a very popular film, and my kids saw it more than once, I will confess. However, when I watched it with them, I pointed out some concerns I had. I told my children that I was bothered by the fact that the hyenas - who were the bad guys of the film - have voices that make them sound like black people and Spanish speaking people. Now, some people would say I'm making too much of that. But think about the fact that young children watch movies like this repeatedly and these messages are seen over and over again. They do have an effect on how we view others.

Now, am I saying that you should never let your children see a film that has a stereotype in it? No. What I'm saying is that you need to help your kids think critically about them so they can recognize them as stereotypes and think critically about whether they make sense or not.

Once, while we were driving through a city not far from where we live, my son saw a young black man running down the street. He said to me, "Why is that kid running?" I said, "I don't know why he's running. Why do you think he's running?" And my son said, "Maybe he stole something." And I was horrified to hear him make that comment. Where would he have gotten that idea?

So I said, "Well, what would make you think so?" He said, "You know, we're in a city. Sometimes people in cities steal things." And I pointed out that we have been in the city many times, parked our car, and never had a problem. I've had one thing stolen from my car in my life, and that happened in the small town, predominantly white, in which I live now. Well clearly he sees the nightly news. He watches television. He had absorbed those messages.

Books, computer games, the Web, television - there are so many places that we can be exposed to stereotypes, that we can be exposed to distorted information. And there is a whole universe of information that we're not getting. Think about these stereotypes, these omissions, these distortions as a kind of environment that surrounds us, like smog in the air. We don't breathe it because we like it. We don't breathe it because we think it's good for us. We breathe it because it's the only air that's available.

And in the same way, we're taking in misinformation not because we want it. When you or your child sits in front of the television on Saturday morning watching cartoons, you're not saying let's have our daily diet of stereotypes today. But you're being exposed to them because they're just there, in the commercials, in the images that you're watching. And it's so pervasive that you don't even notice it sometimes. In fact, a lot of the time you don't notice it.

We're all breathing in misinformation. We're all being exposed to stereotypes, and we all have to think about how we have been impacted by that. You sometimes hear people say there is not a prejudiced bone in my body. But I think when somebody makes that statement, we might gently say to them check again. That if we have all been breathing in smog, we can't help but have have our thinking shaped by it somehow. As a consequence, we all have work to do. Whether you identify as a person of color, whether you identify as a white person, it doesn't matter. We all have been exposed to misinformation that we have to think critically about.

APPENDIX 4

From the Achievement Gap to the Education Debt: Understanding Achievement in U.S. Schools

Gloria Ladson-Billings

I have spent a better part of this year reading the presidential addresses of a number of former AERA presidents. Most take the wise course of giving addresses about something they know well-their own research. Of course, I was not fully persuaded by their wisdom. Instead, I attempted to learn something new, and, unfortunately, the readers will have to determine whether I learned it well enough to share it with my professional colleagues.

The questions that plague me about education research are not new ones. I am concerned about the meaning of our work for the larger public-for real students, teachers, administrators, parents, policymakers, and communities in real school settings. I know these are not new concerns; they have been raised by others, people like the late Kenneth B. Clark, who, in the 1950s, was one of the first social scientists to bring research to the public in a meaningful way. His work with his wife and colleague Mamie formed the basis for the landmark Brown v. Board of Education 1954 case that reversed legal segregation in public schools and other public accommodations. However, in his classic volume Dark Ghetto: Dilemmas of Social Power, first published in 1965, Clark took social scientists to task for their failure to fully engage and understand the plight of the poor:

> To my knowledge, there is at present nothing in the vast literature of social science treatises and textbooks and nothing in the practical and field training of graduate students in social science to prepare them for the realities and complexities of this type of involvement in a real, dynamic, urbulent, and at times seemingly chaotic community. And what is more, nothing anywhere in the training of social scientists, teachers, or social workers now prepares them to understand, to cope with, or to change the normal chaos of ghetto communities. These are grave lacks which must be remedied soon if these disciplines are to become relevant [emphasis added] to the stability and survival of our society. p. xxix)

Clark's concern remains some 40 years later. However, the paradox is that education research has devoted a significant amount of its enterprise toward the investigation of poor, African American, Latina/o, American Indian, and Asian immigrant students, who represent an increasing number of the students in major metropolitan school districts. We seem to study them but rarely provide the kind of remedies that help them to solve their problems.

To be fair, education researchers must have the freedom to pursue basic research, just as their colleagues in other social sciences do. They must be able to ask questions and pursue inquiries "just because." However, because education is an applied field, a field that local states manage and declare must be available to the entire public, most of the questions that education researchers ask need to address the significant questions that challenge and confound the public: Why don't children learn to read? What accounts for the high levels of school dropout among urban students? How can we explain the declining performance in mathematics and science at the same time that science and mathematics knowledge is exploding? Why do factors like race and class continue to be strong predictors of achievement when gender disparities have shrunk?

The Prevalence of the Achievement Gap

One of the most common phrases in today's education literatures "the achievement gap." The term produces more than 11 million citations on Google. "Achievement gap," much like certain popular culture music stars, has become a cross over hit. It has made its way into common parlance and everyday usage. The term is invoked by people on both ends of the political spectrum, and few argue over its meaning or its import. According to the National Governors' Association, the achievement gap is "a matter of race and class. Across the U.S., a gap in academic achievement persists between minority and disadvantaged students and their white counterparts. "It further states: "This is one of the most pressing education-policy challenges that states currently face" (2005). The story of the achievement gap is a familiar one. The numbers speak for themselves. In the 2005 National Assessment of Educational Progress results, the gap between Black and Latina/o fourth graders and their White counterparts in reading scaled scores was more than 26 points. In fourth-grade mathematics the gap was more than 20 points (Education Commission of the States, 2005). In eighth-grade reading, the gap was more than 23 points, and in eighth-grade mathematics the gap was more than 26 points. We can also see that these gaps persist over time (Education Commission of the States). Even when we compare African Americans and Latina/os with incomes comparable to those of Whites, there is still an achievement gap as measured by standardized testing (National Center for Education Statistics, 2001). While I have focused primarily on showing this gap by means of standardized test scores, it also exists when we compare dropout rates and relative numbers of students who take advanced placement examinations; enroll in honors, advanced placement, and "gifted" classes; and are admitted to colleges and graduate and professional programs.

Scholars have offered a variety of explanations for the existence of the gap. In the 1960s, scholars identified cultural deficit theories to suggest that children of color were victims of pathological lifestyles that hindered their ability to benefit from schooling (Hess & Shipman, 1965; Bereiter & Engleman, 1966; Deutsch, 1963). The 1966 Coleman Report, Equality of Educational Opportunity (Coleman et al.), touted the importance of placing students in racially integrated classrooms. Some scholars took that report to further endorse the cultural deficit theories and to suggest that there was not much that could be done by schools to improve the achievement of African American children. But Coleman et al. were subtler than that. They argued that, more than material resources alone, a combination of factors was heavily correlated with academic achievement. Their work indicated that the composition of a school (who attends it), the students' sense of control of the environments and their futures, the teachers' verbal skills, and their students' family background all contribute to student achievement. Unfortunately, it was the last factor-family background- that became the primary point of interest for many school and social policies.

Social psychologist Claude Steele (1999) argues that a "stereo-type threat" contributes to the gap. Sociolinguists such as Kathryn Au (1980), Lisa Delpit (1995), Michele Foster (1996), and Shirley Brice Heath (1983), and education researcher such as Jacqueline Jordan Irvine (2003) and Carol Lee (2004), have focused on the culture mismatch that contributes to the gap. Multicultural education researcher such as James Banks (2004), Geneva Gay (2004), and Carl Grant (2003), and curriculum theorists such as Michael Apple (1990), Catherine Cornbleth (and Dexter Waugh; 1995), and Thomas Popkewitz (1998) have focused on the nature of the curriculum and the school as sources of the gap. And teacher educators such as Christine Sleeter (2001), Marilyn Cochran-Smith (2004), Kenneth Zeichner (2002), and I (1994) have focused on the pedagogical practices of teachers as contributing to either the exacerbation or the narrowing of the gap.

But I want to use this opportunity to call into question the wisdom of focusing on the achievement gap as a way of explaining and understanding the persistent in equality that exists (and has always existed) in our nation's schools. I want to argue that this all-out focus on the "Achievement Gap" moves us toward short-term solutions that are unlikely to address the long-term underlying problem.

Down the Rabbit-Hole

Let me begin the next section of this discussion with a strange transition from a familiar piece of children's literature:

Alice started to her feet, or it flashed across her mind that she had never before seen a rabbit with either waistcoat-pocket, or a watch to take out of it, and burning with curiosity, she ran across the field after it, and fortunately as just in time to see it pop down a large rabbit-hole under the hedge. In another moment own went Alice after it, never once considering how in the world she was to get out again.

Lewis Carroll, *Alice's Adventures in Wonderland*

The relevance of this passage is that I, like Alice, saw a rabbit with a watch and waist coat-pocket when I came across a book by economist Robert Margo entitled *Race and Schooling in the American South, 1880-1950* (1990). And, like Alice, I chased the rabbit called "economics" down a rabbit-hole, where the world looked very different to me. Fortunately, I traveled with my trusty copy of Lakoff and Johnson's (1980) *Metaphors We Live By* as a way to make sense of my sojourn there. So, before making my way back to the challenge of school inequality, I must beg your indulgence as I give you a brief tour of my time down there.

National Debt Versus National Deficit

Most people hear or read news of the economy every day and rarely give it a second thought. We hear that the Federal Reserve Bank is raising interest rates, or that the unemployment numbers look good. Our ears may perk up when we hear the latest gasoline prices or that we can get a good rate on a mortgage refinance loan. But busy professionals rarely have time to delve deeply into all things economic. Two economic terms- "national deficit" and "national debt" –seem to be fuddle us. A deficit is the amount by which a government's, company's, or individual's spending exceeds income over a particular period of time. Thus, for each budget cycle, the government must determine whether it has a balanced budget, a budget surplus, or a deficit. The debt, however is the sum of all previously incurred annual federal deficits. Since the deficits are financed by government borrowing, national debt is equal to all government debt.

Most fiscal conservatives warn against deficit budgets and urge the government to decrease spending to balance the budget. Fiscal liberals do not necessarily embrace deficits but would rather see the budget balanced by increasing tax revenues from those most able to pay. The debt is a sum that has been accumulating since 1791, when the U.S. Treasury recorded it as $75,463,476.52 (Gordon, 1998). Thomas Jefferson (1816) said, "I . . . place economy among the first and most important virtues, and public debt as the greatest of dangers to be feared. To preserve our independence, we must not let our rulers load us with perpetual debt."

But the debt has not merely been going up. Between 1823 and 1835 the debt steadily decreased, from a high of almost $91 million to a low of $33,733.05. The nation's debt hit the $1 billion mark in 1863 and the $1 trillion mark in 1981. Today, the national debt sits at more than $8 trillion. This level of debt means that the United States pays about $132,844,701,219.88 in interest each year. This makes our debt interest the third-largest expenditure in the federal budget after defense and combined entitlement programs such as Social Security and Medicare (Christensen, 2004).

Even in those years when the United States has had a balanced budget, that is, no deficits, the national debt continued to grow. It may have grown at a slower rate, but it did continue to grow. President Clinton bragged about presenting a balanced budget- one without deficits-and not growing the debt (King, J., 2000). However, the debt was already at a frighteningly high level, and his budget policies failed to make a dent in the debt.

The Debt and Education Disparity

By now, readers might assume that I have made myself firmly at home at the Mad Hatter's Tea Party. What does a discussion about national deficits and national debt have to do with education, education research, and continued education disparities? It is here where I began to see some metaphorical concurrences between our national fiscal situation and our education situation. I am arguing that our focus on the achievement gap is akin to a focus on the budget deficit, but what is actually happening to African American and Latina/o students is really more like the national debt. We do not have an achievement gap; we have an education debt.

Now, to be perfectly candid, I must admit that when I consulted with a strict economist, Professor Emeritus Robert Have-man of the University of Wisconsin's Department of Economics, La Follette Institute of Public Affairs, and Institute for Research on Poverty, he stated:

> The education debt is the foregone schooling resources that we could have (should have) been investing in (primarily) low income kids, which deficit leads to a variety of social problems (e.g. crime, low productivity, low wages, low labor force participation) that require on-going public investment. This required investment sucks away resources that could go to reducing the achievement gap. Without the education debt we could narrow the achievement debt. . . . The message would be that you need to reduce one (the education debt, defined above) in order to close the other (the achievement gap). A parallel is trying to gain a growing and robust economy with a large national debt overhang. (February, 2006, e-mail)

In addition to this informal discussion with Haveman, I read a work by Wolfe and Haveman (2001) entitled Accounting or the Social and Non-Market Benefits of Education, which catalogues a series of what they term "non-market effects of schooling." The authors contend that "the literature on the intergenerational effects of education is generally neglected in assessing the full impact of education." Among the nonmarket effects that they include are the following:

- A positive link between one's own schooling and the schooling received by one's children
- A positive association between the schooling and health status of one's family members
- A positive relationship between one's own education and one's own health status
- A positive relationship between one's own education and the efficiency of choices made, such as consumer choices (which efficiency has positive effects on well-being similar to those of money income)
- A relationship between one's own schooling and fertility choices (in particular, decisions of one's female teenage children regarding non marital child bearing)
- A relationship between the schooling/social capital of one's neighborhood and decisions by young people regarding their level of schooling, non-marital child bearing, and participation in criminal activities. (pp. 2-3)

While these economists have informed my thinking, I have taken a somewhat different tack on this notion of the education debt. The yearly fluctuations in the achievement gap give us a short-range picture of how students perform on a particular set of achievement measures. Looking at the gap from year to year is a misleading exercise. Lee's (2002) look at the trend lines shows us that there was a narrowing of the gap in the 1980s both between Black and White students and between the Latina/o and White students, and a sub-sequent expansion of those gaps in the 1990s. The expansion of the disparities occurred even though the income differences narrowed during the1990s. We do not have good answers as to why the gap narrows or widens. Some research suggests that even the combination of socioeconomic and family conditions, youth culture and student behaviors, and schooling conditions and practices do not fully explain changes in the achievement gap (Lee).

However, when we begin looking at the construction and compilation of what I have termed the education debt, we can better understand why an achievement gap is a logical outcome. I am arguing that the historical, economic, sociopolitical, and moral decisions and policies that characterize our society have created an education debt. So, at this point, I want to briefly describe each of those aspects of the debt.

The Historical Debt

Scholars in the history of education, such as James Anderson (1989), Michael Fultz (1995), and David Tyack (2004), have documented the legacy of educational inequities in the Unites States. Those inequities initially were formed around race, class, and gender. Gradually, some of the inequities began to recede, but clearly they persist in the realm of race. In the case of African Americans, education was initially forbidden during the period of enslavement. After emancipation we saw the development of freedmen's schools whose purpose was the maintenance of a servant class. During the long period of legal apartheid, African Americans attended schools where they received cast-off textbooks and materials from White schools. In the South, the need for farm labor meant that the typical school year for rural Black students was about 4 months long. Indeed, Black students in the South did not experience universal secondary schooling until 1968 (Anderson, 2002). Why, then, would we not expect there to be an achievement gap?

The history of American Indian education is equally egregious. It began with mission schools to convert and use Indian labor to further the cause of the church. Later, boarding schools were developed as General George Pratt asserted the need "to kill the Indian in order to save the man." This strategy of deliberate and forced assimilation created a group of people, according to Pulitzer Prize writer N. Scott Momaday, who belonged nowhere (Lesiak, 1991). The assimilated Indian could not fit comfortably into reservation life or the stratified mainstream. No predominately White colleges welcomed the few Indians who successfully completed the early boarding schools. Only historically Black colleges, such as Hampton Institute, opened their doors to them. There, the Indians studied vocation a land trade curricula.

Latina/o students also experienced huge disparities in their education. In Ferg-Cadima's report *Black, White, and Brown: Latino School Desegregation Efforts in the Pre- and Post-*Brown v. Board of Education *Era* (2004), we discover the longstanding practice of denial experienced by Latina/os dating back to 1848. Historic desegregation cases such as *Mendez v. Westminster* (1946) and the Lemon Grove Incident detail the ways that Brown children were (and continue to be) excluded from equitable and high-quality education.

It is important to point out that the historical debt was not merely imposed by ignorant masses that were xenophobic and virulently racist. The major leaders of the nation endorsed ideas about the inferiority of Black, Latina/o, and Native peoples. Thomas Jefferson (1816), who advocated for the education of the American citizen, simultaneously decried the notion that Blacks were capable of education. George Washington, while deeply conflicted about slavery, maintained a substantial number of slaves on his Mount Vernon Plantation and gave no thought to educating enslaved children.

A brief perusal of some of the history of public schooling in the United States documents the way that we have accumulated an education debt over time. In 1827 Massachusetts passed a law making all grades of public school open to all pupils free of charge. At about the same time, most Southern states already had laws forbidding the teaching of enslaved Africans to read. By 1837, when Horace Mann had become head of the newly formed Massachusetts State Board of Education, Edmund Dwight, a wealthy Boston industrialist, felt that the state board was crucial to factory owners and offered to supplement the state salary with his own money. What is omitted from this history is that the major raw material of those textile factories, which drove the economy of the East, was cotton- the crop that depended primarily on the labor of enslaved Africans (Farrow, Lang, & Frank, 2005). Thus one of the ironies of the historical debt is that while African Americans were enslaved and prohibited from schooling, the product of their labor was used to profit Northern industrialists who already had the benefits of education. Consider the real source of New England's wealth (from Farrow, Lang, & Frank, p.6):

- By 1860, New England was home to 472 cotton mills, built on rivers and streams throughout the region.
- Just between 1830 and 1840, Northern mills consumed more than 100 million pounds of Southern cotton. With shipping and manufacturing included, the economy of much of New England was connected to textiles.
- By the 1850s, the enormous profits of Massachusetts industrialists had been poured into a complex network of banks, insurance companies, and railroads. But their wealth remained anchored to dozens of mammoth textile mills in Massachusetts, southern Maine, and New Hampshire.

This pattern of debt affected other groups as well. In 1864 the U.S. Congress made it illegal for Native Americans to be taught in their native languages. After the Civil War, African Americans worked with Republicans to rewrite state constitutions to guarantee free public education for all students. Unfortunately, their efforts benefited White children more than Black children. The landmark Plessy v. Ferguson (1896) decision meant that the segregation that the South had been practicing was officially recognized as legal by the federal government.

Although the historical debt is a heavy one, it is important not to overlook the ways that communities of color always have worked to educate themselves. Between 1865 and 1877, African Americans mobilized to bring public education to the South for the first time. Carter G. Woodson (1933/1972) was a primary critic of the kind of education that African Americans received, and he challenged African Americans to develop schools and curricula that met the unique needs of a population only a few generations out of chattel slavery.

The Economic Debt

As is often true in social research, the numbers present a startling picture of reality. The economics of the education debt are sobering. The funding disparities that currently exist between schools serving White students and those serving students of color are not recent phenomena. Separate schooling always allows for differential funding. In present-day dollars, the funding disparities between urban schools and their suburban counterparts present a telling story about the value we place on the education of different groups of students.

The Chicago public schools spend about $8,482 annually per pupil, while nearby Highland Park spends $17,291 per pupil. The Chicago public schools have an 87% Black and Latina/o population, while Highland Park has a 90% White population. Per pupil expenditures in Philadelphia are $9,299 per pupil for the city's 79% Black and Latina/o population, while across City Line Avenue in Lower Merion, the per pupil expenditure is $17,261 for a 91% White population. The New York City public schools spend $11,627 per pupil for a student population that is 72% Black and Latina/o, while suburban Man has set spends $22,311 for a student population that is 91% White (figures from Kozol, 2005).

One of the earliest things one learns in statistics is that correlation does not prove causation, but we must ask ourselves why the funding inequities map so neatly and regularly onto the racial and ethnic realities of our schools. Even if we cannot prove that schools are poorly funded because Black and Latina/o students attend them, we can demonstrate that the amount of funding rises with the rise in White students. This pattern of inequitable funding has occurred over centuries. For many of these populations, schooling was nonexistent during the early history of the nation; and, clearly, Whites were not prepared to invest their fiscal resources in these strange "others."

Another important part of the economic component of the education debt is the earning ratios related to years of schooling. The empirical data suggest that more schooling is associated with higher earnings; that is, high school graduates earn more money than high school drop outs, and college graduates earn more than high school graduates. Margo (1990) pointed out that in 1940 the average annual earnings of Black men were about 48% of those of White men, but by 1980 the earning ratio had risen to 61%. By 1993, the median Black male earned 74% as much as the median White male.

While earnings ratios show us how people are (or were) doing at particular points in time, they do not address the cumulative effect of such income disparities. According to economists Joseph Altonji and Ulrech Doraszelski (2005),

> The wealth gap between whites and blacks in the United States is much larger than the gap in earnings. The gap in wealth has impli cations for the social position of African Americans that go far beyond its obvious implications or consumption levels that households can sustain. This is because wealth is a source of political and social power, influences access to capital or new businesses, and provides insurance against fluctuations in labor market income. It affects the quality of housing, neighborhoods, and schools a family has access to as well as the ability to finance higher education. The fact that friendships and family ties tend to be within racial groups amplifies the effect of the wealth gap on the financial, social, and political resources available to blacks relative to whites. (p.1)

This economic analysis maps well onto the notion of education debt- as opposed to achievement gap- that I am trying to advance. So, while the income gap more closely resembles the achievement gap, the wealth disparity better reflects the education debt that I am attempting to describe.

The Sociopolitical Debt

The sociopolitical debt reflects the degree to which communities of color are excluded from the civic process. Black, Latina/o, and Native communities had little or no access to the franchise, so they had no true legislative representation. According to the Civil Rights Division of the U.S. Department of Justice, African Americans and other persons of color were substantially disenfranchised in many Southern states despite the enactment of the Fifteenth Amendment in 1870 (U.S. Department of Justice, Civil Rights Division, 2006).

The Voting Rights Act of 1965 is touted as the most successful piece of civil rights legislation ever adopted by the U.S. Congress (Grofman, Handley, & Niemi). This act represents a proactive attempt to eradicate the sociopolitical debt that had been accumulating since the founding of the nation.

Table 1 shows the sharp contrasts between voter registration rates before the Voting Rights Act of 1965 and after it. The dramatic changes in voter registration are a result of Congress's bold action. In upholding the constitutionality of the act, the Supreme
Court ruled as follows:

Congress has found that case-by-case litigation was inadequate to combat wide-spread and persistent discrimination in voting, because of the inordinate amount of time and energy required to overcome the obstructionist tactics invariably encountered in these lawsuits. After enduring nearly a century of systematic resistance to the Fifteenth Amendment, Congress might well decide to shift the advantage of time and inertia from the perpetrators of the evil to its victims. (South Carolina v. Katzenbach, 1966; U.S. Department of Justice, Civil Rights Division, 2006)

It is hard to imagine such a similarly drastic action on behalf of African American, Latina/o, and Native American children in schools. For example, imagine that an examination of the achievement performance of children of color provoked an immediate reassignment of the nation's best teachers to the schools serving the most needy students. Imagine that those same students were guaranteed places in state and regional colleges and universities. Imagine that within one generation we lift those students out of poverty.

The closest example that we have of such a dramatic policy move is that of affirmative action. Rather than wait for students of color to meet predetermined standards, the society decided to recognize that historically denied groups should be given a preference in admission to schools and colleges. Ultimately, the major beneficiaries of this policy were White women. However, Bowen and Bok (1999) found that in the case of African Americans this proactive policy helped create what we now know as the Black middle class.

As a result of the sociopolitical component of the education debt, families of color have regularly been excluded from the decision-making mechanisms that should ensure that their children receive quality education. The parent-teacher organizations, school site councils, and other possibilities for democratic participation have not been available or many of these families. However, for a brief moment in 1968, Black parents in the Ocean Hill-Brownsville section of New York exercised community control over the public schools (Podair, 2003). African American, Latina/o, Native American, and Asian American parents have often advocated or improvements in schooling, but their advocacy often has been muted and marginalized. This quest for control of schools was powerfully captured in the voice of an African American mother during the fight for school desegregation in Boston. She declared: "When we fight about schools, we're fighting for our lives" (Hampton, 1986).

Indeed, a major aspect of the modern civil rights movement was the quest for quality schooling. From the activism of Benjamin Rushing in 1849 to the struggles of parents in rural South Carolina in1999, families of color have been fighting for quality education for their children (Ladson-Billings, 2004). Their more limited access to lawyers and legislators has kept them from accumulating the kinds of political capital that their White, middle-class counterparts have.

Table 1.   Black and white voter registration rates (%) in selected U.S. states, 1965 and 1988.

State	March 1965			November 1988		
	Black	White	Gap	Black	White	Gap
Alabama	19.3	69.2	49.9	68.4	75.0	6.6
Georgia	27.4	62.6	35.2	56.8	63.9	7.1
Louisiana	31.6	80.5	48.9	77.1	75.1	−2.0
Mississippi	6.7	69.9	63.2	74.2	80.5	6.3
North Carolina	46.8	96.8	50.0	58.2	65.6	7.4
South Carolina	37.3	75.7	38.4	56.7	61.8	5.1
Virginia	38.3	61.1	22.8	63.8	68.5	4.7

Note: From the website of the U.S Department of Justice, Civil rights Division, Voting Rights Section *(http://www.usdoj.gov/crt/voting/intro/intro_c.htm)*, "Introduction to Federal Voting Rights Laws."

The Moral Debt

A final component of the education debt is what I term the "moral debt." I find this concept difficult to explain because social science rarely talks in these terms. What I did find in the literature was the concept of "moral panics" (Cohen, 1972; Goode & Ben-Yehuda, 1994a, 1994b; Hall, Critcher, Jefferson, Clarke, & Roberts, 1978) that was popularized in British sociology. People in moral panics attempt to describe other people, groups of individuals, or events that become defined as threats throughout a society. However, in such a panic the magnitude of the supposed threat overshadows the real threat posed. Stanley Cohen (1972), author of the classic sociological treatment of the subject, entitled *Folk Devils and Moral Panics*, defines such a moral panic as a kind of reaction to

> A condition, episode, person or group of persons [that] emerges to become defined as a threat to societal values and interests; its nature is presented in a stylized and stereotypical fashion by the mass media; the moral barricades are manned by editors, bishops, politicians, and other right-thinking people; socially accredited experts pronounce their diagnoses and solutions; ways of coping are evolved or . . . resorted to; the condition then disappears, submerges or deteriorates and becomes more visible. Sometimes the subject of the panic passes over and is forgotten, except in folklore and collective memory; at other times it has more serious and long-lasting repercussions and might produce such changes as those in legal and social policy or even in the way society conceives itself. (p.9)

In contrast, a moral debt reflects the disparity between what we know is right and what we actually do. Saint Thomas Aquinas saw the moral debt as what human beings owe to each other in the giving of, or failure to give, honor to another when honor is due. This honor comes as a result of people's excellence or because of what they have done for another. We have no trouble recognizing that we have a moral debt to Rosa Parks, Martin Luther King, Cesar Chavez, Elie Wiesel, or Mahatma Gandhi. But how do we recognize the moral debt that we owe to entire groups of people? How do we calculate such a debt?

Typically, we think of moral debt as relational between nation-states. For example, at the end of World War II, Israel charged Germany not only with a fiscal or monetary debt but also with a moral debt. On the individual level, Fred Korematsu battled the U.S. government for 40 years to prove that Japanese Americans were owed a moral debt. In another 40-year span, the U.S. government ran a study of syphilis patients-with holding treatment after a known cure was discovered- and was forced to acknowledge its ethical breaches. In his 1997 apology to the survivors and their families, President Bill Clinton said, "The United States government did something that was wrong- deeply, profoundly, morally wrong. It was an outrage to our commitment to integrity and equality for all our citizens. . . .

Clearly racist" (Hunter-Gault, 1997). Today, all human subject protocols reflect the moral debt we owe to the victims of that study.

David Gill (2000) asserts, in his book Being Good, that "we are living today in an ethical wilderness- a wild, untamed, unpredictable landscape" (p.11).We be moan the loss of civil discourse and rational debate, but the real danger of our discussions about morality is that they reside solely in the realm of the individual. We want people to take personal responsibility for their behavior, personal responsibility for their health care, personal responsibility for their welfare, and personal responsibility for their education. However, in democratic nations, that personal responsibility must be coupled with social responsibility.

What is it that we might owe to citizens who historically have been excluded from social benefits and opportunities? Randall Robinson (2000) states:

> No nation can enslave a race of people for hundreds of years, set them free be draggled and penniless, pit them, without assistance in a hostile environment, against privileged victimizers, and then reasonably expect the gap between the heirs of the two groups to narrow. Lines, begun parallel and left alone, can never touch. (p.74)

Robinson's sentiments were not unlike those of President Lyndon B. Johnson, who stated in a 1965 address at Howard University: "You cannot take a man who has been in chains for 300 years, remove the chains, take him to the starting line and tell him to run the race, and think that you are being fair" (Miller, 2005).

Despite those parallel lines of which Robinson speaks, in the midst of the Civil War Abraham Lincoln noted that without the 200,000 Black men who enlisted in the Union Army, "we would be compelled to abandon the war in 3 weeks" (cited in Takaki, 1998). Thus, according to historian Ron Takaki (1998),"Black men in blue made the difference in determining that this 'government of the people, by the people, for the people' did 'not perish from the earth'"(p.21). What moral debt do we owe their heirs?

Think of another example of the ways that the labor and efforts of people of color have sustained the nation. When we hear the word "plantation," our minds almost automatically reflect back to the antebellum South. However, the same word evokes the Palolo Valley on the Hawaiian island of Oahu, where there were camps named "Young Hee," "Ah Fong," "Spanish A," "Spanish B," and "Alabama" (Takaki, 1998). This last camp- "Alabama"-was a Hawaiian plantation worked by Black laborers. Each of the groups that labored in the Hawaiian plantations- the Native Hawaiians, the Chinese, the Japanese, the Filipinos, the Koreans, the Portuguese, the Puerto Ricans, and the Blacks—drove a sugar economy that sated a worldwide sweet tooth (Wilcox, 1998). What do we owe their descendants?

And perhaps our largest moral debt is to the indigenous peoples whose presence was all but eradicated from the nation. In its 2004-2005 Report Card, the Bureau of Indian Affairs indicates that its high school graduation rate is 57%, with only 3.14% of its students performing at the advanced level in reading and 3.96% performing at the advanced level in mathematics. One hundred and twenty-two of the 185 elementary and secondary schools under the jurisdiction of the Bureau of Indian Affairs ailed to meet Average Yearly Progress requirements in the 2004-2005 school year (Bureau of Indian Affairs, Office of Indian Education Programs, 2006).

The National Center for Education Statistics report *Status and Trends in the Education of American Indians and Alaska Natives* (Freeman & Fox, 2005) indicates that the dropout rate among this population is about 15%, which is higher than that of Whites, Blacks, or Asian/Pacific Islanders. Only 26% of American Indi ans and Alaska Natives completed a core academic track in 2000, while 57% of Asian/Pacific islanders, 38% of Latina/os, 44% of African Americans, and 48% of Whites completed core academic tracks during the same year (Freeman & Fox). Taken together, the historic, economic, sociopolitical, and moral debt that we have amassed toward Black, Brown, Yellow, and Red children seems insurmountable, and attempts at addressing it seem futile. Indeed, it appears like a task for Sisyphus. But as legal scholar Derrick Bell (1994) indicated, just because some-thing is impossible does not mean it is not worth doing.

Why We Must Address the Debt

In the final section of this discussion I want to attend to why we must address the education debt. On the face of it, we must address it because it is the equitable and just thing to do. As Americans we pride ourselves on maintaining those ideal qualities as hallmarks of our democracy. That represents the highest motivation for paying this debt. But we do not always work from our highest motivations.

Most of us live in the world of the pragmatic and practical. So we must address the education debt because it has implications for the kinds of lives we can live and the kind of education the society can expect for most of its children. I want to suggest that there are three primary reasons for addressing the debt-(a) the impact the debt has on present education progress, (b) the value of understanding the debt in relation to past education research findings, and (c) the potential for forging a better educational future.

The Impact of the Debt on Present Education Progress

In a recent news article in the business section of the *Cleveland Plain Dealer*, I read that affluent investors are more likely to be educated, married men (Torres, 2006). The article continued by talking about how Whites make up 88% of wealthy investor households, while Blacks and Latina/os make up only 3%. Asian Americans, who are 3.7% of the adult population, make up 5% of wealthy investors. But more salient than wealthy investor status to me was a quote in the article from former Federal Reserve Chair-man Alan Greenspan: "My biggest fear for this country's future, competitively speaking, is that we're doing a poor job in education. If we can resolve our educational problems, I think we will maintain the very extraordinary position the United States holds in the world at large" (Torres, p.G6).

As I was attempting to make sense of the deficit/debt metaphor, educational economist Doug Harris (personal communication, November 19, 2005) reminded me that when nations operate with a large debt, some part of their current budget goes to service that debt. I mentioned earlier that interest payments on our national debt represent the third largest expenditure of our national budget. In the case of education, each effort we make toward improving education is counter balanced by the ongoing and mounting debt that we have accumulated. That debt service manifests itself in the distrust and suspicion about what schools can and will do in communities serving the poor and children of color. Bryk and Schneider (2002) identified "relational rust" as a key component in school reform. I argue that the magnitude of the education debt erodes that trust and represents a portion of the debt service that teachers and administrators pay each year against what they might rightfully invest in helping students advance academically.

The Value of Understanding the Debt in Relation to Past Research Findings

The second reason that we must address the debt is somewhat selfish from an education research perspective. Much of our scholarly effort has gone into looking at educational inequality and how we might mitigate it. Despite how hard we try, there are two interventions that have never received full and sustained hypothesis testing-school desegregation and funding equity. Or field and Lee (2006) point out that not only has school segregation persisted, but it has been transformed by the changing demographics of the nation. They also point out that "there has not been a serious discussion of the costs of segregation or the advantages of integration for our most segregated population, white students" (p.5). So, although we may have recently celebrated the 50th anniversary of the *Brown* decision, we can point to little evidence that we really gave *Brown* a chance. According to Frankenberg, Lee, and Orfield (2003) and Orfield and Lee (2004), America's public schools are more than a decade into a process of re segregation. Almost three-fourths of Black and Latina/o students attend schools that are predominately non-White. More than 2 million Black and Latina/o students-a quarter of the Black students in the Northeast and Midwest-attend what the researchers call apartheid schools. The four most segregated states for Black students are New York, Michigan, Illinois, and California.

The funding equity problem, as I illustrated earlier in this discussion, also has been intractable. In its report entitled *The Funding Gap 2005*, the Education Trust tells us that "in 27 of the 49 states studied, the highest-poverty school districts receive fewer resources than the lowest-poverty districts. . . . Even more states short change their highest minority districts. In 30 states, high minority districts receive less money for each child than low minority districts" (p.2). If we are unwilling to desegregate our schools and unwilling to fund them equitably, we find ourselves not only backing away from the promise of the Brown decision but literally refusing even to take *Plessy* seriously. At least a serious consideration of *Plessy* would make us look at funding inequities.

In one of the most graphic examples of funding inequity, new teacher Sara Sentilles (2005) described the southern California school where she was teaching:

> At Garvey Elementary school, taught over thirty second graders in a so-called temporary building. Most of these "temporary" buildings have been on campuses in Compton for years. The one I taught in was old. Because the wooden beams across the ceiling were being eaten by termites, a fine layer of wood dust covered the students desks every morning. Maggots crawled in a cracked and collapsing area of the floor near my desk. One day after school I went to sit in my chair, and it was completely covered in maggots. I was nearly sick. Mice raced behind cupboards and bookcases. I trapped six in terrible traps called "glue lounges" given to me by the custodians. The blue metal window coverings in the outsides of the windows were shut permanently, blocking all sunlight. Someone had lost the tool needed to open them, and no one could find another.... (p.72)

Rothstein and Wilder (2005) move beyond the documentation of the inequalities and inadequacies to their *consequences*. In the language that I am using in this discussion, they move from focusing on the gap to tallying the debt. Although they focus on Black-White disparities, they are clear that similar disparities exist between Latina/os and Whites and Native Americans and Whites. Contrary to conventional wisdom, Rothstein and Wilder argue that addressing the achievement gap is not the most important inequality to attend to. Rather, they contend that inequalities in health, early childhood experiences, out-of-school experiences, and economic security are also contributory and cumulative and make it near-impossible for us to reify the achievement gap as the source and cause of social inequality.

The Potential for Forging a Better Educational Future

Finally, we need to address what implications this mounting debt has for our future. In one scenario, we might determine that our debt is so high that the only thing we can do is declare bankruptcy. Perhaps, like our airline industry, we could use the protection of the bankruptcy laws to reorganize and design more streamlined, more efficient schooling options. Or perhaps we could be like developing nations that owe huge sums to the IMF and apply for 100% debt relief. But what would such a catastrophic collapse of our education system look like? Where could we go to begin from the ground up to build the kind of education system that would aggressively address the debt? Might we find a setting where a catastrophic occurrence, perhaps a natural disaster- a hurricane- has completely obliterated the schools? Of course, it would need to be a place where the schools weren't very good to begin with. It would have to be a place where our Institutional Review Board and human subject concerns would not keep us from proposing aggressive and cutting-edge research. It would have to be a place where people were so desperate for the expertise of education researchers that we could conduct multiple projects using multiple approaches. It would be a place so hungry for solutions that it would not matter if some projects were quantitative and others were qualitative. It would not matter if some were large-scale and some were small-scale. It would not matter if some paradigms were psychological, some were social, some were economic, and some were cultural. The only thing that would matter in an environment like this would be that education researchers were bringing their expertise to bear on education problems that spoke to pressing concerns of the public. I wonder where we might find such a place?

Although I have tried to explain this notion of education debt, I know that my words are a limited way to fully represent. How can I illustrate the magnitude of this concept? In his 1993 AERA Presidential Address, "Forms of Understanding and the Future of Educational Research," Elliot Eisner spoke of representation- not the mental representations discussed in cognitive science, but "the process of transforming the consciousness into a public form so that they can be stabilized, inspected, edited, and shared with others" (p.6). So we must use our imaginations to construct a set of images that illustrate the debt. The images should remind us that the cumulative effect of poor education, poor housing, poor healthcare, and poor government services create a bifurcated society that leaves more than its children behind. The images should compel us to deploy our knowledge, skills, and expertise to alleviate the suffering of the least of these. They are the images that compelled our attention during Hurricane Katrina. Here, for the first time in a very long time, the nation- indeed the world- was confronted with the magnitude of poverty that exists in America.

In a recent book, Michael Apple and Kristen Buras (2006) suggest that the subaltern can and do speak. In this country they speak from the barrios of Los Angeles and the ghettos of New York. They speak from the reservations of New Mexico and the Chinatown of San Francisco. They speak from the levee breaks of New Orleans where they remind us, as education researchers, that we do not merely have an achievement gap- we have an education debt.

References

Altonji ,J., & Doraszelski, U. (2005). The role of permanent income and demographics in Black/White differences in wealth. *Journal of Human Resources*, 40, 1-30.

Anderson, J. D. (1989). *The education of Blacks in the South, 1860-1935*. Chapel Hill, NC: University of North Carolina Press.

Anderson, J.D. (2002, February 8). *Historical perspectives in Black academic achievement*. Paper presented for the Visiting Minority Scholars Series Lecture. Wisconsin Center or Educational Research, University of Wisconsin, Madison.

Apple, M. (1990). *Ideology and curriculum* 2nd ed.). New York: Routledge.

Apple, M., & Buras, K. (Eds.). 2006). *The subaltern speak: Curriculum, power and education struggles*. New York: Routledge.

Au, K. (1980). Participation structures in a reading lesson with Hawaiian children. *Anthropology and Education Quarterly*, 1 (2), 91-115.

Banks, J. A. (2004). Multicultural education: Historical development, dimensions, and practices. In J. A. Banks & C. M. Banks (Eds.), *Handbook of research in multicultural education* 2nd ed., pp.3-29). San Francisco: Jossey-Bass.

Bell, D. (1994). *Confronting authority: reflections of an ardent protester*. Boston: Beacon Press.

Bereiter, C., & Engleman,. (1966). *Teaching disadvantaged children in preschool*. Englewood Cliffs, NJ: Prentice Hall.

Bowen, W., & Bok, D. (1999). *The shape of the river*. Princeton, NJ: Princeton University Press.

Brice Heath, S. (1983). Ways with words: Language, Life and work in com-munities and classrooms. Cambridge, UK: Cambridge University Press.

Brown v. Board of Education 347 U.S. 483 (1954).

Bryk, A., & Schneider, S. (2002). *Trust in schools: A core resource or improvement*. New York: Russell Sage Foundation.

Bureau of Indian Affairs, Office of Indian Education Programs. (2006). *School Report Cards: SY2004-2006*. Retrieved February 5, 2006, from http://www.oiep.bia.edu/

Christensen, J.R. (Ed.). (2004). *The national debt: A primer.* Hauppauge, NY: Nova Science Publishers.

Clark, K. B. (1965). *Dark ghetto: Dilemmas of social power*. Hanover, NH: Wesleyan University Press.

Cochran-Smith, M. (2004). Multicultural teacher education: Research, practice and policy. In J. A. Banks & C. M. Banks Eds.), *Handbook of research in multicultural education* 2nd ed., pp.931-975). San Francisco: Jossey-Bass.

Cohen, S. (1972). *Folk devils and moral panics: The creation of mods and rockers*. London: McGibbon and Kee.

Coleman, J., Campbell, E., Hobson, C., McPartland, J., Mood, A., Weinfeld, F. D., et al. (1966). *Equality of educational opportunity*. Washington, DC: Department of Health, Education and Welfare.

Cornbleth, C., & Waugh, D. (1995*). The great speckled bird: Multicultural politics and education*. Mahwah, NJ: Lawrence Erlbaum.

Delpit, L. (1995). *Other people's children: Cultural conflict in the classroom*. New York: Free Press. Deutsch, M. (1963). The disadvantaged child and the learning process. In A. H. Passow (Ed.), *Education in depressed areas* (pp. 163-179). New York: New York Bureau of Publications, Teachers College, Columbia University.

Education Commission of the States. (2005). *The nation's report card*. Retrieved January 2, 2006, from http://nces.ed.gov/nationsreportcard

Education Trust. (2005). *The funding gap 2005*. Washington, DC: Author.

Eisner, E. W. (1993). Forms of understanding and the future of educational research. *Educational Researcher*, 2 (7), 5-11.

Farrow, A., Lang, J., & Frank, J. (2005*). Complicity: How the North promoted, prolonged and profited from slavery*. New York: Ballantine Books.

Ferg-Cadima, J. (2004, May). *Black, White, and Brown: Latino school desegregation efforts in the pre-and post-* Brown v. Board of Education *era.* Washington, DC: Mexican-American Legal Defense and Education Fund.

Foster, M. (1996). *Black teachers on teaching.* New York: New Press.

Frankenberg, E., Lee, C., & Orfield, G. (2003, January). *A multiracial society with segregated schools: Are we losing the dream?* Cambridge, MA: The Civil Rights Project, Harvard University.

Freeman, C., & Fox, M. (2005). *Status and trends in the education of American Indians and Alaska natives* (No. 2005-108). U.S. Department of Education, National Center for Education Statistics. Wash-ington, DC: U.S. Government Printing Office.

Fultz, M. (1995). African American teachers in the South, 1890-1940: Powerlessness and the ironies of expectations and protests. *History of Education Quarterly,* 35 (4), 401-422.

Gay, G. (2004). Multicultural curriculum theory and multicultural education. In J.A. Banks & C. M. Banks (Eds.), *Handbook of research in multicultural education* 2nd ed., (pp.30-49). San Francisco: Jossey-Bass.

Gill, D. W. (2000). *Being good: Building moral character.* Downers Grove, IL: Intervarsity Press.

Goode, E., & Ben-Yehuda, N. (1994a). Moral panics: Culture, politics, and social construction. *Annual Review of Sociology,* 20, 149-171.

Goode, E., & Ben-Yehuda, N. (1994b). *Moral panics: The social construction of deviance.* Oxford: Blackwell.

Gordon, J.S. (1998). *Hamilton's blessing: The extraordinary life and times of our national debt.* New York: Penguin Books.

Grant, C. A. (2003). *An education guide to diversity in the classroom.* Boston: Houghton Mifflin.

Grofman, B., Handley, L., & Niemi, R. G. (1992). *Minority representation and the quest or voting equality.* New York: Cambridge University Press.

Hall, S., Critcher, C., Jefferson, T., Clarke, J., & Roberts, B. (1978). *Policing the crisis: Mugging, the state, and law and order.* London: Macmillan.

Hampton, H. (Director). (1986). *Eyes on the prize* [Television video series]. Blackside Productions (Producer). New York: Public Broadcasting Service.

Hess, R. D., & Shipman, V. C. (1965). Early experience and socialization of cognitive modes in children. *Child Development,* 36, 869-886.

Hunter-Gault, C. (Writer). (1997, May 16). An apology 65 years later [Television series episode]. In Lee Koromvokis (Producer), *Online News Hour.* Washington, DC: Public Broadcasting Service. Retrieved February 2, 2006, from *http:// www.pbs.org/newshour/bb/health/may97/tuskegee_5-16.lhtml*

Irvine, J.J. (2003). *Educating teachers or diversity: Seeing with a cultural eye.* New York: Teachers College Press.

Jefferson, T. (1816, July 21). *Letter to William Plumer. The Thomas Jefferson Paper Series. 1. General correspondence,* 651-1827. Retrieved September 11, 2006, from *http://rs6.loc.gov/cgi-bin/ampage*

King, J. (2000, May 1). *Clinton announces record payment on national debt.* Retrieved February 7, 2006, from *http://archives. cnn.com/2000/ALLPOLITICS/stories/05/O1/clinton.debt*

Kozol, J. (2005). *The shame of the nation: The restoration of apartheid schooling in America.* New York: Crown Publishing.

Ladson-Billings, G. (1994). *The dreamkeepers: Successful teachers of African American children.* San Francisco: Jossey-Bass.

Ladson-Billings, G. (2004). Landing on the wrong note: The price we paid for *Brown. Educational Researcher,* 3 (7), 3-13.

Lakoff, G., & Johnson, M. (1980). *Metaphors we live by.* Chicago: University of Chicago Press.

Lee, C. D. (2004). African American students and literacy. In D. Alvermann & D. Strickland (Eds.), *Bridging the gap: Improving literacy learning for pre-adolescent and adolescent learners, Grades 4-12.* New York: Teachers College Press.

Lee, J. (2002). Racial and achievement gap trends: Reversing the progress toward equity. *Educational Researcher,* 1 (1), 3-12.

Lesiak, C. (Director). (1992). *In the White man's image* [Television broadcast]. New York: Public Broadcasting Corporation.

Margo, R. (1990). *Race and schooling in the American South, 1880-1950.* Chicago: University of Chicago Press.

Mendez v. Westminster 64F. Supp. 544 (1946).

Miller, J. (2005, September 22). New Orleans unmasks apartheid American style [Electronic version]. *Black Commentator,* 151. Retrieved September 11, 2006, from *http://www.blackcommentator.com/151/151_millerneworleans.html*

National Center for Education Statistics. (2001). *Education achievement and Black-White inequality.* Washington, DC: Department of Education.

National Governors' Association. (2005). *Closing the achievement gap.* Retrieved October 27, 2005, from *http://www.subnet. ga.org/educlear/achievement/*

National Voting Rights Act of 1965, 42 U.S.C. 1973-1973aa-b.

Orfield, G., & Lee, C. (2004, January). Brown *at 50: King's dream or Plessy's nightmare?* Cambridge, MA: The Civil Rights Project, Harvard University.

Orfield, G., & Lee, C. (2006, January). *Racial transformation and the changing nature of segregation.* Cambridge, MA: The Civil Rights Proj-ect, Harvard University.

Plessy v. Ferguson 163 U.S. 537 (1896).

Podair, J. (2003). *The strike that changed New York: Blacks, Whites and the Ocean Hill-Brownsville Crisis.* New Haven, CT: Yale University Press.

Popkewitz, T. S. (1998). *Struggling or the soul: The politics of schooling and the construction of the teacher.* New York: Teachers College Press.

Robinson, R. (2000). *The debt: What America owes to Blacks.* New York: Dutton Books.

Rothstein, R., & Wilder, T. (2005, October 24). *The many dimensions of racial inequality.* Paper presented at the Social Costs of Inadequate Education Symposium, Teachers College, Columbia University, New York.

Sentilles, S. (2005). *Taught by America: A story of struggle and hope in Compton.* Boston: Beacon Press. Sleeter, C. (2001). Culture, difference and power. New York: Teachers College Press.

South Carolina v. Katzenbach 383 U.S. 301, 327-328 (1966).

Steele, C. M. (1999, August). Thin ice: "Stereotype threat" and Black college students. *Atlantic Monthly*, 284, 44-47, 50-54.

Takaki, R. (1998). *A larger mirror: A history of our diversity with voices.* Boston: Back Bay Books.

Torres, C. (2006, March 19). Affluent investors more likely educated, married men. *Cleveland Plain Dealer*, p. G6.

Tyack, D. (2004). *Seeking common ground: Public schools in a diverse society.* Cambridge, MA: Harvard University Press.

U.S. Department of Justice, Civil Rights Division. (2006, September 7*). Introduction to federal voting rights laws.* Retrieved September 11, 2006, from http://www.usdoj.gov/crt/voting/intro/intro.html

Wilcox, C. (1998). *Sugar water: Hawaii's plantation ditches.* Honolulu, HI: University of Hawaii Press.

Wolfe, B., & Haveman, R. (2001). *Accounting for the social and non-market benefits of education.* In J. Helliwell (Ed.) The contribution of human and social capital to sustained economic growth and well-being (pp. 1-72). Vancouver, BC: University of British Columbia Press. Retrieved September 11, 2006, from *http://www.oecd.org/dataoecd/5/19/1825109.pdf*

Woodson, C.G. (1972). *The mis-education of the Negro.* Trenton, NJ: Africa World Press. Original work published 1933)

Zeichner, K.M. (2002). The adequacies and inadequacies of three current strategies to recruit, prepare, and retain the best teachers or all students. *Teachers College Record*, 05 (3), 490-511.

AUTHOR

GLORIA LADSON-BILLINGS, the 2005-2006 President of AERA, is the Kellner Family Chair in Urban Education in the Department of Curriculum and Instruction, and Faculty Affiliate in the Department of Educational Policy Studies, University of Wisconsin, 225 N. Mills Street, Madison, WI 53706; gjladson@wisc. edu. Her research interests are in culturally relevant pedagogy and applications of critical race theory to education.

APPENDIX 5

Affirmation, Solidarity and Critique: Moving Beyond Tolerance in Education

Sonia Nieto

"We want our students to develop **tolerance** of others," says a teacher when asked what multicultural education means to her. "The greatest gift we can give our students is a **tolerance** for differences," is how a principal explains it. A school's mission statement might be more explicit: "Students at the Jefferson School will develop critical habits of the mind, a capacity for creativity and risk-taking and tolerance for those different from themselves." In fact, if we were to listen to pronouncements at school board meetings, or conversations in teachers' rooms, or if we perused school handbooks, we would probably discover that when mentioned at all, multicultural education is associated more often with the term tolerance than with any other.

My purpose in this article is to challenge readers and indeed the very way that multicultural education is practiced in schools in general, to move beyond tolerance in both conceptualization and implementation. It is my belief that a movement beyond tolerance is absolutely necessary if multicultural education is to become more than a superficial "bandaid" or a "feel-good" additive to our school curricula. I will argue that tolerance is actually a low level of multicultural support, reflecting as it does an acceptance of the *status quo* with but slight accommodations to difference. I will review and expand upon a model of multicultural education that I have developed elsewhere in order to explore what multicultural education might actually look like in a school's policies and practices. (See Sonia Nieto, *Affirming Diversity: The Sociopolitical Context of Multicultural Education*, Longman, 1996.)

Levels of Multicultural Education Support

Multicultural education is not a unitary concept. On the contrary, it can be thought of as a range of options across a wide spectrum that includes such diverse strategies as bilingual/bicultural programs, ethnic studies courses, Afrocentric curricula, or simply the addition of a few "Holidays and Heroes" to the standard curriculum (see James A. Banks, *Teaching Strategies for Ethnic Studies*, Allyn & Bacon, 6th ed., 1997), just to name a few. Although all of these may be important parts of multicultural education, they represent incomplete conceptualizations and operationalizations of this complex educational reform movement. Unfortunately, however, multicultural education is often approached as if there were a prescribed script.

The most common understanding of multicultural education is that it consists largely of additive content rather than of structural changes in content and process. It is not unusual, then, to hear teachers say that they are "doing" multicultural education this year, or, as in one case that I heard, that they could not "do it" in the Spring because they had too many other things to "do." In spite of the fact that scholars and writers in multicultural education have been remarkably consistent over the years about the complexity of approaches in the field (see, especially, the analysis by Christine E. Sleeter & Carl A. Grant, "An Analysis of Multicultural Education in the United States," *Harvard Educational Review*, November, 1987), it has often been interpreted in either a simplistic or a monolithic way. It is because of this situation that I have attempted to develop a model that clarifies how various levels of multicultural education support may actually be apparent in schools.

Developing categories or models is always an inherently problematic venture and I therefore present the following model with some hesitancy. Whenever we classify and categorize reality, we run the risk that it will be viewed as static and arbitrary, rather than as messy, complex and contradictory, which we know it to be. Notwithstanding the value that theoretical models may have, they tend to represent information as if it were fixed and absolute. Yet we know too well that nothing happens exactly as portrayed in models and charts, much less social interactions among real people in settings such as schools. In spite of this, models or categories can be useful because they help make concrete situations more understandable and manageable. I therefore present the following model with both reluctance and hope: reluctance because it may improperly be viewed as set in stone, but hope because it may challenge teachers, administrators and educators in general to rethink what it means to develop a multicultural perspective in their schools.

The levels in this model should be viewed as necessarily dynamic, with penetrable borders. They should be understood as "interactive," in the words of Peggy McIntosh (see her *Interactive Phases of Curricular Revision: A Feminist Perspective,* Wellesley College Center for Research on Women, 1983). Thus, although these levels represent "ideal" categories that are internally consistent and therefore set, the model is not meant to suggest that schools are really like this. Probably no school would be a purely "monocultural" or "tolerant" school, given the stated characteristics under each of these categories. However, these categories are used in an effort to illustrate how support for diversity is manifested in schools in a variety of ways. Because multicultural education is primarily a set of beliefs and a philosophy, rather than a set program or fixed content, this model can assist us in determining how particular school policies and practices need to change in order to embrace the diversity of our students and their communities.

The four levels to be considered are: **tolerance; acceptance; respect;** and, finally, **affirmation, solidarity and critique.** Before going on to consider how multicultural education is manifested in schools that profess these philosophical orientations, it is first helpful to explore the antithesis of multicultural education, namely, **monocultural education,** because without this analysis we have nothing with which to compare it.

In the scenarios that follow, we go into five schools that epitomize different levels of multicultural education. All are schools with growing cultural diversity in their student populations; differences include staff backgrounds, attitudes and preparation, as well as curriculum and pedagogy. In our visits, we see how the curriculum, interactions among students, teachers and parents and other examples of attention to diversity are either apparent or lacking. We see how students of different backgrounds might respond to the policies and practices around them. (In another paper entitled "Creating Possibilities: Educating Latino Students in Massachusetts, in *The Education of Latino Students in Massachusetts: Policy and Research Implications,* published by the Gaston Institute for Latino Policy and Development in Boston, which I coedited with R. Rivera, I developed scenarios of schools that would provide different levels of support specifically for Latino students.)

Monocultural Education

Monocultural education describes a situation in which school structures, policies, curricula, instructional materials and even pedagogical strategies are primarily representative of only the dominant culture. In most United States schools, it can be defined as "the way things are."

We will begin our tour in a "monocultural school" that we'll call the George Washington Middle School. When we walk in, we see a sign that says "NO UNAUTHORIZED PERSONS ARE ALLOWED IN THE SCHOOL. ALL VISITORS MUST REPORT DIRECTLY TO THE PRINCIPAL'S OFFICE." The principal, assistant principal and counselor are all European American males, although the school's population is quite diverse, with large numbers of African American, Puerto Rican, Arab American, Central American, Korean and Vietnamese students. As we walk down the hall, we see a number of bulletin boards. On one, the coming Christmas holiday is commemorated; on another, the P.T.O.'s bake sale is announced; and on a third, the four basic food groups are listed, with examples given of only those foods generally considered to be "American."

The school is organized into 45 minute periods of such courses as U.S. history, English, math, science, music appreciation, art and physical education. In the U. S. history class, students learn of the proud exploits, usually through wars and conquest, of primarily European American males. They learn virtually nothing about the contributions, perspectives, or talents of women or those outside the cultural mainstream. U.S. slavery is mentioned briefly in relation to the Civil War, but African Americans are missing thereafter. In English class, the students have begun their immersion in the "canon," reading works almost entirely written by European and European-American males, although a smattering of women and African-American (but no Asian, Latino, or American Indian) authors are included in the newest anthology. In music appreciation class, students are exposed to what is called "classical music," that is, European classical music, but the "classical" music of societies in Asia, Africa and Latin America is nowhere to be found. In art classes, students may learn about the art work of famous European and European American artists and occasionally about the "crafts" and "artifacts" of other cultures and societies mostly from the Third World.

Teachers at the George Washington Middle School are primarily European American women who have had little formal training in multicultural approaches or perspectives. They are proud of the fact that they are "color-blind," that is, that they see no differences among their students, treating them all the same. Of course, this does not extend to tracking, which they generally perceive to be in the interest of teaching all students to the best of their abilities. Ability grouping is a standard practice at the George Washington Middle School. There are four distinct levels of ability, from "talented and gifted" to "remedial." I.Q. tests are used to determine student placement and intellectually superior students are placed in "Talented and Gifted" programs and in advanced levels of math, science, English and social studies. Only these top students have the option of taking a foreign language. The top levels consist of overwhelmingly European-American and Asian-American students, but the school rationalizes that this is due to either the native intelligence of these students, or to the fact that they have a great deal more intellectual stimulation and encouragement in their homes. Thus, teachers have learned to expect excellent work from their top students, but little of students in their low-level classes, who they often see as lazy and disruptive.

Students who speak a language other than English as their native language are either placed in regular classrooms where they will learn to "sink or swim" or in "NE" (non-English) classes, where they are drilled in English all day and where they will remain until they learn English sufficiently well to perform in the regular classroom. In addition, parents are urged to speak to their children only in English at home. Their native language, whether Spanish, Vietnamese, or Korean, is perceived as a handicap to their learning and as soon as they forget it, they can get on with the real job of learning.

Although incidents of racism have occurred in the George Washington Middle School, they have been taken care of quietly and privately. For example, when racial slurs have been used, students have been admonished not to say them. When fights between children of different ethnic groups take place, the assistant principal has insisted that race or ethnicity has nothing to do with them; "kids will be kids" is the way he describes these incidents.

What exists in the George Washington Middle School is a monocultural environment with scant reference to the experiences of others from largely subordinated cultural groups. Little attention is paid to student diversity and the school curriculum is generally presented as separate from the community in which it is located. In addition, "dangerous" topics such as racism, sexism and homophobia are seldom discussed and reality is represented as finished and static. In summary, the George Washington School is a depressingly familiar scenario because it reflects what goes on in most schools in American society.

Tolerance

How might a school characterized by "tolerance" be different from a monocultural school? It is important here to mention the difference between the **denotation** and the **connotation** of words. According to the dictionary definition given at the beginning of this article, tolerance is hardly a value that one could argue with. After all, what is wrong with "recognizing and respecting the beliefs or practices of others"? On the contrary, this is a quintessential part of developing a multicultural perspective. (*Teaching Tolerance,* a journal developed by the Southern Poverty Law Center, has no doubt been developed with this perspective in mind and my critique here of tolerance is in no way meant to criticize this wonderful classroom and teacher resource.) Nevertheless, the connotation of words is something else entirely. When we think of what tolerance means in practice, we have images of a grudging but somewhat distasteful acceptance. To **tolerate** differences means that they are endured, not necessarily embraced. In fact, this level of support for multicultural education stands on shaky ground because what is tolerated today can too easily be rejected tomorrow. A few examples will help illustrate this point.

Our "tolerant" school is the Brotherhood Middle School. Here, differences are understood to be the inevitable burden of a culturally pluralistic society. A level up from a "color-blind" monocultural school, the "tolerant" school accepts differences but only if they can be modified. Thus, they are accepted, but because the ultimate goal is assimilation, differences in language and culture are replaced as quickly as possible. This ideology is reflected in the physical environment, the attitudes of staff and the curriculum to which students are exposed.

When we enter the Brotherhood School, there are large signs in English welcoming visitors, although there are no staff on hand who can communicate with the families of the growing Cambodian student population. One prominently placed bulletin board proudly portrays the winning essays of this year's writing contest with the theme of "Why I am proud to be an American." The winners, a European-American sixth grader and a Vietnamese seventh grader, write in their essays about the many opportunities given to all people in our country, no matter what their race, ethnicity, or gender. Another bulletin board boasts the story of Rosa Parks, portrayed as a woman who was too tired to give up her seat on the bus, thus serving as a catalyst for the modern civil rights movement. (*Rethinking Our Classrooms* includes a powerful example of how people such as Rosa Parks have been decontextualized to better fit in with the U.S. mainstream conception of individual rather than collective struggle, thus adding little to children's understanding of institutionalized discrimination on our society; see "The Myth of 'Rosa Parks the Tired;'" by Herbert Kohl, in which Kohl reports that based on his research most stories used in American schools present Rosa Parks simply as "Rosa Parks the Tired.")

Nevertheless, a number of important structural changes are taking place at the Brotherhood School. An experiment has recently begun in which the sixth and seventh graders are in "family" groupings and these are labeled by family names such as the Jones family, the Smith family and the Porter family. Students remain together as a family in their major subjects (English, social studies, math and science) and there is no ability tracking in these classes. Because their teachers have a chance to meet and plan together daily, they are more readily able to develop integrated curricula. In fact, once in a while, they even combine classes so that they can team-teach and their students remain at a task for an hour and a half rather than the usual three quarters of an hour. The students seem to like this arrangement and have done some interesting work in their study of Washington, D.C. For instance, they used geometry to learn how the city was designed and have written to their congressional representatives to ask how bills become laws. Parents are involved in fundraising for an upcoming trip to the capital, where students plan to interview a number of their local legislators.

The curriculum at the Brotherhood School has begun to reflect some of the changes that a multicultural society demands. Students are encouraged to study a foreign language (except, of course, for those who already speak one; they are expected to learn English and in the process, they usually forget their native language). In addition, a number of classes have added activities on women, African-Americans and American Indians. Last year, for instance, Martin Luther King Day was celebrated by having all students watch a video of the "I Have a Dream" speech.

The majority of changes in the curriculum have occurred in the social studies and English departments, but the music teacher has also begun to add a more international flavor to her repertoire and the art classes recently went to an exhibit of the work of Romare Bearden. This year, a "multicultural teacher" has been added to the staff. She meets with all students in the school, seeing each group once a week for one period. Thus far, she has taught students about Chinese New Year, *Kwanzaa, Ramadan* and *Dia de los Reyes.* She is getting ready for the big multicultural event of the year, Black History Month. She hopes to work with other teachers to bring in guest speakers, show films about the civil rights movement and have an art contest in which students draw what the world would be like if Dr. King's dream of equality became a reality.

Students who speak a language other than English at the Brotherhood School are placed in special English as a Second Language (E.S.L.) classes where they are taught English as quickly, but sensitively, as possible. For instance, while they are encouraged to speak to one another in English, they are allowed to use their native language, but only as a last resort. The feeling is that if they use it more often, it will become a "crutch." In any event, the E.S.L. teachers are not required to speak a language other than English; in fact, being bilingual is even considered a handicap because students might expect them to use their other language.

The principal of the Brotherhood School has made it clear that racism will not be tolerated here. Name-calling and the use of overtly racist and sexist textbooks and other materials are discouraged. Recently, some teachers attended a workshop on strategies for dealing with discrimination in the classroom. Some of those who attended expect to make some changes in how they treat students from different backgrounds.

Most teachers at the Brotherhood School have had little professional preparation to deal with the growing diversity of the student body. They like and genuinely want to help their students, but have made few changes in their curricular or instructional practices. For them, "being sensitive" to their students is what multicultural education should be about, not overhauling the curriculum. Thus, they acknowledge student differences in language, race, gender and social class, but still cannot quite figure out why some students are more successful than others. Although they would like to think not, they wonder if genetics or poor parental attitudes about education have something to do with it. If not, what can explain these great discrepancies?

Acceptance

Acceptance is the next level of supporting diversity. It implies that differences are acknowledged and their importance is neither denied nor belittled. It is at this level that we see substantial movement toward multicultural education. A look at how some of the school's policies and practices might change is indicative of this movement.

The name of our school is the Rainbow Middle School. As we enter, we see signs in English, Spanish and Haitian Creole, the major languages besides English spoken by students and their families. The principal of the Rainbow School is Dr. Belinda Clayton, the first African American principal ever appointed. She has designated her school as a "multicultural building," and has promoted a number of professional development opportunities for teachers that focus on diversity. These include seminars on diverse learning styles, bias-free assessment and bilingual education. In addition, she has hired not only Spanish and Haitian Creole speaking teachers for the bilingual classrooms, but has also diversified the staff in the "regular" program.

Bulletin boards outside the principal's office display the pictures of the "Students of the Month." This month's winners are Rodney Thomas, a sixth grader who has excelled in art, Neleida Cortes, a seventh grade student in the bilingual program and Melissa Newton, an eighth grader in the special education program. All three were given a special luncheon by the principal and their homeroom teachers. Another bulletin board focuses on "Festivals of Light" and features information about *Chanukah*, *Kwanzaa* and Christmas, with examples of *Las Posadas* in Mexico and Saint Lucia's Day in Sweden.

The curriculum at the Rainbow Middle School has undergone some changes to reflect the growing diversity of the student body. English classes include more choices of African American, Irish, Jewish and Latino literature written in English. Some science and math teachers have begun to make reference to famous scientists and mathematicians from a variety of backgrounds. In one career studies class, a number of parents have been invited to speak about their job and the training they had to receive in order to get those positions. All students are encouraged to study a foreign language and choices have been expanded to include Spanish, French, German and Mandarin Chinese.

Tracking has been eliminated in all but the very top levels at the Rainbow School. All students have the opportunity to learn algebra, although some are still counseled out of this option because their teachers believe it will be too difficult for them. The untracked classes seem to be a hit with the students and preliminary results have shown a slight improvement among all students. Some attempts have been made to provide flexible scheduling, with one day a week devoted to entire "learning blocks" where students work on a special project. One group recently engaged in an in-depth study of the elderly in their community. They learned about services available to them and they touched on poverty and lack of health care for many older Americans. As a result of this study, the group has added a community service component to the class; this involves going to the local Senior Center during their weekly learning block to read with the elderly residents.

Haitian and Spanish-speaking students are tested and, if found to be more proficient in their native language, are placed in transitional bilingual education programs. Because of lack of space in the school, the bilingual programs are located in the basement, near the boiler room. Here, students are taught the basic curriculum in their native language while learning English as a second language during one period of the day with an ESL specialist. Most ESL teachers are also fluent in a language other than English, helping them understand the process of acquiring a second language. The bilingual program calls for students to be "mainstreamed" (placed in what is called a "regular classroom") as quickly as possible, with a limit of three years on the outside. In the meantime, they are segregated from their peers for most of the day but have some classes with English-speaking students, including physical education, art and music. As they proceed through the program and become more fluent in English, they are "exited" out for some classes, beginning with math and social studies. While in the bilingual program, students' native cultures are sometimes used as the basis of the curriculum and they learn about the history of their people. There is, for instance, a history course on the Caribbean that is offered to both groups in their native languages. Nevertheless, neither Haitian and Latino students not in the bilingual program nor students of other backgrounds have access to these courses.

Incidents of racism and other forms of discrimination are beginning to be faced at the Rainbow Middle School. Principal Clayton deals with these carefully, calling in the offending students as well as their parents and she makes certain that students understand the severe consequences for name-calling or scapegoating others. Last year, one entire day was devoted to "diversity" and regular classes were canceled while students attended workshops focusing on discrimination, the importance of being sensitive to others and the influence on U.S. history of many different immigrants. They have also hosted a "Multicultural Fair" and published a cookbook with recipes donated by many different parents.

The Rainbow Middle School is making steady progress in accepting the great diversity of its students. They have decided that perhaps assimilation should not be the goal and have eschewed the old idea of the "melting pot." In its place, they have the "salad bowl" metaphor, in which all students bring something special that need not be reconstituted or done away with.

Respect

Respect is the next level of multicultural education support. It implies admiration and high esteem for diversity. When differences are respected, they are used as the basis for much of what goes on in schools. Our next scenario describes what this might look like.

The Sojourner Truth Middle School is located in a midsize town with a changing population. There is a fairly large African-American population with a growing number of students of Cape Verdean and Vietnamese background and the school staff reflects these changes, including teachers, counselors and special educators of diverse backgrounds. There is, for example, a Vietnamese speech pathologist and his presence has helped to alleviate the concerns of some teachers that the special needs of the Vietnamese children were not being addressed. He has found that while some students do indeed have speech problems, others do not, but teachers' unfamiliarity with the Vietnamese language made it difficult to know this.

When we enter the Sojourner Truth Middle School, we are greeted by a parent volunteer. She gives us printed material in all the languages represented in the school and invites us to the parents' lounge for coffee, tea and danish. We are then encouraged to walk around and explore the school. Bulletin boards boast of students' accomplishments in the Spanish Spelling Bee, the local *Jeopardy* Championship and the W.E.B. DuBois Club of African American history. It is clear from the children's pictures that there is wide participation of many students in all of these activities. The halls are abuzz with activity as students go from one class to another and most seem eager and excited by school.

Professional development is an important principle at the Sojourner Truth Middle School. Teachers, counselors and other staff are encouraged to take courses at the local university and to keep up with the literature in their field. To make this more feasible, the staff gets release time weekly to get together. As a consequence, the curriculum has been through tremendous changes. Teachers have formed committees to develop their curriculum. The English department decided to use its time to have reading and discussion groups with some of the newly available multicultural literature with which they were unfamiliar. As a result, they have revamped the curriculum into such overarching themes as **coming of age, immigration, change and continuity and individual and collective responsibility.** They have found that it is easier to select literature to reflect themes such as these and the literature is by its very nature multicultural. For instance, for the theme **individual and collective responsibility** they have chosen stories of varying difficulty, including *The Diary of Anne Frank*, *Bridge to Terabithia* (by Katherine Paterson), *Morning Girl* (by Michael Dorris) and *Let the Circle be Unbroken* (by Mildred D. Taylor), among others. The English teachers have in turn invited the history, art and science departments to join them in developing some integrated units with these themes. Teachers from the art and music departments have agreed to work with them and have included lessons on Vietnamese dance, Guatemalan weaving, Jewish Klezmer music and American Indian story telling as examples of individual and collective responsibility in different communities.

Other changes are apparent in the curriculum as well, for it has become more antiracist and honest. When studying World War II, students learn about the heroic role played by the United States and also about the Holocaust, in which six million Jews and millions of other including Gypsies (Roill people), gays and lesbians, people with disabilities and many dissenters of diverse backgrounds, were exterminated. They also learn, for the first time, about the internment of over a hundred thousand Japanese and Japanese Americans on our own soil.

It has become "safe" to talk about such issues as the crucial role of labor in U.S. history and the part played by African-Americans in freeing themselves from bondage, both subjects thought too "sensitive" to be included previously. This is one reason why the school was renamed for a woman known for her integrity and courage.

The Sojourner Truth Middle School has done away with all ability grouping. When one goes into a classroom, it is hard to believe that students of all abilities are learning together because the instruction level seems to be so high. Upon closer inspection, it becomes apparent that there are high expectations for all students. Different abilities are accommodated by having some students take more time than others, providing cooperative groups in which students change roles and responsibilities and through ongoing dialogue among all students.

Students who speak a language other than English are given the option of being in a "maintenance bilingual program," that is, a program based on using their native language throughout their schooling, not just for three years. Changing the policy that only students who could not function in English were eligible for bilingual programs, this school has made the program available to those who speak English in addition to their native language. Parents and other community members who speak these languages are invited in to classes routinely to talk about their lives, jobs, or families, or to tell stories or share experiences. Students in the bilingual program are not, however, segregated from their peers all day, but join them for a number of academic classes.

Teachers and other staff members at this middle school have noticed that incidents of name-calling and interethnic hostility have diminished greatly since the revised curriculum was put into place. Perhaps more students see themselves in the curriculum and feel less angry about their invisibility; perhaps more teachers have developed an awareness and appreciation for their students' diversity while learning about it; perhaps the more diverse staff is the answer; or maybe it's because the community feels more welcome into the school. Whatever it is, the Sojourner Truth Middle School has developed an environment in which staff and students are both expanding their ways of looking at the world.

Affirmation, Solidarity and Critique

Affirmation, solidarity and critique is based on the premise that the most powerful learning results when students work and struggle with one another, even if it is sometimes difficult and challenging. It begins with the assumption that the many differences that students and their families represent are embraced and accepted as legitimate vehicles for learning and that these are then extended. What makes this level different from the others is that conflict is not avoided, but rather accepted as an inevitable part of learning. Because multicultural education at this level is concerned with equity and social justice and because the basic values of different groups are often diametrically opposed, conflict is bound to occur.

Affirmation, solidarity and critique is also based on understanding that culture is not a fixed or unchangeable artifact and is therefore subject to critique. Passively accepting the status quo of any culture is thus inconsistent with this level of multicultural education; simply substituting one myth for another contradicts its basic assumptions because no group is inherently superior or more heroic than any other. As eloquently expressed by Mary Kalantzis and Bill Cope in their 1990 work *The Experience of Multicultural Education in Australia: Six Case Studies,* "Multicultural education, to be effective, needs to be more active. It needs to consider not just the pleasure of diversity but more fundamental issues that arise as different groups negotiate community and the basic issues of material life in the same space — a process that equally might generate conflict and pain."

Multicultural education without critique may result in cultures remaining at the romantic or exotic stage. If students are to transcend their own cultural experience in order to understand the differences of others, they need to go through a process of reflection and critique of their cultures and those of others. This process of critique, however, begins with a solid core of solidarity with others who are different from themselves. When based on true respect, critique is not only necessary but in fact healthy.

The Arturo Schomburg Middle School is located in a midsize city with a very mixed population of Puerto Ricans, Salvadorans, American Indians, Polish Americans, Irish Americans, Chinese Americas, Filipinos and African Americans. The school was named for a Black Puerto Rican scholar who devoted his life to exploring the role of Africans in the Americas, in the process challenging the myth he had been told as a child in Puerto Rico that Africans had "no culture."

The school's logo, visible above the front door, is a huge tapestry made by the students and it symbolizes a different model of multicultural education from that of either the "melting pot" or the "salad bowl." According to a publication of the National Association of State Boards of Education *(The American Tapestry: Educating a Nation),* "A tapestry is a handwoven textile. When examined from the back, it may simply appear to be a motley group of threads. But when reversed, the threads work together to depict a picture of structure and beauty" (p. 1). According to Adelaide Sanford, one of the study group members who wrote this publication, a tapestry also symbolizes, through its knots, broken threads and seeming jumble of colors and patterns on the back, the tensions, conflicts and dilemmas that a society needs to work out. This spirit of both collaboration and struggle is evident in the school.

When we enter the Schomburg Middle School, the first thing we notice is a banner proclaiming the school's motto: LEARN, REFLECT, QUESTION, AND WORK TO MAKE THE WORLD A BETTER PLACE. This is the message that reverberates throughout the school. Participation is another theme that is evident and the main hall contains numerous pictures of students in classrooms, community service settings and extracurricular activities. Housed in a traditional school building, the school has been transformed into a place where all children feel safe and are encouraged to learn to the highest levels of learning. While there are typical classrooms of the kind that are immediately recognizable to us, the school also houses centers that focus on specific areas of learning. There is, for instance, a studio where students can be found practicing traditional Filipino dance and music, as well as European ballet and modern American dance, among others. Outside, there is a large garden that is planted, cared for and harvested by the students and faculty. The vegetables are used by the cafeteria staff in preparing meals and they have noticed a marked improvement in the eating habits of the children since the menu was changed to reflect a healthier and more ethnically diverse menu.

We are welcomed into the school by staff people who invite us to explore the many different classrooms and other learning centers. Those parents who are available during the day can be found assisting in classrooms, in the Parents' Room working on art projects or computer classes, or attending workshops by other parents or teachers on topics ranging from cross-cultural child-rearing to ESL. The bulletin boards are ablaze with color and include a variety of languages, displaying student work from critical essays on what it means to be an American to art projects that celebrate the talents of many of the students. Learning is going on everywhere, whether in classrooms or in small group collaborative projects in halls.

What might the classrooms look like in this school? For one, they are characterized by tremendous diversity. Tracking and special education, as we know them, have been eliminated at the Schomburg Middle School. Students with special needs are taught along with all others, although they are sometimes separated for small group instruction with students not classified as having special needs. All children are considered "talented" and special classes are occasionally organized for those who excel in dance, mathematics or science. No interested students are excluded from any of these offerings. Furthermore, all students take algebra and geometry and special coaching sessions are available before, after and during school hours for these and other subjects.

Classes are flexible, with an interdisciplinary curriculum and team-teaching resulting in sessions that sometimes last as long as three hours. The physical environment in classrooms is varied: some are organized with round worktables, others have traditional desks and still others have scant furniture to allow for movement. Class size also varies from small groups to large, depending on the topic at hand. Needless to say, scheduling at this school is a tremendous and continuing challenge, but faculty and students are committed to this more flexible arrangement and willing to allow for the problems that it may cause.

There are no "foreign languages" at the Schomburg Middle school, nor is there, strictly speaking, a bilingual program. Rather, the entire school is multilingual and all students learn at least a second language in addition to their native language. This means that students are not segregated by language, but instead work in bilingual settings where two languages are used for instruction. At present, the major languages used are English, Spanish and Tagalog, representing the common languages spoken by this school community. It is not unusual to see students speaking these languages in classrooms, the hallways or the playground, even among those for whom English is a native language.

Students at the Schomburg Middle School seem engaged, engrossed and excited about learning. They have been involved in a number of innovative long-range projects that have resulted from the interdisciplinary curriculum. For instance, working with a Chinese-American artist in residence, they wrote, directed and produced a play focusing on the "Know-Nothing" Movement in U.S. history that resulted in, among other things, the Chinese Exclusion Act of 1882. In preparation for the play, they read a great deal and did extensive research. For example, they contacted the Library of Congress for information on primary sources and reviewed newspapers and magazines from the period to get a sense of the climate that led to Nativism. They also designed and sewed all the costumes and sets. In addition, they interviewed recent immigrants of many backgrounds and found that they had a range of experiences from positive to negative in their new country. On the day of the play, hundreds of parents and other community members attended. Students also held a debate on the pros and cons of continued immigration and received up-to-date information concerning immigration laws from their congressional representative.

The curriculum at the Schomburg Middle School is dramatically different from the George Washington School, the first school we visited. Teachers take very seriously their responsibility of **teaching complexity.** Thus, students have learned that there are many sides to every story and that in order to make informed decisions, they need as much information as they can get. Whether in English, science, art, or any other class, students have been encouraged to be critical of every book, newspaper, curriculum, or piece of information by asking questions such as: **Who wrote the book? Who's missing in this story? Why?** Using questions such as these as a basis, they are learning that every story has a point of view and that every point of view is at best partial and at worst distorted. They are also learning that their own backgrounds, rich and important as they may be, have limitations that can lead to parochial perceptions. Most of all, even at this age, students are learning that every topic is fraught with difficulties and they are wrestling with issues as diverse as homelessness, solar warming and how the gender expectations of different cultures might limit opportunities for girls. Here, nothing is taboo as a topic of discussion as long as it is approached with respect and in a climate of caring.

What this means for teachers is that they have had to become learners along with their students. They approach each subject with curiosity and an open mind and during the school day they have time to study, meet with colleagues and plan their curriculum accordingly. Professional development here means not only attending courses at a nearby university, but collaborating with colleagues in study groups that last anywhere from half a day to several months. These provide a forum in which teachers can carefully study relevant topics or vexing problems. Some of these study groups have focused on topics such as Reconstruction and the history of the Philippines, to educational issues such as cooperative learning and diverse cognitive styles.

Especially noteworthy at this school is that **multicultural education** is not separated from **education;** that is, all education is by its very nature multicultural. English classes use literature written by a wide variety of people from countries where English is spoken. This has resulted in these classes becoming not only multicultural, but international as well. Science classes do not focus on contributions made by members of specific ethnic groups, but have in fact been transformed to consider how science itself is conceptualized, valued and practiced by those who have traditionally been outside the scientific mainstream. Issues such as AIDS education, healing in different cultures and scientific racism have all been the subject of study.

One of the major differences between this school and the others we visited has to do with its governance structure. There is a Schomburg School Congress consisting of students, faculty, parents and other community members and it has wide decision making powers, from selecting the principal to determining reasonable and equitable disciplinary policies and practices. Students are elected by their classmates and, although at the beginning these were little more than popularity contests, in recent months it has been clear that students are beginning to take this responsibility seriously. This is probably because they are being taken seriously by the adults in the group. For instance, when students in one class decided that they wanted to plan a class trip to a neighboring city to coincide with their study of toxic wastes and the environment, they were advised to do some preliminary planning: what would be the educational objectives of such a trip? How long would it take? How much would it cost? After some research and planning, they presented their ideas to the Congress and a fundraising plan that included students, parents and community agencies was started.

The Schomburg School is a learning center that is undergoing important changes every day. As teachers discover the rich talents that all students bring to school, they develop high expectation for them all. The climate that exists in this school is one of possibility, because students' experiences are used to build on their learning and expand their horizons. Students in turn are realizing that while their experiences are important and unique, they are only one experience of many. A new definition of "American" is being forged at this school, one that includes everybody. Above all, learning here is exciting, engrossing, inclusive and evolving.

Conclusion

One might well ask how realistic these scenarios are, particularly the last one. Could a school such as this really exist? Isn't this just wishful thinking? What about the reality of bond issues rejected by voters?; of teachers woefully unprepared to deal with the diversity in their classrooms?; of universities that do little more than offer stale "Mickey Mouse" courses?; of schools with no pencils, paper and chalk, much less computers and video cameras?; of rampant violence in streets, homes and schools?; of drugs and crime?; of parents who are barely struggling to keep their families together and can spare precious little time to devote to volunteering at school?

These are all legitimate concerns that our society needs to face and they remind us that schools need to be understood within their sociopolitical contexts. That is, our schools exist in a society in which social and economic stratification are facts of life, where competition is taught over caring and where the early sorting that takes place in educational settings often lasts a lifetime. Developing schools with a multicultural perspective is not easy; if it were, they would be everywhere. But schools with a true commitment to diversity, equity and high levels of learning are difficult to achieve precisely because the problems they face are pervasive and seemingly impossible to solve. Although the many problems raised above are certainly daunting, the schools as currently organized are simply not up to the challenge. In the final analysis, if we believe that all students deserve to learn at the very highest levels, then we need a vision of education that will help achieve this end.

The scenarios above, however, are not simply figments of my imagination. As you read through the scenarios, you probably noticed bits and pieces of your own school here and there. However, because the "monocultural school" is the one with which we are most familiar and unfortunately comfortable, the other scenarios might seem farfetched or unrealistic. Although they are **ideal** in the sense that they are not true pictures of specific schools, these scenarios nevertheless describe **possibilities** because they all exist to some degree in our schools today. These are not pie-in-the-sky visions, but composites of what goes on in schools every day. As such, they provide building blocks for how we might go about transforming schools. In fact, were we to design schools based on the ideals that our society has always espoused, they would no doubt come close to the last scenario.

It is not, however, a monolithic model or one that can develop overnight. The participants in each school need to develop their own vision so that step by step, with incremental changes, schools become more multicultural and thus more inclusive and more exciting places for learning. If we believe that young people deserve to be prepared with skills for living ethical and productive lives in an increasingly diverse and complex world, then we need to transform schools so that they not only teach what have been called "the basics," but also provide an apprenticeship in democracy and social justice. It is unfair to expect our young people to develop an awareness and respect for democracy if they have not experienced it and it is equally unrealistic; to expect them to be able to function in a pluralistic society if all we give them are skills for a monocultural future. This is our challenge in the years ahead: to conquer the fear of change and imagine how we might create exciting possibilities for all students in all schools.

Sonia Nieto is Professor of Education in Language, Literacy and Culture in the School of Education, University of Massachusetts at Amherst. Dr. Nieto has published numerous books and articles on curriculum issues in multicultural and bilingual education, the education of Latinos in the United States and Puerto Ricans in children's literature. E-mail: snieto@educ.umass.edu